05871

Date Due

JUN 1981		
MAY 2 5 1983		
JAN 1985		
DEC 2 1 1987		
JAN 3 1991		

DEMCO NO. 38-298

STUDIA MEMORIAE
BELAE BARTÓK
SACRA

STUDIA
MEMORIAE
BELAE
BARTÓK
„SACRA

EDITIO TERTIA

BOOSEY AND HAWKES
LIMITED
LON DON, NEW YORK, SYDNEY, TORONTO, CAPE TOWN, PARIS, BONN
1959

Adiuvantibus
Z. KODÁLY et L. LAJTHA

Curant
B. RAJECZKY et L. VARGYAS

ⓒ *Akadémiai Kiadó, 1958*

Voluminis tegumentum exteriusque involucrum designavit
V. CSILLAG

*

Sole Agents for the United Kingdom of Great Britain and Northern Ireland, its Colonies and Dependencies, the British Commonwealth of Nations, the Irish Free State, the United States of America, France, the French Union, and the German Federal Republic

BOOSEY AND HAWKES
Limited

295 Regent Street, London, W. 1.
New York, Sydney, Toronto, Cape Town, Paris, Bonn

*

Responsible for the edition:
Director of the Publishing House of the Hungarian Academy of Sciences

Responsible editor: G. Dienes
Technical editor: D. Nyári
Subscribed for printing on September 15, 1958: 46.9 (A/5) sheets, two plates, and three supplements
Order: No. 46740

Made and printed in Hungary by the Printing House of the Hungarian Academy of Sciences
Budapest, V. Gerlóczy u. 2.
Director: Gy. Bernát

EFFIGIEM
BELAE BARTÓK
DELINEAVIT
BÉNI FERENCZY

MEMORIAE BELAE BARTÓK,

qui cantus agricolarum Hungarorum, Slovacorum, Rumenorum, Turcorum et Arabum labore immani collegit, melodiasque Meridionalium Slavorum notis musicis mandavit,

qui cantionum popularium complura milia Hungarico aeque ac sermone alienarum nationum contexta opere laborioso notis memoriae tradidit et artem qua carmina popularia conservari debent cura exactissima ac subtili perfectissimam reddidit,

qui cantionibus Hungaricae gentis in ordinem disponendis addictissimus earum descriptionem primam accurate concinnavit et systema aptissimum carminum popularium Slovacorum Rumenorumque rite in ordinem redigendorum elaboravit,

qui populare melos gentis nostrae vicinarumque gentium comparando respexit et scientiae musicam popularem in partibus Europae Orientalis comparanti fundamenta iecit,

qui melodias gentium in artis sublimia evexit,

qui pro plebe populorumque fraternitate nunquam perterritus semper certavit,

qui labore indefessus, animo ad omnia capacissimus viri doctissimi exemplum in aevum nobis praestat,

recurrente die natali septuagesimo quinto
SOCIETAS ETHNOGRAPHICA HUNGARIAE
studia quae sequuntur animo grato dedicat.

SUMMARIUM

9

ZOLTÁN KODÁLY

A PREREQUISITE CONDITION
OF COMPARATIVE SONG RESEARCH

In spite of certain initial results achieved in comparative song research anyone who has a try at it, will find the lack of musically arranged collections a great setback to his work. The research worker must rely on his memory alone and this is known to be likely to fail. Even comparative philology would not have developed had there been no alphabetically arranged dictionaries.

The first arranged collections of songs — not mentioning such earlier attempts as, for instance, Zahn's monumental collection of German ritual songs (see Gy. Kerényi's treatise in this volume, page 443) — are the Finnish collections edited by Ilmary Krohn and his successors, A. Launis and A. O. Väisänen and the *Rätoromanische Volkslieder*, vols, i—ii, (Basel 1945) by Maissen, Schorta and Wehrli.

It is astonishing, indeed, that so few have followed the example set by them. Even in our days collections are being published without even trying to arrange systematically the musical part. The text is, in some of them, arranged one way or other, reflecting a biased literary conception according to which the text is the important part, whereas the melody is considered an incidental addition only.

Even in such collections it would be easy to make a survey of the melodies by means of a musical index or else, at least, to point out whether or not the variants are to be found within the collection in question.

And what is going to happen with the older editions containing a valuable but often inaccessible material? Now and then anastatic reprints are being published (such as *Volkslieder der Sorben* by Haupt and Schmaler, 1953, or the exemplary reprints of the Rupin, Lvov-Pratch, and Trutovsky collections by Beliaev) which ought by no means be short of an up-to-date index of variants. Yet to republish everything would be impossible and superfluous.

Each language community ought to publish its own complete and uniform "Catalogue raisonné", covering all printed collections and possibly manuscripts, and stating the full data of each song. The reprinted edition of G. Raynauds' *Bibliographie des altfranzösischen*

Liedes, Brill, Amsterdam 1955, for instance, which indicates the source of the melodies would have twice its value for research if a systematic survey of the melodies were added to it.

The indexes of the Hungarian folk song collection now being compiled *(Magyar Népzene Tára — Corpus Musicae Popularis Hungaricae*, vols. i—iii) are attempts at giving, beside systematic classification, detailed information about the affinities of the melodies (see vol. i, p. 689). Even where the material had to be arranged on the basis of the text (vols. ii and iii), musical indexes and footnotes give as complete information on the melody as only possible.

Of course, no mechanical or uniform system can be applied; every material claims a system of its own. The best of them, however, will be the one representing the most characteristic features of the different folk tunes, facilitating the discovery of variants and most clearly classifying related melodies which are not necesserily variants at the same time.

The more and the better surveys from the different speech areas will be published, the nearer the time when international collections, like Aarnes and Thompson's *Catalogue* and Thompson's *Motif-Index of Folk Literature* in the domain of tales, will appear in the world of music as well.

Only then will comparative song research yield results illuminating hitherto unrevealed depths of music conserved in oral traditions.

SABIN V. DRĂGOI

MUSICAL FOLKLORE RESEARCH IN RUMANIA AND BÉLA BARTÓK'S CONTRIBUTION TO IT

Interest in collecting musical folklore in our country manifested itself later than in others which did not experience the sufferings of political dependence. The secular Ottoman domination supported by the servile governments of Phanariotes obstructed in every possible way the penetration of culture from east and west, and its propagation in our country. Science and arts could not develop sufficiently to permit us to speak of a Rumanian musical tradition. Only at the end of the 18th and the beginning of the 19th century did some distinguished intellectuals with a national conscience appear, especially in Transylvania and later in the counties of Moldova and Muntenia.

Nevertheless, we find references to the existence and beauty of our musical folklore, especially our dances, in the travel notes of foreigners who visited our country, such as Martin Opitz (17th century), and Paul of Strassburgh (17th century). There are numerous and important descriptions of the epoch in Hungarian documents : Bálint Balassa (16th century), Nicolaus Istvánffy (16th century), *Codex Eszterházy* (Vietoris: 17th century), Péter Apor (17th century). Even two Rumanians left valuable writings, proving their interest in folk song. An anonymous chronicler from the Banat region (18th century) mentions two dances very widespread at that time, and prince Dimitrie Kantemir describes the ritual dance *Căluşul* and some others in his *Descriptio Moldovae* (1715). Very significant is the indignation of the clergyman Andreas Mathesius, expressed in his *Memoires* of 1647, where he complains that the Valachians sang pagan carols at Christmas-time instead of Christian ones.

Up to the beginning of the 19th century we know of only two documents with written melodies : namely a *Codex* by Caioni (a Franciscan monk of Rumanian origin 1629—1687) containing some dances, and a booklet of 11 melodies published by Franz Joseph Sultzer under the title *Walachische Tänze und Lieder* in the *Geschichte des Transalpinischen Daciens* (1781).

13

We can say that Anton Pann was the first Rumanian collector who gathered and published a significant number of songs, which he did not always take directly from the people, but sometimes from the professional popular musicians or the urban circles he frequented. The majority of these songs were of professional origin — written by himself or somebody else.

With the wakening of national consciousness and the thirst for freedom, which fired the imagination of the European peoples as a result of the French Revolution, at the beginning of the 19th century the intellectuals of our country turned their attention toward, and manifested interest in, the people.

But this concern for the people, this interest in their creations could only be considered a romantic approach, devoid of any scientific basis. Therefore the collecting which was carried on chaotically and not always from authentic sources, could not result in the discovery of genuine musical folklore as we know it today. Small, or sometimes more or less comprehensive publications of *"national airs"* arranged for the piano after the fashion and according to the possibilities of the times (since the collected material did not offer anything more or new) did not represent the traditional popular songs connected with the life of the people, with their feelings, customs and struggles, songs that have constantly been polished through the centuries. We could expect no more from these publications because things happened in much the same way even in the case of more advanced peoples. That is why the value of these publications is relative, second rate. We can still consider most valuable — from the point of view of their selection as well as masterful arrangements — those by I. A. Wachmann, Carol Miculi, Erlich Alfred Heinrich, G. Muzicescu, Jacob Mureşianu, G. Dima and D. Vulpian.

Only at the beginning of the 20th century did the collecting of musical folklore start to become a profession when a decisive beginning was made by I. Vidu, A. Voievodea, P. Ciorogariu, P. Pîrvescu, D. G. Kîriac and Tiberiu Brediceanu, the last three having already collected melodies by means of the phonograph. We may say that D. G. Kîriac laid the basis for research in musical folklore in our country. If no more could be done, it was not due to the lack of interest on the part of our musicians, but to the contemptuous attitude of those who assumed the responsibilities of the government.

*

This was the position of folklore research in our country when the powerful personality of Béla Bartók and his love of folk song intervened beneficiently and lent it an impulse that increased interest in folklore and made it an esteemed scientific pursuit.

As a matter of fact, around 1905, Béla Bartók, Zoltán Kodály, László Lajtha and Antal Molnár came to the conclusion that Hungarian professional music would not be able to find its way out of the difficulties brought upon it by completely spent romanticism, by modern alien influences — all of them trying to find new means of expression. They understood that the depleted traditions needed regeneration through contemporary elements to give new life to old values, and these contemporary elements were to be found in the folk song. So they began intensively to collect musical folklore in a scientific and planned way, using the technical means of the time. The more they collected, the more knowledge, love, and appreciation of folk music they gained.

But while Bartók's colleagues limited their activities to collecting and studying Hungarian folk songs, he himself extended his interest also to the musical folklore of the other nationalities living in Hungary, he collected music from Rumanians, Slovaks, Serbs, and Ruthenians with the same scientific care and probity.

He was very much interested in comparison, in mutual influences, likenesses, and differences in the musical folklore of nations living in the Danube Basin (South-East Europe). Later this man with a passion for science extended his research even beyond Europe.

Bartók first collected Rumanian music in the former district of Bihor in 1909—1910. For this he received material assistance from the Hungarian Ethnographic Museum and the Rumanian Academy. The latter also published his collection in 1913. In 1913—1914 he collected abundant material in the forest villages and in Hatzeg, former district of Hunedoara. In 1913 he continued his collecting work in Maramuresh, and the material was published by the Drei Masken Verlag publishing house in 1923. He collected songs also in North Banat, and in various places in Transylvania, among which was a big collection of Christmas carols published in facsimile by the Universal Edition at Bartók's expense (1936). All this material was supplied with explanations and studies which offered a synthesis of his long and careful analyses. He also published several smaller writings about our folk songs, some articles in magazines and lexicons, drawing conclusions that are, in the main, still valid today. But a great number of his collections (he gathered approximately 3500 melodies, 1194 of which are published) and a study written already in America are not yet known to us.

A distinguished musician and progressive composer, Bartók brilliantly and masterfully arranged some of the collected melodies and transformed them in immortal compositions, offering for the first time to the world *genuine* Rumanian folk song.

Thus he did not only teach us how to collect songs but left us indications as to how to arrange them without spoiling their original beauty. These works are : *Sonatina* (1915) for piano, *Rumanian Christmas Carols* (1915) for piano and a *Suite of Bihor Dances* (1917) for piano — all of them published by the Universal Edition. He also used Rumanian dance

15

melodies in his two *Rhapsodies* for violin and piano, and violin and orchestra. The two *Rumanian Dances* (1905) published by the Rózsavölgyi Publishing House are his own themes, which proves the rapidity and the profoundness with which Bartók picked up the characteristics of our folk songs. In his *Cantata Profana* he used the text of a Rumanian Christmas carol.

Bartók loved the Rumanian peasants as he loved all peasants among whom he travelled collecting songs. In order to gain the confidence of the peasants (the principal requisite for a good folklorist), to get to know them in all their manifestations and pursuits, he learned Rumanian, which was very useful to him in his researches into our folklore; it enabled him to acquire his really scientific convictions and conclusions.

Due to his democratic conceptions and his appreciation of our folklore, he was maliciously attacked by Hungarian chauvinistic circles of his country, who accused him of being a traitor to the national interests, while similar circles in our country "recompensed" him by calling him an instrument of Hungarian revisionism. In spite of all the bitterness that such ingratitude and misunderstanding evoked in him, he did not swerve from his path and did not abandon his convictions.

The facts enumerated here speak for themselves. In order to make them clear we have described the man, his work, and the difficulties he had to face. Besides, his being collector and researcher of numerous Rumanian melodies, their scientific and artistic messenger throughout the world, he has a special merit for us Rumanians, for our musicology. We can say without hesitation that he was the folklorist who gave us the first extensive collection, accompanied by scientific studies.

Concomitantly with Bartók's collecting activities, that is, in the second and third decade of our century, there appeared a Pleiade of talented and learned composers under the creative encouragement of George Enescu. Some of them, like C. Brăiloiu and the author of these lines, were galvanised by Bartók's results and teachings, understanding the invaluable services he brought to Rumanian folk art. By awakening our interest, understanding, and love for folk songs, he gave us a strong impetus. Enthusiastically we began to study his collections in order to put them at the disposal of composers who would use them as a basis for creating a national school. Together with us, others came from all corners of the country to give their worthy contribution, though we had no other support than our enthusiasm.

Among them were G. Galinescu, A. Zirra, G. Cucu, G. Fira, Emil Riegler-Dinu, M. Negrea and others.

C. Brăiloiu succeeded in creating a folkloristic archive at the Society of Rumanian Composers, patronized by George Enescu, and proceeded systematically and scientifically to collect our musical folklore by means of mechanical apparatus of the time, maintaining continuous and close contact with Bartók. But in order to work well he needed help. He trained his assistants himself, bringing up disciples in the spirit of Bartók's teaching and method. When the Institute of Folklore was established, we not only received some 30,000 folkloric pieces, documents registered on phonograph cylinders and gramophone records that belonged to the archive of the Society of Rumanian Composers but also Brăiloiu's co-workers turned folklorists, who are the principal supporters of the Institute of Folklore such as Ilarion Cocişiu (1910—1952), Paula Carp, Tiberiu Alexandru, Emilia Comişel, G. Ciobanu, Ion Nicola and Achim Stoia.

With their assistance and always following *Bartók*'s system, the Institute trains new folklorists. Our aim is to create several folkloric circles in the main provincial centres which will help to rear numerous amateur folklorists all over the country, closely guided by us.

On the other hand, Prof. Georgescu-Breazul, our eminent and learned musicologist, who is very passionately interested in collecting and studying our folklore, created an Archive of Phonograms at the Ministry of Arts in 1925, which, owing to the indifference and carelessness of various officials, functioned with interruptions and difficulties. Nevertheless, some 10,000 folkloric pieces were collected and registered. Breazul also trained disciples such as C. Ionescu, G. Bălănescu, C. Mareş, G. Creţoiu and Adriana Sachelarie who joined our Institute when the Archive was put into our care.

These two archives with their documentation and personnel today form the basis of the Institute of Folklore.

This si the rich crop of Bartók's sowing.

*

But we did not limit ourselves only to following Bartók's spiritual footsteps, we undertook vast research (for the time being only in the Hunedoara region) trying to get the same melodies at the same places and from the same persons who sang to Bartók 40 or more years ago, in order to verify scientifically what transformations have taken place during the past half century.

A team of five persons, musical, literary and choreographic experts headed by Emilia Comişel, undertook several expeditions in a group of villages called Pădureneşti. The expeditions were preceded by careful preparatory documentation.

Thorough collecting work has been done in the villages of Cerişor and Cerbăl and in another 22 places only to learn the circulation of different types of melodies. A study will be made of 955 melodies recorded between 1933 and 1955, to which will be added those collected by Béla Bartók and some others written down by ear. Extensive informmative material has been prepared which comprises card indexes indicating the frequency of the songs, repertory of genres of songs and the categories of singers' ages, questionnaires, card indexes with direct observations made at weddings, public merry-makings, Christmas greetings, burials, social gatherings for work, etc. Moreover, where possible, posthumous card indexes were made for singers and for material collected by Bartok. This was done in order to verify whether or not the singers were the most representative.

The villages were visited several times, from 2 to 14 days every time, especially on folkloric occasions. The real life of folklore has been studied in its evolution during the 40 years (from Bartók's first collection). The material gathered by Bartók has been followed up as well as its evolution and the differences from one generation to another (grandfather, father, son) have been analyzed, the continuity of tradition and the present influences, the researches on musical phenomena examined in the society where it originated and developed.

Although research and study of this vast material is still going on, up till now the following problems have been examined:

1. a) The maintenance of dialectal song (old style) in certain social-economic conditions, such as archaic way of life, reserved economy, remote geographical position, etc.

b) Assimilation of some melodies from other regions, due to the vitality of the musical dialect.

No. 1/a

Sung by Maria Costa, aged 15, and another girl. Collected by B. Bartók in 1914 in the village of Cerbel, county Hunedoara. No. M.Gr. 5a.

No. 1/b   **Song**

Sung by Susana (Sana) Crăciunescu, aged 60. Collected by E. Comișel and M. Rabinovici in 1954 in the village of Cerbel, county Hunedoara. Notation by M. Rabinovici. No. Fgr. 14.557b.

The same melody was collected by Bartók in 1914 from the same singer (indicated as "another girl"). From the second verse the rhythm is changed. Only the most important deviations are indicated.

c) Enrichment of the old repertory with Banat and South-Transylvanian melodies. The strong influence of the Banat material has been especially observed in songs and dance melodies.

No. 1/c   Song

Sung by Maria Săracu, aged 48. Collected by E. Comișel and M. Rabinovici in the village of Flugi, county Hunedoara. Notation by M. Rabinovici. No. Fgr. 14.580b.

2. The conservation of dialectal features only in strophical songs[1], and in dance melodies; ritual songs (Christmas carols, wedding and burial songs, ploughing songs), on the other hand, are interdialectals, having a wider zone or circulation.

No. 2.   Song

Sung by Maria Vinea, aged 42. Collected by E. Comișel and O. Bîrlea in 1950, in the village of Cerișor, county Hunedoara. Notation by R. Weiss. No. Fgr. 14.104a.

[1] Here the musical and not the poetical stanza is understood, the *doina* and the ballad not having a strophical structure. Rumanian popular poetry does not know strophes.

21

3. A still lively process of creation (innumerable versions of the same melody by means of creative interpretation.)

4. Survival of the traditional songs (old style) and coexistence with the new melodies.

5. Creation of new melodies even within the ritual genre.

(For instance, in wedding songs by means of reshaping certain old features sometimes through the transformation of one element *(parlando rubato* into *parlando giusto)*, of discarding ornaments or of simplifying the melodic line).

The Song of the Bride

No. 3/a

Sung by Maria Costa, aged 15 and another girl. Collected by B. Bartók in 1914, in the village of Cerbel, county Hunedoara. No. M.Gr. 13c.

The same tune from other singers.

The Song of the Bride

Parlando
Lento - Rubato (♪=94)

și Sa - ra bu - nă,

ieu ,mă du - cu, Nis a

i sa, nu mă cul - cu.

Sung by a group of women — Maria Ticula, aged 27, Maria Pocnita, aged 21, Cosana Goanta, aged 27. Collected by E. Comișel and O. Bîrlea, in 1950 in the village of Cerișor, county Hunedoara. Notation by R. Weiss. No. 14.118.

6. In a vast majority of villages the number of "specialists" knowing ritual songs is steadily decreasing.

The melodies collected by Bartók have survived up to now with some changes.

It has been stated that these transformations differing from one individual to another and from one execution to another occur within the limits of the traditional form of the style, within the limits of the respective genre, region and epoch. But the variations are less frequent in the ritual songs, because they are sung rarely, and by a small number of individuals. The artistic realisation depends on the talent, possibilities and the taste of the singer. (In order to study this problem the same melody has been recorded from the same individual at different intervals and occasions.)

In some villages, under the influence of the city, rituals have disappeared or are disappearing, owing to the transformations of taste (in villages where Christmas carols are no longer in use or are known only by a few old men, ritual song are sung only rarely).

A new tune in the new style.

No. 3/c

The Song of the Bride

Poco rubato (♪=150)

Trăn-dă-fir în cor-nu me-sî, Trăn-dă-fir în

accel.

cor-nu me-sî, Ai hai ia lai la

Ai hai ia lai la Cum mai plîng o -

ki mi-re-sî, Cum mai plîng o - ki mi-re-sî,

a tempo

Cum mai plîng o - ki mi-re-sî Ai hai

ia lai la Ai hai ia lai la.

Sung by a group of girls — Lucuţia Ticula, aged 15, Armina Catrîna, aged 18, Maria Popa, aged 16, and Victoria Bogdan, aged 17. Collected by M. Rabinovici and O. Bîrlea in 1955, in the village of Goleş, county Hunedoara. Notation by E. Comişel. No. Mgt. 503f.

24

No. 4/a

Colinda
(Christmas carol)

Pe su' poa-la ce-riu-lu-iu Doam-ne,
dai Dom-nu-lui Doam-ne, Prim-blă-ji Mai-ca
Dom-nu-lu-iu.

Sung by two men, aged 20 and 25. Collected by Bartók in 1914, in the village of Cerbel, county Hunedoara. No. M.Gr. 8a.

No. 4/b

Colinda
(Christmas carol)

Plim-bă, plim-bă mai-ca sfîn-tă Dom-nu-
lui, Dom-nu-lui Doam-ne Pă cěst plai, pi-čior de ra-i.

Sung by Josif Spăriosu. Collected by I. Cocișiu, in 1946 in the village of Ruda, county Hunedoara. Notation by E. Comișel. No. Fgr. 10.198a.

Bartók collected the same tune from another singer. *Tempo* and original *finalis* cannot be indicated as it was not recorded.

7. Tendency to disappearance of some popular instruments like the flute and the bagpipe, and their substitution by city instruments such as the *taragot*, the clarinet, the trumpet and string instruments. If the instrument still exists, it is no longer used, not even at village festivities.

8. Tendency to disappearance of the dialectal repertory in some villages densely populated by workers, like Ghelari, Topliţa and Govajdia, under the influence of broadcasting and of professional choral songs (in these places the national costume has also disappeared).

9. Changes in some occasions for singing and dancing: *a)* Sunday village merriments tend to disappear owing to the scarcity of young people (decrease in population); *b)* wedding is usually celebrated without music ("night feast"); *c)* for funeral songs mourners are called in from neighbouring villages.

No. 5/a   **Dirge**

Sung by Maria Costa, aged 15, and another girl. Collected by Bartók in 1914, in the village of Cerbel, county Hunedoara. No. M.Gr. 13a.

Sung by Pătruța Ispas, aged 25. Collected by I. Cocișiu in 1946 in the village of Cerbel, county Hunedoara. Notation by E. Comișel. No. F.Gr. 10.268.

10. Dependence of the text on the melody; among ritual songs of the same village several texts are sung to the same melody (in villages where the ritual is disappearing). The same thing happens to the simple songs in the first phases of their penetration from other regions.

*

I. It is necessary to add that there exist some genres that are absent from Bartók's collections. Their existence in his time is indisput-

---

* Double elision (of two syllable).

able but they escaped his attention. Thus there have been found and collected :

    a) children's songs and dances,

    b) ritual songs for drought *(babaluga ploii, băbăruţa)*,

    c) reaping songs,

    d) songs used on occasions of collective social work and sung to the melodies of strophic songs,

    e) cradle songs (sung to the melodies of funeral or strophical songs),

    f) songs for St. Theodore's day (help the hair grow), the old, original melody being substituted by some strophic song,

    g) funeral ritual songs, of the *Fir tree* type, mourning songs like *Daybreak* and *Watchsongs* existing in the North.

II. Epic texts, few in number, are sung by the peasants to the melodies of strophic songs. Here neither the style of professional interpretation nor the epic recitative, which is characteristic of the old monarchy, are known. Besides, even music to dancing is performed by peasants, whereas semi-professional musicians have appeared very rarely, and only in the last decades.

III. The six-syllable verses are very frequent in ritual songs *(Fir-tree, Daybreak, Paparude,* Christmas carols) and even in some strophic songs.

IV. As an answer to Bartók's statement made in *Rumanian Folk Music*, in an article published in *The Dictionary of Modern Music and Musicians*, London 1924, and in *Das neue Musiklexikon*, Berlin 1926, where he maintains that for centuries no new melodies have been created — with the exception of Maramuresh and neighbouring regions — we may refer to a new wedding melody (see no. 3) created in recent decades and influenced by the strophical song. This melody is not executed with other texts.

*

People remember Bartók with affection. Among the many references that have been written down, we reproduce here one by the peasant Bistrian Alexandru from the village Feregi, now 52 years old, who was a child when he met Bartók: "He was a kind man, who spoke gently. It was evident that he strove to speak Rumanian with the people. He offered them money and tobacco. He came to see the dances and described them afterwards."

Ilarion Cocişiu, a learned collaborator of the Institute of Folklore, also undertook, on his own initiative, a trip to retrace Bartók's footsteps in Bihor. There he found people who had sung for Bartók and remembered him with love. But Cocişiu's premature death prevented him from sharing his findings with us.

In 1950 the collecting expedition to Maramuresh, village Ieud (where Bartók also worked in 1913), found the *Hora lungă*, for example, to have disappeared in some villages owing to changes in taste and mentality.

Bartók not only maintained close contact with the Rumanian peasants but also carried on an extensive correspondence with Rumanian folklorists such as Constantin Brăiloiu, I. Buşiţia I. Bianu, I. Bîrlea, D. G. Kîriac, Tiberiu Brediceanu and Octavian Beu.

Though the scope of the present paper does not permit us to express our entire appreciation for Bartók's numerous deeds for the benefit of our people's culture, I still wish it to testify to our gratitude which I express in the name of the Institute most authorized to do so.

EMILIA COMIŞEL

THE RUMANIAN POPULAR BALLAD

Rumanian folk art is characterized by a great variety of forms, regional styles and variants, owing to the complexity of life therein reflected, to the changes and to the continuous transformations — peculiar to folk art — it undergoes in the course of different periods in different places and under different circumstances.

Rumanian popular epic poetry is particularly rich in content and musical idioms. Generally, it is still living and performed on various occasions.

We distinguish several categories: epic poetry connected with rites and ceremonies, and epic poetry proper, the ballad called "old song" *(cîntec bătrînesc)* in popular terminology.

Among the songs connected with rites and ceremonies, many have a more or less epic character: thus, the funeral songs like *Zorile* (Song of Dawn), *Al Bradului* (Song of the Fir) and *Priveghiul* (Song of the Vigil); the nuptial epic poetry sung or recited, like *Cîntecul Miresii* (Song of the Bride), *Oraţia* (greeting songs or recitals); the agrarian epic poetry, like *Cîntecul Secerii* (Harvest Song). A real epic character can be found in the songs connected with the winter festivals, like *Colinde*, *Pluguşorul*, (ritual ploughing), the greeting song *Urarea*, while in the spring songs, *Lăzărel*, the *Toconele*, it is less marked.

In the collection of Macedonian folklore another category is mentioned, the one connected with dances; epic songs performed during the dance at important festivals.[1]

The majority of these folklore compositions are sung in groups by women, men, young and old or adult, and children; either accompanied or unaccompanied by certain rites. The *colinde*, the funeral songs, and the songs accompanying dances are sometimes performed in an antiphonic manner (by two or three alternating groups). The lines of six (five) and eight (seven) syllables, belonging to the trochaic type, are isometric.

[1] T. Papahagi, *Antologie Aromînească* (Arumanian Anthology), 1922, pp. 365—370.

The greetings recited at a wedding and in winter are heterometric. Without having the epic ampleness of the ballads, some of them run into many lines (300). In the *colinde* a heroic epic art may be observed : the young man leads the "tied up lion" "unharmed", he struggles with the stag, with the maiden from the fortress, etc. The conciseness of the melody and the varied *giusto* rhythm impart to some of these songs an optimistic character, while others, having a richly ornamented melodic line and extending at some length, have a solemn, dramatic character, an artistic polish. Some themes circulate in several art forms : in the tale, the ballad, the song.

Epic poetry proper — "the old song" — owing to the variety and great wealth of motifs and themes, as well as to the way of composing which is still kept alive in certain districts, occupies an important place in Rumanian folk art.

The ballads are only sung for the "public" on certain occasions (without having a ritual character) : at festivals, family gatherings, inns, taverns. In the districts where the genre is still kept alive, the performance of the ballad at the wedding, particularly at the great feast of Sunday evening, constitutes the most important moment. Having a declamatory character, the ballad cannot be rendered in a true manner without two essential elements : the performer and the audience. The ballad is sung by a single performer, by a peasant or a country musician,[2] with or without accompaniment (by a single instrument : the *cobza*, a kind of guitar ; the cymbalum ; the violin ; and the *taraf*, a group of instruments). The peasant performer is sometimes accompanied by the *taraf*.

The performance of the ballad is based, for the most part, on improvization within the frame of certain traditional procedures and formulas. This demands a gifted singer having a good memory and being acquainted with the specific poetical and musical requirement of the art form. To enhance this art form, some performers also use, in a masterly manner, dramatic means, — mimicry, gestures, declamation. Today the real preservers of this genre are the country musicians contributing to the maintenance, propagation, and development of the "old song". They possess an extraordinary memory, they know from 30 to 40 ballads, which means about 12,000 lines.

The ballad cannot be understood perfectly in all its complexity and expressive value unless heard in its proper environment, in the atmosphere where it is recited. Usually the recital of the ballad requires and produces a very high tension, both in the audience and the performer, and is performed in perfect silence. The moment the ballad is "requested", the performer assumes a dignified air, just like a rhapsodist of ancient times. "Those who listen, fascinated by the face, the gestures

---

[2] The opinion that had called in question the value and authenticity of the ballads collected from gypsy musicians was later refuted.

and the inspired look, lend their ears motionless and their thoughts wander to the places, persons and deeds the singer describes or relates."[3]

The ballads being known to the audiences, the listeners may intervene and sometimes correct the performer. Thus, in the artistic realization of the ballad, besides the knowledge of style and rules of the performance, the audience play an important part by stimulating the singer's creative imagination and his gift of improvization.

Moreover, the performing of the ballad being an important moment in collective life, we have to stress its ideological value. Like other art forms, also the ballad reflects in specific artistic images, the people's way of thinking and feeling, their conception of the world and life, folklore having formerly been almost the only form of expression of their culture. That is why the ballad always has a topical aspect, even if composed in previous epochs, and features facts and aspects of the days of yore. The ballads of the Heyducks (men who took arms individually or in groups against an unjust or foreign rule) and the heroic ballads, — perfect examples of patriotism which preserve the best traditions of the people's heroic past, — maintain the will to a happy and free life.

Even today they can influence human conscience in an active way, thus constituting a means of raising the intellectual level of the masses.

Though the existence of the ballad is attested in chronicles and publications, Rumanian and foreign, as early as the 16th century[4], the first collections of Rumanian ballads were compiled as late as the 19th century[5]. Conceived under the influence of the esthetic and historic principles of the romantic school, the folkloric value of the material is rather uneven. Certain collectors took the liberty of "correcting", of changing the names of the heroes to make them correspond to certain historical characters, and even of composing, in popular style, ballads with a historical theme.

Concerning the documentary value of the ballad for history, the conception adopted by the literary critics, philologists and historians — of whom the most fervent adepts are B. P. Haşdeu and N. Iorga — still survives in our country in the 20th century.

The most important problems that arise in connection with the ballad are : origin, veracity, genuineness, relation with the epics of other peoples, connection between ballad an epic, between ballad and written literature. But the studies made according to different conceptions and methods, relying on publications and only very seldom on living reality, have not always yielded results of value. Monographs,

---

[3] G. Dem. Teodorescu, *Poezii populare romîneşti* (Rumanian Folk Poetry), 1885, p. 418.
[4] B. P. Haşdeu, *Archiva Istorică a Romînilor* (Historic Archives of the Rumanians), vol. ii, 1865, p. 7.
[5] For collections see enumeration on p. 52.

treatises, and essays published so far do not cover all the problems of the genre to be solved[6].

Essays on the music of the ballad appeared as late as 1954[7], the only musical monograph has been left unpublished.[8] The latest researches made under the auspices of the Institute of Folklore are completed with the study of musical idioms.

Among the old songs some have subjects taken from the life of the Rumanian people and some have motifs originating from the South-East of Europe, and related to those of the ancestral Indo-European layer having universal circulation.

The classification of the ballad, from a literary point of view, presents great many difficulties ; owing to the different aspects of the same motif, which arise from interpenetrations, constant transformations and adaptations, from superpositions in the course of time, a ballad may belong to different categories. Nevertheless, bearing in mind the subject matter which may relate an imaginary plot or a real event seen by the people, or else the thoughts and feelings of communities and performers, three groups may be distinguished : the *fantastic ballad*, drawing on myths, legends and tales ; the *heroic ballad*, *i. e.*, the *ballad of the Heyducks* or the *historical ballad*, as well as the *news ballad* which tells about everyday events in the life of an individual or a family from certain aspects of the epoch, etc. N. Iorga has made an attempt at classifying the ballads according to cycles.[9]

Versification and Poetics

The ballads are sung in isometric verses of the "trochaic" type, having six (five) and eight (seven) syllables. There is great variety in the grouping of the lines, according to rhyme or assonance governing two, three, or four, etc. lines. The internal rhymes add a pulsation and impart suppleness :

Doi	Two
cotoi	tomcats
în loc de boi	instead of oxen
Stejar drept	Straight oak
tare-n piept	full-chested
'Nalt la stat	The stature tall
mare la sfat	sensible the behaviour
Şi viteaz cum n'a mai stat	And brave like never there was.

[6] For monographs see enumeration on p. 54.
[7] E. Comişel, *Recitativul epic al baladei* (The Epic Recitative of the Ballads), in *Rev. Muzica*, vol. vi, 1954.
[8] O. Bîrlea and E. Comişel, *Balada haiducească Radu Anghel* (The Heyduck Ballad Radu Anghel), 1953, manuscript.
[9] N. Iorga, *Balada populară romînească* (Rumanian Folk Ballad), 1910, pp. 25—65.

Professor N. Iorga has, with remarkable intuition, described the way of alternation and coupling of the lines : "a too flat rhyme repeated in every couplet would be an obstacle. Too much would be demanded from the person who speaks (recites or sings), if he had to know by heart so many ballads. Besides, there are rhymes which one meets in the same song performed by different persons. These rhymes represent such important technical achievements that they cannot be easily forgotten. They please too much not to become imprinted in the memory. And they are useful, serving as a cue. From time to time a remarkable rhyme springs up, reassuring the singer that he is on the right way and, indeed, without following to the letter the footsteps of his predecessors, he has nevertheless reached the point he had to reach from where the way unfolds itself."[10]

The majority of the ballads have a great number of lines, sometimes over 1000. (*The Ballad of Tanislav* — 1042, *Badiu* — 1020, etc).,

When dictating the singer scans the lines in several ways. Usually the stressed syllables are the 1st, the 5th, or the 3rd, the 7th (the 7th rarely).

$$\acute{-} \, \cup - \cup \acute{-} \cup - \cup \qquad\qquad \overset{\prime\prime}{-} \, \cup - \cup - \cup$$

$$- \cup \overset{\prime\prime}{-} \cup - \cup \overset{\prime\prime}{-} \cup \qquad\qquad - \cup - \cup \overset{\prime\prime}{-} \cup$$

$$- \cup - \cup - \cup \overset{\prime\prime}{-} \cup$$

The completion of catalectic verses (of 5, 7 syllables), the anacrusis, the elisions taking place during the performance, according to the requirements of the melody, follow the same rules as in the other literary genres.

In the old ballads the action, having achieved a perfectly crystallized form and complete balance, forms an integral whole in all the versions. The action takes place in an epic atmosphere of tales, of grandeur which strongly impresses the audience. Hyperboles, personifications, allegories, detailed descriptions, repetitions of certain groups of typical verses, dialogues, alternation of pathetic passages with gay ones, constitute only part of the poetical procedures.

Groups of typical lines, crystallized in the course of centuries, circulate in different ballads so as to render certain moments, descriptions and characters analogous. Thus in the ballads *Antofiţă al lui Vioară* and *Miu*, the feast is described by the same verses, etc.

The people have created their heroes, their types, their characters, The Heyducks all have the same characteristics : bravery, courage, love, and pity for the humble, physical beauty and strength, tenderness for comrades-in-life and -in-arm, for their horses and for the nature in which they live. But the love and admiration that the people feel for their heroes make them exaggerate their qualities, they attribute them super-

---

[10] N. Iorga, *op. cit.*; idem. *Istoria Literaturii* pp. 33—34.

natural power, invulnerability, etc. We see a child of 12 killing, all by himself, 16,000 enemies in the course of a battle he wages against the Tartars ; Gruia slays 100 Turks with his club weighing a hundred kilograms ; Doicin, the invalid, tosses his club weighing 5000 kilograms into the air and catches it with his other hand ; the weapon and saddle of Miu the Youngster are so heavy that none of the 50 strong lads can lift them.

The exaggerated traits of the persons of positive and negative character intensify the dramatic conflict. The tendency to archaize the facts of the present and to actualize the events of ancient times, the elements of tales which often attenuate the reality of facts, are to be found everywhere in the ballad (magic horse, animals and plants that can speak, prophetic dreams, allegories, metamorphoses, etc.).

The atmosphere in which the ballad takes place, the characters, the clothes, hunting with falcons, etc. recall the feudal age.

Certain performers show a remarkable talent in epic construction, to make the most of the moments of scenic effect, rendering them more and more dramatic. These procedures of composition are used much less in the ballads of recent origin.

The most excellent fantastic ballad based on the popular belief concerning the serpent of the hearth is *The Serpent* or *The Dragon*.

The brave young man, whom his mother has cursed to be devoured by the serpent of the hearth, departs :

Intr-o joi de dimineață	A Thursday morning
Pe rouă și pe ceață	Through dew and fog

(typical lines to be found in several ballads) with falcons and greyhounds

Tot la vînătoare	Always a-hunting
Pentru-nsurătoare	For the wedding
Vînat să găsească	To find game
Masă să-și gătească	To prepare the feast

In certain versions he pursues a dove — his soul — who begs him not to pierce it with his arrow. He wants to roast it and, imagining to see a great fire in the distance, he comes across a dragon.

Cu șolzii de aur	With scales of gold
La soare sclipind	Glittering in the sun
Ca focul lucind	Gleaming like fire

who advises him to lay down his arms, for the struggle between them is of no avail, his mother having destined him for the dragon since his early childhood. The serpent half swallows him :

Jumătate nu mai poate	The other half [he] cannot [swallow]
De armele-ncărcate	Because of the loaded arm
La brîu întesate	Girded round his waist

After three days he is saved by a young Moldavian, with whom he make friends as "frate pîn' la moarte" (brother till death), though the dragon had promised his rescuer

Șoimei	Falcons,
ogărei	greyhounds
Și arme cu zale	And armoured weapons
Și murgul din vale	And the bai [horse] from the valley
Pietre nestemate	Precious stones
Și comori bogate	And rich treasures

In certain versions the Moldavian burns the serpent which he lures among the reeds ; from its ashes grows a plant similar to the pearls worn by the young girls. Other versions make the brave young man die, poisoned by the spittle of the dragon, although his rescuer had dipped him in milk.

The action takes place in an atomsphere of tales and is developed into a text of considerable proportions (560—700 lines).

In *Antofiță al lui Vioară*, the aspects of the fishermen's life are given in a fantastic atmosphere. Antofiță fishes in the Vidros, in deep water that "reaches from heaven to earth". The sovereign of the waters, Vidra, helps him because the fisherman has captured her only offspring and tortures him. Certain versions are interlaces with the themes of blasphemy and the death of the father, and the scene of the bride asking him to bring her

Știucile	Pike
ca vacile	like cows
Morunii	Sturgeon
ca bivolii	like buffalos

The poetic images describing Antofiță's father recall those describing Corbea :

Cu bărbuța pîn' la brîu	The whiskers till the waist
Barba-i bate brațele	The beard covers his arms
Genele	The eyelashes
sprîncenele	his eyebrows
Și chica călcîile	And his hair his heels

Toma Alimos "Heyduck of the Lowlands" — a wealthy shepherd in certain versions — wounded in a cowardly way by Manea,

| Stăpînul moşiilor | The owner of the lands |
| Si domnul cîmpiilor | The lord of the fields |

takes revenge and dies. The great love of nature is rendered in poetic images of unparalleled grandeur. The hero drinks to the health of the trees :

Că-mi sînt mie frăţiori	Because they are my little brothers
De poteri ascunzători	Who hide me from the sight of the patrols
De-oi muri	If I have to die
m-or tot umbri	their shade will cover me
Cu frunze m'or înveli	Their leaves will enfold me
Cu freamătul m-or jeli	And their rustling will lament for me

As he raises his glass "the forest trembles".

Fagi şi paltini se pleca	Beeches and maples bowed down
Fruntea de i-o răcorea	To cool his forehead
Mîna de i-o săruta	They kissed his hand
Armele din teci ieşea	The arms sprang from the scabbard
Murguleţul necheza	The bai [horse] neighed

The horse's affection for his master assumes touching human aspects. It is the horse that digs the grave of the heyduck

Cu copita cînd săpa	When he dug with his hoof
Groapă mică că-i făcea	A small pit he made for him
Floricele că-i sădea	He planted little flowers
Cu trei lacrimi le stropea	He watered them with his tears

Iovan Iorgovan, the brave man who goes hunting followed by his falcons and his greyhounds, kills the serpent; poisonous flies issue from its skull. This ballad, which is known all over the country, has numerous versions. The subject is interwoven with the theme of the brothers who find each other again, with the motif of the metamorphoses, and that of incest (between brother and sister), etc.

The young man, arriving at the Cerna (a river in the Banat), asks the river to stop its course that he may cross ; on the other bank he finds the young savage girl. In spite of her protests, as she identifies him as her brother, Iorgovan rapes her. The young man is drowned, while the young girl saves herself by swimming. In other versions she is transformed into a flower, or killed by Iorgovan ; or the emperor promises a reward to him who will kill the serpent. Iorgovan after having burnt the serpent receives :

| Jumătate din cetate | Half of the fortress |
| Şi din sate-a treia parte | And a third of the villages |

The Ballad of Meşterul Manole is a masterpiece of the epic genre composed in superior artistic form ; it is related to the building of Arges monastery. Borrowing the principal motif — the offering of human sacrifice to the protecting divinity of a new building — from the peoples of South-Eastern Europe with whom this subject has become typical in the ballad[11], the Rumanians have given it an autochton form. Studies and monographs relating to this ballad have been published by D. Caracostea[12] P. Caraman,[13] I. Popovici,[14] and D. Găzdaru.[15] This ballad circulates in many versions.

The prince Negru-Vodă, accompanied by

Nouă meşteri mari	Nine great artisans
Calfe şi zidari	Apprentices and masons
Cu Manole zece	Ten with Manole
Care-i şi întrece	Who surpasses them all,
Stă inima rece	[Your] heart would be [paralized] with fear

seeks a site for the monastery he wants to build. A little swineherd, whom they meet on the way, shows them an "old forsaken wall" or, according to other versions, a little mountain lake. Unfortunately, what they build during the day is demolished in a mysterious way during the night. Manole, the central figure, has a dream in which it is revealed to him that as long as the wife of one of the artisans is not walled in alive, their work would not last. After being bound by a solemn oath not to betray the secret, the masons go home. Only Manole stays near the wall and struggling between his given oath and his love for his wife, he writes her to prepare a dish "made of the meat of an ox lost a year ago". The author of the ballad describes the love and devotion of the young woman who fulfils the wish of her husband — a wish that Manole thought to be unrealizable — and brings him the food. The other masons did not keep their oath. When Manole perceives his wife from the top of the scaffolding, he prays to God to send a rainfall

Brazii să-i despoaie	That would strip the firs
Paltinii să-ndoaie	That would bend the plane trees

[11] Kurt Schladesbach, *Die Aromunische Ballade von der Artabrücke*, in *Jahresbericht des Instituts für rumänische Sprache*, vol. i, 1892.
[12] Caracostea, *Material sud-est european şi formă romînească* (South-East-European Material and Rumanian Form), in *Rev. Fund. Reg.* 1942.
[13] Caraman, *Consideraţii critice asupra genezii şi răspîndrii baladei Meşterului Manole în Balcani* (Critical Reflections on the Origin and Diffusion of the Ballad of Meşter Manole in the Balcans), in *Bul. Inst. Fil. Al. Philippide*, vol. i, 1934.
[14] I. Popovici, *Balada Meşterul Manole* (The Ballad of Meşter Manole), in *Rev. Transilvania*, 1909, pp. 5 — 19.
[15] D. Găzdaru, *Legenda Meşterului Manole* (The Legend of Meşter Manole) in *Arhiva*, 1932.

like a tempest. Other versions speak of thorny thickets, of a she-wolf and a poisonous beast. His wife, Caplea (the name is not the same in all versions), overcoming all obstacles, joins Manole. The latter, though in despair, respects his oath. While Caplea is being walled in, the following lines, which like a *leitmotiv* are repeated through the whole ballad, can be heard :

Var şi cărămidă	Lime and bricks
Că-i pustie multă	We have much to build
Că-i lucrare lungă	Our work is long

These lines alternate with the sighs of the young woman being sacrificed :

Manole, Manole	Manole, Manole
Zidul rău mă strînge	The wall embraces me
Trupuşoru-mi frînge	It crushes my body
Tîţişoara-mi curge	Milk streams from my breast
Copilaşu-mi plînge	My little child cries

The popular poet finds words of dramatic force ; while Manole works with his trowel he hears :

Un glas răguşit	A husky voice
Un vaet topit	A smothered groan

When the monastery is completed, the prince asks the artisans whether they are able to construct a building that surpasses this one in beauty. Receiving an affirmative answer, the prince has the scaffolding removed and lets the masons die on the roof. The artisans make themselves wings of laths, but they sink heavily. The masons are changed into stone statues and Manole into a well

Cu apă curată	Having clear water
Trecută prin piatră	Sifted by pebbles
Cu lacrămi udată	Watered by tears
De Caplea vărsate	Shed by Caplea

The invasions of the Turks and Tartars have left their traces in the ballads.

Tanislav,

Măcelarul turcilor	The butcher of Turks
Hîngherul tătarilor	The slayer of Tartars

sometimes an innkeeper, admired for his bravery, is pursued by the Turks. Real situations intermingle with fantastic elements. Coming across young girls washing linen, the Turks ask them where Tanislav is

40

hidden. His former, jilted sweetheart shows them the hiding place of the young hero, who is sleeping in a kayik [boat] "inlaid with silver letters, the naked sword on his chest". The description of the sleeping hero, that of the Turkish captain, and the answer of the young girls are given in typical repeated lines. The Turks with the help of Nedea, the servant of Tanislav whom they have bribed, tie the hero to a millstone and throw him in the Danube. Tanislav awakes after three days, lifts the millstone to his shoulders, and rises to the surface of the water. Noticed by a young girl he is saved by her father. After having taken revenge on the Turks by slaughtering and burning them, after having punished Nedea, Tanislav marries and gives up his profession of Heyduck. In other versions the hero punishes his unfaithful sweetheart by burning her. The action is developed with ever growing tension.

The ballads of the heyducks — which reflect their organized struggle against social injustice, against native and foreign oppressors — are numerous. The revolt of the Heyducks "a form of struggle and social resistance, becomes more intense in the second half of the 17th century. The popular compositions of later origin, dedicated to the Heyducks, are conceived in the same line."[16] Though, in general, the action, owing to the local character, is the same, the name of the Heyduck and the secondary episodes vary: from an artistic point of view these latter ballads are presented with less reality. In spite of the real events underlying the subject "in proportion to the distance from their place of origin, the details linking them to their point of departure fade away . . . the plot begins to be generalized, mythical elements take the place of accidental, local elements".[17]

Music

Musical investigations have revealed that the ballads represent two distinct melodic idioms; some have a free structure, others have a fixed texture. Nevertheless the specific idiom of this art form is the free style, the epic recitative. The rich and dramatic contents of the ballad, its dimensions and declamatory character have, in the course of time, determined the formation and development of the means of expression and of the specific structure on this art form. The means of expression — subordinated to the sense of the contents — are reduced to an utmost simplicity, thus creating a recitative style, a *melodic recitation* in an adequate architectonic form which permits great freedom to the singer.

[16] T. Ionescu-Nişcov, *Haiducia şi cîntecul haiducesc* (The Heyducks and the Heyduck song) in *Studii şi Cercetări de Istorie, Literatură şi Folclor*, vol. ii, 1953 pp. 267—268.
[17] O. Bîrlea, *Procesul de creaţie al baladei* (The Process of Ballad Creation), in *Rev. Fundaţiilor Regale*, vol. viii, 1941, p. 584.

Thus the specific melody of the ballad proper is the epic recitative, the basic elements of which are : *a)* the simple recitative, the verse sung on a single tone — *recto tono; b)* the melodic recitative, characteristic melodic formulae of narrow compass, corresponding to a line or a hemistich; *c)* the so-called *parlato*, the declaimed, recited, related verse (marked ⅃).

These elements are combined quite freely, in an improvised manner, with unlimited possibilities. Each element has an exactly determined sense. Thus, the role of the melodic and simple recitative is to bring into relief the text — the fundamental element — without attenuating it, and to contribute to the development of the action in a relatively short time, in a narrative, epic atmosphere. In keeping with the text the recitative becomes especially expressive when using simple means : identic or varied repetition, irregular alternation, etc. The singer employs in turns the melodic recitative and the simple recitative to prevent monotony, he repeats a melodic formula to emphasize an idea, a verse ; he then passes to another formula, keeping the attention of the audience continually alive. At the climaxes when the action develops rapidly, he "speaks", recites the verses imparting a sonorous timbre to his voice and, thereby, according a relaxation to the audience; then, accompanying himself on his instrument, he again takes up the thread of his narrative which develops in a continually varied and vigorous form till the end of the theme, owing to an expressive and suggestive formula, generally a *melisma "cantabile"* (the final formula).

The numerous procedures of variation are determined by the requirements of the expressiveness of the melody or the text, by the possibilities, by the talent and fancy of the singer, within the limits of tradition. The most frequently used procedures are : *a)* transpositon of a formula to different pitches, *b)* the modification of one or several notes, *c)* the repetition of one note to make an accent tonic or expressive, *d)* the expressive gradation achieved by duration, pitch, etc.

The architectonic form belonging to this genre of great dimensions, besides allowing great freedom of creative improvisation, eliminates, by imposing a coherent and fixed structure, the monotony that would result from the unchanging repetition of a melody having a fixed outline. In folk music, when determining structure, one has to take into account the number and alternation of the melodic lines (by melodic lines we mean a melodic fragment that corresponds to a verse of the poetic text), their similarity or dissimilarity in the contents. In general, the length of the line determines the musical phrase which can be constructed of one or two melodic formulae identic or dissimilar ; the melodic formula may develop over two lines though very seldom.

In the ballad the melody is arranged in "periods" (a provisional term, because we cannot assimilate these musical fragments with the stanza which is based on a fixed number of melodic lines that follow each other in the same order). The "periods" are formed by a varying number of melodic lines (in the ballads studied so far, from 3 to 16), arranged in groups of symmetrical or asymmetrical phrases, the repetition and succession of which are arbitrary. Thus the first period may have six phrases, the second three, the third four, etc. (each one having 2—3—4 different formulae).

The initial formula (which is often in the high register), the first in a "period", and the final formula which concludes it, have specific features and are not subject to transformations of great importance. The median formulae undergo a wide range of transformations, owing to the principle of identic or varied repetition and of free sequence. Generally they are kept in the middle register reaching the high notes to mark the stress, while the notes of lower pitch are reserved for recital.

The forming of phrases into groups generally depends on the theme and the talent of the singer. With good performers the "period" corresponds to a literary episode.

The scales are very varied as to range and structure. Beside the pentachords and hexachords, gapped scales occur, archaic modes, the most frequent ones being *la, re, mi*. The chromatic scales (whith one or more augmented seconds) of the major and minor type are the most frequent in this genre. They are characterized by a great mobility of the degrees — particularly of those chromaticized — sometimes indicating modulations, and sometimes an ambit that often begins at VII. The ambit which is extremely varied (1—5, 1—6, 1—8, VII—5, VII—6, etc) rarely goes beyond the octave.

Generally the melody does not modulate ; it often has a bi-modal character, or it "modulates" from a diatonic scale to a chromatic scale.

The final cadences are generally made on the repeated prime, less ferquently on the second or on the VII, in *parlato*. The internal cadences are variable, nevertheless certain descending melodic formulae can be observed which design the final cadence, repeated here in the same way.

Miorită

(Initial formula)

Pe-un pi - čior de   pla   iu   *finalis*

Corbea

finalis

Corbea, Badiu, Crivăt, Voica, etc.

finalis

Ion ăl Mare

finalis

Radu Anghel

(Final formula)

Pă - du - rea   să je - lu - ia, măi

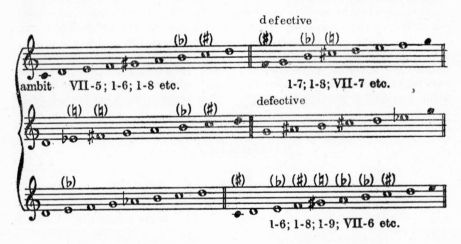

defective

ambit VII-5; 1-6; 1-8 etc.   1-7; 1-8; VII-7 etc.

defective

1-6; 1-8; 1-9; VII-6 etc.

finalis

44

Rhythm. The epic recitative evolves in a lively manner with free rhythm, *parlando*, in which ♪ and ♩ alternate in various ways. The long values and the rests occur rather in the initial formulae and in the finales or at the end of the melodic line. This rhythm influenced or determined by the verse or by the tonic and expressive accent, does not adhere to the strict isochronism of the strong beat, as it cannot be fitted into the measures. Our schematic way of notation cannot render all the wealth of expression that the good singers are able to display by different procedures.[18]

In certain ballads a tendency may be observed at attaining a greater rhythmical precision by the use of triplets, metrical accents, which is partly due to the instrumental accompaniment. Besides, the ballads are generally sung throughout in metrical rhythm.

The tempo varies between ♪ = 160—380 (approximately).

The adaptation of the epic recitative to the different folkloric areas has led to regional dissimilarities; thus one distinguishes a Walachian style (belonging also to Little Walachia), a style of the Banat (influenced partly by the melodic character of the song proper and by Serbian music); this indicates a phase of disintegration of the old style. The problem, however, remains open because sufficient researches in this field have not yet been undertaken.

In general the Rumanian epic recitative is reminiscent of the Gregorian liturgical recitative and of that of the psalms, as well as of the Ukrainian and Bulgarian ballads.

It has been observed that certain ballads have their own melodies (*Miorița, Manole, Corbea,* etc.), others have borrowed melodic formulae common to several ballads. But it happens that the same ballad is sung in different districts to different melodies. A tendency of a cyclic formation of the ballads has been found, in the sense that the ballads having similar contents are sung to melodies consisting of identical formulae (*Badiu, Tanislav, Voica,* etc. use the same melodic formulae). The study of the formation of the musical types of the ballad *Miorița*[19] has revealed that the majority of the versions circulate with a melody of their own, sometimes having a fixed structure, while others use the epic recitative with different formulae; in Moldavia and Transylvania they are sung to the melodies of the *colinde*. The ballad has some 500 variants.

The ballads of recent origin, especially those concerned with the Heyducks and those relating the events of everyday life, are adapted

---

[18] O. Bîrlea and E. Comișel, *op. cit.* (in note 8.) p. 214.

[19] E. Comișel, *Tipologia baladei Miorița* (The Typology of the Ballad Miorița), manuscript.

to the melodies of the *"doina"*[20]. The adaptation of the epic text to the melody of the *doina*, in which recitatives alternate with richly ornamented and melismatic melodic lines, has brought about some changes in the melodic structure of the *doina*. Owing to the great number of recitatives and *parlatos*, the organization of the melodic lines into lengthy "periods" as well as to the meaning and the places where the ballad is performed, to its literary contents, a new quality has arisen. Nevertheless, thanks to the melismatic formulae, the ballad proceeds in a more intense and more lyrical atmosphere.

In the ballads of everyday life, and very rarely in the older ballads, the words are adapted to the folk songs of the respective districts. The same epic melody to which lyrical texts and themes are sung in different districts, is adapted to different texts. The epic text rarely circulates with the same melody in different districts. Recently a tendency has been observed to replace the epic recitative by melodies of songs or to crystallize the recitative in forms requiring stanzas, which shows a decline of the art form.

When the ballad is performed by country musicians, the vocal recitative is preceded by, and alternates with, instrumental parts. This has been observed also in the case of peasants accompanying their recital with the bagpipe or the shepherd's pipe. This manner of performance has an expressive and practical function. In this way the singer can more easily hold the attention of the audience during a musical performance of such dimensions ; as the instrument stimulates the fancy of the singer, he may thus convey more powerful images, obtain a wider range of expression. At the same time he may rest his voice and he can recall the following lines. Sometimes, during the vocal performance, the singer makes use of the violin to complete certain melodic lines, to stress the melismatic formulae, thus enriching and embellishing the melodic line.

Four parts have to be observed :

1. *The instrumental introduction*, of variable dimensions, based on the melody of the ballad, but enriched, according to the technical possibilities and skill of the singer, with different ornaments, flourishes, shakes, etc. Sometimes it is built on two contrasting movements. Certain country musicians call it *"taxîm"*.

2. *The vocal "period"* is accompanied, in an extremely varied manner, by instruments.

3. *The instrumental interlude* — called *"vivart"* by the country musicians — is composed of some chords of a new melody, having a tempo more *vivace* or *guisto*, or by a variation of the instrumental introduction. The "periods" alternate with the instrumental interludes.

---

[20] Rich *melopoeia*, improvised freely on the basis of certain traditional elements and procedures

4. *The instrumental finale* is a dance melody or the instrumental introduction in a more lively tempo. Sometimes it is lacking.

The methods of accompaniment differ according to performer or district. In course of time the country musicians have established certain formulae of accompaniment which differ according to idiom, local custom, the talent and the technical skill of the performer. Here are a few of them :

a) the simple accompaniment in which rhythm predominates ;

b) the rhythmico-harmonic accompaniment forming a harmonic texture above which the voice freely asserts itself;

c) the accompaniment combined with different heterophonic and polyphonic procedures, etc.

The present situation. Today the ballad is still kept alive in the west and the south of Walachia, in the south of Little Walachia, and in the north of Dobrudja. The old people still remember the exploits of certain heyducks whose ballads are much "in demand" and are listened to with great interest. In general a tendency of decline of this art form can be observed ; some ballads have disappeared, others circulate only in fragmentary forms and still others are performed only on instruments, their words having been forgotten.

By reason of their rich and varied contents expressed in a specific adequate form, their high artistic standard, the popular ballads form part of the treasures of our national culture. They constitute authentic, classical values that may serve as models and encouragement for artistic composition. The artistic appreciation of this art form has greatly contributed to the composition of certain works of high value, works of literature, music and sculpture.

The creative use of the epic recitative of the ballad in different genres — chamber music, instrumental and dramatic music — has, since the last century, interested our best composers. Beside the simply harmonized ballads, the arrangements for voice and pianoforte, voice and symphonic orchestra, chorus (G. Dima, T. Brediceanu, T. Rogalski, P. Constantinescu) mention should be made of larger works :   the *Oratorio-cantata Tudor Vladimirescu* by G. Dumitrescu, the opera *Napasta* by Sabin Dr. goi, the opera *Pană Lemnea Rusalim* by P. Constantinescu (libretto by Victor Eftimiu).

Being acquainted with the epic recitative of the ballad and its manner of performance we can also enrich the vocal style by its manner of singing, by its natural and simple tone — impressive in its simplicity. The performance of the popular ballad itself is a problem that must interest our singers.

The popular ballad represent, both for the composers and the performers, a remarkable source of inspiration.

Corbea

Parlando. Rubato M.M. ♪=180

Fo - i - ci - că de-un mă - criş,   La tem - ni - ţa lui O - priş,

Un-de za - ce Cor-bea-n chis   De no ani si ju-mă - ta - te,

De cînd în tem-ni-ţă-mi za-ce, De cîn' în tem-ni-ţă-mi za'.

A - co - lo cînd l-a bă - gat,   E - ra ti - ne - rel bă - iat,

Dar a - cu moş-neag bă-trî - nî,   Ie cu bar - ba pîn' la brî - u,

Şi cu bar - ba pîn la brîu,   Bar-ba-i ba-te bra-ţi-li

Şi chi-ca căl-că - i - li,   Mus-tă - cioa-ra u-me-ri - i,

De i-au us-cat je - li - li.   A - co-lea cîn' l-a bă - gat,

Şerpi ie - ra ca a - ci - li,   S-a cu sin' ca grin-zi - li.

Broaş - te le ca nu - ci - li,

Ş-a cu sîn' ca ploş-ti - li . a-poi Dar o oa-ţă de bros-coai, că

s-a o-uat ş-a îm - pu - iat. In gu-ra caf-ta-nu-lui,

Fun-du bu-zu-na - ru - lui. Co-pi-laş' cu ce şî-i creş-te?

Sîn - ge din iel că ciu-peş-te, Sîn - ge din iel că ciu-peş-te.

Sung by Dobrică Cius, aged 42, collected in Ploeşti by E. Comişel, notation by E. Comişel and V. Dosios. No. Fgr. 9334a

Radu Anghel

Foa-ie ver-de bo-bi-lor măi hei

Sus pe dea-lu Gre-ci-lo-rî, Sus pe dea-lu Gre-ci-lo-rî,

Dea-lu Cîr-ste-ie-ni-lo-rî, Pe sub um-bra nu-ci-lo-rî,

Stă sta-ros-tea ho-ţi-lo-rî. La cel fag ver-de din coa-stă-î,

Şa-de Ra-du ca-ntr-o ca-să, Şa-de Ra-du ca-ntr-o ca-să,

Şi lui Ra-du că nu-i pa-să, Şi lui Ra-du că nu-i pa-să.

accel.

Prin cră-ci-le fa-gu-lui, măi Prin cră-ci-le fa-gu-lu-i,

Pis - toa-li - li Ra-du - lu - i,   La tul - pi - na fa - gu - lu - i,

Ca - ra - bi - na Ra - du - lui.   Nu ştiu goa - lă sau e pli - nă,

Ba - gă po - te - ra - n i - zi - nă,   Ba - gă po - te - ra - n i - zi - nă.

Ia - ră Ra - du ce fă - cea?

De - get în gu - ră bă - ga,   Şi-n ce - pea d-a şu - e - ra,   î

Si-n ce - pea d-a su - e - ra,   Multi voi - ni - ci că să strîngea,

Ca frun - za şi ca iarba î   Si la Ra - du că ve - nea.

Ia - ră Ra - du le spu - nea î   Hai bă - eţi pî - nă co - lea, î

Să mer-gem la po-pa Sta-n, Că mai ți-ne cî-te un ban

si cî-te un pui de cîr-la-nî Si cî-te-un pui de cîr-la-nî.

Sung by Alexandru Chirită, aged 38, collected in Bărbătești-Vedea-Pitești'
notation by E. Comișel. No. Disc. 803.
Prelude, interludes and postlude on violin.

COLLECTIONS OF BALLADS

Anton Pann, *Poezii deosebite sau cîntece de lume* (Different Poems and Secular
Songs), 1831 (with notes).

V. Alexandri, *Poezii populare ale Rominilor, Balade (cîntece bătrînești, adunate
și îndreptate)* (Folk Poetry of the Rumanians, Ballads [Old Songs, Collected
and Revised]), 1852−53, 1866.

A. Marienescu, *Balade culese și corese* (Ballads Collected and Edited) vols. i—ii,
1859−1867.

S. F. Marian, *Poezii populare din Bucovina* (Bucovinian Folklore), 1869.

N. Pompiliu, *Balade populare rominești* (Rumanian Popular Ballads), 1870.

A. Caramfil,*Cîntece populare de pe valea Prutului* (Folk Songs from the Prut Valley),
1872.

T. T. Burada, *Un călător în Dobrogea* (A Traveler in Dobrudja), 1880.

G. Dem. Teodorescu, *Poezii populare romîne* (Rumanian Popular Poetry), 1885.

D. Vulpian, *Balade, Colinde, Doine, Idyle* (Ballads, Christmas Carols, Chants and
Idylls), vol. i, 1884, vol. ii, 1885 (with notes).

T. Frîncu — G. Candrea, *Romînii din Munții Apuseni* (Rumanians in the Western
Erzgebirge), 1885.

E. Sevastor, *Cîntece Moldovenești* (Moldavian Songs), 1888.

N. Canianu, *Poezia populară, doine culese și publicate întocmai cum se zic* (Folk
Poetry, Doinas Recorded and Published as Recited), 1888.

C. Rădulescu-Codin, *Din Muscel, cîntece populare*, I (Folk Poetry from Muscel, I),
1896.

C. Rădulescu-Codin, *Literatură, tradiții și obiceiuri* (Literature, Traditions, and
Customs), 1929.

C. Rădulescu-Codin, *Chira Chiralina, cîntece bătrînești* (Chira Chiralina, Old
Songs), 1924.

52

C. Negoescu, *Poezii populare alese. Balade adunate din diferite colecțiuni și reviste* (Selected Folk Poetry. Ballads Collected from Different Collections and Reviews), 1896.

I. Bibicescu, *Poezii populare* (Folk Poetry), 1893.

E. Hodoș, *Poezii populare din Banat* (Folk Poetry from the Banat Region), 1892.

A. Corcea, *Balade poporane* (Folk Ballads,) 1899.

Gr. Tocilescu, *Materialuri folcloristice* (Folkloric Material), 1900.

P. Papahagi, *Din literatura populară a arominilor* (From the Folk Poetry of the Arumanians), no year.

Al. Tiplea, *Poezii populare din Maramureș* (Folk Poetry from County Maramuresh), 1906.

Iosif Popovici, *Poezia populară romînă* (Rumanian Folk Poetry) vol. i. *Balade* (Ballads), 1908.

T. Bud, *Poezii populare din Maramureș* (Folk Poetry from County Maramuresh), 1908.

C. N. Mateescu, *Balade* (Ballads), 1909.

Al. Vasiliu, *Cîntece, urări și bocete de ale poporului* (Folk Songs, Congratulations, and Dirges), 1909 (with notes).

C. Ciobanu-Plenița, *Cuvîntări adînci. Cîntece din vechime* (Voices from the Depth. Old-Time Songs), 1909.

I. N. Păsculescu, *Literatura populară romînească* (Rumanian Folk Literature), 1910 (with notes).

C. Rădulescu-Codin — St. Tuțescu — T. Chirilieanu, *Cîntece voinicești și ostășești* (Heroic and Soldiers' Songs), 1910.

T. Panfile, *Cîntece de țară* (Peasant Songs), 1913.

T. Panfile, *Cîntece bătrînești, doine, mustrături și blesteme* (Old Songs, Doinas, Scolding Songs and Maledictions), 1926.

Gh. Giuglea — G. Vîlsan, *Dela Romînii din Serbia* (Rumanians of Serbia), 1913.

O. Densușianu, *Graiul din Țara Hațegului* (The Dialect of the Hațeg Region), 1915.

O. Densușianu, *Flori alese* (Selected Flowers), 1920.

G. Cătană, *Balade populare* (Popular Ballads), 1916.

T. Chirileanu, *Comoare sufletului, Cîntece populare* (The Treasures of the Soul. Folk Songs), 1920.

T. Papahagi, *Antologia Aromînească* (Arumanian Anthology), 1922.

T. Papahagi, *Graiul și folclorul din Maramureș* (Dialect and Folklore in Maramuresh), 1925.

Pr. I. Bîrlea, *Balade, colinde și bocete din Maramureș*, I (Ballads, Congratulations, and Dirges from County Maramuresh, I), 1924.

D. Furtună, *Cîntece bătrinești din părțile Prutului* (Old Songs from the Prut Region), 1927.

N. Georgescu, *Tistu — Folclor din jud. Buzău* (Tistu — Folklore from County Buzau), 1928.

C. Brăiloiu, *Cîntece bătrinești din Oltenia, Muntenia, Moldova și Bucovina* (Old Songs from Oltenia, Muntenia, Moldavia and Bucovina), 1932 (with notes).

I. Diaconu, *Ținutul Vrancei* (The Vrancea Region), 1932.

I. Diaconu, *Folclor din R. Sărat* (Folklore from R. Sărat), 1934.

C. S. Timoc, *Poezii populare ale Romînilor din Valea Timocului* (Folk Poetry from the Timoc Valley), 1943.

Din folclorul nostru (From Our Folklore), ESPLA in collaboration with the Inst. de Folclor (with notes).

Antologia de muzică populară (Anthology of Folk Music), vol. i, *Poezia* (Poetry), ed. Acad. RPR, 1953.

Balade populare (Popular Ballads), ESPLA, 1955.

Ballads have been published in calendars, reviews, literary gazettes, particularly in *Columna lui Traian, Convorbiri literare, Familia, Grai și Suflet, Archivele Olteniei, Rev. pentru Istorie, Archeologie și Filologie, Anuarul Archivei de Folclor* (Cluj) 1932—1945, etc.

Poezii populare culese din valea Timocului (Folk Poetry Collected in the Timoc Valley), C. Sandu Timoc, 1943

MONOGRAPHS ON BALLADS

H. G. Ubicini, *Introduction aux ballades et chants populaires de la Roumanie*, 1955.

Al. Odobescu, *Cîntece poporane ale Europei răsăritene în raport cu țara, istoria și datinile Romînilor* (East-European Folk Songs on Rumanian Soil, History and Customs).

Al. Odobescu, *Răsunete ale Pindului în Carpați* (The Echo of the Pindus in the Carpathians), 1861.

B. P. Hasdeu, *Cuvinte die bătrîni* (Discourses from Old Times), 1879.

Al. Philippide, *Incercări asupra stării sociale a poporului romîn în trecut* (Investigations of the Social Situation of the Rumanian People in the Past), 1881.

M. Găster, *Literatura populară romînă* (Rumanian Folk Literature), 1882.

M. Găster, *Cucul și turturica* (Cuckoo and Turtle-Dove), a comparative study in *Convorbiri Literare*, vol. xiii, 1879, pp. 229−234, 322−344.

L. Săineanu, *Studii folcloristice* (Studies in Folklore).

Al. Russo, *Poezia poporală* (Folk Poetry) in *Scrieri*, 1909.

N. Iorga, *Balada populară romînească* (Rumanian Popular Ballad), 1910.

N. Iorga, *Istoria literaturii romînești* (History of Rumanian Literature), 1929.

D. Marmeliuc, *Figuri istorice romînești în cîntecul popular al Romînilor* (Rumanian Historic Characters in Rumanian Folk Poetry), 1914.

A. Densușianu, *Epopea noastră populară* (Our Popular Epopee), in *Revista critică literară*, vol. iii, p. 351.

P. Cancel, *Origina poeziei populare* (The Origin of Folk Poetry), 1922.

O. Densușianu, *Viața păstorească în poezia noastră populară* (Shepherds' Life in our Folk Poetry).

D. Caracostea, *Cours universitaire 1936−1937*.

D. Caracostea, *Miorița în Moldova* (The Ballad Miorița in Moldavia) in *Convorbiri Literare*, vol. xlix, 1915, pp. 1214−1250; vol. 1, 1916, pp. 77−101, 181−196.

D. Caracostea, *Miorița în Muntenia și Oltenia* (The Ballad Miorița in Muntenia and Oltenia) II, *Contaminări în epica Munteniei* (Contaminations in the Epical Poetry in Muntenia) in *Convorbiri Literare*, vol. lii, 1920, pp. 1613−1634, 715−723 ; III *loc. cit.* vol. liii, 1921, pp. 144−149 ; IV, *Legătura cu lirica bocetelor* (Connections with Lyric Dirges), *loc. cit.* vol. lv, 1923, pp. 465−485 ; *Totalizări* (Summing up) with Densușianu's comments *loc. cit.* vol. lvi, 1924, pp. 811−839.

M. Ștefănescu, *Din trecutul Iugoslavilor și Romînilor. Despre haiduci și haiducie* (From the Past of the Rumanians and Yugoslavs. About the Heyducks and their Character), 1931.

D. Găzdaru, *Legenda Meșterului Manole* (The Ballad of Meșterul Manole), in *Archiva*, pp. 88−92.

P. Caraman, *Contribuții la cronologizarea și geneza baladei populare la Romîni* (Contributions to the Chronology and Genesis of the Rumanian Folk Ballads).

O. Bîrlea, *Procesul de creație al baladei* (The Process of Ballad Formation), in *Rev. Fundațiilor Regale*, vol. viii, 1941.

T. Ionescu-Nișcov, *Haiducia și cîntecul haiducesc* (The Life of the Heyducks and Heyduck Ballads), lecture in *Studii și Cercetări de Istorie, Literatură și Folclor*, vol. ii, 1953, pp. 267−268.

A. Stoia, *Folclor din Sibiu − Miorița* (Folklore from County Sibiu − Miorița), in *Ethnos*, 1941.

JOZEF KRESÁNEK

BARTÓK'S COLLECTION OF SLOVAK FOLK SONGS

Bartók's collection of Slovak folk songs, beside representing the outcome of a large-scale field-work, is a systematic arrangement and classification of the rich Slovak musical folklore and, thus, a scientific achievement of the highest order. The manuscript constitutes an imposing volume of 1121 pages (densely filled foolscaps), completed by introductory chapters (28 and 8 pages), the key to signs (6 pages) and a great number of notes (25 pages in the first part alone). And all this is the harvest of a work that could not have been reaped without a still greater amount of preparatory work. For instance, Bartók does not include close variants in his collection, contenting himself with making references to deviating notes and verses. Yet, to be able to do so, he must have previously prepared a complete collection of all variants, taken down tunes in musical notation from phonographic records, corrected existing notations and so forth. In his philological studies, Bartók had gathered all Slovak folk songs available in collections thitherto published and the greater part of Moravian and Czech collections.[1]

This work of Bartók cannot fail to compel admiration. If we remember that he performed, in addition, a huge amount of other activities such as the collection of Hungarian, Rumanian, Jugoslav and other folk songs, the creation of musical compositions, the giving of concerts, teaching etc., we are really at a loss to see how he could find the time necessary for all these things.

[1] Of the Slovak collections : two parts of the *Sborník slovenských národných piesní...* (Collection of Slovak National Songs), three parts of the *Slovenské spevy* (Slovak Songs), the monograph *Detva* by Medvecký, a few melodies from the Hungarian review *Ethnographia*. Of the Czech and Moravian collections : Erben, *Nápěvy prostonárodních písní českých* (Melodies of Czech Popular songs) ; Sušil, *Moravské národní písně* (Moravian National Songs) ; three parts of the *Nové národní písně moravské* (New Moravian National Songs) by Bartoš ; Peck, *Valašské národní písně* (Walachian National Songs) ; Vaclavek, *Valašská svadba* (Walachian Marriage); Vikoukal, *Česká svadba* (Czech Marriage); Bartoš, *Naše deti* (Our children) ; Černik, *Zpěvy Moravských kopaničárů* (Songs of Moravian Peasants of Detached Farms).

The fact that the collection under review has been kept under lock and key and remained unprinted up to now is a serious loss not merely to Slovak folklorists but to the entire science of Central European folklore as well. So far, nobody has been in a position to form an idea of the abundance of melodies contained therein, nor were composers — except the author himself — able to draw from the rich source hidden in the collection. Therefore we cannot speak of any kind of influence Bartók's collection may have had upon the development of Slovak music.

It would seem rather difficult to report on an unpublished work in such a manner as not to impress readers as being either too long-winded or too subjective. Hoping, as we do, that at least the first part will be published before long, we think we can dispense with paraphrasing the work in question even by way of introduction. Therefore, we propose to restrict ourselves in this short essay to just making a few references to the first volume of Bartók's work which is to appear in three parts. We were prevented from presenting at this juncture an analysis of the second and third parts because their manuscript was at the press at the time of writing the present article. We hope we shall be able to make up for this deficiency in a future essay.

We cannot appreciate Bartók's work without forming at least a rough idea of the position of Slovak views on folklore at the time when Bartók was busy collecting Slovak folk songs.

It was in the seventies of the last century that — after a few earlier, rather insignificant attempts (Füredy, Sucháň) — the Society Matica Slovenská at Turčansky Sv. Martin achieved the first results by collecting and publishing Slovak folk songs. Edited by Michal Chrástek, the first volume appeared in Vienna in 1870 under the title *Sborník slovenských národných piesní, novestí, prísloví₁priekadiel atd.* (Collection of Slovak Folk Songs, Legends, Proverbs, Witticisms, etc.). Edited by Pavel Dobšinský and published at Turčansky Sv. Martin, the second volume followed as early as 1874. Being rather of an ethnographic character, neither of these compilations contained exclusively musical material, as is evident from their very title. The first volume contained 66 melodies and the second 65.

After the dissolution of the Matica Slovenská in 1875, a special committee, the Priatelia Slovenských Spevov (Friends of Slovak Songs) was formed which launched the *Slovenské Spevy* (Slovak Songs) at Turčansky Sv. Martin in 1880. It appeared in periodical booklets, and most of the collectors were village teachers. The first volume was edited by Ján Kadavý, the second and part of the third by Karol Ruppeldt. While the earlier compilations were meant to be, as far as possible, scientific collections, and bore an ethnographic rather than a musical character (the same as Kolberg's series *Lud* in Poland), the *Slovenské Spevy* were more in the nature of a series of popular songbooks, a fact that endowed them with the character of a normative collection, serving as a guide to show the kind of songs to be sung at social gatherings and offering instruction as to the manner in which they were to be performed. Such a tendency will surprise nobody who knows the conditions in which the *Slovenské Spevy* appeared. It was a time when the people had to be aroused, when a disclosure of the riches of the people's culture appeared to be the appropriate means of reviving national consciousness. Since a Slovak aristocracy was at that time practically non-existent, the *Slovenské Spevy* were meant, in the first place, for the petty bourgeoisie which relied upon its strongest support, the people.

It was in 1906, at a time when the *Slovenské Spevy* had already arrived at their third volume, that Béla Bartók and his collaborators (Z. Kodály, M. Vikár, A. Baník) began their field-work in Slovakia. Bartók's original idea was to bring about an arrangement of cooperation with the editors of the *Slovenské Spevy*, and, with this end in view, he approached the responsible executives of the periodical ; as a first step, he offered them gratuitously 400 songs collected, most of them, in the former county of Nitra and some in that of Gemer, his sole condition being that 4 or 5 free copies should be reserved for himself. Bartók was at that time already thinking of a comprehensive scientific study of Slovak folk songs and wanted to use various parts of the free copies for his planned compilatory work.

The negotiations between Bartók and the *Slovenské Spevy* began in 1910, dragged on and on and ended dismally in 1913. It is, of course, probable that a certain mistrust, evidenced by the *Slovenské Spevy* against the "professor of the Royal Hungarian Academy of Music" played some part in the failure of the negotiations ; the principal cause of the failure to come to an agreement was, however, the fact — duly recorded in the notes — that the editors of the *Slovenské Spevy* (after the decease of Karol Ruppeldt) were absolutely at a loss to comprehend the system of Bartók's notations. The contributors of the *Slovenské Spevy* made no real efforts to record songs in any systematic and accurate manner : they were, on the contrary, quite proud if they succeeded in ridding the melodies of all vulgarities of popular representation (*glissando*, fluctuating intonation, rhythmic irregularities), and satisfied if they managed to present in their collections the bourgeois variants of folk songs. Even Karol Ruppeldt, a comparatively erudite musician (he had studied music in Prague), was in the habit of modifying notations and justified these arbitrary corrections in his *Notes* to Part II by affirming that "changes were unavoidable, for no writing of music can be published with such arbitrary songs that defy all rules".

Bartók took a completely different attitude toward this problem. Disdaining to record urbanized variants and to regard them as the norm, he endeavoured to record genuine folk songs as living on the lips of village peasants, and to render them in their true original form. Bartók never resorted to mediators. Desirous of recording a certain song, he refrained from addressing himself to, say, the village teacher who had learned the song from the villagers: he contacted the peasants themselves, and preferably those peasants who had remained innocent of urban influences. What he was especially after was the peasants' culture as preserved in the villages. And it is this moment, *i. e.* his concentration on peasant culture, that must be regarded as the principal characteristic of Bartók's work, the feature that distinguishes his collection not only from the *Slovenské Spevy* but also from nearly all hitherto published anthologies of Slovak folk songs.

The visible consequences of this attitude are particularly pronounced in the songs collected in the quondam county of Zvolen. It had become a custom with us to look out for archetypes in alpine pastures and not in villages. It was in sheep-pens, among shepherds, that we were wont to hunt for characteristic folk songs in the region of Zvolen, Detva and Očová, forgetting that—though the Walachian life of these shepherds did undoubtedly represent the special cultural characteristic of the region — it far from exhausted the store of folkloristic treasures.

In order to convey a better idea of the characteristic features of Bartók's collection let us quote a few figures. The first part contains 421 groups of variants, within wich 761 melodies recorded by Bartók himself were published (apart from data concerning further variants). Most of the songs in this collection originated from the county of Zvolen (426), many from the county of Hont (133), and a number from the counties of Nitra (75), Gemer (74), Trenčin (32), Tekov (10), Pest (6), Bratislava (2) and Szilágy (1), together with two soldiers' songs of unknown origin as regards county. In respect of tonality (Table I) and he nature of the songs (Table II), the collection presents the following distribution :[2]

[2] The classification here applied follows the system which, in the course of my researches into Slovak folk songs, I attempted to establish and evolve in my essay *Slovenské ľudová pieseň zo stanoviska hudobného* (The Slovak Folk Song from a Musical Point of View), SAVU, Bratislava 1951. Not content with a mere lexicographic arrangement, I was especially keen on penetrating the tonal structure of the melodies. Relying on this system which enables us to set off everything that is formal and historically essential in the domain of Slovak folk songs we show in Table I the evolution from a central note to harmonic arrangement. If there is but a single central note, the melody will remain within a small range. To the pentatonic group belong melodies in which the line-cadences follow the pentatonic scale (principal cadence usually being the minor third above the final note). This type, probably of Hungarian origin, is rare in Slovakia while songs of the tetrachordal system occur with greater frequency. In the latter, melody is supported by two notes at a distance of a perfect fourth. There exist, of course, various combinations of the tetrachords which allow a greater number of such "pillar" notes and impart to the melody a wider flourish and ambit. In the pentachordal system we often encounter major and minor triads as "pillar" notes of the melody. Such triads sometimes form various combinations and may even be interwoven with tetrachords, thus giving rise to the mixed system of tetrachords and pentachords. Certain songs have, on account of tonality, been placed in the harmonic category : in these one feels a latent harmonic cadence of the type TST_6^4DT.

Table I

	Zvolen	Hont	Nitra	Gerner	Trenčín	Tekov	Pest	Bratislava	Military	Silágy	Total
A single central note	5	—	—	—	—	—	—	—	—	—	5
Pentatony	5	4	1	—	—	—	—	—	—	—	10
Tetrachords	33	3	3	4	—	1	—	—	—	—	44
Intermediary system between tetrachords and pentachords	70	21	11	20	4	6	3	—	—	—	135
Pentachords	214	72	35	39	15	3	—	—	—	—	378
Songs with harmonic structure	99	33	25	11	13	—	3	2	2	1	189

Table II

	Zvolen	Hont	Nitra	Gerner	Trenčín	Tekov	Pest	Bratislava	Military	Silágy	Total
Lullabies	7	1	—	—	—	1	—	—	—	—	9
Harvest songs	5	—	—	—	1	—	—	—	—	—	6
Haymaking song	15	—	—	1	—	1	—	—	—	—	17
Nuptial songs	41	4	4	5	3	3	—	—	—	—	60
Midsummer-night songs	2	2	—	1	—	—	—	—	—	—	5
Epic songs and ballads	61	22	16	16	5	1	1	—	—	1	123
Dances	100	31	15	7	7	—	3	1	—	—	164
Soldiers' songs	25	10	4	5	2	1	—	—	2	—	49
Shepherd's and highwayman's songs (rebels' songs)	40	3	—	7	—	—	—	—	—	—	50
Spinning-room songs	1	—	—	—	—	—	—	—	—	—	1
Children's play songs	—	2	—	1	—	—	—	—	—	—	3
Christmas songs	1	—	—	—	—	—	—	—	—	—	1
Carnival songs	—	1	—	—	—	—	—	—	—	—	1
Diverse (love songs, comical songs, satirical songs)	128	57	36	31	14	3	2	1	—	—	272

Of course, these figure should be viewed with some precaution and should in no case be accepted as *pars pro toto*. We must bear in mind that the figures are taken from a third of the whole collection and that the entire material of collection was selected according to special considerations in keeping with special, largely musical, criteria. It is only the quota of each particular region that we may regard as applicable to the whole material. Though each county has its own individual musical features, *i. e.* any musical system must take into account the regional characteristics, yet they are not very distinctly expressed, especially not in the factors upon which Bartók's classification is based, *i. e.* matters of form and the number of syllables. Figures relating to the latter show hexasyllabic verses to be characteristic of the whole of Slovakia, a fact which is corroborated by the six-syllable songs and variants taken over by Bartók from the *Slovenské Spevy*. None of the songs quoted in the first part of the collection by Bartók upon the evidence of his own recordings, comes from the areas of Turiec, Liptov, Orava, Špis or Šariš, and only two from the neighbourhood of Bratislava. On the other hand, the great number of songs originating from the county of Zvolen allows us to conclude that a similar distribution will be found throughout the collection. It is seen that Bartók extended his field work also to the counties Hont, Nitra, and Gemer, while Vikár collected for him in the county of Trenčin : he, however, did not get farther north than Ilava and Poruba. Neither Bartók, nor his collaborators did any field work in the rest of Northern Slovakia.

According to Bartók's classification, the first part of his collection comprises the four-line songs with undotted rhythm and an identical number of syllables in each line (isometric verses). The following table will convey better idea in this respect.

Table III

Number of syllables in a line	*Parlando-rubato*	Isometric verses	Heterometric verses	Number of songs in the collection
Five	—	1— 5	6— 10	19
Six	11—53	54— 97	98—214	378
Seven	—	215—232	233—261	76
Eight	262—279	280—302	303—351	166
Nine	—	352—364	365—366	16
Ten	—	367—384	385—397	63
Eleven	—	398—401	402	9
Twelve	—	403—408	409—416	22
Thirteen	—	417	418—419	5
Fourteen	—	420	—	4
Fifteen	—	421	—	3

The distribution of the songs in the second and third volume is this : the second volume contains four-line songs with undotted rhythm but a different number of syllables in the lines (heterometric verses). This applies to the groups of variants between nos. 422 and 1077. The third volume contains four-line songs with dotted rhythm : the verses are first isometric and then heterometric. These are followed by songs of the architectonic structure AAA, AABA with undotted and dotted rhythm. Then we have three-line melodies with undotted and dotted rhythm ; two-line melodies ; melodies of no definite form ; children's songs and children's playsongs; finally, instrumental music. The volume covers groups of variants from no. 1078 to no. 1620.

Due to this arrangement, the most typical Slovak melodies are included in the first volume, a fact which was emphasized by Bartók himself. The other two volumes contain creations of a more recent date and also modern songs, new Hungarian songs in particular. That is why we think our concentration upon the first volume is justified both from a scientific and from an artistic point of view. The songs contained in the first volume represent pronounced types in respect of each stylistic feature, which is to say that each given tonal type commands a definite form, a definite rhythm, a definite manner of representation, etc. Thus the criteria upon which Bartók based his system of classification led — of course, by a different path — to more or less the same results as do the criteria we nowadays endeavour to apply. In the classification of Bartók, who was concerned with form and metrics in the first place and only in the second place with the final notes of particular sorts and types, these different sorts and types of melodies form the same groups as if governed by our present principles, although the latter are chiefly based on tonality. This is a fact not devoid of significance.

The collection is headed by melodies (nos. 12b to 15f ; sixteen in all) sung on festive or special occasions (called "ceremonial songs" in the Slovak language) : 7 songs during the work in the fields, 4 harvest songs, 3 nuptial songs, a lullaby and a melody sung at Midsummer celebrations. Of these songs, 14 come from the county of Zvolen and 2 from that of Hont. As regards the tonal aspect of these songs, two of them are built upon a single central note (nos. 14a, 14d) ; six melodies reveal a tetrachordal and two a pentachordal structure, while three of the songs represent a transition from the system of tetrachords to that of pentachords. Two nuptial songs, showing the tonal change from the tetrachordal to the pentachordal system, come from the county of Hont, and all the rest from Zvolen. If we rely on other Slovak collections, — in the present case on Valaštan's[3] in particular — we find the county of Zvolen to be an area dominated by Walachian pentachords

[3] Ján Valaštan — Dolinsky, *Slovensé spievanky* (Slovak Song Melodies), Matica slovanská, Turčansky Sv. Martin 1940.

and Hypoionian (Mixolydian) modes. As Bartók's interest was focused on the musical culture of the peasantry, he recorded also in this area typical expressions of the farmers' culture with the characteristic tetrachordal system. The nuptial song *Leťia pávi, leťia* (no. 13b) testifies to the tetrachordal system (as also to the care with which Bartók handled the melody). It would be impossible to find melodies so carefully recorded in the *Slovenské Spevy,* and it is therefore not so surprising that Bartók's manner of notation seemed to be unacceptable to the publisher of the *Slovenské Spevy.*

No. 1

As a further example of the same system and the manner of notation, we quote a song which is sung at the time of the Midsummer celebrations (June 24th) — *Na vrchu, na Ďieľe* (no. 15e).

No. 2

The song *Hrabajže len, hrabaj* (14f) is a pentachordal one, characterized by an augmented B♭—C♯ second. It is remarkable that this second is encountered in our ceremonial songs of the alpine shepherds' song type (as also in the cowherds' song *Kebyich ja vedela* in *Slovenské Spevy* vol. ii, no 359 and in the harvest song *Žnica som ja, žnica,* in *Slovenské Spevy,* vol. ii. no 234). It would be incorrect if, in connection with songs of this kind, we tried to ascribe some importance to the influence of gipsy music : we have to do here with the culture of

62

the fields and pastures which had always remained innocent of gypsy music.

No. 3

Tempo giusto ♩= 160

Hra-baj - že len, hra-baj to ze - le - nuo se - no!

Ve bi ja hra- ba- ua: ne- mám na- ko- se - nuo.

Further songs from the county of Zvolen belong to the ceremonial songs of the foregoing group. Elements of the tetrachordal system are predominant in the song *Hrabala, hrabala* (no. 19d).

No. 4

Parlando ♩= 106

Hra- ba- la, hra- ba- la, čer- ta na- hra- ba - la,

od vel- kí - ho spa- nia hra- ble do- lá - ma- la.

It will be seen from the two following songs — the lullaby *Búvaj že mi, búvaj* (no. 20) and the highwayman's song *Ved sa kasír nazdá* (no. 25c) — that also songs with a Lydian fourth are also familiar in the villages around Zvolen, *i.e.* not only Hypoionian, but also Hyperionian songs which have always been regarded as a speciality of the north-western part of Slovakia.

No. 5

Parlando ♪= 180

Bú- vaj že mi, bú- vaj, len ma ňe- u - nu - vaj;

lep- šie ti je spa- ti, a - ko u- nú - va- ti.

63

This is particularly striking in highwayman's songs for such songs are indigenous mainly in Walachia. Also this song begins with the Lydian fourth.

No. 6

Finally, in the nuptial song *Bula to ňevesta* we encounter an instance of Hypoionian ceremonial song, the like of which had never before been found in this region.

No. 7

But for the county of Zvolen, the tetrachordal type of song is everywhere characteristic of agricultural communities. And from these other areas too, Bartók has produced new, so far unknown, and original types. The song *A taďe hor* (no. 51) from the county of Hont, for example, illustrates the authentic connection of tetrachords which here occurs in a *parlando* song and not in a dance song where a structure of this kind is more usual.

No. 8

a - zda je moj mi - ľi   šti - ri vo - ľi   že - ňie.

The nuptial song *Vienok, vienok* (no. 286b) from the county of Tekov is, tonally, a transition from the tetrachordal to the pentachordal system. Its whole character qualifies it for the preceding ceremonial songs, although it consists of eight-syllable lines. This concurrence of six and eight-syllable songs is one of the general characteristics we are made avare of by Bartók's collection (see samples of the *parlando-rubato* type).

No. 9

Rubato

Vie - nok, vie - nok maj - rán - ko ví   de ho vi - la?

čí - rom   po - li   vi - la že ho spie - va - jú - ci

a skla - da - la   ho pla - čú - ci.

Investigations hitherto performed have shown Western Slovakia (Záhorie) to be the home of the plagal arrangement of tetrachords (F—C, C—G). The Zvolen material in Bartók's collection offers a most instructive example from Central Slovakia, the song *Leťela kačička* (no. 160).

No. 10

Tempo giusto ♩ = 87

Le - ťe - la   ka - čič - ka,   ľe - ťe - la zvi - so - ka,

šu - haj do - brí stre - ľec   stre - ľiu jej do bo - ka.

Another such example with a displaced lower tetrachord is the song *Dolu dolinami* (no. 47a) from the county of Gemer.

No. 11

A similar displacement (but in an inverse sense) is found in the dance song *Divča pod tancovať* (no. 185). So far, all examples of such tetrachordal displacement at the beginning of the second part have come from East-Slovakia: Bartók presented a similar phenomenon from the county of Nitra.

No. 12

A different picture is revealed by the shepherd-highwayman's songs from the region of Detva.

Relying chiefly on Valaštan's *Slovenské spievanky*, experts have always held that such songs begin almost exclusively with the higher octave and then show a descending tendency. And yet, out of a total of 34 Walachian songs in Bartók's collection only 19 have this initial note while that of the other 15 songs is different. The explanation is again given by the agricultural peasant character of the songs in Bartók's collection. The predominance of the higher and lower fifth (in Bartók's songs these are the notes G in C major) seems to be attributable to the shepherd's pipe, the so-called *fujara*. It was this instrument—facilitating as it does, a peculiar *vibrato* of the notes $G^2 G^1$—that exerted a strong influence upon the songs in the region of the mountain pastures where the collectors, inspired and impressed by the peculiar manner of life in these isolated spots, were fond of hunting for songs. In the villages, on the other hand, there arose variants which were not exposed to this influence and did not, therefore, follow the rule of predominant higher and lower fifths. And this was duly put down on paper in Bartók's collection. To offer a good example, let us quote the dance song *Vo hajduche* (no. 217c) which presents at the same time an instructive instance of a connection of the major common chords D—F#—A and G—B—D. Although this type is rare, Bartók has collected two more songs of this category (nos. 328 a, b).

No. 13

We encounter in Walachian songs the same correspondence of six-, seven-, and eight-syllable verses as in songs from other regions, and thus three groups of variants, namely no. 16 (six-syllable verses), no. 217 (seven-syllable verses), and no. 328. (eight-syllable verses) correspond in Bartók's collection. A division according to the numbers of syllables is of secondary importance in the matter of Slovak folk songs, and it must be admitted that Bartók's classification, based on this system, has rather scattered homogeneous groups and separated closely related elements.

Ballads — epic songs (songs in which some story is told that need not invariably have a balladic, *i. e.* tragic, ending) are arranged in heterorhythmic groups. To the hexasyllabic group belong songs no. 184 to 191c ; to the heptasyllabic, nos. 246 to 259g ; to the octosyllabic, nos. 312 to 316c and 329a to 345c. Beside the heterorhythmic groups there are among the octosyllabic *parlando-rubato* songs, three from the county of Gemer. A few further songs of this class are scattered throughout the work. The largest group is that of octosyllabic heterorhythmic songs (30 epic-balladic songs out of a total of 36).

A comparison of these three groups shows that the first group of hexasyllabic songs is dominated by the preharmonic tonal system to the ratio of 7 : 1 ; while the ratio of preharmonic and harmonic tonality is still 13 to 5 in the second group of heptasyllabic songs, but we can detect no traces of a tetrachordal system among the songs of this group; as regards the third group (octosyllabic songs), the number of preharmonic tonalities is not more than the double of harmonic ones (24 : 12). We find in nearly all epic-balladic songs a rhythmic contraction in the middle which (termed by Bartók "the Slovak rhythm contraction") may, therefore, be regarded as a typical feature of epic-balladic songs. It should be noted that this rhythmic contraction occurs also in hexasyllabic songs with a tetrachordal-pentachordal structure. There are not less than four songs of this kind in the collection (nos. 186 a, b, c, d) of which we present here the song *Chceu sa Jaňik ženiť* (no. 186b).

No. 14

Only partly does the rhythmic contraction become manifest in the ballad *Bola jedna hrdlička* (no. 254b, heptasyllabic), while its beginning is akin to that of the preceding song.

No. 15

But the most beautiful ballads are those in which there is no rhythmic contraction at all, in which — instead of intruding itself as an additional and independent element — musical rhythm gives way to the rhythm of the words. Example of this kind are the ballads *Ore,*

ore šesť volou (no. 249a) and *Čo sa stalo tam dou* (no. 76c), both from the county of Zvolen.

No. 16

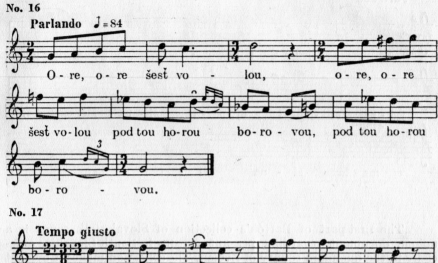

No. 17

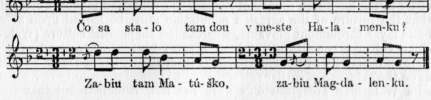

Two further examples, likewise from Zvolen, are the ballads *Kod sa milí od milej brav* (no. 267) and *Ej, bola jedna mlinárka* (no. 345c) in which we encounter both tetrachord and pentachord.

No. 18

Parlando

Ej, bo-la jed-na mli-nár-ka, ej, bo-la jed-na mli-nár-ka, ej, ma-la si-na Mi-chal-ka, ej, ma-la si-na Mi-chal-ka.

The first part of Bartók's collection of Slovak folk songs is a unique document regarding peasant culture in South Slovakia, especially in the quondam county of Zvolen. The collection makes it evident that the culture of the agrarian population must be looked upon as a basic layer throughout Slovakia, whereas the shepherds' culture (Walachian culture) constitutes, at best, a second stratum. Inclined as we were — especially in the light of songs from the region of Detva as well as on the evidence of earlier researches — to regard the county of Zvolen as a Walachian area, Bartók's work has now demonstrated that the typical villages of the county bore, prior to 1918, the characteristic marks of agrarian and not pastoral culture. What better proof of this is there than the fact that the collection from Zvolen contains 41 nuptial songs against 40 shepherd-highwayman's songs, 61 ballads and 15 shepherd's songs (sung while stacking hay, etc.; see Table II). The idea that the former county of Zvolen interrupts the continuity of agrarian culture in South Slovakia has turned out to be an erroneous assumption, one, no doubt, that bore all the semblance of reality until Bartók's revelations. To have disclosed the falsity of such an assumption is a great scientific achievement by Bartók.

The cultural layer mentioned is very fertile soil for the seeds of modern civilization, and it is due to this that songs of the agrarian type have died out since 1918, while the original folklore has survived in the mountains, in isolated spots, in sparsely populated places, in logged forest-land, mountain pastures and the like. Even after 1918 there was time enough to trace this culture, and it is still possible to collect and record its manifestations. Yet, Bartók's work undoubtedly is, and is sure to remain, the most beautiful and most valuable collection of this kind.

When reviewing the collection from a scientific point of view we cannot restrict ourselves to mere research work, to simple evaluation and comparison. Whether we want to or not, we gain insight into a new world that stands above pure science, one that we must acknowledge as the final aim, the *raison d'être* of music and song. Much as one tries to pigeonhole songs according to schemes of form, number of syllables, final notes, ambit and the like, all these scientific analyzes fail to bring home what is most important and essential, namely the artistic quality of the songs. Our forefathers, and even our fathers, approached folklore and its manifestations in this manner, and we think we deserve credit for having put a stop to their flowery oratory, to have begun to analyse folk melodies on the basis of palpable characteristics, of what can be measured and defined. Bartók, the first scholar to take this new path, solved the whole problem in a manner befitting the man that he was above all — the composer. In his collection he appears as a man of science *par excellence* but — in his quality as a composer — he was able to recognize and disclose all the artistic qualities of the songs he collected. And what he did both as a scientist and a composer, was being done in a way that is accessible only to men of genius.

RAINA KACAROVA–KUKUDOVA

PROPAGATION AND VARIANTS OF A BULGARIAN FOLK DANCE

Four dances with their many variants and under diverse names keep spreading all over Bulgaria and wherever Bulgarians live :

Pravo horo (simple round), in 2/4 time ;

Paidushka in 5/16 time ♪♪. ;

Povărnato horo (hither-and-thither round dance) also called *Naprednasad* (forward-backward), in 9/16 time ; ♪♪♪♪. ; and

Răchenitsa, a pair dance in 7/16 time ♪♪♪. ; danced also as a round dance in the same rhythm.

In addition to the above, we may mention, the round dance *Eleno Mome* (Elena, my girl) performed in 7/8 time ♩♩♪♩ which became popular between the two World Wars.

These dances are danced not only to instrumental accompaniment but also to songs : this tradition is kept alive in many places in Bulgaria.

Besides these wide-spread dances each region has its own characteristic rounds and folk dances. The round dances, as well as the folk dances penetrate by way of migration into the bordering and also into more remote regions. They are spread by shepherds who lead their flocks in winter to warmer flatlands, by harvesters who descend in groups from the mountains into the villages of the flatland, by itinerant musicians — Bulgarians and gypsies, — by potters and artisans who carry their products into remote villages and sell them on fairs. Visits, weddings and fairs are also good opportunities for learning new round dances.

The round dances spread also across the borders of the country. In the villages along the Danube and on the Danube Plain they dance also tripping dances, named *Vlaski hora* (Walachian rounds). In the southern regions we find variants of the Greek *Hasapiko* as well as variants of the *Sirto* known by different names, or nameless. In North-Western Bulgaria the names of certain rounds indicate a Serbian origin. Two or three "Macedonian" round dances belong to the permanent dance repertoire of the whole country. Thousands of Macedonian immigrants, who settled in Bulgaria, dance also Bulgarian rounds, besides their own and Albanian dances. The *Lases* (a Caucasian tribe which in ancient times, while fishing on the far south-eastern coasts of the Black Sea, came as far as the Bulgarian coast) brought their dances with them. Our fisher-folk dance even today *Las Havasă* in the characteristic 7/8 time. A mutual exchange of dances took place during the Turkish domination among the enslaved Balkan peoples.

Certain dances are nowadays performed only sporadically in places scattered all over the country, forming a rather loose net. In other places they are still remembered though no longer danced. This proves that in earlier times they had formed a fairly tight net.

To these belong the wedding dances *Zaicheskata* (Rabbit dance), *Kak se sadi pipera* (How to plant red pepper), the pleasant *Idi mi, mamo, poiskai* (Ask the girl's hand for me, mother) and the variants of a dance known to Bulgarian folklorists by the name *Ovchata* (Sheep dance).

I saw and noted the Sheep dance first in 1941, in Hlevene, district Lovech (Northern Bulgaria). Researches have revealed that it is danced also in the Dobrudja in Northern and Western Thrace, in the Eastern and Middle Balkan Mountains, in the region of the Sredna-Gora Mountains and are denoted by quite different names : *Ovchata* (Sheep dance) in the district Lovech ; *Zaicheskata* (Rabbit dance) in Sinemorets in the Strandja Mountains ; *Kukuvichka* (Cuckoo dance) in Omurtag, *Topchiyska* (Gunner dance) in Spahievo, district Haskovo. The dance is often named by the first line of the song to which it is danced : *Dobre mi doshel, Ivancho* (I welcome you, Ivancho) in the village of Mrachenik, district Levskigrad ; *Mari babo Hadjiyke*[1] (On mother Had-jiyka), *Kak se chuka cher piper* (How to crush red pepper) in Dobrudja ; *Mări momichentse, măninko* (Oh my girl, my little girl) in the village of Yakovtsi, district Elena, in Shipka, district Kazanlik, in Gramatikovo in the Strandja Mountains and elsewhere ; *Kako Măriyke kakva si* (Mariy-ka, my sister, how are you) in Koprivshtitsa and elsewhere ; *Chicho Kolyo ima dve shterki* (Father Kolyo has two daughters) in the villages of Evrenozovo, Fakiya, and in the Strandja Mountains.

In 1941 this dance was no longer danced in the village of Hlevene, district Lovech. Some elderly folk dancers, who knew it from early youth, have later revived it. It is known by young and old in the Strandja Mountains, in the districts of Elena and Haskovo, in Dobrudja. The dance has been recorded from elderly dancers in the Sredna Gora Mountains, but has disappeared from the everyday and holiday reper-toire. It is remembered occasionally at family festivities.

Originally the Sheep dance was performed to a song. Later on, instrumental accompaniment was introduced, which reproduced the melo-dy sung with slight modifications. It is only in the village of Hlevene that people remember having once danced it to a song. There it is danced to

---

[1] *Hadjiya* (masc.), sometimes *Hadjiyka* (fem.) is the title of pilgrims to Jerusalem.

a metrically changed instrumental melody with many reminiscences of the well-known sung variants which are rendered more colourful by dotted rhythms, syncopes, 1/16 notes, trills and *appoggiaturas* (see no. 8), depending on the individuality of the musicians.

The melody of the dance consists of four lines, and each line of four bars. The Bulgarian round-dance melodies consist usually of two lines. Four-line dance melodies are seldom to be found.

The second line of the melody is a repetition of the first line with slight or no modifications ; the fourth melodic line is a repetition of the third line.

This is a descending melody within the range of the Aeolian penta-chord, the most popular ambit of the Bulgarian round-dance songs, completed (with G) by a major second under the keynote.

The fundamental rhythm is 2/4 ♩♩. At the beginning of the first and second melodic line the 2/4 rhythm is divided into the following rhythmic figures : ♪ ♪ ♪ ♪ or ♩ ♪⌣♪

The last rhythmic figure, consisting of ligatured or non-ligatured quavers, is characteristic of the Bulgarian dance melodies in 2/4 time.

The second part of the melody, the refrain, has, in one of the variant groups, an undulating structure of fourths and fifths (see nos. 4 and 7). In an other group it is arched, but the great interval appears generally in the 11th bar (see nos. 3 and 5). In the third group, the third melodic line is undulating, while the fourth is arched (see nos. 1 and 10).

Less rhythmic deviations from exact 2/4 time appear in the refrain. All four melodic lines end in the rhythmic formula ♩♩|♩. A rhythmic "contamination" ♩|♩♩|| appears only in one song from Strandja at the end of the first and second melodic line (see no. 10).

While the melodies of all known variants are closely related to each other and genetically connected, the words are heterogenous (they have only one common characteristic : humour).[2] Only in two variants are the words uniform, in Dobrudja where for the most part the song *Mări, babo Hadjiyke* is sung (see words in no. 5) and in the Strandja Mountains where besides the widespread words *Chicho Kolyo ima dve shterki* (see words in no. 3) sometimes other words are sung as well (see words in nos. 7 and 10).

The lines of words have seven syllables (see no. 5). In the first two lines the isometry is often infringed, because the verse sometimes has eight or nine syllables (see nos. 1, 4, etc.).

[2] In only one of the hitherto known cases does the melody have a mechanical variety of the words of the known theme : "Conversation with the closest relative of the buried person", in this case between the wife and the sister of the husband.

The verses of the refrain are isometric. They consist, as a rule, of short words of one or two syllables accentuating the steps which are stamped on the spot:

Che tăi, che tăi, che pak tăi (Like this, like this and again); see no. 7, or

Ay tos, păk tos, păk tos, tos (one [foot], this one, this again); see no. 1, or

Aha, aha kundurki (Aha, aha little boots); see no. 4, or

Lyava, lyava, ‖lyavata, dyasna, dyasna, ‖dyasnata (Left, left‖ *the* left [foot], right, right‖ *the* right [foot]); see no. 3.

Performance. The dance is performed by a few dancers (8—10 persons) who, standing close together, hold on to each other's belts. In two villages, Gramatikovo in the Strandja Mountains, and Iakovtsi in the district Elena, it is danced in a circle. In some villages it is executed by men, in some by women, in others by men and women together.

The dance begins on a strong beat. It consists of two distinct parts.

No. 1

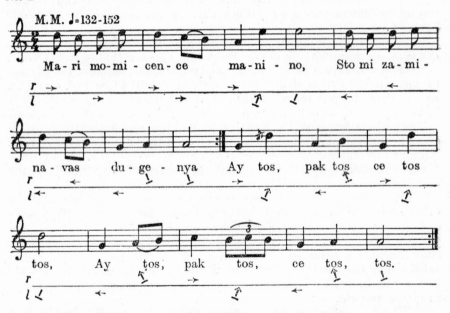

Sung and danced in June 1955 by Nikola Petkov Georgiev, aged 42, born in the village Iakovtsi, district Elena.

The first part has two dance figures performed to four bars to the left and four to the right. The second part is danced on the spot. Each dance figure ends by stamping twice with the left or the right foot. Also the steps to the second part of the 9th, 10th, 13th and 14th bars are performed by stamping either with the right or with the left foot.

In the region of Omurtag both dance figures performed on the spot (Part II) are replaced by forward and backward movement without stamping. At the end of every second bar there is a rocking step.

No. 2

In the village of Kochmar, district Tolbukhin, among the immigrants for Northern Dobrudja (village of Adjilartsi, district Tulcha), the dance figures with right and left movement are replaced by forward and backward movements. All the four dance figures end in stamping with the heel four times:

No. 2a

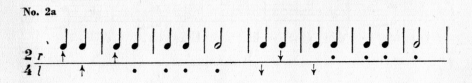

In the variant from the village of Evrenozovo, district Malko Tăr-novo, the second part of the dance is performed in two different ways with a corresponding modification of the melody; first by stamping on the spot seven times with the right foot and seven times with the left, and when repeated, the stamping is replaced by forward and backward steps (diagonally to the right and diagonally to the left). The forward steps are accentuated. The posture does not change, or is slightly inclined to the left or to the right.

No. 3

djas-na - ta,   ·Lja - va,   lja - va,   lja - va - ta.

Sung and danced in July 1955 by Anastasia Andreeva Panaiotova, aged 18, born in the village of Evrenozovo, district M. Tărnovo.

The *Topchiyskata* (Gunner dance) of Spahievo, district Haskovo, is compressed into two dance figures, both beginning with three vigorous stamps. The dancers maintained that the gunners had stamped in the same manner with their clogboots. But the bantering and chaffing have nothing to do with the content which the people ascribe to the dance.

No. 4

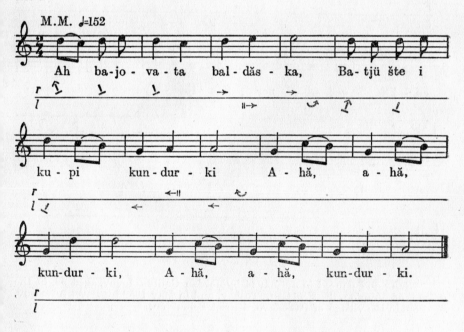

Ah ba-jo - va - ta bal - dăs - ka,   Ba- tjü šte i

ku - pi   kun - dur - ki   A - hă,   a - hă,

kun-dur - ki,   A - hă,   a - hă,   kun-dur - ki.

Sung and danced by Kina Stilianova, aged 18, and Petra Ivanova, aged 25, born in the village of Spahievo, district Haskovo. Noted at the mass in the Batskovski Monastery, August 28, 1946.

In the Dobrudja dance *Mari, babo hadjiyke* we find a figure taken from the dance *Kak se sadi cher piper*, a reminiscence due to the accidental conformity of the words. At the words *"tăi se chuka cher piper"* ("red pepper is crushed like that") in the 13th to 16th bars the men perform a knee-bending and "crush *red pepper*" with the alternative knee. Sometimes they begin to "crush *red pepper*" already at the 9th bar.

This dance was also interwoven with the original dance *Kak se chuka cher piper* (How black *pepper* is crushed).[3] At many places the name was accepted together with the steps, while sometimes, instead of *"pepper"*, "salt and *pepper*" was "crushed", and the dance soon became known also as *Sol, piper* (Salt, *pepper*).

No. 5

Sung and danced in July 1954 by Jordan Gantsev Iovov, aged 98, in the village of Vranino, district Gen. Toshev, and in May 1952 by Pavel Atanasov, aged 86, in the village of Paskalevo, district Tolbukhin.

[3] A ritual wedding dance to the song, performed on the bridal night of the newly married couple.

In some villages in Dobrudja *Mari, babo hadjiyke* is performed to the Rumanian melody

No. 6

Ha - lo ne - lo, ha - lo ne - lo, haï la jok
Să ne fi - e, să ne fi - e   cu no - roc,

Ci - ne   o - ra   nu sâ   joa - ce
Ma - re   ma - re   nu să   fa - ce.

which comes from the time of the Rumanian rule when it was taught to the children in the elementary schools.

The variant from the village of Gramatikovo *Mări, Momichko, Mănina* (Hallo little girl) is danced in a circle. The first part is performed twice : it is extended to 16 bars while both dance lines end in only one stamping to the last measure, however, in the second half of the dance, which is again extended to 16 bars, there is a treble stamping — characteristic in Gramatikovo — at the end of the dance lines.

No. 7

Mă - ri mo - mič - ko   mă - nin - ka,   Mă - ri mo -

mič - ko   dreb - nin - ka.   Če tăj,   če tăj,

6   *81*

čе pak tăj, Ce tăj, čе tăj, čе pak tăj.

Sung and danced in July 1955 by Iana Kostadinova, aged 58, in the village of Gramatikovo, district M. Tărnovo.

The variant *Ovchata* (Sheep dance) from Hlevene begins with figures performed on the spot (1st to 8th bars). The figures performed to the left and to the right, unlike in variants hitherto mentioned, are divided by figures danced on the spot. The dance-figures on the spot to the first two bars are performed with rocking steps instead of stamping steps. The dance leader commands the rocking step by calling out "up". The dance develops in two twelve-time periods. The dance period grows from two to three lines. The instrumental melody too is now detached from the fundamental metric and has an asymmetrical structure. The first period has become three-lined. The dance is performed within 24 bars; the melody consists of 20 bars.

No. 8

Danced to flute in January 1948 by the men of the dance collective in the village of Hleneve.

A whole melodic line is wanted to complete the last dance figure which is executed to the repetition of the first melodic line. At this repetition the dance begins in the middle of the melody. The lack of conformity in the structure of the melody and of the dance has no influence upon the performance, since a complete conformity exists within little metric units, *i. e.* between the melodic and dance lines. A race begins between melody and dance which maintains the tension until the end of the dance.

In the Elena district, in many places of the Strandja Mountains, in the Sredna-Gora Mountains, and in many villages of Dobrudja the dance is performed in the same form which may be regarded as the original type (see nos. 1, 10). *Ovchata* (Sheep dance, no. 8) from Hlevene, *Topchiyska* (Gunner dance, no. 4) from Spahievo, *Kukuvichka* (Cuckoo dance, no. 2) from Omurtag *(Chicho Kolyo ima dve shterki* (Uncle Koljo has two daughters ; no. 3) from Evronozovo, *Kak se chuka cher piper* (How to crush *pepper*, no. 5) from Dobrudja are variants of this type.

The variant from Hlevene has an additional element, a dance figure, and has been named the "Sheep dance". The inhabitants of Hlevene maintain that the sheep stamp with their hoofs in the same manner when they scent danger. Instead of one step to a crochet, two small steps on sole are performed in this variant

a good imitation of the dainty steps of a flock of sheep.

The Thracian variant of the *Topchiyskata* (Gunner dance, no. 4) has become choreographically poor to the advantage of the pantomimic features. Two figures are omitted from the usual dance and the triple "gunner-stamping", which starts the dance, is separated by some steps to the left and to the right.

It is difficult to establish the age of this dance. Sixty, seventy-year old peasants in the village of Hlevene learned it from their grand-fathers. A singer from Dobrudja, the ninety-year old clergyman Pavel Athanasov learned it from his parents. The two best known songs that accompany the dance *Mări, momiche măninko, kato tropash horoto* (Hallo, little girl, when you stamp the round dance) and *Mari, momi-chentse măninko, shto mi zaminuvash dyukenya* (Hallo, my little girl, why do you pass by my shop) and have the same melody, belong to the category of the round-dance melodies which are nearly 150 years old.

On the strength of the available material, we feel entitled to presume that the song came in vogue together with the dance and spread through-out villages and towns. When people had accepted and learned to like it, diverse words were invented to it, (a practice still quite com-mon with our folk too) but the dance has remained for the most part unchanged. In some places the melody has spread without the dance and been attached as an accompaniment to rhythmically corresponding round dances.

In other places the new dance has not only been introduced in the dance repertoire of the village, but has also had an influence on the local dance folklore. Thus the inhabitants of the village of Zvezdets, in the Strandja Mountains, have started to dance, to an old song with lines in five-time, round dances in which the dance lines end in stamping steps as in the recently adopted "new dance". The new dance is called, according to the content of its words, *Mechkinata* (Bear dance).

No. 9

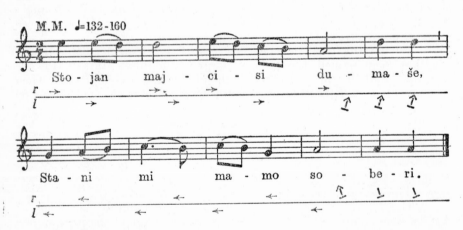

Sung and danced in July 1955 by Irina Stankova Lambova, aged 46, in the village of Zvezdets, district M. Tărnovo.

The local style influences, in turn, the melody of the "new dance", *i.e.* the final rhythmic formula, while the first two lines show the above-mentioned contamination.

No. 10

Sung and danced in July 1955 by Irina Stankova Lambova, aged 46, in the villaged of Zvezdets, district M. Tărnovo.

Is there any connection between the Bulgarian dance and the above-mentioned Rumanian *Halo Nelo* (no. 6) and what is this connection?

From the scarcity of Rumanian material at our disposal we know that the song *Halo Nelo* had been taught fifty years ago to children in the Rumanian schools of Transylvania and in other places. They danced *Sărba* to it (a round dance with many participants), the steps and style of which are closely related to the Bulgarian dance discussed above.

The melody of both dances is a descending one. The Rumanian melody has a wider range, a whole octave, the Bulgarian, a sixth. Both are characteristic folk tunes. We may presume a distant genetic connection between the Rumanian and the Bulgarian dance. Which of the two peoples has borrowed the dance from the other? Or should we, with strong reserve, consider this dance a "*gesunkenes Kulturgut*"? In any case the dance lives on in its supposed place of origin as well as in its new home, it is popular and susceptible to changes according to the environment and the taste of the dancer.

When, not long ago, these dances met again, the Rumanian melody took root in the dance repertoire of some villages of Dobrudja. Today the inhabitants of Dobrudja dance the same dance to two melodies. The Bulgarian melody is mostly sung, the Rumanian melody is played on instruments. The Rumanian text is not as wide-spread as the melody, it has fallen into oblivion. Only in a single case could I note the first four lines of the song. (See no. 6.)

From the investigation of the life and propagation of this dance, known by so many names, we may come to the following conclusions :

1. When a dance is to the people's liking, it propagates quickly together with the accompanying melody;

2. Melody and dance, when connected, find their way into the dance repertore of the people and are submitted to changes from which new variants arise. These reflect a tendency to development and a creative activity of outstanding dancers ;

3. In some places a dance, newly introduced, wins a hearty welcome and influences the dance folklore of the region; thus new round dances of the same style arise ;

4. The words are not so firmly connected with the melody as with the dance and may be replaced by new, topical words which become permanent in the local repertoire. The new words spread together with the dance ;

5. The dance forms have an extraordinary vitality. Even if they penetrate foreign areas, they take root in the new environment without essential alteration and are perpetuated in many variants.

Signs for the steps of the round dances here discussed

ʔ	right foot
ℓ	left foot
I	step on the spot
←	usual step in the
→	direction indicated by the arrow
)←	leaping step in the
→(	direction indicated by the arrow
O	on tiptoes
●	on heel
∪	foot raised from the ground
I̱	stamping of foot
L	accentuated step

rocking step of the left foot before the right foot
rocking step of the right foot before the left foot
step crossing the left foot before the right foot
step crossing the right foot before the left foot
step crossing the left foot behind the right one

step crossing the right foot behind the left one

slight and brisk elastic bending and stretching
    of the knee

one foot pulled to the other

right leg raised with knee bent

left leg raised with knee bent

sudden lifting of right knee

sudden lifting of left knee

crossing of arms and holding of belts

No. 1

Мъри, момиченце мънинко,	Oh girl, my little girl,
Що ми заминуваш дюкеня	Why do you go past my shop,
Ай тос, пък тос, пък тос, тос (2)	*This one, this one, this again*
Що ми заминуваш дюкеня,	Why do you go past my shop,
Що не пазаруваш от меня?	Why don't you buy from me?
«Арбе бачо Иване,	"My sister sends me always
Меня ма кака пруводи	To the lower end of the village,
Долу в долнята махала,	There are the most youngsters".
Дету има най баш иргени.»	

No. 2

Кукувичката кукува	(2)	Listen how the cuckoo calls
Във Янкината градина,		In our garden Jana,
Кукувичката кукува,	(2)	Listen how the cuckoo calls,
Кукува още хортува :		Calls and says the words :
Чуваш ли, Янке, чуваш ли	(2)	Can you hear, Jane, can you hear,
Кукувичката кукува.		Can you hear, how the cuckoo calls,
Кукувичката кукува,	(2)	Can you hear, how the cuckoo calls,
Кукува, още хортува.		Calls and says the words?

Чувам я, мале, чувам я,	(2)	Listen, mother listen to him,
Ала не мога да изляза.		I can not go out now,
Платно на стана ме чака,	(2)	Linen awaits me at the loom,
Либе на чешма ме вика		My darling calls me at the well...[4]

No. 3

Чичо Кольо има две щерки,	Uncle Kolyo has two daughters,
Чичо Кольо има две щерки,	Uncle Kolyo has two daughters,
Лява, лява, лявата,	*Left, left, the left,*
Дясна, дяна, дясната.	*Right, right, the right,*
Едната ще е на тебе,	One of them will be for you,
Другата ще е на мене.	The other will be for me.

No. 4

Ах байовата балдъзка,	Ah little, fine sister-in-law,
Батю ще й купи кундурки,	I shall buy nice boots for you,
Ахъ, ахъ кундурки. (2)	Aha, aha, little boots.
Ах байовата балдъзка,	Oh little, fine sister-in-law,
Батю ще й купи коланче,	I shall buy a little belt for you
	Aha, aha, a little belt.
Ах байовата балдъзка,	Ah, little, fine sister-in-law,
Батю ще й купи герданче.	I shall buy a necklace for you,
	Aha, aha, a necklace.
Ах байовата балдъзка,	Ah little, fine sister-in-law,
Батю ще й купи пръстенче.	I shall buy a ring for you,
	Aha, aha a ring.
Ах байовата балдъзка,	Ah, little, fine sister-in-law,
Батю ще й купи чехлички.	I shall buy slippers for you,
	Aha, aha slippers.

No. 5

«Мъри, бабо хаджийке,	"Oh, you mother pilgrim,
Къдей дядо хаджия?»	Where is father pilgrim?"
«Ей гу гори — на таваня,	"Eh, there above on the roof,
Пипер чука в гаваня.»	There he crushes pepper in mortar."
«Мъри, бабо хаджийке,	"Oh, you mother pilgrim,
Как са чука чер пипер?»	Say, how they crush pepper?"
«Със лявото коляно,	"With the left knee, look at it,
Тъй са чука чер пипер.»	So they crush pepper."

---

[4] Kyril Djenev, Tojko Küchukov, Kyrill Haralampiev, Peter Zahariev, *Terminologie der Bulgarischen Choreographie*. State Publisher *Nauka i Izkustvo* 1952, p. 60.

No. 7

— Мъри, момичко мънинка,
Мъри, момичко дребнинка,
Че тъй, че тъй, че пак тъй. (2)
Ти като тропаш хорото,
Кой ша ти тупа платното?
— Ас ша си тропам хорото,
Мама ша ми тупа платното.
— Мъри, момичко мънина,
Мъри момичко дребнинка,
Ти като носиш киткитe,
Кой ша ти жъне жетвата?
— Аз ша си носа киткитe,
Мама ша ми жъне жетвата.

— Oh, you little girl,
Oh girl, you pretty girl,
Like this, like this, and again.
When you stamp in the round dance,
Who shall weave linen for you?
— I shall stamp in the round dance,
Mother will weave the linen.
— Oh you little girl,
Oh girl, you pretty girl,
When you bring the small bouquets,
Who shall gather in the crops?
— I bring the little bouquets,
Mother will gather in the crops.

No. 9

Стоян майци си думаше:
»Стани ми, мамо, събери,
Моята гержик прямена,
Да се применя наредя,
Че я ще, мамо, да ида,
На един чуен панаир,
С мечката да се бориме.«
Пък майка си му думаше:
«Тук седи, сино, ие ходи,
Че мечката е лошава,
Мечката шега не знае,
Мечката хатър не гледа.»
Стоян майка си не слуша,
Че стана Стоян, та тръгна,
На панагирет отиде,
Като от далек вървяше,
Тия като го видяха
Всички му диван станаха,
Всички му силям дадоха.
Мечка му диван не стана,
Мечка му силям не даде,
А се с Стояна залови,
Та се борили, борили,
Три дена, до три вечера,
За харман място извили.
Нито мечката надвива,
Нито Стоян надвива.
На Стояна му се наяди
И хвана мечката през кръст,

Stoyan spoke to little mother:
"Get up, mother, and give me
My smartest clothes,
I shall dress for a feast,
I will, mother,
Go to the fair,
I will there wrestle with the bear."
But little mother answers him:
"Here you stay my son, don't go
Since the bears are always bad,
They do not take a joke,
The bear won't spare you."
Stoyan didn't obey mother,
Stoyan was ready to go,
And he went to the fair,
He should go far away,
All the people, who saw him,
Treated him with great respect.
And welcomed him.
The bear didn't respect him,
And did not welcome him,
It threw himself on him,
And they wrestled and wrestled,
Three days and three nights,
They trampled the earth,
Neither won the bear,
Nor did Stoyan overcome it,
Stoyan became furious,
He seized the bear by the chine,

В синьо я небо издигна,
В черна я земя удари,
Та девет педи потъна.
Мечката се силно изрева
И на Стояна продума :
«Халал да ти е момата,
Момата хубавелката!»

He raised it to the blue sky,
And smashed it to the black earth,
Driving it in nine fathoms.
The bear howled mightily
And spoke to Stoyan :
"The little girl may be yours,
The little girl, the pretty bride".

No. 10

»Мъри, бульо, мъри, милна бульо,
Стани ме, бульо, соплети,
Ситното гръцко плетене.»
«Мъри, лейко, мъри милна, лейко,
Не мога, лейко ле, да стана,
Змёя ми очи испила,
Руса ми коса скосила,
На сърце гняздо извила.»

"Oh sister, oh my dear sister,
Get up, sister and plait me
Thick Greek tresses."
"Oh little sister, sweet little sister,
I can't get up, little sister,
The snake drank out my eyes,
Bit off my blond hair,
And nestled down in my heart."

BOŽIDAR ŠIROLA

THE FOLK MUSIC OF THE CROATIANS

I. Kuhač' Investigations

It was Franjo Š. Kuhač, the first outstanding Croatian musicologist, who undertook the job of summarizing the characteristic features of the South-Slavic song with the intention of making a guide to the domestic composers in matters of style. He has come to the following conclusions :

1. Croatian folk tunes exhibit non-tempered scale structure.

2. They are characterized by small interval*, especially by seconds, the sequence of which is scarcely interrupted by greater intervals : minor thirds are infrequent and perfect fourths or fifths appear even less. Also sixths are very rare and octaves never occur. The augmented second is characteristic of South-Slavic music ; the diminished fifths are borrowed by the Slovenes from the cadences of Alpine songs.

3. The construction of the Croatian tunes is indicated in Kuhač' *Musical Syntaxis*, as follows :

a) Upbeat is completely missing ; every melody begins with the strong beat.

b) Textual structure and melodic pattern correspond to a latent harmonic action (a thesis untenable today).

c) Melodic motives meet the poetical tropes and figurations and affect the architectonic formation of the small two-section form or three-section form. The frequent insertion of exclamatory syllables and words (some sort of tropes) points to the considerable influence of purely musical architectonics upon poetry.

4. Kuhač has thoroughly investigated the connection of the melody of the speech and its flexions under different emotions with musical melody and found that the melodic line in Croatian folk tunes, in most of the instances, corresponds to the melody of speech. As regards the

---

* A statement of his professor at the Budapest Conservatory (Nemzeti Zenede), Karl Thern.

formation of recitatives, Kuhač requires strict conformity with the way the *guslar*, singer of national heroic songs, performs his recitative-like chant. Here the melody of the speech is scarcely heeded, for the performance consists of a number of ten-syllable verses in equal metrical scansion.

5. According to Kuhač the stanza, *i. e.* a melody in the form of a short song, is built up in two ways ;

a) a litany-like series of equal but short melodic phrases ; as in children's songs and in the recitation of heroic songs ;

b) the shaping of the small form, consisting of two or three sections, from one stanza of the poem by repeating whole verses or only parts thereof, further by shorter or longer introductions, insertions and additions, and by a special refrain with or without insertions respectively.

These statements have been confirmed by later research.

Kuhač' investigations were based on the idea that melody comes from elevated speech and thus the tune is, so to say, a kind of enhanced speech melody. Still, the investigation of the *melopoeia* seems to have proved that the tune has been brought to life by the laws of its own.

II. The Tonal Basis of the Bosnian-Herzegovinian Folk Song as Investigated by Ludvik Kuba

Arranging his numerous records of (mostly secular) folk songs from Bosnia-Herzegovina, Ludvik Kuba, a well-known editor of folk songs of Slavic origin, applied a method never used before. Folk songs had earlier been arranged according to their contents, and classified as love songs, satirical songs, drinking songs and ceremonial songs. As a basis for his classification Kuba selected the musical construction alone, *i. e.* the tonal quality of the tune. He endeavoured to discover the scale and thus reveal the inherent latent harmony, the tonality proper. He found the scales, well known from common European music, but succeeded in tracing some infrequent ecclesiastic and unusual modes as well. In the Bosnian-Herzegovinian folk songs he discovered eleven scales altogether which, however, he reduced to five scale schemes. By transposing the constituent tetrachords of same and by stressing notes other than finals he obtained all the eleven scales. In naming these scales, he made use of the Old-Greek scale names, for he supposed there must have been a close connection between the ancient Greek musical tradition and the Croatian folk tunes.

In Kuba's opinion the first scale scheme is a major scale, consisting of two disjunct Lydian tetrachords.

The second scheme is a minor scale, termed harmonic in the theory of music with the leading note on the seventh grade and an augmented second between the sixth and seventh grades. (Kuhač had already termed "Slavic" the minor scale of this type and introduced a new key signature for it in his great song collection : thus in A minor he applied a sharp on the second line for G♯; in D minor he used the same for C♯ and a flat for B♭.)

The third scheme is the following :

$$\text{A-B-C}♯\text{-D} \parallel \text{E-F-G}♯\text{-A}$$

ascending and descending, with the last grade sharpened.

The fourth scheme is :

$$\text{A-B-C-D} \parallel \text{E-F}♯\text{-G}♯\text{-A}$$

ascending and descending with the last two grades sharpened.

The fifth scheme is :

$$\text{G}♯\text{-A-B-C-D}♯\text{-E-F-G}♯$$

(the same scheme is to be found in gypsy music, as F. Liszt called it), more clearly :

$$\text{A-B-C-D}♯\text{-E-F-G}♯\text{-A}$$

with A as final note. This scale consists of two conjunct "oriental" tetrachords with an augmented second in the middle.

These are the five scale schemes, from which Kuba develops all the eleven scales found by him to be the fundament of melody in Bosnian and Herzegovinian folk songs.

From the first scheme he deduces six scales, which are the following : Major scale (ancient Greek Lydian; medieval Ionian) :

$$\text{C-D-E-F} \parallel \text{G-A-B-C}$$

Ancient Greek Phrygian (medieval Dorian) :

$$\text{C-D-E}♭\text{-F} \parallel \text{G-A-B}♭\text{-C}$$

Ancient Greek Dorian (medieval Phrygian) :

$$\text{C-D}♭\text{-E}♭\text{-F} \parallel \text{G-A}♭\text{-B}♭\text{-C}$$

Ancient Greek Hypophrygian (medieval Mixolydian) :

$$\text{C-D-E-F} \parallel \text{G-A-B}♭\text{-C}$$

Ancient Greek (and medieval) Hypodorian :

$$\text{C-D-E}♭\text{-F} \parallel \text{G-A}♭\text{-B}♭\text{-C}$$

Ancient Greek Mixolydian (medieval Hypophrygian) :

$$C-D\flat-E\flat-F \parallel G\flat-A\flat-B\flat-C$$

(All the scales here are built on C; thus the places of the whole tones and semitones within the scales can readily be seen.)

The following two scales are derived from the second scheme : Harmonic minor scale :

$$C-D-E\flat-F \parallel G-A\flat-B-C$$

Minor dominant scale :

$$C-D-E\flat-F \parallel G-A\flat-B\flat-C$$

The third scheme yields but one scale, the major-minor scale :

$$C-D\flat-E-F \parallel G-A-B\flat-C$$

The fourth scheme again yields but one scale, this being the minor-major scale without *diazeuxis:*

$$C-D\flat-E\flat-F\flat-G\flat-A\flat-B\flat-C$$

Finally, the fifth scheme represents the so-called oriental scale :

$$C-D\flat-E-F \parallel G-A\flat-B-C$$

The new names for these scales were devised by Kuba on the basis of their tonal affinity which follow from the melodic and harmonic quality of each scale. The name "minor dominant scale", for instance, originates from the fact that the relevant melodies, belonging to a minor scale in harmonic respect, have a dominant cadence. Kuba found the last scale exclusively in folk melodies collected in larger settlements where the Moslem element prevails. Here not only folk tunes exhibit a stronger oriental influence, but so do all the other manifestations of the life of the people. The minor dominant scale, the major-minor scale and the minor-major scale are said to be characteristic of the Slavs (both of Catholic and of Moslem faith) in Bosnia and in Herzegovina as well as of the Serbians not only in the aforesaid two provinces but also farther eastwards, in Serbia (in the neighbourhood of Levče) as proved by Mokranjac. The subdominant in minor form is especially characteristic because in melodies it tallies with the descending leading note on the sixth grade.

Kuba's system of scales was unfit for the oldest folksongs having a tonal range not exceeding a fourth or a third. In such cases the relation to the *nota finalis* alone was indicative. These melodies have, however, other characteristic features showing their remote age, such as simplicity in rhythm and melody, the syllabic compliance of the wording with the notes of the melody and a melody without ligatures and without any ornaments.

Kuba found two reasons for the alterations of a note in a scale. The first is a reason inherent in singing : sometimes it is easier for the singer to produce a flattened note ; the second reason refers to modulation : the melody passes from one key to another, mostly from the major scale to one having an augmented second.

Kuba found harmony proper in but a few Bosnian-Herzegovinian folks songs ; in most of them it is the vocal character that prevails ; the final notes are considered tonics. In some melodies he discovered a tonal change because, when spreading from one folklore area to another, the melody is likely to lose its pure vocal features (*e. g.* its Dorian tonality) and assumes the qualities of the major tonality with a final dominant. This is the case in areas where folk melody has assumed a harmonic character (East Slavonia, Sirmia, Bačka).

III. *Problems of Harmony*
(*The "Istrian" scale, pentatony, ecclesiastic modes*)

In some of the scales, according to which Croatian folk melodies are formed, there is no trace of the most important relation of fifths. The so-called "Istrian" scale has an ambit extending, at best, to the sixth, this being a sure sign of the age of this tradition in a considerable part of South-Western Croatia. P. Ignacije Radič considered the following scale fundamental :

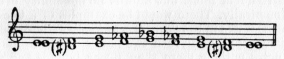

Another musician, Ivan Matetić Ronjgov, enlarged this scale with another minor second :

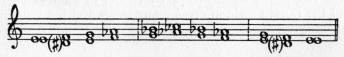

The third in this scale and the leading note are somewhat different from those in pure major and minor tonality, which makes it difficult to illustrate the usual final cadence with common notes. According to Matetić :

95

Though this final cadence shows a marked resemblance to the one in the medieval Phrygian tonality, the "Istrian" scale can by no means be qualified as a Phrygian one (as was done, *e. g.*, by Žganec, Dugan, and Matetić), all the less so since in the Phrygian scale there is no sign of a constant lowered fifth grade.

Matetić constructed the "Istrian scale" from trichords, without applying *"diazeuxis"*:

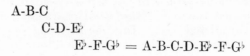

$$A\text{-}B\text{-}C$$
$$C\text{-}D\text{-}E^\flat$$
$$E^\flat\text{-}F\text{-}G^\flat = A\text{-}B\text{-}C\text{-}D\text{-}E^\flat\text{-}F\text{-}G^\flat$$

The scale thus formed points definitely to the melodic construction of the old Istrian folk songs but affords no possibility of expressing its tonality harmonically. These would be examples of a two-voice heterophony in which — like in the *"cantus gemellus"* of the Middle Ages — no harmonic quality appears. In such two-part singing we find between the subsequent notes nothing more than linear bounds and a tendency to reach easily and smoothly the final note.

Kuhač himself was bound to discover old ecclesiastic modes in the melodies of several folk songs. The existence of such modes in folk songs was recognised by Žganec even clearer in those of Medumurje. He found the Dorian scale in great many songs and the Phrygian scale less frequently.

The folk songs of the neighbouring areas, Hrvatsko Zagorje and Gornja Podravina, for instance, show exactly the same conception of harmony. In his collection from Medumurje, Žganec published also folk songs, the melodic lines of which show definite signs of anhemitonic *pentatony*.

No. 3.

Zvi-ra vo-da   iz   ka-me-na

Whether this ancient scale scheme was later enriched with elements of heptatony by the folk tunes of these areas to create a melodic idiom of their own is a musicological problem that will, for lack of historical material, probably remain unresolved.

Dr. fra Branko Marić has found definite traces of pentatony also in the Bosnian-Herzegovinian folk songs collected by Ludvik Kuba. Marić interpreted the occurrence of notes missing in pentatony as pentatonic modulations. He has also pointed out the following definitely pentatonic features: the frequent repetition of a melodic motive (consisting of steps to the minor third and to the perfect fourth) within the range of a fourth; the dissonance of notes filling the span of the augmented fourths; the wavering of the melody between different modes; and finally, the melody ending on the second note of the scale. Thus Marić has come to the conclusion that this type of pentatony must be closely related to the medieval Dorian scale.

Under the influence of instrumental music and especially of the justly intoned bagpipe, Croatian folk tunes assumed, over a restricted area, in East Slavonia, in Sirmia and the Bačka, characteristics in consequence of which their harmony yields cadence formations exhibiting definite signs of the major and minor systems (IV—V—I).

No. 4.

Ko- lo ma-lo   Ma- ri- ce,   ig ra po-la - ga - no,

ko- lo ma-lo,   Ma- ri- ce,   ig- ra po-la - ga - no.

IV. Two-Part and Polyphonic Folk Music

Croatian folk music — be it vocal or instrumental — is (with very few exceptions) two-part music; it is performed in common by several male and female singers. Homophony can rarely be found (*e. g.* in Medumurje). If, for instance, a folk song is performed by women it splits up into alto and soprano. In male choirs we find tenors and basses. Somewhat different is the position with mixed choirs. In the coastal areas and in Istria the female voices are in the alto range, whereas the male voices belong to the tenor range. This produces two-part music: both melodic lines move in parallel sixths, with a pure final octave, as it has already been shown. Female voices in Slavonia and in the neighbouring areas sing in parallel thirds and so do the male voices. Thus, a double biphony is obtained at an octave distance. The performances of such choirs are strong and full. Each of the verses is usually started by an expert female singer who thereby gives the just intonation to the whole choir. The final dominant of these folk songs is justified: it imparts an uncertainty to the final through which the litany-like sequence of new verses become comprehensible to the listener.

However, an even more unusual type of biphony flourishes in a large part of Bosnia and almost in the whole mountainous region of Dalmatia. This type of chorus performance was called by Kuba "a duet in seconds". Here, one voice separates only intermittently from the other and only at a distance of a major or minor second (whence the denomination) and soon unites again.

No. 5.

Maj-ka cer-cu giz-do-va-la, giz-do-va-nu i u-da-la,

giz-do-va-nu i u-da-la oj ————— !

Very often the final consists of sustained parallel seconds, as for instance, in the performance of the *guslars* in some districts of Dalmatia, and also in the performances of some ceremonial songs in Zumberak. The *guslars* play preludes and interludes on the *gusle*, while the singer, after a long recitation, gives his voice a rest. The *sevdalinke* (love song) sung by the Moslem youngsters in Bosnia under the windows of the beloved girl and accompanied on the *tamburica* is similarly performed. It is exactly like the performance of the rhapsodes in ancient Greece as described by Plato: "κρούσις ὑπὸ τήν ᾠδήν."

On the *diple*, with or without a bellow, and on the *dvojnice* (double flute) two-part melodies are played; since the accompaniment needs a smaller range of notes, the accompanying pipe has a small number of holes. The blowing of bag pipes used in Macedonia and in Bulgaria passes the air through a single-melody pipe, on which a unison melody sounds above the sustained bourdon. The central empty string of the Dalmatian and Macedonian string instruments *(lirica, g'dulka)* is also sounded as a bourdon during the whole performance.

Where has this biphony come from? How long has it been used by Croatians and by the other Southern Slavs?

This biphony, if we may apply here the name of the ancient European musical usage, the first signs of polyphony, is a particular feature of Croatian musical folklore. It is only surpassed by the chorus performances of the Russian peasants (as it appears from the recordings made by Mrs. Linev). Many European musicologists have been induced to inquire into the heterophonic character of this biphony (such as Guido Adler who recognised heterophony in it, Robert Lach, *et al.*), by the living example of ancient *contrapunctus a mente* in folk melody. Robert Lach found notes of some biphonic ecclesiastic songs in Lošinj and published them in vols. IV. and VI. of *Sammelbände der Internationaler Musikgesellschaft*. A two-part *Sanctus* written in punctum neumes was found by Viktor Novak in the *Codex S. M. Jadrensis*, in Zadar, Dalmatia, dating from the end of the 11th century. Lach tried to account for the biphony in the Croatian folk songs by explaining that the people must have learned them from the many church choirs which performed their songs biphonically as early as the 11th and 13th centuries all over Istria and the Quarnero Islands. The church choirs having disappeared, the people themselves began to replace them in the church ceremonies and were thus prompted to apply the biphonic performance in secular folksongs as well.

The Bulgarian musicologist Vasil Stojin tried to find another explanation for the appearance of biphony in the folk songs of the Southern Slavs. (In the remotest settlements of the Rhodope Mountains in Bulgaria the same biphonic performances are to be discovered.) In his opinion, the Bulgarian immigrants must have brought along this musical practice from their ancient home in Asia and maintained it up to now: moreover, the Bulgarian soldiers serving under the Longobardian rulers are likely to have introduced this way of performance to Italy where it probably had a great influence upon the appearance of polyphony in West European music.

In the light of our present knowledge of musicology neither of these explanations is acceptable. First, because polyphony already existed at that time in Northern Europe, and second, because the singing of the people, living in the remote localities of the mountain-areas, could by no means have been influenced by church choirs.

It is in biphony that Croatian folk melodies find their appropriate expression because this is the mode of performance the people have adapted and conserved as a precious legacy from their ancestors.

In the performance of urban songs even tetraphonic features can be observed. This applies especially to some of the bigger localities along the Dalmatian coastline. Kuba proves this by songs recorded in some of the towns of the area. The most characteristic feature of this kind of polyphony, Kuba tells us, is the homophonic simplicity of the harmony. The use of chords is limited to the tonic and the dominant chord; subdominants are scarcely heard. The subdominant chord is connected with the dominant chord by the parallel shifting of all voices, resulting in perfect-fifth and octave parallelisms. In any similar performance, the singers of the accompaniment, if improvised, attain the next note by the smallest melodic step unless, in changing the chord, they are bound to sustain the common note. Only very gifted singers are willing and able to embellish their part. Parallelism at all voices to a given melody, always sung in the upper voice, remains the only governing factor of singing. Kuba was unable to detect where and when this practice came into existence.

V. The Connection between Metrics and Musical Rhythm

Non-metrical forms in the Croatian folk melodies only appear in songs with liturgic wording sung in Catholic churches, where, on the basis of old traditions, Church Slavic still is or was used (as in the dioceses of Senj and Krk, for instance, but also in other localities in the montainous area of Dalmatia, where Church Slavic has been replaced by the more common colloquial Croatian). The *melopoeia* of these songs resembles that of the Gregorian chorales. When performing these songs in the course of the religious ceremony, almost the whole population, including men and women, take an active part. The tradition is passed on verbally from one generation to the other. Some minor melodic alterations arise from the differences in accentuation, whereas more important changes are due to another factor, the distribution of breathing. Apart from this, the syllabic arrangement in conformity with the individual notes of the melody prevails as in the psalmody or the lectures of the Gregorian chorale.

No. 6.

Svet, svet, svet Gos-pal Bog Sa - va - ot.

It is the accentuated syllable that carries the whole weight of the rhythm and also the stress, even if the relevant note of the melody is not emphasized either by a melodic step or by the duration.

All the other folk songs are definitely rhythmical: now and then almost non-metrical forms can be found in dirges in Slavonia, especially in those of the so-called *narikuse* (hired mourning women.).

The accentuation of folk poetry has had a direct influence upon the development of musical rhythm. An accentuated syllable corresponds to a strong beat (thesis) and an unaccentuated one to a weak beat (arsis): this is the way two-beat and three-beat bars have arisen. Croatian folk melodies have, in strict compliance with folk poetry, produced such elementary metric patterns as trocheic and dactylic lines without upbeat. The upbeat to be found in the folk tunes of the Slovenes must, in Marko Bajuk's opinion, be considered an anacrusis. In the Croatian, Serbian, and Bulgarian music the upbeat in a melody is the proof of its foreign origin; it occurs only in the urban songs — so called by Kuhač. Songs like this have developed as a result of the amalgamation of domestic and foreign traditions and this is the reason why the urban songs of Dalmatia are reminiscent of Italian folk music and those of Bosnia and Herzegovina exhibit oriental influences.

The dactylic metrics to be found in the folk music of the Romanic and Germanic peoples leads up to three-beat bars, whereas with the Croatians they result in different two-fourth measures where the accent is in most cases on the strong beat.

From Medumurje:

Do - ri - ca pla - če, kaj ji je?

From Hrvatsko Zagorje:

ne sha- jaj   mi ra - no

The same applies to the trocheic metrics in folk poetry, leading up to three-beat bars:

s o - ne   stra-ne

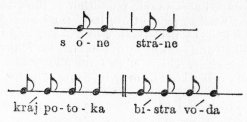

kraj po- to - ka   bi- stra vo - da

In the performance of the *guslars* and also in some girls' songs, the musical scansion is playing a more important part than verbal metrics.

If the musical rhythm in older non-metrical folk songs (without measure schemes) is governed solely by accentuation in speech, then singing in chorus, — as in the case of people working together, for regulating their movements in common, — is bound to lead up to even rhythms. The non-metrical schemes come from the prosaic recitation whereas the rhythmical ones are rooted in the metrics of poetry. When the accent affects the *melopoeia*, the stressed syllable is placed on the strong beat. When equal measures, readily conceivable, follow each other, the sense of measure diminishes the importance of the accent factor, in fact reduces it to nil. Thus the melody takes the upper hand and the melodic line develops according to its own rhythmical laws.

The five-beat measure, appearing in the form of 5/4, 5/8 or even 5/16 is not uncommon in Croatian folk melody. It could be regarded as a combination of either 2/4 + 3/4, or 3/4 + 2/4 (see example no. 2).

Five-beat measures are often found in the old ritual songs of the Northern coastline. Here, the final note is sometimes sustained like the *mora ultimae vocis* in the Gregorian chorale.

Polyrhythmical measures can also be heard in the Croatian folk tunes. Unequal measures follow each other, but a tendency toward symmetry can still be observed, as, for instance in the repetition of the three-bar phrase 5/8 + 3/8 + 5/8 (see no. 2).

VI. The Problem of Architectonics
Smaller Units in Litany-like Succession

The shaping of the melody, *i. e.* of the *melopoeia* takes place according to special, purely musical laws, regulating the form of both vocal and instrumental sentences.

The simplest sentences consist of notes of equal duration and are at the same time isometric. The connection between the words and the melody is considerably strong: the accent factor emphasizes the alternation of strong and weak beats. The sentences are made up of two-bar phrases constituting, so to say, the only elements of the *melopoeia*. Simple forms like these are to be found in children's songs and old ritual songs. These folk songs are but a simple repetition of the two-bar phrase (A), which yields the whole architecture, its form being AAAA .... This form governs the lengthy performance of a *guslar* and this is where the special applicability and suitability of this simple architecture for certain purposes becomes clear. This simple form allows the quick recitation of the *guslar*. Any other kind of melody, being of necessity more complicated, would unnecessarily spin out the narration of an exciting story; listeners want to learn the developments as soon as possible; they have little interest in the performing melody itself. This type of architecture is the one that governs the arrangement of verses in a dance tune or the sequence of shorter sentences in the instrumental accompaniment of the dancers to their lively steps.

In lyrical folk songs there is, naturally, an effort to form more complex melodies ; while even forms of *durchkomponiertes Lied* occur, yet there is a striving to construct melodies of more clearly outlined units. Though the singer richly embellishes certain phrases, he does it because he wants them to blend in proper entity. That is why there is a great variety, even a bright abundance of forms in the Croatian folk songs, although the songs are built up of the regular two-bar, rarely three-bar, motives in the form AB. It is exactly owing to this abundance of forms that a folk song poet may get confused when constructing a complete musical sentence. He has one short verse at his disposal to use for building up a song. In Croatian folk poetry there are no stanzas ; stanza-like forms occur only in the so-called urban songs, which is a sign of recent origin and very often a sign of foreign influence as well.

How does a complex stanza develop from a single verse? Partly by the repetition of the words and partly by the insertion of exclamatory syllables, or words.

The repetition of the text can be performed in several ways. There is a difference between simple repetition and complex repetition (*i. e.* of what has already been repeated), and there is another difference between partial and complete repetition. When a two- or three-bar melodic phrase (A) is repeated, the result gives the impression of a closed musical sentence (2A) When two sentences (A and B) thus repeated follow each other, we gain the impression of a complete period. This is how the architectonic scheme 2A + 2B is obtained.

Repetition may, however, take place in the reversed way, the scheme being : AB + BA. For instance :

> Više sela zelena dubrava
> zelena dubrava više sela

A partial repetition may occur either at the beginning or in the middle of the verse :

> Djevojka se,
> djevojka se krivo kunijaše.

Some of the syllables may be repeated :

> Kupi ko-
> kupi konja

or

> Kiša pa-
> pade dolje na livade.

If the partial or complete repetition does not yield enough syllables to cover the whole melody, and some final notes of the melody would remain without words, the necessary syllables can be taken from the beginning of the next verse. This will immediately show that the song is not finished and a continuation is to be expected.

The structure of the stanzas in the folk songs of Bosnia and Herzegovina has been investigated by Kuba who found complicated architectonic schemes indeed as, for instance, 2 AB + 2 (2A + B), etc. These analyses have thrown light upon the richness and brightness of architectonics in Croatian folk music. As an example let us quote a part of the folk song *Popuhnul je tihi vetar* from the Croatian coastline :

> Popuhnul je,
> Popuhnul je tihi vetar,
> popuhnul je ;
> trajna nena,
> nina nena, trajna nena,
> tihi vetar.

The application of the inserted meaningless exclamatory syllables here becomes clear.

No. 7.

Certain exclamatory words have a meaning but are not related to the words of the poem. Such are, for instance, *djevojko* 'lassie', *draga dušo moja* 'my sweetheart', *more* 'heigh-ho', *aman* 'apparently', and the like. (Some of the words mentioned here are of Turkish-Arabic origin and can be heard especially in the songs of Bosnia and Herzegovina.) Now and then also exclamatory syllables will be used, such as *oj! ej! ih!.* Particularly common is the use of the word *oj !* in rich melismatic variations (see Ex. no. 5). The inserted meaningless exclamatory syllables of this type are called in the Istrian folk songs, *ta rankanje.*

The structure of the musical sentence presents complete or partial repetitions of the musical phrase as well ; in case of a repetition of this kind either purely rhythmical or also melodic variations may appear. The melodic embellishment of a musical phrase is not uncommon either. The inserted exclamatory syllables and words interrupt the narrative (since they are required by the *melopoeia)* and may occur in many Bosnian-Herzegovinian folk songs, sometimes exceeding the extent of the verse itself. In many Dalmatian folk songs especially long melismata extend over the syllable *oj* but within very small intervals, in trill-like sequences or in *staccato* tones of very short duration. Melismatic forms of this type are usually found at the beginning of the musical strophe and serve also to end the musical sentence. Between such extended melismata there is only a syllabic recitation of the verses of the folk song. In fact, it is the distribution of breath that affects the *melopoeia* and forms the melody. Music dominates poetry, though the words of the text are arranged on the basis of the accent factor. According to Dobronić, this is the case when the song of three sections becomes the most apparent: ABA.

Regular refrains are very common in Croatian folk melodies. They have an architectonic importance of their own by ensuring a stronger and more expressed unity owing to their regular recurrence.

The richness in minute details of the short two-section forms, the commonest in folk poetry, is a proof of the great creative power of the unknown folk composer.

The repetition of some parts of the melody (motives or phrases, etc.) may render the performance monotonous. This risk is easily avoided by applying a diminution when repeating (the diminution of the metric units of all or some notes in one motive). Although this eliminates symmetry, the melodic line will become much livelier. Both this means and the variation already mentioned (by which the range of the motive is likely to change) serve to produce the required effect.

Finally: the large form of all Croatian folk melodies is the song consisting of strophes — the most developed form of musical expression in the life of all peoples — *i. e.* a sequence of strophes following each other at shorter or longer intervals. In purely vocal songs the intervals between the strophes are not long : these serve to give the singer's throat a rest. The *guslar* plays the interludes on the strings of his *gusle,* while the piper blows embellished interludes between the strophes of his dance song.

This great stanza-form was called by Robert Lach the litany form, and rightly so : it is the succession of short musical sentences linked by a common refrain and by the same melodic cadence (which may, now and then, replace the refrains as well). And this, indeed, is the form of a litany.

*

LITERATURE

Franjo Š. Kuhač, *Osebine pučke glazbe naročito hrvatske* (The Properties of Folk Music, Especially of the Croatians), Rad Jugoslavenske Akademije, Book 160, pp. 174, 176.

Ludvik Kuba, *Narodna glazbena umjetnost a Dalmaciji* (Folk Song Art in Dalmatia), in *Zbornik za narodni život i običaje* (Collection of Folk Life Customs), Books iii and iv.

Franjo Š. Kuhač, *Turski živalj u pučkoj glazbi Srba, Hrvata i Blgara* (Turks in the Serbian, Croatian and Bulgarian Folk Music), in *Glasnik Zemaljskog muzeja*, Sarajevo 1898.

Ludvik Kuba, *Cesty za slovanskou pisni* (For Slovak Songs), vol. ii, Praha 1935.

Milovan Gavazzi, *Pregled karakteristika pučke muzike južnih Slavena* (Survey of the Characteristics of South-Slavic Folk Songs), in *Lud slovianski*, vol. iii, 1927.

Božidar Širola, *Problemi našeg muzičkog folklora* (Problems of our Musical Folklore), in *Zbornik za narodni život i običaje*, Book xxviii.

Božidar Širola, *Cod. S. M. Jadrensis*, in *Sveta Cecilija*, vol. xxxvii, 1943.

Marko Bajuk, *Mera v slovenski narodni pesni* (Metrics in Slovene Folk Songs), Ljubljana 1925.

Robert Lach, *Studien zur Entwicklungsgeschichte der ornamentalen Melopcie*, Kahnt, Leipzig 1913.

Guido Adler, *Über Heterophonie*, in *Jahrbuch der Musikbibliothek Peters*, vol. xv, 1909.

Vasil Stojin, *Hypothèse sur l'origine bulgare de la diaphonie*, Sofia 1925.

Vinko Žganec, *Hrvatske pučke popijevke iz Medumurja* (Croatian Folk Songs from Medumurje), published by the Yugoslav Academy of Sciences and Arts, 1924.

Antun Dobronić, *Ojkanje*, in *Zbornik na narodni život i običaje*, 1915.

St. St. Mokranjac, *Srpske narodne pesne i igre (iz Levča)* (Serbian Folk Songs and Dances from Levča), in *Ethnografski zbornik*, Serbian Royal Ac., Belgrade 1902.

Ivan Matetić—Ronjgov, *Još o bilježenju istarskih starinskih popijevki* (Again about the Collection of Ancient Istrian Songs), in *Sveta Cecilija*, vol. xx, 1926

TIBERIU ALEXANDRU

THE TILINCA
AN ANCIENT RUMANIAN
FOLK INSTRUMENT

The Rumanian people have, in the course of their history, produced a great variety of musical instruments adapted to the necessity of giving expression to their wonderful and inexhaustible art.

Among the various categories of traditional Rumanian musical instruments, the wind-instruments have spread widest. They have, presumably, developed in close connection with the centuries old life of the shepherds, a way of life that has gradually disappeared since the beginning of the last century. According to the latest researches, we know to-day of five types of alphorns, distinguished by the form of their sound-tube (cylindrical or conical, straight or bent), five kinds of bagpipes with shawms of different construction (simple or double, and with a changing number of finger-holes), and a family of flutes consisting of thirteen members.

The flutes are the most common and, at the same time, the most popular instruments with the Rumanians. According to an old popular belief, the flute is of divine origin: God created the flute and the sheep, the devil the bagpipe and the goat. In old Rumanian *colinde* (Christmas carols), God is represented as an old shepherd with white hair and beard, grazing his flock of sheep while playing the flute. A variant of the Prometheus myth in Rumanian folklore says that God and St. Peter purloined a piece of coal from the fire belonging to the impure spirit and handed it to the people, concealed in a flute ; therefore — the legend says — the flute is evidently of divine origin. The Rumanian folk songs tell of a shepherd who would not for anything part with his beloved instrument and would remember his flute in the last moment of his life ; he expresses the wish that it should be planted on his grave with the blow-hole windward ; then, as the wind blows, the flute will sound and the sheep will gather round his grave to shed bitter tears.

The various kinds of flutes known by the Rumanian people differ according to :

a) the construction of the sound-producing parts : blow-whole placed horizontally or laterally, with or without fipple ; without or with (five, six, seven, or more) finger-holes ; simple flutes (with one tube) or double ones (with two tubes) ;

b) the outer form of the sound-tube: slightly conical or cylindrical ;

c) the manner of holding it while playing: vertically (with fipple), half horizontally (without fipple), and horizontally (with blow-hole placed horizontally) ;

d) the material used: whether made of wood ash, willow, plum-tree, hornbeam, hazelnut, elder, cherry-tree, sour-cherry tree, plane-tree, osier, and others), of reed, of metal (brass, aluminium, iron, and others), or very rarely of bone ;

e) their length: short (up to 30 cm) middle-sized (35—50 cm) and long (over 50 cm).

As to the number of finger-holes the following should be mentioned : flutes with 6 finger-holes are constructed with fipple, without fipple, or with laterally placed blow-hole ; those having 5 finger-holes are provided with a fipple, those having 7 finger-holes are constructed with fipple, without fipple, or with laterally placed blow-hole, and those having more than 7 finger-holes again without fipple.

All these peculiarities have, of course, made the classification of the flute family rather difficult. Besides, there is no uniform folk terminology, for one and the same term is applied all over the country for different kinds of instruments, or one and the same instrument has a different name in different places. Thus we were obliged to make our choice. We have selected the commonest terms and made an attempt to generalize them as shown in the appended table of systematization.

Each type is made by the performer himself or by artisans living in the village and is used all over the country. There are some communities in Rumania, real flute centres, as *e. g.* the Transylvanian village of Hodac, district Reghin, where some 90 semi-professional instrument-makers manufacture over 100,000 flutes a year. Most of them offer their instruments for sale while wandering from fair to fair.

Owing to the primitive method of construction based on empiric measurements with the fingers, a piece of thread, a twig, or a finished flute, and so on, almost every flute produces a different scale. Very few instrument-makers manufacture equally intoned flutes, conforming to an absolute pitch. One rather finds craftsmen who take great pains in constructing richly ornamented instruments, such as beautifully carved flutes, set in metal, bone, or the bark of cherry-trees, truly valuable objects of folk art.

The numerous peculiarities, resulting from the many different ways of construction, account for the fact that each performer prefers to play on his own instrument and not on any other, insisting that others are incorrect.

		Designation	Finger-holes	Size	Material
With horizontal blow-hole	without fipple (half horizontal)	1. Tilinca	—	long	wood, metal
		2. Flute of Moldova	6	short long	
		3. Flute of Dobrudja	7 (7th at back)	short middle-sized	wood, reed
		4. Bulgarian flute (caval)	8	long (three parts)	wood mounted in bone
	with fipple (vertical)	5. Tilinca with fipple	—	long	wood, (very rarely of metal or bone)
		6. Caval	5	long short	
		7. Flute	6	long middle-sized short	
		8. Double flute (equal tubes)	6	short middle-sized	
		9. Double flute (equal tubes)	7 (7th on accompanying tubes)	short middle-sized	
		10. Double flute (with short tube of accompaniment)	6	short middle-sized	
		11. Flute (very rare)	7 (7th at back)	short	
With lateral blow-hole	transverse flute	12. Popular flute	6	short long	wood
		13. Popular flute	7 (all in front)	long	

Note: The Panpipe *(naiul)* has not been entered into this table, though it is related to the family of flutes.

The flute is played chiefly by shepherds. Their musical repertoire consists of tunes closely connected with their daily occupation and a few airs that have lost their magic significance long ago: such as *Milking the Sheep, Distributing Milk, Curdling Milk* or *Cheese-making;* wanderers' airs: *Departure, When the Sheep Move up the Mountains, When they Leave the Fold, When the Sheep Descend into the Valley,* etc; pasturing airs: *When the Sheep are Grazing on the Mountain-Slope, Song of Grazing;* and signals: *Calling the Sheep together to the Sheep-Farm, When the Sheep are Called to Graze, When the Sheep are Called from the*

Mountains, Return of the Sheep, or dances: *The Shepherds' Bătuta, The Sheperds' Belt-dance* (Brîul), *The Shepherd (Ciobănasul), The Shepherds' Dance (Ciobăneasca),* and others.

The "musical narrative", *The Shepherd who Lost his Sheep,* is also often performed on the flute. It is played in many parts of the country without words, but the simple content of this genuine musical popular poem is known by everyone. The sequence of melodies — lament — dance — lament — dance — is interpreted as follows: a shepherd, while looking for his lost flock, begins to sing a lament. Suddenly he imagines he sees his flock in the distance. His sad song changes into a lively dance. But the shepherd was mistaken, he was deceived by some white stones. The plaintive melody is resumed. At last he finds his sheep and the narrative ends with a dance "full of joy that he has found them". The story of the shepherd who, on the summit of the mountain, died of longing for his sheep, is also performed on the flute.

The sorrowful folk songs *(doina),* slow melodies, rich with embellishments, are mostly played on long flutes, the dances preferably on short ones. Formerly they danced in the Rumanian villages to the flute and the bagpipe. Nowadays the flute is played to the festive *Hora* in some parts of the country only as *e. g.* in a few villages of county Hunedoara. But on the other hand, peasant gatherings generally end in dancing to the sounds of the flute. The traditional good wishes of the *Plough* are often recited to the sounds of the flute and around New Year the popular plays *Goat* and *Bear* are performed in disguise. Finally, the flute is also played in some parts of the country at funeral ceremonies.

*

The simplest flute is the *tilinca* or *telinca,*[1] a tube about 60—70 cm, open at both ends, without any finger-holes, and with narrowed blow-end.

To blow the tilinca, which is held somewhat crosswise, the lips are slightly pursed to give the column of air the desired form in diverting it against the narrower end where it is divided and set in vibration. The various overtones of the fundamental are produced by stronger or weaker blowing, as well as by opening or closing the lower end of the tube with the help of the forefinger.

The oldest description of this primitive instrument is by Franz Joseph Sulzer[2]: ". . . The third (flute or pipe) called tielinka, has neither fipple, nor holes, is made of willow, and gives the required tones according as one knows how to cover the lower opening more or less with the finger".

---

[1] Read: teelinca.
[2] *Geschichte des transalpinischen Daciens,* Rudolf Gräfer, Wien 1781, vol. ii, p. 419.

A century later the Rumanian researcher Teodor T. Burada described this instrument more exactly in his treatise[3]:

"Having examined the flutes used by the people, we believe that the tilinca is our primitive wind-instrument and belongs to the family of flutes. It consists of a cylindrical tube of elder, plane, or willow-wood bored through ; the old people say that formerly it was also made of the bark of the lime-tree *(tilia)*. Several (flutes) are mounted on some places with cherry-tree bark, that they should not crack. The tilinca is 65 cm long and 66 mm thick ; shepherds while grazing the sheep play on it by blowing into one end, touching the other end with their forefinger, producing in this way different notes, according to the extent the lower end is covered. This instrument is the most imperfect among all flutes used by our people. The notes produced on it have a rather shrill and unclear sound ; only a few, monotonous songs are played on it because it can produce only the following notes :

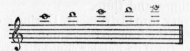

To play on the tilinca one has to hold it rather crossways to the lips".

Another detailed description comes from Béla Bartók in the introduction to his monograph on the folk music of the Rumanians of Maramuresh.[4] Bartók has discovered in Maramuresh also a tilinca with fipple; this is a device which facilitates blowing and consists of a plug which shuts one end of the tube, leaving a small square opening — called "light" — as well as of a square or rectangular "window" cut into the wall of the tube — similar to the recorder. Such a tilinca was also discovered by Burada in 1894 among the shepherds of Rumanian origin in Moravia.

We are quoting Bartók's description of the two kinds of tilinca :

"The *'tilincă cu dup'*, a thin wooden slit-flute, about 80 cm long, without finger-holes."

,,The *'tilincă fără dup'*, similar to the former, a long flute without finger-holes or slit. This is substituted by a special pursing of the lips, holding the flute somewhat tilted (like the North-African *gsba*). On both tilincas only natural tones can be produced since the finger-holes are missing. While playing, the lower opening of the flute is shut from time to time for a moment with the forefinger of the left hand with a definite purpose. What effect this shutting has and at which notes it occurs, I could not find out either on the spot, or from the phonograms. It is said that on both tilincăs only the *Horă lungă* can be played."

[3] *Cercetari asupra danţurilor şi instrumentelor de musică ale Românilor* (A Study of the Dances and Musical Instruments of the Rumanians) in *Almanah Musical*, H. Goldner, Jaşi 1877, vol. ii, p. 71.
[4] Béla Bartók, *Volksmusik der Rumänen von Maramureş*, in *Sammelbände für Vergleichende Musikwissenschaft* published by Carl Stumpf and E. M. von Hornbostel, Drei Masken Verlag, München 1923, vol. v, p. xxvi.

Bartók informs us in the *Zenei Lexikon*[5] that the bottom-note of the tilinca is :

while the diameter and the length of the tube permit the production of the series of natural overtones till the 12th harmonic. At the same time we get to know that "the Székelys of Mureş-Torda know a degenerate form of the tilinca : In spring the children cut a branch of the willow-tree, about the length of the hand, the bark of which is loosened up to the middle of the branch and in such a way they get a pipe closed at one end. At the opposite end a fipple is inserted and at the lower end a hole is cut. This tilinca produces a single shrill and crying tone". Bartók is of the opinion that probably the Székelys were also acquainted with the original form of the instrument, since in their speech there is a precise distinction between tilinca and flute.

The tilinca is a very rare instrument. During a quarter of a century the *Arhiva de Folclor* of the former Rumanian Association of Composers and since 1949 the Institutul de Folclor could discover only three tilinca-players, among whom Mihai Lăcătuş (who was 49 years old in 1951) is the most gifted. Mihai Lăcătuş, a peasant from Cîmpulung-Suceava, could attend only 3 grades of the elementary school. He worked in forestry and was shepherd for many years. He is an enthusiastic instrument-maker and an efficient folk-instrument player. He can play with the help of a leaf, or a piece of birch-bark, he blows the alphorn, the tilinca, the flute without fipple, the flute with fipple, he plays the *cobza* (a sort of lute) and the violin ; at the same time he has a thorough knowledge of the popular art of his district. At present Mihai Lăcătuş is head of a cultural centre at of Capu Satului, the western district of the town, where he has been working for many years.

Lăcătuş' activity in the house of culture consists of training young players of folk instruments ; he is also constantly striving to raise the artistic level of his Moldavian flute ensemble : for that purpose he has also constructed a flute family.

The tilinca on which Mihai Lăcătuş played for tape-recording and which is now part of the instrument-collection of the *Institutul de Folclor*, is an elder-wood tube, 69 cm long, with an inner diameter of about 2 cm, with irregular profile and a non-centred opening. Lăcătuş explains that

[5] *Zenei Lexikon* (Encyclopedia of Music), edited by Bence Szabolcsi and Aladár Tóth. Győző Andor, Budapest 1931, vol. ii, p. 61, in the entry *Magyar népi hangszerek* (Hungarian folk instruments). Unfortunately we could not discover the two writings of Bartók in which he probably speaks about the *tilinca*, namely : *A hangszeres zene folklórja Magyarországon* (Folklore of Instrumental Music in Hungary), published in *Zeneközlöny*, Budapest 1911—1912 and *Primitiv népi hangszerek Magyarországon* (Primitive Folk Instruments in Hungary), published in the periodical *Zenei Szemle*, Temesvár 1917.

Mihai Lăcătuş

(Facing page 112)

the length of the tube was determined according to the length of the arm in such a way that he should be able to shut the lower end of the tube with his finger easily ; the inner diameter of the tube corresponds about to the thickness of the little finger : "a bit more than the little finger", "up to the nail", so that "the little finger should fit into the opening of the tube".

The tilinca can also be made of willow, the bark of the willow or some other wood, *e.g.* of plane, osier, hornbeam, etc. or of metal. The instruments made of wood have to be wetted before playing to obtain an evenness of *the walls*. Playing requires a certain effort and attention on the part of the performer that the constant change of strength of the *air current* should coincide with the opening and closing of the tube-end. Tape-recording shows the following result with open tube :

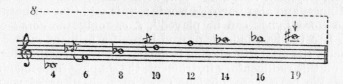

with closed tube :

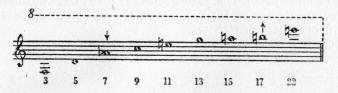

with alternately opening and closing of the tube :

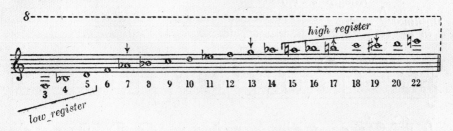

The overtones 18 and 20 were only performed at the third recordings (with alternately opening and closing of the tube); on the other hand, on this occasion the overtones 3, 11, 16 and 17 were not produced. Yet in our third example we have included the complete series of overtones played by Mihai Lăcătuş on his tilinca. The 13th overtone should be noted : G which sounds unclear, instead of G♭.

The performer, while playing, never used extreme notes (*i. e.* the overtones 3 and 4 and those from 16 upwards) ; the deep notes have a dull sound and are hard to blow, the high notes sound shrill and are also hard to produce. The sound of the tilinca is, in general, shrill, as if hissing and rather harsh.

The melodies are sometimes accompanied by an *isonus* (accompanying voice) called "murmur", which the Rumanian flute-players produce from the throat while blowing and interweave in the melody. This technique of performance is characteristic of all kinds of flutes and serves to set off the melody better. Sometimes the height of the accompanying voice *(isonus)* is adapted to the melody, mostly in the melodies "after the bagpipe".

The *doinas,* songs and dances played by Mihai Lăcătuş, contradict T. Burada's opinion that only "few, monotonous songs" can be played on the tilinca, and also Bartók's words : 'it is said that on both tilincas only the *Horă Lungă* can be played", *i. e.* only the *doina* of Maramuresh. Lăcătuş has, indeed, proved himself a brilliant *virtuoso* on his instrument. His masterly playing is delightful. The artistic effect he can achieve on this rudimentary instrument, the simplest flute imaginable, is amazing. We have here obvious proof of a gifted artist who, owing to his efforts, his skill, and ingenuity, has achieved the greatest results with the simplest tool. The art of Mihai Lăcătuş was awarded the first prize in the summer of 1953, on the occasion of the national competition of folk-instrumentalists.

Here is a melody recorded in his performance :

Bătuta Dance

(Resp.)

Played by Mihai Lăcătuş, aged 49, in Capu Satului, county Cîmpulung-Suceava. Collected by T. Alexandru on 23th March, 1951, notation by P. Bentoiu and B. Marcu. No. Mg. 30g.

Unlike the tilinca without fipple, the tilinca with fipple is easy to blow. The tones produced on the latter are limited to a section of the series of overtones, just like on the tilinca without fipple. The tilinca with fipple tuned to A, discovered by Bartók in Maramuresh, produced the following series of overtones, as noted by him in his afore-mentioned monograph (Melody 23i, p. 24):

$G^{\sharp 2}$ was produced by the performer in a way that has slipped from the memory of the collector. This note seldom appears as forefall to A^2.

Here follows a melody played on such a tilinca and noted by Bartók:

Horă lungă — Doină

Played by Josif Ilies, aged 25, in Poienile Glodului, county Vișău-Baia Mare, collected by B. Bartók in 1913. No. F. 2157a (Budapest).

117

The tilinca is also known by the "Ciangăi"[6]. During a research undertaken in 1950 by the branch establishment in Cluj of the Institute of Folklore (Bucharest) the folklorist János Jagamas discovered two tilinca-players. Gábor János Anton of Luizi Călugăra, county Bacău, a 23 year old peasant who attended the elementary school for six years, plays the tilinca and the violin, and Antal Kotyorka of Cleja, county Bacău, a 52 year old worker, without any schooling, learned to play the flute in his early years when he was a shepherd.

Gábor János Anton's tilinca is made of a bent metal tube, about 80—90 cm long. The diameter of the instrument corresponds to an ordinary waterpipe and is open at both ends. The technique of performing is the same as that of the tilinca without fipple. The bending of the tube has no influence on the series of overtones which can be produced by the instrument.

Antal Kotyorka's tilinca is constructed in a different way: it is an intermediary between the tilinca with fipple and without fipple and consists of a straight tube of poplar-bark, some 60 cm long, with a diameter similar to that of the ordinary flute. At the blow-end a "window" is cut at the edge of the tube-wall, as on the flutes with fipple.

The performer takes the blow-end in the mouth putting his tongue as far as the side-opening of the tube. The tones are produced by closing and opening the lower end of the tube with the help of the finger. The folklorist János Jagamas related that he had made two records with electric phonograph. When first recording he placed the microphone against the lower end of the instrument, but on listening to the phonogram he found that only a few notes of the melody were audible, namely those produced with open tube. At the second recording, he turned the microphone against the upper end of the instrument and only in this way was it possible to record the complete melody. This proves that the overtones produced with closed tube sound only in the upper part of the instrument (which is quite obvious).

From each of these two tilinca-players we could record only one melody, whereas Mihai Lăcătuş played six melodies for us.

In the following we reproduce a melody played on a metal-tube tilinca; it is a love song in free, improvised form, related to the *doina*.

From the notation we could gather the following series of notes:

---

[6] From the Hungarian *Csángó*. These are Hungarians settled in Moldavia. They call this instrument *Cilinka* (read: tzilinca).

Leánycsalogató
(For Cajoling Girls)

Played by Gábor János Anton, aged 23, in Luizi Călugăre, county Bacău collected by J. Jagamas, on 17th September, 1950. No. Fgr. 253a (inv. 1650),

The unsteady pitch of some tones is explained in some cases by the inexact intonation of the overtones (11 and 14), in other cases (overtones 9 and 10) perhaps by changing the hold of the instrument while playing : it has been found, for instance, that through different tiltings of the flute-tube without fipple, with closed or open blow-end, it is possible to produce tones of different pitch.

The tilinca is supposed to have formerly been widely used. Today this ancient folk instrument — called "grandfather" of flutes by Mihai Lăcătuș — is a veritable rarity. According to information which has reached us, the tilinca is still blown today in Moldavia, Bukovina, and the Northern part of Transylvania. Among the nationalities it is said to be known also to the Hutzuls.

LUIS–HEITOR CORRÊA DE AZEVEDO

THE ARCHAIC GUITAR IN BRAZIL

Two forms of the guitar are used in Brazil by the folk musicians: the *violão* and the *viola*. The *violão*, which is popular in towns, is exactly the type of guitar known everywhere, with its six simple strings tuned *E—a—d—g—b'—e'*. The *viola*, of smaller size, having five double strings, all of metal, is the instrument of the peasant.

The origin of these two instruments is Iberian, the *viola* being nothing else but the primitive Spanish *guitarra*, in use till the 18th century. Fallen into disuse in Spain, this type of guitar continued to be a favourite of the Brazilian peasant who has remained faithful, up to this day, to the instrument of his ancestors. Very often — particularly in the southern part of the country — he makes his instrument himself.

The shape of the *viola* is essentially that of the ordinary guitar, with variants determined by the provenance of the instrument (frets more or less near the neck, diameter of the rose, number of pegs and nuts). It varies according to size.

The number of strings varies between 4 and 14, the most frequently used instruments being those with 10 strings. These distributed in groups of two (tuned to unison or to the octave) generally are the same as the chords of the ordinary guitar, without great *E: a—d—g—b' —e')*. The three lowest ones *(a—d—g)* are doubled at the octave and the other two in unison, with the result that the highest one (*e'*) is below the chord that doubles the third (*g'*). Unlike the *violão*, the chord of which is invariable, there are several ways to tune the *viola*. The style of the music determines the choice of the chord. The greatest fantasy is displayed in the tuning of the pairs of strings; the interval of a fifteenth (two octaves) is used besides the octave and unison. The tuning of a pair of strings in unison often leads to the disappearance of one of the strings (the instrument in this case will have double strings and simple strings). Generally the distribution of the intervals of the chord is retained (starting from the lowest: fourth—fourth—major third—fourth) to whatever pitch the series is transposed (in the North of Brazil the *violas* have a much lower register). But different distributions can also be found. I could note the following: fourth—fifth—major third—minor third; fifth—major third—minor third—fourth; fifth—fourth—major third—minor third.

Even less common chords are sometimes used: D—G—b—d—g$^\sharp$; a—e—b'—e'—f'$^\sharp$.

In the South of Brazil the *violeiro (viola* player) knows two positions for holding the instument: sitting, with the instrument resting on his thigh, when he accompanies dances or profane songs; standing, with the instrument almost vertical, pressed against the chest and under the chin, in case of popular religious rites with which the instrument is associated (Saint Gonçalo, patron saint of the *violeiros,* is often represented in the peasant imagery with this archaic guitar).

Collected in Goiânia, Brazil, by the author.

122

(Facing page 122)

PAUL COLLAER

CARIBAN AND MAYAN MUSIC

When listening to the music recorded by the four-member commission (Pierre Gaisseau, Alain Gheerbrandt, Luis Saenz and Jena Fichter) of an expedition to the Orinoco-Amazon region (1948—1950), one can discern a similarity between the music of this region and that of the Mayas. It would be more correct to say that the resemblance concerns the music of the Puinavis, Guaharibos, Piaroas and Maquiritares, on the one hand, and the music of the Caribs of the State Lara (Venezuela) and of the Maya-Quiches of Guatemala, on the other. At first hearing one is inclined to ascribe this likeness to the melodic flexion and structure, to the scales employed and even to the proportion of the intervals, as well as to the style of the performance. And it is the more suprising that the geographic regions inhabited by these tribes lie at a considerable distance from one another.

The most striking resemblance can be detected in songs belonging to the fully developed melodic types of these tribes : for instance in those recorded in the musical documents attached to the present paper under the signs F (Mayan melody) and J (Puinavian melody).

*

A likeness as striking as that cannot be attributed to a fortuitous chance or coincidence : it is the reflection of several elements of the musical idiom. But we may ask whether this is an isolated phenomenon or an inherent common feature of Mayan and Puinavian music. And if so, the question arises whether it is logically possible to assume the existence of a common musical conception.

In order to elucidate this question we have investigated the music of the regions concerned. This investigation, however, was limited, both in its extent and importance, by the number of the available and accessible phonographic recordings : such documents are scarce for the time being. In order to draw some conclusions, inevitably temporary, we have undertaken to examine also anthropological and cultural data presented in recent scientific works.

123

"The third colonizing invasion of America took place in the neolithic age", writes S. Canals Frau. "That is how the more or less brachyoid tribes of medium civilization developed on the continent, and spread over the tropical regions of the North and the South. This invasion, as well as the fourth, are of South-Asiatic origin and of a Mongoloid type" ... "The adaptation to the American conditions of these allochthonous brachyoid elements and the incorporation of autochthonous dolichoids gradually created new groups which, from a somatic point of view, soon took an aspect of collective biologic forms" ... "The southern type which is the oldest, *i. e.* the Brazilides, inhabit the forests of the Amazon and the Orinoco. In the Antilles they are almost extinct. The largest group of this type is to be found among the Arawaks and the Caribs."

"Linguistic and ethnographic arguments seem to indicate that there had been an important Arawakan substratum underlying the great civilizations of Mexico and Guatemala."[1] Schuller[2] and Lothrop,[3] too, share the view of Canals Frau.

The Arawakan family includes the Goajiros. The Cariban family comprises the tribes of Venezuela and of the Guianas, among others the Maquiritares.

Let us add the information given by Joseph Grelier.[4]

In the Guianan massif the oldest stratum of the population lives along the Upper Orinoco and its affluents. They are the Guaharibos, Waikas and Shirishanas. They make their living by fishing, hunting and gathering.

The Arawaks form the second stratum. They are an agricultural and seafaring people. We can find among them the Banivas, Puinavis, Barès, Kuripakos and Piapocos. They are the most mixed race anthropologically and originate from the South and South-East.

The Caribs form the third stratum : Maquiritares, Makus, Yavaranos, Mapayos. They came from the North, from the Antilles, approximately a century before the Spanish Conquest.

The tribes of the first stratum are the most primitive representatives of present-day humanity. Iron or weaving are unknown to them.

The Brazilides and Centralides are two varieties of the same group. For their charactheristics see the above Table.

---

[1] S. Canals Frau, *Préhistoire de l'Amérique*. French translation by Marc. S. Sauter, Paris 1953, pp. 235, 252—253, 311—312.
[2] R. Schuller, *Zur sprachlichen Verwandtschaft der Maya-Quittsé mit den Carib-Aruac*, in *Anthropos* nos. 14—15, pp. 465—491. (Mödling 1919—1926.)
[3] S. K. Lothrop, *South America as seen from Middle America*, New York 1940, pp. 417—430 : *The Maya and their Neighbours.*
[4] J. Grelier, *Les Indiens Guaharibos et Waikas*, in *Geographia* no. 42 (Paris, March 1955).

	Brazilides	Centralides
Average height of men	160	157
Average height of women	147	143
Moderately short and low head		
Cephalic index	82	85
Index of medium height	80	81
Relatively large face		
Facial index	about 79	
Medium nose		
Nasal Index	about 82	80
Figure	round contours	less round than the Brazilides

These anthropological characteristics probably take their origin from the Proto-Malayans, and appear together with cultural elements of archaic neolithic origin. The centre of their dispersion seems to be near the Isthmus of Panama.

The physical characteristics of the constituent elements, displayed at the beginning of the third invasion, are still more distinct with the majority of the Centralides having a great civilization, than with the Brazilides who have persisted in a medium civilization. Canals Frau attributes the reason of this phenomenon to a process of dilution to which all original elements are exposed according to the distance from the natural centre of dispersion.

In the South-American cultural forms of neolithic type which have been preserved until the historical period, we may distinguish three subsequent strata :

1. The oldest cultural stratum represented by numerous tribes speaking unrelated languages, of vaguely defined somatic aspect and of a somewhat heterogenous civilization, being dispersed in the Western half of the Amazonian region. These tribes have not been much influenced by the great impulses of expansion.

2. A medium cultural stratum to which belong the groups and tribes of Arawakan substratum, having a medium civilization.

3. A recent Cariban and Tupi-Guarani culture as a regression to the preceding culture, and which can be regarded as a reaction of non-Arawakan tribes.

These data on cultural relation complete the anthropological data furnished by Joseph Grelier.

It is the Arawaks who spread farthest from the Isthmian region the principles of American neolithic age and the substratum necessary to the formation of the great American civilizations. We can add that after the dispersion of the Antillean Caribs, part of them settled in the forests of Central America, and produced a Mayan-Cariban hybridization.

We conclude this exposition of the anthropological and cultural situation on the relevant territories by ascertaining the homogeneous character of numerous elements common to the tribes of the Upper Orinoco (Maquiritares, Guaharibos, Puinavis), to the Caribs of Venezuela (Lara State) and to the Maya-Quiches of Guatemla. — We refer especially to these tribes because it is their music that we could compare. We must include here the Piaroas, who are, properly speaking, Andeans, but the Piaroan music known by us, even according to the Piaroas themselves, continues Puinavian traditions.

The Andeans, who are of the mountaineer type, have a distinct stature and a different culture from that of the tribes here considered, owing to the Polynesian element in them instead of the South-Asiatic element. The music of the Andeans is markedly different from that of the Mayas and Caribs, and this difference between the music of these two groups, by contrast, brings into prominence the resemblance within the groups here studied.

Musical Inquiry

The following recordings were studied by us :

Library of Congress (Archive of American Folk Song) : *Music of Venezuela* (1940—1942), five records 78 revolutions, 18 musical documents. AAFS/71 to 75.

Instituto Nacional de Antropologia e Historia, Mexico (Archivo de Musica Indigena) : *Musica indigena de Guatemala* (1943—1944), twelve records 33 revolutions, 157 musical documents. Copies of the Institut National de Radiodiffusion, Bruxelles. INR/Volk 73/Audiodisc. 1—12.

Musée de l'Homme, Paris : *Musique indienne d'Amérique* (1948—1950), five records 78 revolutions, 18 musical documents. MH/51.

The copious material from Guatemala presents a homogeneous musical culture. The same can be said of the material of the Musée de l'Homme. From among the Venezuelan records of the Library of Congress we had access to recordings of typically Cariban origin. We have selected examples that best illustrate our argumentation by the clearness of their performance and recording. Besides, each example contains a number of musical features recurring in the recordings which have not been transcribed.

The examples enable us to make a comparative examination. Being aware that the music of the Venezuelan Caribs and that of the tribes of the Upper Orinoco belong to a more or less archaic phase free of European influence, we have selected our Mayan examples from among pieces corresponding to the same stage of development, *i. e.* among those preserved from Spanish influence, the only influence that had penetrated the Mayan country. The Iberian music is so characteristic and its character differs to such an extent from that of Mayan music that, in principle, the hybrids can readily be distinguished. It is, however, important to direct our attention to a fact which makes things more complicated.

The Mayas often adopted Iberian tunes and rhythms. These elements, however, assumed a thoroughly Indian character : the Iberian music pieces were reduced to their skeleton, stripped of every decoration in order to suit the austere mentality of the Indians. In most cases nothing more is left of the Iberian tune than the notes used in the Mayan musical idiom. This regression of the Iberian music towards a more primitive stage induces us to go slow with the discrimination of purely Indian elements and those due to foreign influence.

Before starting the analysis of the songs we have to make another observation. The power of tradition is perhaps stronger among the Indians than among any other people. And it is especially strong in the domain of music, as stated by Alan P. Merriam.[5] Consequently their music and the mode of performance are not likely to have changed ever since the *Conquista*. That is why we can still find the use of Pre-Columbian instruments among the Mayas of Guatemala and of Chiapas (Mexico): the sedge-pipe *(flauto de carrizo)*, the drums called *tun* and *huehuetl*, the tortoise-shell struck with an antler ; the rasps and maracas, the conchs, the trumpets of wood or of rolled-up bark. And even where the metal trumpets gained the upper hand over the wooden ones, the former remained without keys or valves. The present-day Mayan orchestra consisting of these instruments is represented on several of our recordings, especially on those made among the Ixils. This orchestra, by the way, has been described more than once also by Raul G. Guerrero[6] and by Karl Gustav Izikovitz.[7]

This orchestra corresponds exactly to the one so meticulously depicted on one of the Bonampak frescoes[8] dating from the 8th century. This is a remarkable example of the persistence of tradition with the minimum of evolution.

The cultural indifference of the Indians towards foreign influence is emphasized also by Simone Dreyfus-Roche :[9] "Piaroas and Maquiritares have, for several decades, maintained commercial relations with the merchants of adjacent regions, but this contact has remained superficial and has not considerably modified the life of the villages. Espe-

[5] A. P. Merriam, *Songs and Dances of the Flathead Indians*, in *Album P 445* of Ethnic Folkways Library, Notice, New York 1953.
[6] R. G. Guerrero, *Musica de Chiapas*, in *Revista de Estudios musicales,* vol. i, no. 2, p. 143 (Mendoza 1950).
[7] K. G. Izikovitz, *Musical and Other Sound-Instruments of the South-American Indians*, in *Göteborgs Kungl. Vetenskaps- och Viterhets-Samhälles Handlingar*, Femte följden, Ser. A, vol. 5, no. 1 (1935).
[8] Agustin Villagra Caleti, *Bonampak*, Mexico 1949.
[9] S. Dreyfus-Roche, *Musique indienne d'Amérique*, in *Album* (same title) of Musée de l'Homme, Notice, Paris 1953.

cially the musical instruments of these tribes have remained typically Indian and do not bear any traces of European or African influence."

The strange concert of wooden flutes without holes or with three holes and of long spiral rolled-bark trumpets with wooden mouthpiece is always to be heard along the Upper Orinoco and in the Amazonian forests. The photographs of these trumpets and the pictures of trumpets at Bonampak show that we have to do with closely related instruments, if not with the same ones. Besides, we can sometimes find basket-rattles and tambourines with a single membrane.

The Puinavis, on the other hand, use Panpipes which are unknown by the Mayas: the Northern limit of the diffusion of the Panpipe is the Isthmus of Panama. The Puinavis and Piaroas have their Panpipe from the Guahibos, who belong to the Amazonian group.

Taking into consideration that along the Upper Orinoco as well as along all the rivers in the forests north of the Amazon the population is divided into small riparian groups, that these groups are strictly isolated from each other, and consequently their interrelation is rather scarce ; and realizing that the distance separating the Mayas from the Orinoco Caribs is considerable and the land is impassable, we are inclined to think that the parallel features in the music of the two groups are due to an ancient common source, very likely to the culture of the third wave of colonization. Besides, the music pieces which appear to be directly related come from the zone of archaic culture in its most primitive stage represented by archaic statuettes dating from the beginning of the invention of pottery.[10]

*

On analysing the archaic forms of Indian music, as they have come down to us, we find musical entities consisting of two notes separated by an interval approximately equaling a wholetone, and others where the ambit goes beyond the octave. This latter type is especially interesting because the proper octave interval is rare in this music and the intervals exceeding the octave either downwards or upwards are not octaval replications of notes contained in the basic octave. (Or to put it more correctly : in the octave to which we are inclined to attribute a basic function.) Finally, we can observe a weak stability of the size of the intervals ; yet the difference or, if you prefer, the variability of a given interval remains within the limits of ten cents, *i. e.* a twentieth part of a tone. This relative instability[11] cannot be attributed to the variety of the traditions of the different regions or localities. These divergences can be observed both in the music coming from one region or locality

[10] Spinden, *El Norte de Mexico y el Sur de Estados Unidos*, Mexico 1944; p. 343 ; Raphael Girard, *Le Popol-Vuh, Histoire culturelle des Mayas-Quichés*, Paris 1954, pp. 40—42.

[11] *I. e.* compared to our conception of precision and to our keenness of perception.

and in various music pieces of different origin, always within the same order of magnitude. This characteristic instability may be the consequence of the construction of the instruments still rather primitive and of a musical conscience scarcely developed or not requiring strictly fixed intervals.

Listening to the music of these regions one has the general impression that as its ambit extends, it tends to a gamut embracing not eight but ten degrees. It is impossible to transcribe, however approximately, the notes and the intervals of this music in our graphic system. Even the signs $+$ and $-$, superposed to the notes, are unfit for rendering the size of these intervals and, consequently, the nature of this music.

Thus we have undertaken to transcribe this music in the order of the growing number of notes occurring in the scales. The written notes are identical with those of our European system which most approach the actually heard sounds.

Table I

References to the transcriptions

Class	Indication of sources	Transcribed documents
A	MH 61—27 E_3/I, end.	Piaroas. To accompany the rasping of the manioc
B	MH 61—28 E_3/II, first reel	Maquiritare, Ritual song
C	MH 61—28 E_3/II, second reel	Guaharibos. Ritual song
D	INR/Audiod. I/B, first reel	Quiches of Nahuala, Sololà. *Baile del Venado*
E	AAFS 71 A/1	Venezuelan Caribs (Lara). *Baile de las Turas*
F	INR/Audiod. IV/A, third reel	Kekchi of San Pedro Carcha, Alta Verapaz. *Baile de Cortès*
G	INR/Audiod. IV/B, seventh reel ...	Quiches of Cantel, Quetzaltenango. *Baile de los Moros*
H	INR/Audiod. IV/B, reels 4, 5, 6	*idem*
I	AAFS 71/A, third reel	Venezuelan Caribs (Lara). *Maremare*
J	MH 61—31 E_4/II, first reel	Puinavis. Panpipes

Table II

The transcriptions with the reservation made on account of their approximate character

Table III

*The frequency of vibration of the notes constituting the tunes, set forth
in cycles/sec, and the size of the intervals given in cents*

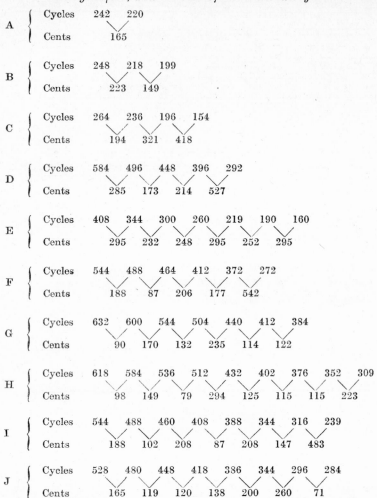

A { Cycles 242 220
    Cents   165

B { Cycles 248 218 199
    Cents   223 149

C { Cycles 264 236 196 154
    Cents   194 321 418

D { Cycles 584 496 448 396 292
    Cents   285 173 214 527

E { Cycles 408 344 300 260 219 190 160
    Cents   295 232 248 295 252 295

F { Cycles 544 488 464 412 372 272
    Cents   188 87   206 177 542

G { Cycles 632 600 544 504 440 412 384
    Cents   90   170 132 235 114 122

H { Cycles 618 584 536 512 432 402 376 352 309
    Cents   98   149 79   294 125 115 115 223

I { Cycles 544 488 460 408 388 344 316 239
    Cents   188 102 208 87   208 147 483

J { Cycles 528 480 448 418 386 344 296 284
    Cents   165 119 120 138 200 260 71

The indicated frequencies are the average of a series of measurements made peri-
odically with a set of 54 diapasons, each at a distance of four cycles, provided by the
Ragg Tuning Forks Co., Sheffield. The successive measurings of one note remained
within the four-cycle limit of measurability imposed by the composition of the set of
diapasons. We have justified the use of this method in another context.[12]

[12] P. Collaer, *Les phénomènes primitifs de l'invention musicale*, in *Acta medica
belgica*, 1954, Fasc. I (Bruxelles).

Table IV

The scales corresponding to the transcribed music pieces

The notes actually heard are shown in the first column, in order to render possible their comparison with the recordings; then in the second column these notes are reduced to a uniform tonality, in order to allow the comparison of the scales.

From these tables we may come to the following conclusions :

1. Up to type E the primitive phases of the Mayan and Cariban music correspond to what can be observed almost all over the world : starting from a music on two notes separated approximately by a whole-tone, we obtain the structure of unhemitonic pentatony.

2. The types from F to J develop a scale extending over an interval of approximately ten degrees within which the octave of none of the notes occurs.

3. The intervals of the Mayan-Cariban music do not conform with those of the Western system.

In order to convince ourselves about the reality of this last fact, let us group the values of the measured intervals in a series within which they do not differ more than by 12 cents, a degree of indetermination due to the limit of the sensibility of the average ear.[13] We obtain the average values given here below :

Table V

Average values of measured intervals

Measured size (cents)	Average (cents)	The maximum divergence between the measured size and the average (cents)
71—79	75	4
87—87—90	88	2
98—102	100	2
114—115—115—119—120—122—125	118	7
132—138	135	3
147—147—149	148	1
165—165—170—173—177	170	7
188—188—194—196—200	193	7
206—208—208—214	209	5
223—223—232—235	228	7
248—252—260	253	7
285—294—295—295—295	292	7
321		
418		
483		
527		
542		

[13] P. Collaer, *Etat actuel des connaissances relatives au fonctionnement de l'oreille, à l'émission vocale et à la mémoire musicale. Questions relatives à la mesure des intervalles et des rythmes*, in *Les Colloques de Wégimont*, vol. i, (Bruxelles 1955).

4. The fourth, having an important structural role in this music gives the following data of measuring :

Table VI
Average values of measured fourths

Measured size (cents)	Average (cents)	The maximum divergence between the measured size and the average (cents)
453—458—458	456	3
470—471—481—483	476	7
498—498—503—515	503	12
522—527—527—531—534	527	7
537—543—547—547	543	6

Hence, the fourth is considered a physical, natural fourth measuring 498 cents. But we find other values too, deviating by I/4 or I/8 of a tone above and below this physical fourth. The average of the measured fourths is generally 501 cents. This proves that in this system (if it is a system at all) it is the physical fourth that forms the basis of the scale, as nearly everywhere, and that the particularities of the Cariban scale come from the peculiar way of dividing the interval of the fourth.

5. The relationship of the melodic structure of types F and J is rather close. It has a predominantly tetrachordal structure where steps by conjoint degrees of a wholetone or a semitone alternate with leaps of empty fourth either ascending or descending, the latter having nearly always a cadence character. Such structures are common with the Puinavis, the Caribs of Lara, and the Maya-Quiches.

6. If we look for analogies of the intervals employed in this music we shall find most of them in the Javanese Pelog. Let us confront our measurements with those relating to the Pelog, made by Jaap Kunst.[14]
Average of contemporary Pelog : 165, 250, 120, 150, 270, 115 cents.
Average of contemporary Cariban scale : 170, 253, 118, 148, ... 118.
That is to say out of six intervals characteristic of the Pelog five are to be found in the Cariban scale. The order of succession, however, is different.
Certain fourths of what we call, for want of a better denomination and with the usual reserve pending further information, the "Cariban scale", which are very important constituting elements in it, are obviously the same as those of the Pelog :[15]
Penunggul-Pelog interval : 120+150+270 = 540. Cariban : 543(+3).
Nem-Gulu Bara-Nem interval : 535. Cariban : 527 (— 8).

[14] J. Kunst, *Music in Java*, The Hague 1949, vol. i, p. 14.
[15] *Loc. cit.*

The great Pelog major thirds, the Gulu-Pelog and Bara-Lima interval : 420.

Nem-Penunggul : 415. We find with the Caribs : 418 ($+$ 3).

After these statements let us quote what Jaap Kunst says of the Pelog. "I incline to the view", he writes, "that Pelog was introduced in these islands by the ancestors of the present Javanese and Balinese peoples themselves, and that the Slendro did not come until later, probably as late as the 8th century A. D. . ." Speaking of the present recurrence of the Pelog, after it was eclipsed by the Slendro, the author goes on : "It might be an interesting hypothesis that we have to do here with a phenomenon parallel to what we see in literature and still more in architecture and the plastic arts, namely, a reassumption of rights by the ancient Indonesian elements — in this case long delayed — from the foreign Hindu, Hindu-Malay, and Hindu-Javanese cultural influence" . . . „It is probable that both the Pelog and the Slendro systems originated in the ancient Chinese series of successive fifths (the so-called blown fifths) derived from the harmonic tones of stopped bamboo flutes" . . . "from which the structure of a large number of tonal systems, spread over a great part of the world, may be explained : not only do the Javanese and Balinese scales seem to derive from it, but — as von Hornbostel was able to show — also the tuning of Central-African, Siamese and Birmese xylophones and metallophones, and of Melanesian, Polynesian, North-West Brasilian and ancient Peruvian Panpipes."[16]

Conclusions

There is a close relationship between the music of the Orinoco Caribs and that of the Mayas. The measurings made in connection with their music ; the concordance of these measurements with those made on the Javanese Pelog scale for certain constituting notes of the Cariban scale ; the fact that this Indian music goes back to a precisely defined and determined cultural era belonging to the third wave of the colonization of America, of Proto-Malayan origin ; the fact that the Javanese Pelog scale is attributed to the same Proto-Malayan origin, permits to presume that the system according to which the music pieces here studied are composed, was very likely imported by Proto-Malayan immigrants constituting the third wave of the colonizers of America, the centre of dispersion of which is to be looked for in the region of the Isthmus of Panama.

Discussion

— The views expounded in the preceding text are necessarily meant to be a first approximation only. At present we cannot do more than that, because the Indian tribes of South America, from where we have taken our recordings and on which exact data are available, are

[16] *Op. cit.* vol. i, pp. 18, 22, 24.

few in number and the enormous geographic space separating them is, for the time being, "musically bare" for us.

— In spite of these deficiences in our information, it seems that the style here described is limited to the Mayas and the Venezuelan Caribs. We may presume that it has spread to the Guianas, East of the Venezuelan massif. Certain cultural indices seem to corroborate this assumption[17] yet we must wait until we shall dispose of recordings[18] made in this region, in order to prove or disprove this hypothesis.

— The available recordings made along the Upper Amazon, the Uyacala and in the Peruvian Andes show an obviously different style as to melodic patterns, rhythmical structure and the size of the intervals. The same applies to the music of the regions further south, as in Mato Grosso, where tritony and tetratony prevail and where pentatony is the most "modern" stage of development. There is only one exception to be noted, but a rather important one: the Iawa music (trumpets or horns and long flutes) for the magic ceremony of the "Nian", which, unlike other music pieces of this people, belongs to the G—H—I—J type of our examples. Hence, it is related to the Cariban type, whereas the music of the neighbouring Boras reveal a distinctly Andean character.

— The shamanistic music of the Yaruros is entirely pentatonic, without any semitones. This strict pentatony and the ternary symmetrical rhythm relate this music to the Andean music of Bolivia, of Peru and of Columbia, the character of which has been revealed by Isabel Aretz.[19]

The following recordings made in these regions were accessible for comparative studies :

Musée de l'Homme : *Séance de Chamanisme* (Yaruros), one record 33 revolutions, MH LD/1.

Musée de l'Homme : *Amazone* (The Iawa and Bora tribes), one record 33 revolutions, MC 20096.

Ethnic Folkways Library : *Music from Mato Grosso*, one record 33 revolutions, P 446 (The Kayabi, Camayura, Chavante, Iwalapeti tribes).

Ethnic Folkways Library : *Indian Music of the Upper Amazon* (The Cocama, Shipibo, Campa, Conibo tribes), one record 33 revolutions, P 458.

Ethnic Folkways Library : *Music of Peru* (The Quechua and Amayra tribes), four records 78 revolution, EFL 1415.

— One can note that the similarity of certain cultural elements does not necessarily imply the resemblance of other elements of culture. The same applies to musical culture : the ritual music on trumpets and

[17] Francis Mazière — Dominique Darbois, *Indiens d' Amazonie*, Paris 1953.
[18] Clifford Evans — Betty J. Meggers, *Life among the Wai-Wai Indians*, in *Nat. Geogr. Mag.* March 1955 (Washington).
[19] I. Aretz, *Musicas pentatónicas en Sudamérica*, in *Archivos Venezolanos de Folklore*, vol. i, no. 2 (Caracas 1952).

137

flutes, which is to be found on vast territories in South America, presents different musical features on the Orinoco, on the Upper Amazonas and on the Mato Grosso. The Panpipes of Orinoco and those of the Andes produce intervals of different size.

— The dances *Las Turas* (the flutes) and *El Maremare* are now considered by certain Venezuelan experts, such as Miguel Acosta Saignes,[20] to be typically Cariban music of ancient origin. Their origin is recognizable through the numerous variants of the poetical texts and of the choreography : these dances are actually spread all over Venezuela and presumably in Guiana. The music of the versions here reproduced belong to archaic traditions.

— One may raise certain questions : may we attach primary importance to a quantitative analysis (the size of the intervals)? Has the size of the intervals a predominant role in the musical idiom of a people?

It seems to be impossible to give an answer which would hold good for all places and cultures. In a number of cases the melodic structure is predominant and typical, and the size of the intervals has but a subordinated significance. That is the case, for instance, with certain songs that have been spread for a long time over vast areas of dispersion. In our case the resemblance between F and J, and between H and I is due to melodic features without any regard to the interval of the seconds and thirds occurring in them. — In other cases it is the size of the intervals that has a decisive importance. These measurements in reality are an average : a fact to be borne in mind lest one should misinterpret the real significance of the numbers. Bearing in mind that the intervals are considered as average values, the study of the scales, on its way to perfection, seems to show that the space of sonority is organized for the whole mankind according to a limited number of great types, such as pentatony, or to put it more correctly, several pentatonic systems, the western diatonic system, and the Pelog. It is important to know to which type of scale the music of the different peoples belongs. Each of these types diffused over enormous territories seems to be a common heritage pointing to a common cultural origin of the peoples having otherwise a music of markedly different melodic and rhythmical structure. Hence we think that the size of intervals deserves a meticulous examination. A large number of scientific investigations of that kind, and a synthetic essay will only enable us to assess their real value.

In the present paper we have classified the songs according to the enrichment of scales. This method seemed quite natural to the founders of ethnomusicology because it proceeds from simpler forms to complex ones. This point of view, however, is no longer unanimously accepted. Some prefer the contrary, saying that the most primitive music is often

[20] M. A. Saignes, *Las Turas*, Caracas 1950 ; Idem, *El Maremare: Baile de Jaguar y la Luna*, in *Archivos Venezolanos de Folklore*, vol. i, no. 2 (Caracas 1952).

complex, and the rudimentary forms of two or three notes are nothing but remnants conserved by regression, degeneration, oblivion, or other reasons. We are not willing to endorse this new conception which is a rough simplification just as is the former view. We admit that really primitive music is often complex. But this complexity is to be found above all in such idioms which do not yet manifest the notion, conscience, or desire to produce notes in fixed and determined intervals. As soon as the notion of fixed intervals asserts itself, the apparent complexity turns into a very limited choice of what we call "notes". This passage from apparent primary complexity to the simplicity of the first choice is observable in Australia. On the other hand, certain tribes formerly regarded as primitive are no longer considered such and, consequently, their music thought to be primitive is, in fact, not primitive at all.

The decisive argument which makes us persist in the idea of primitive simplicity is this : the tribes known for certain to be primitive, such as the Weddas and the Fuegians, have a music on two or three notes at rather constant intervals. — As to the phenomenon of regression, there are numerous data from Oceania clearly showing that the evolution is irreversible. Complex musical forms of superior cultures may well return to a more primitive stage, but not to the point of becoming a music of two or three exactly measured notes. Regression is due to the carelessness of the performance, to oblivion, and confusion of details. A music piece of primitive appearance which, in reality, is a music of regression is easily recognizable for its irregularities and the resulting lack of homogeneity, and one can also find in such degenerated music the traces of the previous, higher stage.

It seems to be indicated to quote finally the opinion of Marius Schneider[21] on the music of the Mato Grosso. The author has transcribed and analyzed a number of songs of the Yabuti, Huanyam, Cabixi, Movima, Chiquitos, Macurap, and Tupari tribes living north of the river Guaporé. Schneider's opinion on the music of these tribes is much the same as ours, inasmuch as he observed the extremely primitive character of a number of music pieces collected among them. But he has found also more developed ones as, for instance, the music of the Macuraps. Schneider states that the characteristics of the latter differ considerably from those coming from the Cariban group. They belong to the Andean group. Schneider presumes a South-Asiatic origin, with certain features which can be found also in Polynesia. This view conforms completely with the anthropological and historical data quoted by us in support of our thesis.

[21] M. Schneider, *Contribución a la música indígena del Mato Grosso (Brasil)*, in *Anuario Musical* vol. vii (Barcelona 1952).

JAAP KUNST

FRAGMENT OF AN ESSAY ON "MUSIC AND SOCIOLOGY"

All over the world it is found that certain musical instruments are reserved for the exclusive use of either men or women. Take the flute for instance : among most peoples, past and present, playing the flute — almost any kind of flute — is regarded as a masculine prerogative, while sometimes prejudice has gone so far in this connection as to forbid a woman even to look at this instrument on pain of death. Yet on the other hand, for some inscrutable reason that rather rare variety, the central-hole flute, may be played only by women. I noted this myself among the Ngadanese and Nagas of Mid-Western Flores[1] and Van der Tuuk records the same custom among the Toba-Bataks.[2] The same applies to the use of the Panpipes in some regions, as for instance among the Macao Indians in Venezuela and the Tinguians in North Luzon (Philippines).[3]

On the island of Nias, off the West coast of Sumatra, the *doli-doli*, a primitive xylophone, is only used when the rice is ripening and the fields are guarded, and then by women only.[4]

The above-mentioned Batak tribe also makes a distinction between the kind of mouth harp played by girls and that reserved for the use of the young men. For instance, among the ornaments suspended from the little instruments meant for the youths there is always a miniature bamboo spring clapper which is never found on the girls' harps.

Among the Bunun tribe on the island of Formosa, the musical bow is solely for the use of the male ; the mouthharp usually for the female ; the flutes restricted to male use are played only on occasion of triumphal head-hunting, but not for amusement.[5]

---

[1] J. Kunst, *Music in Flores*, Leyden 1942, p. 150 ff.
[2] *Bataksch Woordenboek*, p. 152a.
[3] Curt Sachs, *Geist und Werden der Musikinstrumente*, Berlin 1929, p. 49 ff.
[4] J. Kunst, *Music in Nias*, Leyden 1939, p. 23.
[5] Takatomo Kurosawa, *The Musical Bow of the Bunun Tribe in Formosa and Suggestion as to the Origin of the Pentatonic Scale*, Tokyo 1952.

Regarding the flutes of the Venda of Northern Transvaal, Kirby[6] states: "They are made in a special area, which is protected by special sacred ceremonies and taboos, by a specialist maker, and their sale is a monopoly. They are constructed in sets, and are always placed in charge of a selected individual. The players are always males."

The Central African marimba (m'bila, timbila, balafon) is a typically male instrument; the same may be said of the wooden slitdrum of Indonesian culture.[7]

In Surinam, women, the principal singers, never play drums. They believe that if they break the taboo their breasts will grow to the ground.[8]

On Manam Island (New Guinea) girls are called upon to sound a single death beat but do not use drums at any other time.[8]

Among the Kissi (French West Africa) the seo, a rattle made of a gourd, is a women's instrument in that it is made as well as played by women only, and furthermore is used, except sporadically in very special cases, exclusively for accompanying women's dances;[9] the Baganda (British East Africa) have castanets made of a particular kind of seeds which only girls are allowed to play,[10] while the Big Nambas (Malekula, New Hebrides) consider the musical bow a definitely woman's instrument.[11]

In how far this assigning the use of a given kind of instrument to one sex or the other is connected with the sex-suggestion inherent in some instruments I do not know. Sometimes such a connection seems quite evident, as in the case of the flute, which is commonly regarded as a phallic symbol and to which naturally — one is reminded of certain equivocal expressions in many Western languages — male characterristics are ascribed, even though the word itself — in West-European languages at least — may be feminine. But in other cases no such connection exists — or perhaps we should say exists no longer.

In Indonesia and elsewhere the drum itself is felt to be feminine. In those regions this instrument belongs to a group of concepts including darkness, an empty cavity, moisture, the maternal womb, the moon — ideas obviously related in the subconscious in true Freudian fashion. Yet for all that the beating of the drum is not confined to one sex only. On the islands of Java and Bali the instrument is played by men exclu-

[6] Percival R. Kirby, The Musical Instruments of the Native Races of South Africa, London 1934, p. 168.
[7] D. H. Meijer, De spleettrom, in Tijdschrift van het Kon. Bataviaasch Genootshap, vol. lxxix, 1917, p. 415 ff.
[8] Sophie Drinker, Music and Women, New-York 1948, p. 57.
[9] André Schaeffner, Les Kissi. Une société noire et ses instruments de musique, Paris 1952, p. 9.
[10] K. P. Wachsmann and Marg. Trowell, Tribal Crafts of Uganda, Oxford University Press 1953, p. 325.
[11] A. Bernard Deacon, Malekula, a Vanishing People in the New Hebrides, London 1934, p. 42.

sively, but in Timor and West Flores I saw it oftener, though not always, being played by women. It is quite possible that the cultural phase still manifesting itself on the Lesser Sunda Islands — and perhaps the same may be said of Borneo, where the Dyak priestesses often beat a narrow, high one-headed drum *(ketobung belian)* — is an older one which clings more closely to the original view of things. The fact, as stated by Marius Schneider,[12] that drums were originally used to produce rain, accords with the above in so far that it is suggestive of one of the components of the group of concepts already mentioned, namely, moisture.[13]

[12] Marius Schneider, *Australien und Austronesien,* in *Die Musik in Geschichte und Gegenwart,* vol. i, col. 877, 1950.
[13] The bronze kettle-drums of South Eastern Asia are also said to have originally served for the magical production of rain.

LAURENCE PICKEN

TWELVE RITUAL MELODIES OF THE T'ANG DYNASTY

The total volume of medieval (eighth to fourteenth century) music surviving in China is remarkably small considering the length of the Chinese musical tradition and the constant efforts of successive dynasties since the beginning of the Christian era to maintain a faithful performance of the Confucian Rites. The chief reasons for this paucity, apart from political disturbances, are first, that music other than ritual music was rarely regarded as worthy of preservation before the beginning of the fifteenth century; secondly, the repertoire of ritual music was probably small enough to be memorized, and what was committed to paper was little more than a mnemonic of which the *cognoscenti* had no need. It is certain that ritual melodies underwent in performance the sort of elaboration and transformation observable at the present time in the expansion of the cantus of a Balinese *gamelan*-composition, or of the written parts in a Japanese *gagaku*-performance. There is no evidence, however, that any Chinese before Prince Chu Tsai-yü (late sixteenth century) ever compiled a full-score of the performance of a ritual melody, so that music of the Rites must have been highly sensitive to the destruction or dispersion of sets of instruments in a particular clan-shrine or temple, or to the premature decease of musicians and masters of ceremonies.

Of the music which has survived, the greater part was intended for ritual use and probably owes its preservation to that intention. Very little of this music has as yet been transcribed into staff-notation, either in the West or in China, and until recently, four ritual melodies from a set of ten by Chiang K'uei,[1] dating from the first years of the thirteenth century and transcribed by J. H. Levis,[2] were the only examples available in the West. The ritual tunes in Courant's famous essay[3]

---

[1] Chiang K'uei, *Pai-shih Tao-jen Ko-ch'ü, Yüeh chiu ko.*
[2] Levis, J. H., *Foundations of Chinese Musical Art*, Peip'ing 1936.
[3] Courant, M., *Essai historique sur la musique classique des chinois*, Lavignac & La Laurencie, *Encyclopédie de la musique*, Paris 1931, vol. i, pp. 77—211,

are taken from Prince Chu's treatise of the late sixteenth century[4];
but while it may fairly be claimed that in Prince Chu's day they
were reputedly ancient, they do not occur in any earlier source known
to us. Prince Chu's statement, that one of the melodies is taken from
the stone-engraved classics set up in 853—857, and surviving to the present in the *Pei Lin* (Forest of Inscriptions) at Hsi-an, is not supported
by the stones. This stone-text of the *Book of Songs (Shih Ching)* was
recently (December, 1954) examined on my behalf by Professor E. G.
Pulleyblank of the University of Cambridge, who subsequently learned
that Chinese musicologists have searched in vain for evidence in support of Prince Chu's claim.

There survive, however, twelve melodies for poems from the *Book
of Songs* which may be somewhat earlier in date even than Prince Chu's
unconfirmed example. The earliest text in which they occur is a post-
humously printed work of the Sung philosopher Chu Hsi (1130—1200),
the *I-li Ching-chuan T'ung-chieh* — the title may be paraphrased as
A General Survey of Ritual. The preface to the first edition is dated
1223, but the work was reprinted on several occasions in Ming times,
and again in early Ch'ing times — for example, the *Lü-shih Pao-kao
T'ang* edition of *ca.* 1700, which I have consulted.[5] These twelve melodies
were also printed by Hsiung P'eng-lai (1246—1323) in the *Sê P'u
(Large-Zither Scores)*, of which the earliest surviving print is that in
the *Yung-lo Ta Tien*, the Ming encyclopedia, finished in 1407, of which
fragments only of a single copy survive ; from this it has many times
been reprinted. The text in the *Yüeh-ya T'ang Ts'ung-shu* (1829) has
been used here. The first section of this as yet unexplored source of
Chinese medieval music reproduces Chu Hsi's tunes, both in pitch-pipe
notation and in flute-notation. Hsiung's version in the pitch-pipe notation does not indicate the octave of the fundamental or of any higher
degree, though these are unambiguously indicated in the flute-notation.
In the transcriptions given here, it may be assumed that wherever
f' or *g'* occurs, Hsiung's pitch-pipe version has *f* or *g*. A third version
of the twelve melodies, ostensibly derived from Chu Hsi, occurs in the
Yüeh Tien (Encyclopedia of Music) of Huang Tso, printed in 1544 ;
a reprint of 1853 has been consulted. This also gives the tunes in pitch-
pipe and flute-notations. Huang Tso, however, like Chu Hsi, discrimi-
nates between *f* and *f'* and *g* and *g'* ; he differs chiefly from the latter in
that two of his melodies are shorter by one or more stanzas than Chu Hsi's
version. In the transcriptions given here, the text followed is that of
Chu Hsi, and it may be assumed that *Sê P'u* and *Yüeh Tien*
agree with the transcription unless the contrary is expressly stated.

[4] *Chu Tsai-yü:* See in particular the volumes *Hsüan Kung Ho Yüeh P'u*
and *Hsiang Yin Shih Yüeh P'u.*
[5] Edited by Lü Liu-liang, 1629—1683. The rarity of this print may be
due to burning of his work because of hostility to the Manchus.

In several places in Chu Hsi's text, lexigraphs have been deliberately obliterated in the *Lü-shih Pao-kao T'ang* edition — a usual practice when blocks are worn. The gaps have been filled from *Sê P'u* and *Yüeh Tien*.

Chu Hsi states that his text derives from the Sung scholar, Chao Yen-su, who had the songs from a source dating from the K'ai-yüan period (713—741) of the T'ang dynasty. This attribution is accepted both by Hsiung and Huang. The writings of Chao — who took the degree of Chin-shih in the period 1165—1173 — were extensively used by Chu Hsi as a source of information on matters of ritual. There is no reason to doubt Chu Hsi's ascription of the transmission of the songs to Chao, but in view of the 'Golden Age' halo which hung about the K'ai-yüan period already in Sung times, the ascription of the songs to precisely that period can only be accepted with reservations.

A single melody from this set of twelve has twice been printel in recent historical surveys of Chinese music published in China. The melody to the first poem in the *Book of Songs* (no. 1 in the standard order of Mao) was transcribed into the common flute-notation by T'ung Fei[6]. More recently, Professor Yang Yin-liu, head of the Institute for Musicological Research in Peking, has transcribed the same melody into staff-notation[7]. Both T'ung, and Yang accept Chu Hsi's ascription of the tunes to the K'ai-yüan period.

The transcription of the tunes, so far as the relative pitch of the notes is concerned, is a simple matter because the note to which a word is sung is unambiguously shown by the name of one of the twelve pitch-pipes. In theory, the chromatic series of the pitch-pipes was generated as a cycle of pure fifths from a fundamental, reduced to the space of an octave, the thirteenth fifth yielding the (slightly sharp) 'octave'; but it seems very likely that some degree of tempering of the series was practised from early times. In any case, the complex sounds of bell-chimes and stone-chimes must surely have obscured the fine edge of intonation in the ensemble. The ritual orchestra furthermore included large zithers, and it is difficult to believe the Chinese did not use consonant octaves on these. If, moreover, heterophony was practised, as described by Moule[8] in the last century, and as argued for the past by Prince Chu, it must have been difficult, if not impossible, to distinguish between a 'chromatic octave' generated by the cycle of fifths and an equal-tempered chromatic octave. It is therefore probably legitimate to

---

[6] *Chung Yüeh Hsin-yüan* (Fundamental of Chinese Music), Shanghai 1926, Book 2, pp. 1—3.
[7] *Chung-kuo Yin-yüeh Shih-kang* (Historical Summary of Chinese Music), Shanghai 1952.
[8] Moule, G, E., *Notes on the Ting-chi, or Half Yearly Sacrifice of Confucius*, in *Journal of the North China Branch of the Royal Asiatic Society*, Shanghai, vol. xxxiii, 1901, pp. 37—73.

transcribe the melodies in terms of an equal-tempered chromatic octave.

The question of the absolute pitch of the fundamental of the system is more difficult. Professor Yang has recently calculated values for the fundamental, at all periods in Chinese history, from the lengths of the standard pipes adopted by successive dynasties, and from supposed values of the standard 'foot' and 'inch' of each period. For the K'ai-yüan period of the T'ang he proposes $f^\sharp$ as fundamental. His transcription is printed in facsimile (without acknowledgement) in Achilles Fang's introduction to Ezra Pound's version of the *Shih Ching* entitled *The Classic Anthology*.

The melodies are settings of lyrics taken from two main sections of the *Book of Songs (ca.* B. C. 800): from the *Hsiao Ya* (Lesser Elegancies) and from the *Kuo Feng* (Airs of the Principalities), which latter is represented by songs from two sections only: *Chou Nan* (Chou State and South thereof) and *Chao Nan* (Chao State and South thereof). Following Waley's grouping,[9] the themes of the songs are: Courtship (9), Marriage (7, 8, 10, 11, 12), Blessings (4, 5, 6), Welcome (1), Public Life (3), Warriors and Battles (2).[10] For the traditional meaning of the songs, the general reader may consult Couvreur.[11] A first attempt to translate certain of the songs without reference to their traditional interpretation was made by Granet[12]; but it was Waley who carried through this attempt to its logical conclusion, making use of the philological researches of Simon and Karlgren; as indicated here, he groups the songs for comparative purposes according to their social function. For all that is known about the ancient sounds of the poems, the reader is referred to Karlgren.[13]

The form of the lyrics is variable, but a majority exhibit a small number of stanzas (two to five) of from four to eight four-word lines. The rhyme-schemes vary; but the same rhyme may occur at the end of each line throughout a stanza. On occasion the rhyme occurs on the penultimate word (see Song 4, for example); in these cases, the last words of the rhyming lines are identical. There are a few places where a reduplicative binome is rhymed, for example, in Song 8, stanza I, where *ts'iər-ts'iər* rhymes with *kɛr-kɛr* (sound-values from Karlgren). In three of the poems (1, 4, 5) the lines are occasionally lengthened to six or seven words, or reduced to three or even to two.

Musically the songs are of great interest. The melodies are strictly syllabic (more accurately: one-note-to-one-word), and are ascribed to

[9] Waley, A. D., *The Book of Songs*, London 1937.
[10] The numbers in brackets are the serial numbers of the songs in the set of twelve.
[11] Couvreur, S., *Cheu King*, Sien Hien 1896, 1926.
[12] Granet, M., *Fêtes et Chansons anciennes de la Chine*, Paris 1919.
[13] Karlgren, B., *The Book of Odes*, Stockholm 1950.

two modes only, both heptatonic : *huang-chung ch'ing kung* (mode 1) and *wu-i ch'ing shang* (mode 2).[14] In respect of note-series only (that is, of their relative pitches), these are Lydian on *f*, with *f'* as final (nos. 1—6) and Mixolydian on *f*, also with *f'* as final (nos. 7—12) but for two exceptions.

Though all the melodies make use of semitone steps, it is clear that the extent to which they do so varies from example to example. Some, indeed, appear to be a patchwork consisting of phrases from a purely pentatonic series mingled with others from a heptatonic series (no. 7 for example). The ritual melodies of Chiang K'uei, previously mentioned as dating from the thirteenth century, are more consistently heptatonic.

Most of the tunes show instances of the repetition of entire musical lines — particularly marked in nos. 5 and 6. This is also observable in the tunes of *Chiang K'uei*.

From the nature of the verse, it might be excepted that each musical phrase, corresponding to a single line — that is, to a complete sentence — would itself be complete and self-contained. It is known from Prince Chu's exposition that the lines of the stanzas were separated from each other in performance by several beats of percussion, sometimes equal to the duration of the line itself (see Courant, p. 129). This would lead us to expect that the last note of a four-note phrase would possess 'final' or at least 'subfinal' (secondary final) quality. Examination of the songs showed in fact that a limited number of degrees of the mode occur as line-finals, and that the number of stanza-finals is even more restricted. While picking out line- and stanza-finals, however, I noticed that the half-lines also tend to end on the same few degrees as the lines, so that each four-note phrase is made up of two two-note phrases. This seemed at first sight so remarkable that a detailed analysis of all the tunes in mode 1 was undertaken, setting out for each nature and frequency of the degrees that act as stanza-finals, line-finals and half-line finals. A similar enumeration was made of the various stanza-initials, line-initials and half-line initials. A complete analysis is shown for Song 2, p. 151 ; for the remaining songs, a summary analysis follows each transcription.

In setting out the transcriptions, the following data are given for each song : (1) A transcription into staff-notation on the basis of *f* as fundamental. Bar-lines mark the ends of lines ; double bar-lines mark the ends of stanzas. The notes are of equal duration ; this is in accordance with nineteenth century practice and with that recorded by Prince Chu.

---

[14] The meaning of the phrases : *huang-chung ch'ing kung* and *wu-i ch'ing shang* will be considered later (p. 168). For the present it will be sufficient to remind the reader that *kung* is the basic series in root position, while *shang* is the modal inversion on the second degree of the basic series.

(2) The rhyme-scheme, based on the sound-values given in Karlgren (*op. cit.*). This is given in full only for Song 2. (3) For all the songs, notes on rhyming syllables are marked with a small circle over the note. If two different rhymes occur in the same stanza, one is marked with a dot, the other with a circle. (4) The figures in brackets above the notes refer to alternative readings given below the transcription, either from *Sê P'u* (SP) or *Yüeh Tien* (YT). The *I-li Ching-chuan T'ung-chieh* is referred to as IL. The word 'flute' in brackets indicates that the reading derives from the flute-notation. Where no alternative is given, the text is attested by three versions: IL, SP (pitch-pipe and flute), YT (pitch-pipe and flute); where an alternative is given, the text is attested by two versions, one of which is that of Chu Hsi. (5) For each song, the number of repetitions of entire musical sentences is recorded as 'line-repeats'. (6) For Song 2, a complete list of steps and leaps to and from each degree of the mode is also given. (7) For all songs, the information derived from such a list is summarized in a staff-notation diagram. Arrows mark the direction of movement, and the value of the note (following von Hornbostel's notation) is proportional to its frequency of occurrence as subfinal; the final is marked by a pause-sign.[15]

An important point in the transcription of the songs is that (as shown in the notes to the transcriptions) the lexigraph '*ta*' is occasionally used in error for '*t'ai*' — the difference amounts to one dot, and the confusion is a common one. These words are abbreviations for the expressions *ta lü* and *t'ai ts'ou*, f# and g respectively (*f* being the fundamental). The error is of little significance here, since we have the flute-notation as a check; but it suggests that similar emendations would not be inappropriate in certain ritual songs of Chiang K'uei, where a strict adherence to the text would lead to a note-series that transgresses the limits defined by the nominal mode.

Song 2: My Four Steeds are Weary
(Mao 162; Waley 146)

No. 1

[15] This diagram is only complete for Songs 2 and 10. For the others it is reduced (for ease of reproduction) to conjunct steps and the most frequent steps and leaps, these latter indicated by heavy arrows.

(1) SP *d* (2) YT *f* (3) YT *a* (4) SP *f'* (flute) (5) SP *d*

Rhymes : I *p'įwər, d'įər, kįwər, pįər.* II *p'įwər, kįwər; må, ko, î'io.* III *g'å, χįwo, ko, b'įwo.* IV *îįəg, k'įəg, məg.* V *iš'įəm, śįəm.*

Line-repeats : I. 2, III. 4, V. 4.

Stanza-finals : *f' f f' f f'.* Line-finals : 7*a* 7*d* 2*f* 2*f'* 2*c.* Half-line finals : 8*a* 7*d* 5*f* 2*e* 1*c* 1*b* 1*g.* All-finals : 15*a* 14*d* 9*f* 5*f'* 3*c* 1*b* 1*g.* Stanza-initials : *f f f' f' f.* Line-initials : 8*c* 5*b* 3*g* 2*e* 1*a* 1*f.* Half-line initials : 7*b* 6*c* 4*e* 3*g* 3*g'* 1*f* 1*f'.* All initials : 14*c* 12*b* 6*e* 5*f'* 3*f* 3*g'* 1*a.*

Steps and leaps to and from each degree. Movement occurs from left to right ; forms in brackets occur only *between* phrases. Minor second : *ef' bc.* Second : *gf fg (ag) ba (ab) cd (dc) ed (de) g'f'.* Minor third : *(ac) ca bd (db) (df').* Major third : *fa (bg) ce (ec).* Tritone : *fb (f'b).* Fourth : *f'c (cg) (dg').* Fifth : *cf ae.* Sixth : *f'a (df).* Seventh : *ef.* Octave : *(ff') (f'f).* Ninth : *(fg').*

No. 2

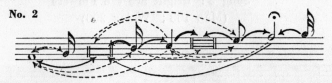

Arrows indicate the direction of movement. This diagram includes only movement *within* phrases (not between phrases). The weight of the arrow indicates the frequency of occurrence of a particular step or leap. Dotted arrows mark movement of least frequency.

Song 1 : 'Yu, Yu', Cry the Deer
(Mao 161, Waley 183)

No. 3

(1) YT *a* (2) YT *a* (3) SP *f'* (flute).

Line-repeats : I. 6+7, III. 6+7.

The six- and seven-note lines are broken down, following the structure of the text, as follows : (II. 6) *ef' ab ad;* (II. 8) *cd ed g'f';* (III. 8) *cdf ed g'f'* (see p. 171).

No. 4

Song 3 : Bright are the Flowers
(Mao 163 ; Waley 290)

No. 5

(1) SP *f'* (flute) (2) SP *d* (3) IL obliterated (4) YT *f d g' f'*-end of stanza and song ; this presumably arose as a contraction of the first note of stanza IV, line four, and the last three notes of stanza V, line four.

Line repeats : I. 4, V. 4 ; II. 2+3, IV. 2+3.

No. 6

Song 4 : The Fish Caught in the Trap
(Mao 170 ; Waley 168)

No. 7

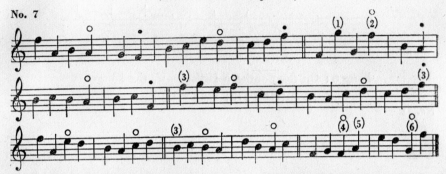

(1) SP a (flute) (2) SP f (flute) (3) YT f (4) SP a (5) SP f (6) SP g' (flute).
Line-repeats : I. 4, III. 4.; II. 3, V. 1.; III. 3, IV. 2.

The rhyme-scheme clearly indicates six stanzas, and these are marked in all three texts. Nevertheless, the last three stanzas are combined to form a single musical unit, a 'stanza' of six lines ; for the purposes of analysis, this has been treated as a single stanza. The three-note lines have been broken down as : $cd\ f'$ and $bc\ f$.

No. 8

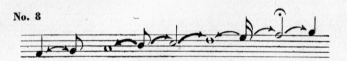

Song 5 : In the South there are Lucky Fish
(Mao 171 ; Waley 169)

No. 9

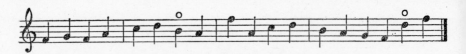

(1) YT *e* (2) '*ta*' for '*t'ai*'.
Line-repeats : I. 3, IV. 2 ; III. 3, IV. 1.
The six-note lines are broken down as 2 + 2 + 2.

No. 10

Song 6 : On the Southern Hills Grows the Nutgrass
(Mao 172; Waley 170)

No. 11

SP *g'* (flute) (2) SP *f'* (flute) (3) SP *d* (4) YT *f*.
Line-repeats : I. 3, III. 3, IV. 3, I. 6, II. 2 ; II. 3, IV. 3 ; II. 5, IV. 5 ; II. 6,
III. 2 ; III. 4, V. 4.

No. 12

154

From the full analysis of Song 2, it is evident that the half-line finals include a greater number of different degree than the line-finals; but in all six songs in this mode, *d* and *a* are the degrees which occur most frequently as subfinals, whether as half-line or line-finals. The songs in mode 1 do not all show the same frequency of occurrence of the same subfinals. Whereas in 1, 3, 4 and 6, the most frequent line- or half-line finals are *d*, *a*, *c* and *f'*, for 2 and 5, the most frequent are *d*, *a*, *f'* and *f*. In 4, and even more so in 6, *c* is of greater relative weight, and in 6 challenges both *a* and *d* as line-final.

The commonest line-initials are *e*, *b* and *c*, and the frequency of occurence varies in different songs. Again, as for half-line finals, there is a greater number of degrees acting as half-line initials than as line-initials, but the frequency of occurrence of degrees other than *e*, *b*, *c* and *g*, is low. A glance at the list of line- and half-line initials in Song 2 shows that these include the two auxiliary notes *(pien)*, *b* and *e*, which convert the pentatonic to a heptatonic series. They also include, among the most frequently occurring initials, *c*, *g* and *g'*. All these act, as we shall see, in a general sense as 'leading notes' or 'passing notes' to one or other subfinal or final. What is true, with regard to initials, of Song 2, is also true of Songs 1, 3—6.

When the half-line structure of 'initial' and 'final' was detected, lists were made of all half-lines in each song. These showed that the number of two-note motifs actually used was far smaller than the possible maximum. Accordingly, for each of Songs 1—6, a list was prepared of the various possible steps or leaps to or from each note throughout the note-series. An example of such an analysis is given in full for Song 2. The movement in each case is from left to right; brackets indicate that the movement occurs only between four-note or two-note phrases, never within a two-note phrase. For the Songs 1—6, the results of this analysis are shown in staff-notation diagrams. Although the diagrams are never identical, there is a common pattern of permitted steps and leaps:

No. 13

For conjunct movement, this diagram is valid for all six songs, save that the step *b* to *a* is reversible in Song 1. For leaps, the diagram is valid for at least five songs, but not necessarily for the same five for each leap. It shows the essential dynamic structure of mode 1. Clearly, *f'*, *d*, *a* and *f*, are focal points towards which movement occurs; while *g'*, *e*, *c*, *b* and *g* are points to be quitted, sometimes in a specific direction only. These are the 'finals' and 'initials' isolated by the analysis of half-lines.

A distincion between line-initials and line-finals was established by *Levis*[16] in his analysis of certain purely pentatonic, and in part melismatic, *tz'ŭ* melodies of the nineteenth century. In the pentatonic series : *c d f g a c' d'*, for example, he showed that when *d* is final, *a* and *d* alternate as line-finals ; while the line-initials in a nine-line song are : 3*f* 3*c'* 1*c* 1*f* 1*g*. His attention was first directed to the 'harmonic relationship' between line-initials and line-finals by *Prince Chu*'s remarks in the *Üüeh-lü ch'üan shu* (1595) ; but since *all* combinations of the degrees of the pentatonic series are harmonious in the Chinese sense (c. f. the beneficient harmony of tinkling jade pieces tuned to the pentatonic series and hung at the girdle[17]), what is important is surely the distinction between line-initials and line-finals, rather than their 'harmonious relationship'. We shall return to Chinese rules for composition later.

Leaving now the detailed structure of the mode, it is convenient to consider the types of melodic movement deducible from Songs 1—6. In classical western contrapuntal melody — as to some extent in Turco-Arabic melody — the melodic line is controlled by prohibition of leaps of augmented or diminished intervals, of sevenths or of ninths, or of direct conjunct movement following a leap, etc. The musical line of the four-note phrases of these T'ang melodies is evidently not controlled by this sort of prohibition (phrases of other lengths will be dealt with subsequently). It might be supposed that the leaps arise from gross corruption of the text (they could not arise from simple graphic confusion of similar characters) ; but against the view that they are spurious is the fact that such leaps also occur in the flute-versions of the *Sê P'u* and *Yüeh Tien*, as well as in the ritual tunes of Chiang K'uei. If we analyse the movement from note to note in the four-note phrases in terms of the nature of the steps — whether conjunct or disjunct — and the direction of movement in relation to previous movement — whether direct or contrary — the unexpected fact emerges that, with two or three exceptions only, every logical alternative is realized. This does not mean that all possible groups of four notes from the note-series are used ; but that the movement of the musical line at any point does not depend on the nature of the previous movement or its direction as such. Whether the second of the three steps in a four-note phrase is conjunct and contrary, for instance, is unrelated to whether the first step is disjunct ; and this is true for the third step as well. At each point, all possibilities of movement are open ; and which movement actually occurs depends on factors other than the character of previous movements as defined by the criteria : conjunct or disjunct ; direct or contrary. The evidence for this assertion can best be presented as a table ; in this, the terms 'direct' or 'contrary' are used with respect to the immediately preceding step, and 'conjunct' implies a step of a

---

[16] Levis, *op. cit.* p. 120.
[17] *Li Chi*, Song 9 '*Yü Tsao*', Szŭ Pu Pei Yao edition : folio 9 v°.

Note-to-note movement in a four-note line

| FIRST | SECOND | THIRD | Reference |

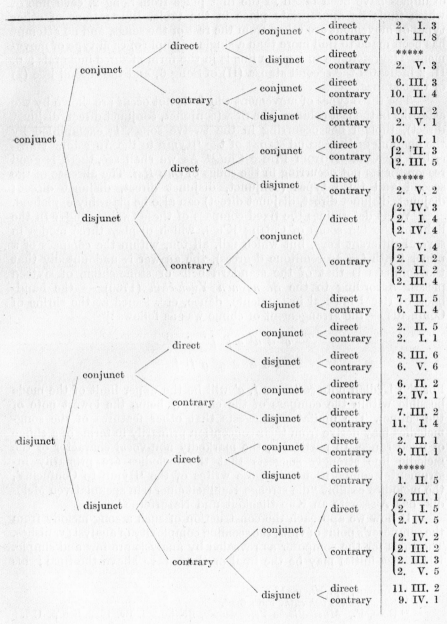

FIRST	SECOND	THIRD		Reference
conjunct	conjunct	direct	conjunct < direct	2. I. 3
			contrary	1. II. 8
			disjunct < direct	*****
			contrary	2. V. 3
		contrary	conjunct < direct	6. III. 3
			contrary	10. II. 4
			disjunct < direct	10. III. 2
			contrary	2. V. 1
	disjunct	direct	conjunct < direct	10. I. 1
			contrary	{ 2. II. 3 / 2. III. 5
			disjunct < direct	*****
			contrary	2. V. 2
		contrary	conjunct direct	{ 2. IV. 3 / 2. I. 4 / 2. IV. 4
			conjunct contrary	{ 2. V. 4 / 2. I. 2 / 2. II. 2 / 2. III. 4
			disjunct < direct	7. III. 5
			contrary	6. II. 4
disjunct	conjunct	direct	conjunct < direct	2. II. 5
			contrary	2. I. 1
			disjunct < direct	8. III. 6
			contrary	6. V. 6
		contrary	conjunct < direct	6. II. 2
			contrary	2. IV. 1
			disjunct < direct	7. III. 2
			contrary	11. I. 4
	disjunct	direct	conjunct < direct	2. II. 1
			contrary	9. III. 1
			disjunct < direct	*****
			contrary	1. II. 5
		contrary	conjunct direct	{ 2. III. 1 / 2. I. 5 / 2. IV. 5
			conjunct contrary	{ 2. IV. 2 / 2. III. 2 / 2. III. 3 / 2. V. 5
			disjunct < direct	11. III. 2
			contrary	9. IV. 1

minor or major second. Each type of movement is illustrated by the individual song-lines listed in the column on the extreme right. The examples have been taken in the first place from Song 2, each line of which finds its appropriate place in the table. Illustrations of other types of movement are taken from the rest of the songs, and no attempt has been made to find more than a single example of each type of movement. The reference to a given line is in the form of three numerals; 6. II. 2 indicates the second stanza (II) of Song 6, and the second line (2) of that stanza.

The three types of movement which do not occur are shown by the asterisks in the last column. The first (conjunct, conjunct direct, disjunct direct), though not occurring in the twelve songs, is exemplified by the opening of the second stanza of the 'Hymn to the Ancestors' transcribed by Courant from Prince Chu.[18] As we shall see, there is good reason for its not occurring in the songs of *Chu Hsi*. The absence of the second and third types (conjunct, disjunct direct, disjunct direct; disjunct, disjunct direct, disjunct direct) can also be plausibly explained.

What determines the fixed compass of these twelve songs? In the light of the ten songs of Chiang K'uei, which display three modes in several different keys, but which fall, all ten, within the compass of a minor tenth (= 16 semitone degrees), the answer is undoubtedly that the compass is that of the standard bell- or stone-chime of sixteen pieces. According to the *Sheng-men Yüeh-chih* (1766) — the handbook of ritual musical instruments, dance, etc. issued at the shrine of Confucius — the arrangement of chime was as follows :[19]

$$c^\sharp\ d\ d^\sharp\ e\ f'\ f^\sharp{}'\ g'\ g^\sharp{}'$$

$$c\ b\ a^\sharp\ a\ g^\sharp\ g\ f^\sharp\ f$$

For the Lydian note-series on *f*, *g'* will be the upper limit of the mode possible within the compass of the chime (*f* being the lowest note of the chime). The limitation suggests that other features of the song-melodies may derive from their conception primarily in terms of a chime of fixed range. In particular, the markedly non-vocal character of the melodic line strongly suggests that the melodies are primarily instrumental compositions. As Bose writes of the 'Hymn to Confucius', the melodies exhibit "die strenge Kahlheit einer rein spekulativen Melodik, das Äusserste an Künstlichkeit und Naturferne".[20]

If now we approach the construction of such a song-melody from the composer's point of view, the seeming complexity of analysis vanishes. The rules for the composer as revealed by analysis are few and simple. His stanza-initial may be the final or the octave above the final; his

---

[18] Courant, *op. cit.* p. 130.
[19] *Sheng-men Yüeh-chih*, folio 6 r°.
[20] Bose, F., *Musikalische Völkerkunde*, Freiburg i. Br. 1953. See p. 126.

stanza-final may be the octave of the final, but in his last stanza must be the final itself. In a four-note phrase he has on the whole to respect the 'final' qualities of *f'*, *d*, *a* and *f*, and the fugitive or leading note properties of *g'*, *e*, *c*, *b* and *g*. In stanzas of a large number of lines, or in songs of a large number of stanzas, an 'initial' may occasionally occur in half-line final position, approached from a 'final' (cf. 2. IV. 5.).

The 'impossible' movements already referred to are : (1) conjunct, conjunct direct, disjunct direct ; such a movement is impossible with the dynamics shown in Example 13, where *ag* and *gf* are not reversible. But Prince Chu's example[21] shows that this movement could occur in other variants of mode 1 ; (2) conjunct, disjunct direct, disjunct direct ; here too there is no point in the series (Example 13) at which such a movement can begin and end without disturbing the 'initial' and 'final' relationships. Finally, (3) disjunct, disjunct direct, disjunct direct ; this again is impossible in this mode ; but in Chiang K'uei's Sixth Song such a movement occurs.

We can now see the major restraints which impose order on the seeming freedom of movement suggested by the Table. Movement in a four-note phrase can occur in any of the logical alternatives shown in the Table provided only that, in each half-line, movement occurs from an 'initial' to a 'final' according to the permitted movements summarized in Example 13.

Although with three exceptions all types of movement are possible, it is clear from the analysis of Song 2, shown in the Table, that some patterns are used more frequently than others, presumably because they offer a larger number of melodic alternatives. They are, in particular, the oscillatory types of movement with mutually compensating contrary leaps, such as : conjunct, disjunct contrary, conjunct direct or contrary ; and disjunct, disjunct contrary, conjunct direct or contrary.

The analysis thus far has proceeded without reference to any previously recognised type of modal structure, or to the modal functions recognised by the Chinese themselves. We may begin with the function of the two *pien*, indicated by the term *pien* itself. The fourth degree of the basic Lydian series is *pien chih*, 'becoming *chih*', that is, leading to the fifth degree ; while the seventh degree is *pien kung*, 'becoming *kung*', that is, leading to the octave of the fundamental. The question whether the Chinese basic note-series was anciently heptatonic or pentatonic has been hotly disputed — by the Chinese themselves as early as the sixth century A. D. As Courant has pointed out[22], the fact that the names for the fourth and seventh degrees are not distinct (as are those of the other degrees) in itself suggests that the *pien* were acquired later. The observed tendency for the degrees *b* and *e* in Songs 1—6 to 'resolve' on *c* or *a*, or *f* or *d*, respectively, accords with the view of them as 'leading' or 'passing' notes, though their observed resolution either by ascent

[21] Courant, *op. cit.* p. 114.
[22] Courant, *op. cit.* p. 93.

or descent indicates that the functional analogy with leading notes must not be pressed too far. Levis's translation of *pien* as 'side' has little justification; and Courant's 'modifié' does not convey the notion of self-transformation implicit in *pien* — this is its customary use in Taoist texts, for example. Van Aalst[23] also gives the meaning 'changing into *kung* (or *chih*)'.

The scheme in Example 13 shows, however, that in the complete note-series of mode 1 the *pien* are not the only degrees to be treated as passing notes; the degrees *c* and *g* or *g'* are treated in a similar way. If we abstract *b* and *e* from the note-series, there remains the pentatonic *kung*-mode series. Now in purely pentatonic tunes, such as the Ritual Hymns in Prince Chu's treatise[24], it is clear that within the pentatonic series itself, a *pien*-like function is performed by both *c* and *g*. This can be seen in the first stanza of Song 7, and in parts of Songs 11 and 12. In more extended purely pentatonic specimens, it can be seen that *g* and *c* (or more generally, the second and fourth degrees of the basic pentatonic series) are also the degrees least frequently occurring as line-finals. Within the basic pentatonic series itself, there is evidently a system of modal dynamics such that (for the *kung*-mode on *f*) *f'*, *d*, *a* and *f* are focal points, and *g'*, *c* and *g* are points of departure.

The treatment of the pentatonic degrees as line- or sub-finals is supported by Chu Hsi (quoted by Prince Chu[25]): "If the note at the head is the *kung*-note, the note ending the tail will also be the *kung*-note; this then is the *kung*-mode. If there are places midway where the beat is arrested, there the five degrees — following ancient usage — are all employed [as finals] and not only and exclusively *kung*". Prince Chu gives three examples. A much later compilation, the *Ch'in Ting Ta Ch'ing Hui Tien* (Statutes of the Ch'ing Dynasty) (1818)[26] gives a further illuminating definition: "The two *pien* degrees established in each *yün* (= the basic series in one of twelve keys) are not modal initials *(ch'i tiao)*. The note established in the fifth degree position *(chih)* [that is, *c* in the series with *f* as fundamental] also is not initial. The note established in the sixth degree position *(yü)* [that is, *d* in the series with *f* as fundamental] is identical with the modal dominant *(chu tiao)*". Two points merit comment: 'modal initial' also implies melody initial, so that this text informs us that there are neither modes nor melodies beginning on the *pien*. Secondly, the modal dominant with which the sixth degree is identified is defined as the note in the sixth-degree position

[23] van Aalst, J. A., *Chinese Music*, Shanghai 1884, p. 14.
[24] Courant, *op. cit.* p. 103.
[25] Courant, *op. cit.* p. 114. I have translated from Prince Chu, *Yüeh-hsüeh Hsin Shuo* (1595) folio 18 v°. *Prince Chu* gives the reference as *Chu Hsi Yü Lu*, but the passage is not be found in the *Lu* (Lecture Notes) and, in fact, occurs in the music section of the complete works. In the *Yü-tsuan Chu Tzü Ch'üan Shu* (1714), the passage will be found under *Yüeh, Chüan* 41, folio 6 v°.
[26] *Op. cit.* folio 8 v°.

two places before *kung*, the fundamental of the *yün*. Accordingly, the observed conspicuous role of the sixth as line- and half-line final in the T'ang melodies here receives verbal authority. According to *Han Pang-ch'i*[27] there existed a tradition that the initial of every mode in Chou times was the sixth of the basic note-series.

These references will not, on this occasion, be pursued further. They are given only to show the extent to which the observed structure of the six tunes in mode 1 accords with principles stated in Chinese texts, for which illustrative material from sources earlier than the sixteenth century has hitherto been lacking. The avoidance of the fifth degree as melody-initial agrees with the *pien*-like use of *c*; a similar avoidance of *g* would be in accordance with the tradition of Chou,[28] for this is the nefast *shang* degree. Combining the citations, it is clear that there is textual support for much of the observed dynamic structure; there is, however, no textual support thus far for the observed detailed line-structure, with alternation of 'initial' and 'final'.

Turning now to the modal functions as revealed in Songs 7 to 12 inclusive, it is evident that they differ from those of mode 1.

Song 7 : 'Fair, Fair', Cry the Ospreys
(Mao 1 ; Waley 87)

No. 14

(1) SP *f'* (flute).

Line-repeats : I. 1, II. 1, 5.

Stanza-finals : *f' f' f'*. Line-finals: 5*d* 3*a* 3*c* 2*f* 2*f'* 1*g* 1*g'*. Half-line finals: 8*d* 4*a* 3*b♭* 3*c* 1*f* 1*e♭*. Stanza-initials : *f' f' f'*. Line-initials : 4*c* 4*f'* 3*a* 2*f* 2*g* 1*b♭* 1*g'*. Half-line-initials : 6*c* 4*d* 4*e♭* 3*g* 2*a* 1*f'*.

[27] *Yüan Lo Chih Yüeh* (1508). See Courant, *op. cit.* p. 107.
[28] Courant, *op. cit.* p. 101.

11   161

No. 15

Song 8: How the Cloth-Plant Spreads
(Mao 2 ; Waley 112)

No. 16

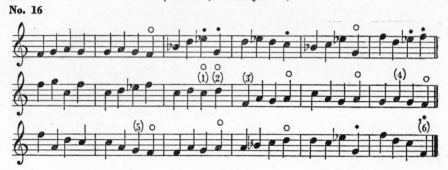

(1) YT *d* (2) IL obliterated ; YT *b♭* (3) IL *f a g* obliterated (4) IL obliterated
(5) '*ta*', but flute confirms '*t'ai*' (6) *f'* (flute).
Line-repeats : I. 2, II. 6 ; II. 4, III. 3.

No. 17

Song 9: Thick Grows the Cocklebur
(Mao 3 ; Waley 40)

No. 18

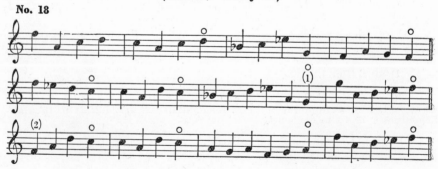

162

(1) SP '*ta*' for '*t'ai*' (2) YT omits this stanza.
Line-repeats : I. 4, IV. 2 ; II. 2, III. 2.
The six-note lines are broken down as *bcd eag; aga fga;* and the five-note lines as *g'c def', f'c def'*.

No. 19

Song 10 : Now the Magpie had a Nest

(Mao 12 ; Waley 89)

No. 20

(1) SP '*ta*' for '*t'ai*'.
Line-repeats : I. 2, III. 1.
Stanza-finals : *f' f f'*. Line-finals : *5c 1f 1g 1a 1f'*. Half-line finals : *5c 2f 2e♭ 1g 1a 1d*. Stanza-initials : *f f f'*. Line-initials : *3f' 2c 1g 1d 1b♭ 1g'*. Half-line initials: *6d 2g 1a 1b♭ 1c 1e♭*.

No. 21

Song 11 : See, She Gathers White Aster

(Mao 13 ; Waley 98)

No. 22

(1) ⅜YT *a;* this melody is hexatonic.
Line-repeats : I. 3, III. 3.

No. 23

Song 12 : Here We are Gathering Duckweed

(Mao 15 ; Waley 76)

No. 24

(1) SP *f'* (flute).
Line-repeats : I. 3, II. 3.

No. 25

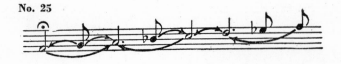

Songs 9, 10 and 12, show clear dominance of *c* as subfinal; in Song 11, *c* is less important than *a* and *d*, which are of about equal importance. In Song 8, the most frequent line-finals are *g* and *a*, while in Song 7, *d* is the most important subfinal. The mode evidently embraces a number of *rāga*-like variants.

The occurrence of the same notes as subfinals in both groups — with the exception of Song 8 — is surely very remarkable, since in the *shang*-mode (that is, the modal inversion commencing on the second degree of a Lydian series) the position of the auxiliaries *(pien)* ought theoretically to be different. Instead of the *kung* series: first degree, second, third, *pien*, fifth, sixth, *pien*, first degree *(8va)*; that is, on *f*, for example:

$$f \; g \; a \; b \; (= pien) \; c \; d \; e \; (= pien) \; f',$$

the series runs: second degree, third, *pien*, fifth, sixth, *pien*, first *(8va)*, second *(8va)*. For the *shang*-mode on *wu-i (e♭)* this is:

$$e^\flat \; f \; g \; a \; (= pien) \; b^\flat \; c \; d \; (= pien) \; e^{\flat'} \; f'$$

The observed dynamics are not at all what would be expected: *a* and *d* (by analogy with the *kung*-mode) should be initials (since they are the *pien*), not subfinals; while *b♭* and *e♭* might be expected to act as sub-finals. Clearly in spite of being classified as *shang*, this mode is merely a variant of *kung* in which both *pien* are flattened *(b♭* and *e♭)*. The true *pien (a* and *d)* are not treated as *pien* — except to some extent in Song 10, where *d* sometimes resolves on *c;* but the example is very short and is largely pentatonic.

When writing in the *shang*-mode then, the composer's practice — judging by these six examples — was to treat *b♭* and *e♭* as if they were *pien*, ignoring the auxiliary nature of *a* and *d*, and forgetting that *e♭* is the upper octave of the fundamental of the entire *wu-i* system, and *f'* merely the modal final.

All this would seem to suggest that by the time these tunes were composed the significance of the old classification of the modes, with its complete set of modal inversions, had been forgotten. The names *shang* and *kung* define note-series; if they ever implied those changes in dynamics which the inversion of the pentatonic series would lead us to expect, these implications have been obliterated. Mode 1 and mode 2 are nothing more than two versions of the *kung*-mode with different auxiliaries. But if the earlier modal system seems to be in decay, there can be no question that heptatonic construction is incompletely assimi-lated, as shown by the long stretches of purely pentatonic writing in the twelve songs. It would seem a point of great importance then, that as late as (or later than) the eighth century A. D., and in spite of intercourse with India and Central Asia, the auxiliary degrees are used with such diffidence.

Although the pentatonic skeletons of the *kung* and *shang* modes are identical, once *b*, *e*, *b*♭ and *e*♭ are removed (cf. p. 165), there is nevertheless a profound difference between the two — apart from the flattening of *b* and *e* — for *shang* tends to break into conjunct tetrachord and pentachord (Song 10), and *kung* does not. This behaviour may be related to the persistent dominant role of the sixth degree of the basic series in all modes of any given system, implied in the passage from the *Ta Ch'ing Hui Tien* already cited (p. 160); for *c* is the sixth degree *(yü)* of the basic series starting on *e*♭. But it must also be pointed out that the basic note-series of heptatonic *shang* approximates to the descending form of the Persian mode *rast* (in the ascending form the seventh is sharpened); *kung*, on the other hand, is without parallel in the Perso-Turco-Arabic system. Is it possible that an original structural similarity — namely, the role of the fifth above the initial as dominant — in *shang* and *rast*, led to a re-inforcement of the popularity of *shang*, because foreign melodies in *rast* (or a *rast*-like mode) could be assimilated, owing to their affinities with *shang?*

The Lydian note-series of heptatonic *kung*, on the other hand, occurs in classical and medieval Indian music; for example, the *ga* modes as defined in the *Nāṭyăśhāstră* (first centuries A. D.) and in the *Saṅgītă Ratnākară* of Śhārṇgadevă (thirteenth century).[29] Grosset's account of the constitutive elements of the *jātis* (the *lakshanas)* reads like a summary, using Indian technical terms, of the analysis of the T'ang melodies presented here; in particular the Indian discrimination of initial, final, medials-phrase-finals and sub-finals, and the recognition of a group of tonic-initials, some or all of which can act as subsidiary finals, suggests that the technique of melodic composition in eighth-century China may have been influenced by ideas still potent in thirteenth century India. The greater richness of the Indian vocabulary (as compared with the Chinese) in terms for functional elements of melody, suggests that the analysis (and the technique of composition) may be Indian rather than Chinese in origin.

On the other hand, if — as seems reasonable — the basic Chinese pentatonic series is to be thought of as an assembly of overlapping three-note (tritonic) structures,[30] certain degrees of the series are likely to retain the character of passing notes, and we need not appeal to an Indian model for the basic dynamics of the Chinese pentatonic modes.

It has been shown that a common modal dynamic unites the six *kung*-melodies (and to some extent the six *shang*-melodies as well), so that we can define the Chinese *kung*-mode, for example, just as we

[29] Grosset, J., *Inde*, in Lavignac & La Laurencie, *op. cit.* vol. i, pp. 257—376. See p. 305 *et seq.*
[30] Bose, *op. cit.* pp. 110, 111.

can define a Turkish or Arabic *maqam* or an Indian *rāga*. Moreover, these Chinese modes share yet another characteristic with *maqam* and *rāga*, namely, the recurrence of entire phrases (four-note phrases in this instance) in different songs in the same mode. Thus in the *kung*-tunes, the following four-note phrases occur in two or more different songs : *b a c d* (3. IV. 2) (4. III. 3, IV. 2) (5. II. 2) ; *f g f a* (2. V. 1) (6. IV. 1) (4. VI. 1) (5. IV. 1, III. 3) ; *b c b a* (3. I. 3) (4. II. 3) (6. III. 5, V. 5) ; *f a b a* (2. I. 1) (3. II. 1) (6. II. 1) ; *c d g' f'* (II. 8, II. 2) (2. III. 5) (6. II. 6, III. 2, IV. 4) ; *e f g' f'* (2. V. 5) (3. III. 4) (6. V. 2) ; *f' d b a* (1. I. 1) (5. II. 1). (No attempt has been made to record all occurrences of a given phrase or even all phrases recurring in this way.)

In the *shang*-melodies, the following phrases occur in two or more songs ; again the list is not necessarily complete : *f' d e♭ f'* (8. I. 6) (7. III. 4) ; *f' e♭ d c* (7. IV. 1) (9. II. 1) (10. I. 2, III. 1) ; *f' d e♭ f* (11. I. 4) (12. III. 4) : *b♭ c e♭ g* (8. I. 5.) (9. I. 3) (10. I. 3) ; *f' d c d* (7. I. 1, II. 1, III. 1) (11. I. 1.) ; *a b♭ c d* (7. IV. 3) (8. III. 4.).

It is striking to see how frequently, both in *kung* and *shang*, the same phrase is used in the same position in the stanza in different songs. In one and the same song this is also true to a large extent (see the lists of line-repeats following each song). For example, the same fournote phrase may tend to recur in initial, or medial or final position in a stanza. Thus, *f g f a* and *f' e♭ d c* are initial lines in three out of four occurrences ; *f' d e♭ f'* is final in both its appearances ; *b a c d* is medial in three out of four occurrences, and so on.

I have suggested that the *shang*-mode was in effect only a variant of *kung* with two different auxiliaries. This view is supported by the fact that a number of medial four-note phrases are common to *kung* and *shang* tunes, as shown here : *f a g f* (6. I. 6, II. 2) (5. II. 4) (7. I. 2) (12. I. 4) (9. I. 4, III. 2) ; *f a g a* (11. I. 3) (12. II. 1) (8. II. 4, III. 3) ; *f' a c d* (3. II. 2) (9. I. 1) (5. IV. 4) ; *c a g f* (8. III. 2) (2. II. 5) (10. II. 2) (12. III. 2) ; *c a c d* (3. I. 2) (7. V. 2) (9. I. 2) ; *f' c d f'* (5. II. 4) (7. I. 4) (10. I. 4).

An important implication of these three lists of 'stock' phrases is that both *kung* and *shang* tend to use purely pentatonic stock phrases in *medial* positions — that is, neither as initial line, nor as final line of the last stanza. The stock of *initial* and *final* phrases in use in both modes tends to include the functional auxiliaries, and are therefore characteristic of the particular mode. This generalization only applies to the stock phrases, not to the structure of the ritual melodies in general. The sequence and relative frequency of purely pentatonic phrases, and of phrases with auxiliaries, varies from stanza to stanza and from song to song. A song such as No. 11 with twelve four-note phrases is purely pentatonic save for two final phrases ; while Song 2, with twenty-five four-note phrases, exhibits one or other auxiliary in all but six of these. In general, the modal dynamics of mode 1 show less variation in the six songs than do those of mode 2.

From a passage in the Music Section of Chu Hsi's works, it is evident that he could make no sense of the description : *huang-chung ch'ing kung*, defining mode and key. If the description were *huang-chung kung*, there would be no difficulty ; this would be the usual formula indicating that the mode is the *kung*-mode of the system whose fundamental is the pitch-pipe *huang-chung (f)*. *Huang-chung* defines the key and *kung* the mode. Now the expression *huang-chung ching* normally means the octave of *huang-chung* — the note given by a pipe of half the length. And Chu Hsi reads *huang-chung ching kung* as : 'the octave of *huang-chung* acts as *kung (huang-chung ch'ing wei kung)*'.[31] But this seems to him preposterous, because in his view the modal final, *kung*, must be at the bottom of the note series ; if its octave were allowed to take precedence, there would be confusion in the social order! He does not refer, however, to the description of mode 2 : *wu-i ch'ing shang*, which should be read (if he is right about the first) as : 'the octave of *wu-i* acts as *shang*'. But such a reading is explicitly contradicted by the note-series of this group of songs, unambiguously defined by the pitch-pipe notation. The note-series is that of a *shang*-mode ; and *wu-i (e♭)* is not *shang* (the final) but the fundamental of the system. *Shang* is in fact *huang-chung (f)*.

I conclude that Chu Hsi's reading is wrong, and that *ch'ing-kung* and *ch'ing-shang* are specified variants of the *kung* and *shang* modes. The tunes themselves show that the final degrees, *kung* and *shang* respectively, are indeed '*ch'ing*' for they occur at the top of the modal series in ten out of the twelve songs. The fact that Chu Hsi did not recognise *ch'ing-kung* and *ch'ing-shang* as modal variants seems to me to increase the probability that these songs are indeed of pre-Sung date.

The existence of the set of six melodies in *ch'ing-shang* is of great interest in view of the literary associations of what has usually been thought of as the 'upper *shang*-mode'. In an open letter to me, published in the *Pei-p'ing Ching-shih Jih-pao*, October 29th, 1947, Professor Yin Fa-lu recognises five different meanings of the term *ch'ing-shang*. They are : (1) A *shang*-mode transposed up a semitone. The term *ch'ing-shang* (as well as *ch'ing-chih*, *chih* being the fifth degree) occurs already in *Han Fei Tzŭ* (third century B. C.). [Transposition is not implied by this text, however (L. E. R. P.).] (2) A type of music evoking a nostalgic ('autumnal') emotional response. This is suggested by seasonal correlation in the *Yüeh-ling* section of the *Li Chi (ca.* third century B. C.) and also by the passage from *Han Fei Tzŭ* already mentioned. (3) A class of melodies, recognised from Han times onwards, for a chamber-ensemble of strings and wind and in three modes : *p'ing tiao*, *ch'ing tiao* and *sê tiao*. (4) A particular mode of this set of three, namely *ch'ing tiao*, in which *shang* was 'dominant'. (5) A general term in Sui and T'ang times for old tunes in use in the Music Bureau *(Yüeh-fu)* under the

---

[31] Chu Hsi, *op. et editio cit.* folio 11 v°.

Southern Dynasties (*i. e.* Sung, Liang etc.) ; as used in the Music Section of the *T'ung Tien* (early ninth century). In the light of the ritual melodies preserved by Chu Hsi, it would seem probable that a sixth meaning can be added to Yin's list : that at some time prior to the twelfth century, *ch'ing-shang* was the name for a mode on the second degree of a Lydian note-series with the final at the top of the mode. That is to say, the qualifying '*ch'ing*' does not refer, as has been supposed, to the *tessitura*, but to the upper position of the final in the note-series. This implies a special modal dynamic and suggests that at one time the Chinese had something of the attitude to modal structure which Middle Eastern and Indian peoples have today.

It is sometimes held[32] that the nostalgic quality of *shang* melodies cannot have resided in musical attributes, but was due to cosmological associations. This may well be ; but it is plain that the *ch'ing-shang* mode possessed a peculiar dynamic, as well as a characteristic note-series ; and it is difficult to believe that the musical quality of the rising final cadence, for example, had nothing to do with the literary associations of *ch'ing-shang* during so many centuries. Moreover, there would seem to be no reason why all modes should not occur in '*ch'ing*' forms ; we have already noted *ch'ing-chih* from *Han Fei Tzŭ*, and the Songs exhibit *kung* as well as *shang* with upper finals.

The fact that no less than half the songs should be in this mode adds weight to the view that they are indeed music of the T'ang dynasty. For cosmological reasons, the *shang*-mode was not inimical to the T'ang dynasty, as it had been to the Chou, and a certain *Chao Shen-yen*[33] is reported to have expressed the view in 720 A. D. that the *shang*-mode should be added to those used in the great sacrifices.

Hsiung P'eng-lai, writing in the thirteenth to fourteenth centuries, also gives the modes of the twelve songs as : *huang-chung kung* and *wu-i shang*, as if (like Chu Hsi) he no longer saw the significance of *ch'ing*, though he adds a note to the effect that the old score gives the modes as *huang-chung ch'ing kung* and *wu-i ch'ing shang*.

It has been shown that the note-to-note movement within the four-note phrases, each corresponding to a four-word line, consists of a twice-repeated movement from 'initial' to 'final'. This segmentation of the phrases is surely linked with the tendency of the four-word lines of the Chinese text to split up into meaningful binomes or two-word phrases. Without embarking on a full discussion of the matter, it is fair to say that the first member of such a word-pair carries a different psychological weight from the second in that, in the most general sense, it qualifies the second member. In lines of five, six or seven words, the placing of the words on initial or final degrees seems again to be related to the meaningful articulation of the text. As a single example,

[32] Bose, *op. cit.* p. 122.
[33] Courant, *op. cit.* p. 101.

we may take the last line of the third stanza of Song 1. The text in Kuo-yü, with commas to mark natural breaks, runs : *I yen lo, chia pin, chih hsin*. The notes are : *c d f e d g' f'*. If commas are inserted in accordance with the meaning, the initial-to-final movement is preserved : *c d f, e d, g' f'*.

On several occasions[34], it has been suggested that the fitness of music for words, so stressed in ancient China, was related in some way to the inherent melodic accent (tone) of each word of the text. There is no evidence that the tones played any part in the construction of the ancient verses of the *Shih Ching*, however ; nor is it easy to see how a one-note-to-one-word melody could be related to the tonal structure of the language, inasmuch as the 'tone' is not merely a pitch but a neume — a melodic accent. On the other hand, an unexpectedly close parallel exists between the structure of the four-word lines and the articulation of the musical phrases corresponding to each line of the verse ; the dynamics of the individual melodic phrases would seem to be immediately related to the tendency of the verse to break into binomial units.

While it must be remembered that the four notes constitute a *line* and not a *bar*, there would seem nevertheless to be a sense in which this unit of four is a *measure* with 'good' and 'bad' beats. May not the excellence of ancient Chinese song have resided in the psychological matching of the text with the movement of tension and relaxation in the melody? In order to establish this point, however, a more detailed study of the correlation of text and music in the earliest sources would be necessary.

The principles of melodic composition as they emerge from this analysis of the twelve songs may now be summarised as follows : (1) The first line of the first stanza must begin on the final or its octave. (2) The last line of the last stanza must end on the final ; medial stanzas may end on the octave of the final. (3) For variety, stanzas may begin alternately on the final or its octave. (4) Within a stanza, the line-finals will be chosen from the first, third, fifth, sixth or eighth degrees. These are also the most frequent half-line finals ; but in one or other of the six *ch'ing-kung* songs all notes of the series may occasionally act as subfinals, though some do so but rarely. (5) The frequency of use of the various line-finals varies. While first and eighth degrees are relegated for the most part to initial and final lines, the third, fifth and sixth may occur with equal frequency or the sixth or third may dominate. There is no evidence here that the Chinese distinguished between the different resultant *rāgas*. (6) The most frequent initials in medial or final lines are the fifth, fourth and seventh degrees in *ch'ing-kung*, or fifth, eighth and first degrees in *ch'ing-shang*. With descending frequency,

[34] Levis, *op. cit.* Chapter III, p. 47 ; Bose, *op. cit.* p. 92 *et seq.*

170

all notes of the series can act as initials. (7) Each four-word line (one note to each word) includes two phrases of two notes. Each of these phrases involves movement between an 'initial' and a 'final' — ascending or descending, conjunct or disjunct ; there is no instance of a repeated note. (8) Subject to the movement within two two-note phrases of a four-note line being (in general, from a note of the 'initial' group to one of the 'final' group, the musical line in medial phrases is restricted only by the compass of the standard bell- or stone-chime of sixteen semitone degrees. (9) Repetition, independent of the text, of entire musical lines, often in the same position in different stanzas, helps to give coherence to the melody. (10) In *ch'ing-kung* as in *ch'ing-shang* there are certain characteristic melodic formulae which can be used in any melody in that mode. (11) The notes of the melody never transgress the note-series of the nominal mode.

In view of this highly organized and largely instrumentally conceived structure, these melodies can as little be claimed as 'folk' songs as their verses can be as 'folk' poetry.[35] Nevertheless, analysis reveals certain features which may surely be regarded as echoes of a very ancient musical tradition, held with great tenacity. For example, in spite of the note-series being heptatonic, the modal structure is basically pentatonic. Furthermore, both in *ch'ing-kung* and *ch'ing-shang* there is a tendency for the sixth degree of the basic series to act as dominant ; this is in accordance with a tradition associated with the Chou dynasty. Again, melodies nominally in the *shang*-mode tend to revert to the *kung*-mode with the same initial ; this might be expected in view of the great popularity of the *kung*-mode in China. Lastly, the four-note phrases are surely a very ancient feature, shared with certain syllabic folksongs of Japan and Indo-China, and with the majestic bases of Indonesian *gamelan*-compositions. They may be regarded as a manifestation of that standard quaternary rhythm so typical of Chinese melody,[36] and as such they embody an ancient folk trait.

ACKNOWLEDGEMENTS

My debt to Chinese musicians and musicologists, incurred during a visit to China on behalf of the British Council during 1944 and 1945, cannot adequately be expressed here. I am greatly indebted to Dr. *A. D. Waley, C. B. E., F. B. A.*, and to Mr. *Thurston Dart*, for their comments on the manuscript ; to Mr. *Piet van der Loon* for drawing my attention to the availabil.ty of a text of the *I-li Ching-chuan T'ung-chieh* in the John Rylands Library, Manchester, England ; and to the Librarian of that library for permission to examine this rare work.

[35] Karlgren, B., *Glosses on the Kuo Feng Odes*, in *The Museum of Far Eastern Antiquities, Bulletin* No. 14, Stockholm 1942, pp. 71—247. See p. 75.
[36] Bose, *op. cit.* p. 86.

WERNER DANCKERT

MELODIC STYLES OF THE FINNO—UGRIC PASTORAL PEOPLES

In making a comparative survey of the songs and instrumental airs of the Finno-Ugric pastoral peoples, we, as a rule, meet with two basic elements of remote antiquity (if we do not consider the recent and latest strata of style). One of them is a *melos*, near to speech, so to say engendered by speech, of narrow to moderate compass : a recitative *melos*, "*parlando* style" (Bartók), "litany type" (Lach). In the Hungarian folk song this type of melody is embodied in the ritual tunes, particularly in dirges. They have, as a rule, a pentachordal range and consist of five notes, so they are of diatonic structure. Szabolcsi has grouped Hungarian carols *(regös énekek)* with dirges and a part of the children's songs in a melody-class ("ritual melodies") of archaic character. These airs move within the range of a major, pentachord or hexachord, are rhythmically recited but almost without ornamentation. Their structure is loose and litany-like. Also in the older melody strata of the Estonians and Suomi Finns, *e. g.* in the dirges and *runo* airs, this type is widely represented. The five strings of the older Finnish *kantele* point, among others, to a pentachordal compass and stock of note. The Estonian *runo* airs confine themselves to the tetrachord (filled out diatonically). The recitative *melos* of narrow to medium range fills up the Ob-Ugric dirges too; it appears (besides other elements) also in the heroic lays and bear song.

Opposed to this relatively narrow recitative melodics, stands a tensely rhythmicized, measured *melos* with isometric lines, a type of stanza-melody of a generally wider compass. The older forms of this second type, called "Central Asian" by Szabolcsi, often show pentatonic scales without semitones or at least pentatonic "outlines". Already Bartók, who considers pentatony as a characteristic of the "old style" of Hungarian folk-music, thinks of a relation with the pentatonic melodies of the Tartars and the Cheremiss. Kodály says : the four-line melody stanza of the Cheremiss is formed through the repetition of the first two lines in the lower fifth. The transposition however is not achieved quite so schematically as that : the two zones of tonal range are not quite equivalent. In any case the *zonal arrangement* is structurally characteristic often to such an extent that each of the two superposed tonal ranges carries its own pentatonic system with itself. One may then speak of the interlocking of two pentatonic systems with a common central stock.

The latter is connected with the peculiar zonal structure which can be most clearly distinguished in the music of Turkic peoples, as the Kazan-Tatars, Mishers, the West-Siberian Tatars and the Kirghizes : the total range of notes consists of *two* superposed *zones*. These tonal zones are either completely separated, or more frequently have a common central note ; often, especially in the case of zones having a wide compass, they overlap and so have several central notes in common. The zones may appear as tetra-, penta-, hexa- and heptachords. They may have a span of an octave or even more. The melody of this "two-zone *melos*" is distinctly descending.

I first coined the term "two-zone *melos*" in two musical-ethno-logical essays in 1937.[1] "Terrace-type" has also been suggested, as mentioned by Lach in his publication of 1952. This expression, however, can hardly be recommended ; it would be far more adequate for certain descending North-American Indian melodies of wide compass and extension interrupting the descent at certain intervals by pulsation or by the repetitions of a note. In the two-zone *melos*, however, the distinguishing mark is *dualism, i. e.* the temporal sequence and the confrontation of *two* sharply demarcated tonal zones. There are, of course, certain (mainly Turco-Tatar) melodies of this kind which, after a perfunctory analysis, give the impression that the descent is performed not in two, but in three or four phases. On closer analysis, however, two large zones can generally be detected as decisive structural marks.

The wide-ranging two-zone *melos* is evidently the style of a comparatively more recent Asiatic pastoral stratum, that of the equestrian peoples ; the nomadic cattle-breeders. This style is most distinctly expressed with the *Turkic* peoples free from Islamic influence. The two-zone *melos* is not quite so sharply marked with the *Mongols*. Frequently they still compose in a more spacious compass, not so briefly and rationally as the Turkic peoples. Their melodies are in general more flourishing, frequently also more melismatic, *cantabile:* all these are traits that, to my mind, can be traced to the millenary cultural relations, partly even symbiosis, with the Chinese great culture.

The occurrence of the split two-zone melody type in North-Chinese songs cannot mean that it was indigenous in China. On the contrary, it is the strong influence of pastoral elements, to be observed also in other respects in Northern China, that manifests itself here.

Both groups of pastoral peoples, Mongols as well as Turks have certainly borrowed anhemitonic pentatony from the Chinese ; yet not

---

[1] *Musikwissenschaft und Kulturkreislehre*, in *Anthropos* vol. xxxii, 1937, 1 ff. — *Musikethnologische Erschliessung der Kulturkreise*, in *Mitteilungen d. Anthropol. Gesellschaft in Wien*, vol. lxvii, 1937, 52 ff.

all pentatonic modes, just a few of them. Most probably it was from China that a strong stimulus came towards rational rhythm and periodicity though hardly from the chime-like oscillating Old-Chinese hymns consisting of long notes, but probably from different melody types of more recent style which also show a marked two-bar or four-bar periodicity.

Anhemitonic pentatony was, to my opinion, originally the musical realm of a highly developed *agriculture*.[2] That it has been faithfully preserved in China up to the present, in spite of the always renewed pressure of the heptatonic scale, may be ascribed, on the one hand, to the survival of the old agricultural basis ; on the other hand, to the deliberate fixation, in fact, canonization in which Confucianism may have played a role, as suggested by Hermann Schneider.[3]

Pentatony was by no means originally pastoral. As I have already suggested in my book *Das europäische Volkslied*[4] it was probably borrowed comparatively recently by the cattle-breeding peoples. It is characteristic that Chinese musical tradition speaks at different times of *seven-note scales* or heptatonic instruments brought to China by the invading pastoral tribes from the West or North West. In the mythic-religious symbolism of the herdsmen it is the number seven and not the number five that is strikingly predominant.[5] The early music of the Mongols and Turkic peoples must have been seven-note diatonic much rather than pentatonic. The melodics of European bark-trumpets also points to heptatonic scales. The bark-trumpet, however, which is known to have been carried along as a relic by the Maoris from New Zealand, is undisputedly a leading instrument of the older pastoral culture.

It is also striking that a great number of Turkic melodies are *not of purely pentatonic* structure, but half diatonic (frequently in the high notes), half pentatonic (in the low notes). In others as already mentioned, two *different* anhemitonic zones interlock : here it becomes manifest that pentatony represents so to say an instrument only, and not a closed tonal system, as is usual with the agricultural civilization.

The split style, the confrontation of two melody zones cannot be traced back to Chinese models. Chinese melodies of the most different ages show, as a rule, precisely a uniform centralized conception of tonal range, despite their extensiveness. The split tonal range is not and has never been, as far as we can see, a Chinese peculiarity. Nor can it be expected that the original, archaic forms of Chinese melody-building

[2] See my essay : *A Félhangnélküli Pentatónia Eredete* (The Origin of Anhemitonic Pentatony), in *Emlékkönyv Kodály Zoltán hatvanadik születésnapjára* (Treatises in Honour of Zoltán Kodály's 60th Birthday), Budapest 1943, pp. 9—18.

[3] *Die Kulturleistungen der Menschheit,* vol. i, Leipzig 1927, p. 649 ff.

[4] Berlin 1939, p. 354 note 2.

[5] Friedrich v. Andrian-Werburg, *Die Siebenzahl im Geistesleben der Völker;* Gesammelte Abhandlungen, Wien 1915, p. 359 ff.

should have been preserved in the Mongolian *melopoeia*.[6] True enough, the Chinese *melopoeia* had received stimuli from the steppe peoples; yet we do not know whether the symmetrical period-structure belongs to them. The splitting of the tonal range, however, seems to me positively a characteristic mode of expression of the herdsmen. This pastoral or Central-Asian split style is undoubtedly connected with the cosmological dualism which these herdsmen of later stamp profess. In the splitting of the tonal range, as well as in the rational and stressed rhythm in the music of the Turkic peoples, impulses of power, domination and submission are displayed. The extensiveness of the compass, the strongly stressed descent and the splitting of the tonal range may be considered the original characteristics of this recent pastoral style embodied to an extreme degree in the Turkic peoples.[7]

The split style adopted by the Finno-Ugric pastoral peoples has undergone considerable changes. It can be felt that the melodic range of the Finno-Ugrians had originally been more restricted, that the melodic action is much more strongly bound to a centre in the tonal range. Thus the adopted two-zone *melos* often shows moderation in splitting. The comprehensive unity remains noticeable. Often an intermediate nuclear second, less frequently a nuclear third, forms the centre of the compass.

The following Cheremiss maid's song *Pleasure in Beautiful Clothes*, still shows clearly in its descent, in its rhythmically pointed, hammered low-pitched final, the two-zone model. But the central bars circumscribe, over and over again, the centre of the compass, the nuclear second A^1—G^1. Thereby the antagonism of the cadence notes A^1 and G^1, which are so prominent in many Turkic melodies, are softened. The nuclear second is the centre and axis of the whole. A circumscribing, back-reaching, oscillating type of movement is opposed to the descending tendency of melodic conduct. Therefore the two zones C^2—A^1—G^1 and A^1—G^1—E^1—D^1 appear, after all, as secondary formations. On the rhythmical level the change of time: $^4/_4$ $^3/_4$, shows a *parlando* effect (proximity to speech).

[6] According to D. Bartha, *Neue ungarische Literatur zur vergleichenden Melodieforschung*, in *Acta Musicologica* vol. viii, 1936, p. 49.
[7] Compare this interpretation with my review of R. Lachs' *Publikation von Gesängen turktatarischer Stämme*, in *Die Musikforschung*, vol. vii, pp. 499—502.

Lach, 1929, p. 25, no. 16.

The structural formulae after the melodies here quoted indicate the melodic-zonal relations in a condensed manner. The signs have the following meaning:

⌐‾‾‾¬	melodically realized steps of fifth
⌐‾ ‾ ‾¬	latent relations of fifth, to be felt only as a frame
⌐__¬	realized fourths
⌐_ _ _¬	frame-fourths
⌐......¬	latent affinity by fourths of minor grade
∧	nuclear second or nuclear third
⌣	tonic
⌢ ⌢	two zones
───	real steps of third
-------	latent relations of third
⌣	real semitone steps
⌣---	latent semitone relations

Different *lengths* of the scale notes signify the estimation of their value or rank in the whole.

The *Mordvine* songs published by Väisänen (Helsinki 1948) show an almost exclusively circumscribing *melos*, having for the most part a narrow to medium compass (third, fourth, fifth, sixth, seventh, rarely more), among them, strangely enough, can be found many songs without semitones: *e. g.* tritonic airs in the compass of a fourth, tetratonic airs within the range of a fifth, pentatonic melodies in the hexachord, *etc.* Thus anhemitony appears here in a very loose connection with the two-zone *melos*. The occasionally recurring hypothesis, that we have to do here with the bichordal or trichordal prototypes in the "evolution" to pentatony, seems to me absolutely untenable. If such evolutions exist, we must look for them elsewhere, eventually in the music of the ancient agricultural civilization. The anhemitonic tri- and tetratonic melodies of the Mordvines, however, are to be conceived altogether as a synthesis of Old-Finnish narrow melodies and of extensive pentatony brought from the East. To put it in a formula : it is not a question of evolution, but of involution, regression, reduction. A parallel to this is the *reduction of compass* which can be often observed in the transformation of *Russian* songs and dances when adopted by the Mordvines.

Structural formulae of some Mordvine melodies (Väisänen 1948) :

No. 17, *Wedding lament*   Nos. 18—21, *Dirges*

No. 23, *Dirge*   No. 62, *Nuptial song*

The Ob-Ugrians, Vogules and Ostyaks, occupy a special position also from a musical point of view.

The circumscribing, centered *"parlando melos"* in speech proximity is, here too, a *pièce de résistance;* it appears narrow, of medium width as well as extensive in all forms. But also other traits become prominent which are not specifically Finno-Ugric, but seem generally *North-Asiatic.* The most striking is perhaps the peculiar flickering, fluctuating agitation. This often appears as a *vibrato* in a single sustained note and is even more conspicuous in trill-like *tremolandos* in seconds or minor thirds. This unsteadiness of melodic structure, characterizing a considerable number of melodies, is due to the fact that the tonal range lacks a scale-like, modal frame (mostly so, perhaps in the bear songs and the melodies of dramatized bear performances). Nevertheless one cannot speak of tonal uncertainty (Väisänen), for the tonal centre (tonic, final) can always be felt. The movements within the tonal range are usually condensed around a nuclear second, less often around a nuclear third. This is the case in the example to follow.

F[1] tonic-final, G[1] confinal or counter-cadence note ; both notes together form the central nuclear second. Each of these two intermediate notes, both F[1], and G[1] however, attracts a lower semitone E[1] and F[1]. To the confinal G[1] is added the supertonic and topnote A[1], connected with the low note E[1] by a latent fourth-relation. Compare construction formula.

Performance at a Vogule Bear Festival

Väisänen, 1937, no. 58.

The same nuclear second with the same added subsemitones appear in this example:

Performance at a Vogule Bear Festival

Väisänen, 1937. no. 72.

But another low note D^1 is added to it (as lower fourth of the tonic G^1), as well as the upper fifth D^2 of the tonic. It is characteristic that the division of the pentachordal upper space D^2—G^1 is variable: it is divided either by the major third B^1, or the minor third $B\flat^1$.

We have to content ourselves with these few examples. Väisänen's publication offers a great many melodies similarly constructed, having either a narrower or wider compass and stock of notes. In all melodies of this type besides some fixed frame-notes, other variable tones will be found; sometimes the exchangeable notes are limited to variants of a "quarter-tone" only.

Melodies of non-modal type with partly "variable" filling notes, exist also elsewhere: in the East, in the Old-Scandinavian "*Skaldmelos*"[8] having survived especially in Norway, also in the old strata of the Moravian song. But the variability of the Ob-Ugric *melos* is of a specific kind. It should not be confused with the accidental wavering of intonation of untalented singers. Here we have most probably to do with an ancient phenomenon of North Asiatic style.

Middendorf noted by ear a *Giliak* tune:

Giliak Tune

H. Schurtz, *Urgeschichte der Kultur*, Leipzig—Wien 1900, p. 516.

It comprises a complete tetrachord, containing besides the predominant major third also the minor third, in a pronouncedly chromatic way. On all main notes the singer develops either swift or slow, rhythmic shakes. According to the description of the recorder he (the singer) trilled, besides a guttural shake, also a nasal *falsetto* shake. Quite typical examples of the vibrating performance of the Palaeo-Siberians were contained in the songs of the *Oroches* or Amur-Tunguses, taken down by Rudel.[9] I have the intention of publishing a preserved rendering of one of the pieces at another place in the near future. A Samoyed soothsayer's

[8] I refer to my study: *Die ältesten Spuren germanischer Volksmusik*, in *Zeitschrift für Volkskunde*, vol. 48, Berlin 1939, pp. 137—180.
[9] Phonograms of the Berliner Lautarchiv, destroyed during the war.

song (Väisänen 1937, no. 167) condenses this form of movement entirely into a chromatics as revealed by the structural formula:

The melodic vibration, fluctuation, quivering, shake-like circumscription may be explained first of all as the expression of a peculiarly constituted psychical situation. It is the arctic unsteadiness which often extends over the Sub-Arctic, the expression of primitive life that manifests itself, among others, also in the well-known bird-costume of the shaman and in his "rides" to the upper and lower realm of ghosts.

Already Gräbner[10] emphasized the "boundlessness" of the "all-animated" world as conceived by the Arctic peoples, of a world lacking aggressiveness. Gräbner speaks of the "defensive" or passive character of the Arctic languages. In this early strata man had no "master's relation" to animals. On the contrary: "no doubt, the animal had once been generally considered by the North-Asiatics to be far superior to man."[11]

The frequent occurrence of the fluctuating type of melody, not bound by any fixed diatonic scale in the *bear songs* of the Vogules and the Ostyaks as well as in the performances at the bear festivals, can only confirm our opinion that we have to do with a phenomenon of the earliest times. From the Lapps to the Ainus, as is generally known, bear cult and brear songs appear as archaisms. The few preserved bear songs of the Lapps[12] certainly have a different structure, more defined in rhythm and compass (semitoneless tetratony), than those of the Vogules.

According to the state of things, I should not regard the flickering-vibrating element of so many Ob-Ugric songs as an original property of the Finno-Ugric circle. I should rather see in it a later acquisition of the Ugrians driven to the North, a formation of contact brought about by a longer intercourse with the Palaeo-Asiatic neighbours. But we must not forget that opposed to this vibrating, unsteady movement there is a permanent tendency *towards the centre* realized above all in the tonic and the nuclear second. Also the extensive melodies of the Ob-Ugrians, in which most probably later foreign influences are reflected, are regularly "centered". In this, however, the ancient psychical legacy of this ethnic group is always revealed anew.

---

[10] *Das Weltbild der Primitiven*, München 1924, pp. 98, 102.
[11] Hans Findeisen, *Nordasien*, in H. Bernatzik, *Die Grosse Völkerkunde*, vol. II, Leipzig 1939, p. 62.
[12] Karl Tirén, *Die lappische Volksmusik*, Stockholm 1942, p. 90, nos. 5 and 6.

WALTER WIORA

OLDER THAN PENTATONY

Two- to Four-Note Scales in the Music of Ancient Europe and of Primitive Peoples

The first volume of *Corpus Musicae Popularis Hungaricae*, this comprehensive work dedicated to the memory of Béla Bartók who had such a large share in it, quotes several tunes of the simplest pattern; children's songs consisting of but a small number of notes. But even many of the songs connected with calendar customs, published in the second volume, have a compass not exceeding two to four notes. Melodies using less than five notes are to be found among the folk songs of almost every European country, though, mostly among in those sung to children's games or to calendar customs, or else surviving in remote regions unaffected by international routes. Such tunes were currently sung, e. g. in Gotschee, this one-time island of the German language in Slovenian surroundings. Let us compare, for instance, the following songs[1] both having the word "carnival" *(Fassang, Voshog)* at the beginning.

No. 1

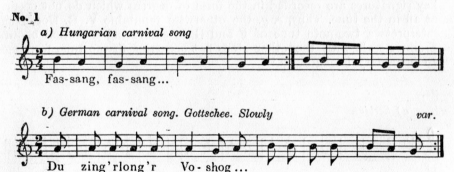

a) Hungarian carnival song

Fas-sang, fas-sang...

b) German carnival song. Gottschee. Slowly   var.

Du   zing'rlong'r   Vo-shog...

How to interpret such melodies in tonality? Are they sections of five- or seven-note scales like the three-note song in Rousseau's lyrical

---

[1] Sources : 1*a*. Bartók—Kodály, vol. ii, no. 71. — *b*. Deutsches Volkslied-archiv A 110 091, published in Moser, p. 207.

drama *Devin du village*, or do they represent self-contained scales where the limitation to two, three, or four notes is an essential characteristic ?

In West-European theory of music and its developed forms we find, besides the seven- and twelve-note scales, pentatony at best. Patterns of children's songs such as *so la so mi(re)* are said to be essentially pentatonic, meaning that they are not self-contained scales but sections of other scales. Thus, from the historical angle they should be considered either reductions or primitive forms that have not yet attained independence, as compared to the complete form evolution was striving after. In the latter interpretation they cannot be regarded as, let us say, a complete three-storey building, but only as a five-storey one under construction, with only three storeys finished. This conception seems even more odd if pentatony were supposed to have been arisen from theoretical considerations : the first persons singing in pentatony should have constructed their scale first, joining perfect fifths and reflecting the steps so obtained within the frame of an octave. In this manner, how could children's and primitive peoples' music be understood psychologically ? Was the circle of fifths actually at the origin ? Was the pentatonic scale at the origin ?

Not only theorists, however, but also students of musical folklore often referred tunes consisting of a few notes to five- or seven-note scales. Thus, one of the famous musicologists includes the two- and three-note tunes of North-East Europe in pentatony. I have read in an unpublished treatise that several Bulgarian melodies of a narrow compass do not belong to any definite mode, since at least six or seven degrees are required to speak definitely of modes. And such kinds of prejudices are responsible for the fact that in collections of folk songs key signatures are recorded in the form of degrees which do not occur at all in the tune. Thus, *e. g.* the otherwise reputable V. R. Đorđević interprets a two-note tune of F and G as embracing a section of an F-minor scale with the other steps not occurring in the tune forming an imaginary background.[2]

No.

   a) Serbian

In fact similar two-note tunes may be found outside Europe, too, thus for instance, among Fuegians, in rituals of initiation.[3]

[2] Đorđević, vol. ii, no. 300.
[3] Hornbostel (5), no. 3.

b) Tierra del Fuego

Such tunes could hardly be recorded as sections of A-minor or A-major. But even to-day there are globe-trotters who talk of the melancholic "scales in minor" of dark-faced singers, and even such a superior mind as Carl Stumpf happened to analyze once an Indian tune in the following manner: "Theme I: F-sharp and G-flat major all along, using only four steps."[4] His controversy with Gilman in 1892 is still instructive as regards method. Both were wide off the mark: Gilman, out of pure empirism, failed to bring into relief the melodic stucture intended by the singers, and, thereby, the musical essence of the song. On the other hand, Stumpf, though trying to grasp it, failed to recognize the scale system used by Indians and measured them against European categories. He fought against the erroneous conception of constructing a new scale whenever a note is omitted from a mode underlying a melody. *E. g.* the song *"Kommt ein Vogel geflogen"* — he says — is in major and not in a scale of six notes. Nonetheless he arrived at another erroneous conclusion: he generalized such cases from the realm of the major scale extending them to exotic styles far off this scope; alleging the entire treasury of Indian melodies published by Gilman to be classified "without exceptions among seven- and five-note major and minor scales".

But slowly dawn began to break upon the trackless woods of prejudices and there appeared a growing comprehension towards the peculiar character of sub-pentatonic modes. Persistent research has revealed their prevalence in the music of many peoples, especially of most primitive tribes, and also in Europe: with Finno-Ugric and Baltic peoples, in Bulgaria, on the Balkans, a great treasure of such melodies is available for comparative studies.[5] This may serve to overcome prejudices rooted in the western systems as well as the evolutionism of Rowbotham and Lach who regarded the one-, two-, three-, and more-note systems as corresponding to successive historical periods: they alleged music to have consisted of one note, then of two, and so on. C. Stumpf, E. M. von Hornbostel and other authorities of the Berlin circle tried to discover the "primitive forms of the scale" in the typology of primitive melodics.[6] B. Szabolcsi sketched the course of evolution, beginning with the modulation of the voice, through the different forms of two- and three-note

[4] Stumpf (2), pp. 122 *et seq.*
[5] For instance, Lach's collections (see esp. I/2, pp. 106 *et seq.*); Väisänen, Launis, Tampere, Stoin, Đorđević, Rihtman, Žganec, etc.
[6] Hornbostel (1), p. 23; Schneider (1), pp. 145 *et seq.*; Sachs, pp. 30 *et seq.*; etc.

melodies to pentatony. W. Danckert speaks of three- and four-note scales, and, surveying the narrow-ranged melodies of different European peoples, interprets the basic forms of the tonal system in the sense of *Kulturkreislehre*.[7] In his attempt to understand the original forms of tonal function, Z. Estreicher falls back on the two-note melodies, particularly Eskimoes. B. A. Kremenliev stresses the independence and archaism of the few-note scales in South-East Europe.[8] I have pointed out myself on several occasions the existence of such keys.[9] But it was Brăiloiu first of all who, after a thorough study of a rich material, called attention to three systems preceding pentatony, to wit tetratony, tritony and bitony.[10] Besides this paper pointing far ahead, it was particularly R. Lachmann[11] who drew a parallel between the music of primitive peoples and that of Europe when he stated that the formula G A G E in children's songs was equally usual in working and cradle songs of women on all the continents (see Ex. no. 10).

It is odd that this significant initiative should not have been followed up until now, when further research in this line would be obvious. But it would be the task of one branch of research to bring to fruition the germs of well done preliminary work.

The issue raised has a systematic and a historical aspect.

1. *To what extent* do two- to four-note melodies have underlying *modes of their own*, different from other, say, five-note scales ? To what extent are these modes self-contained entities with *characteristic structural properties ("Prägnante Gestaltsqualitäten")*, and in what do they differ from the sections of, say, the major or Dorian scale. In what sense do they "underlie" singing and how do they "exist" in opposition to scales logically defined in theory and optically represented on instrument ?

2. Which of the two- to four-note scales reach back as primitive modes into the early days of music, as far as the age preceding the great civilizations ? Which are *older* than pentatony ? Which belong to the ancient European music preceding the *Ars Musica* of Western Europe and how has the latter affected it in the course of time ?

As regards methods, we face the task of attaining a comprehensive grasp of the material ; in their systematized catalogue the musical department of the *Deutsches Volksliedarchiv* (German Archives of Folk Songs) have already begun to set up a systematic compilation of such melodies originating from Europe or other continents. What matters is, without indulging in conjectures with regard to the pattern of evolution, a thorough analyzis of the material and of variant formation which

---

[7] Danckert (3), p. 200 ; (1), pp. 79 *et seq.;* etc.
[8] Kremenliev, p. 53 ; see also Bartók—Lord, p. 52.
[9] Wiora (1), pp. 60 *et seq.*, 23 *et seq.*, 35 *et seq.;* (3), p. 155, etc.
[10] Brăiloiu, p. 370 *et seq.*
[11] See p. 8 ; cf. also Werner, Chapter on the extensive congruity between the keys underlying the singing of "small children and low-cultured primitive peoples" (p. 74).

may furnish information as to the psychological aspect of tonal forms. Further studies should be devoted to the currency of such modes and "comparative"[12] studies of the different characteristics should establish their age and origin. This would lay the foundation to the first chapter of the general history of keys both in Europe and on other continents.

The following brief contribution is meant to be a survey of basic modes, and, with respect to Lachmann's statement quoted above, the comparison of European and primitive peoples' melodies. I am, of course, far from believing that it is always "the same melody" which appears here and there having wandered from continent to continent; such a supposition would be nonsensical. The same stock of notes may be embedded in different styles; the identity of what can be recorded does not mean the perfect identity of the relevant phenomena. Strange coincidences may sometimes be explained by affinities of civilization as, e. g., between Indians and Eskimoes, but more often can they be explained polygenetically: elementary musical ideas of mankind may have cropped up on different points of our globe without any historical connexion. It is the same in other fields of life, where in similar conditions some elementary forms are always generated anew. In lack of other evidence conclusions as to affinity of civilizations or historical correlations cannot be drawn solely on the ground of formal likeness between primitive formations. The likeness in form of European primitive music and the primitive music of other continents, however, throws a light upon the similitudes inherent in human nature and the fundament of music. At the same time it is a touchstone of our problem, namely to what extent are we allowed to interpret European melodies consisting of a small number of notes as rudiments of five- and seven-note modes, or else as originating from more ancient, primitive modes.

*

The adjacent degress of a "scale" are situated at intervals of a step or a leap from each other. "Thirds" are in an intermediate position between the two, looking alternately like long steps or short leaps. Scales built up of steps are called, according to the number of steps, bi-, tri-, tetra-, penta-, or hexachordic modes. Those, on the other hand, that consist of leap-intervals, or where leaps and steps alternate, are called bi-, tri-, tetra-, or pentatonic.

Tunes built on a few notes are not necessarily of a narrow compass; if the intervals are large, the gamut will be large even with a small number

[12] It will be well to stress the meaning of this word in terms such as "comparative" musicology, linguistics, study of religions. Is comparative linguistics with its methodological inferences, e. g. concerning Primitive Indo-European, something quite different from the study of the individual primitive peoples? Same is true of the difference between the method of "comparative musicology" and the field of "ethnomusicology (of primitive peoples)". See also Wiora (2); (4); (5).

of notes, particularly when the steps are repeated in other octaves, as it is the case with fanfare melodics ("*Durchlaufende Fanfarenmelodik*", M. Schneider). Narrow melodies have often a rather close compass while the compass of melodies covering a wider space is alternating; the voice moves within varying amplitudes. In this sense one may speak of *close* or *open* scales besides *short* and *long* scales.

In primitive music the leaps are mostly successive consonances or intended as such, in the sense of significant relations, even when the pitch vacillates. Steps, on the contrary, before becoming intervals distinctly heard in differentiated systems, *i. e.* small seconds,[13] are merely approximative "seconds" or "thirds". The difference between shorter or longer steps, is still of purport and has an influence on the formation of "keys".

The "scale" or, more generally, the tonal stock is the inventory of occurring notes. The "key" indicates, in addition to this, also the tonal structure, that is the distribution of the different accents between the steps, the position of the final and so on. The keys possess structural properties of their own such as the harmonic differentiation or the equilibrium in the play of tonal forces. These can not be expressed in pure scales, but in structural formulae as those of Hornbostel, and by means of characteristic phrases.

1. From Bichord to Tetrachord. Our 2nd example is a bichordic tune having two notes at an interval of one step. The next example differs from it in the span between the steps being shorter.[14]

No. 3

a) *Indian, British Columbia*

b) *Algeria*

c) *Bulgaria*

[13] For explanation *cf.* Collaer, p. 10 *et seq.*
[14] Sources: 3*a*. Abraham—Hornbostel (1), no. 34 (= 174 with drum accompaniment in 3/4); *b*. Bartók—Lord, p. 54; *c*. Stoin, no. 4000 (pitch there: C'...).

188

In the dance music no. 3*a* and in the nuptial song no. 3*b* the span is uncertainly larger than a small second, in the Bulgarian dance tune however, it appears as an intentional semitone. Here the limitation of the whole tune to two steps appears to be rather deliberate in connection with a delicate rhythm and within the range of an idiom, where chromatics have a character of usual, intentional restriction. With regard to its likeness to 3*a* and 3*b* it seems that we have here an ancient type altered under later influence.

The duality of pitch, rising and falling by one step, is in primitive music obviously related to accent. "The singer gives way to the natural tendency to sharpen ot flatten the note simultaneously as it grows weaker or stronger."[15] It is more natural to change the level in such a manner than to maintain it, that is to repeat a note continuously from beginning to end of a song. It this sense two-note melodics (bichord) is more primitive than one-note singing (*i. e.* in a unaltered pitch), in the way as the smaller difference of voices in a "choir for one voice" is more primitive than perfect unison.

Already two-note singing produces embryonic "keys" depending on the „second" being minor or major and whether singing ends on the lower or the upper note. The upper note corresponds to the raising or stressing of the voice or expresses impetus.[16] It is further influenced by the primitive forms of melodic movement: recitative repercussion,[17] regular oscillation between the two notes,[18] a song-like flat curve,[19] the differentiation in open and close cadences,[20] etc.

The primitive phenomenon of middle position is first encountered in the trichord: a central note is surrounded by a lower and an upper note. Its importance as centre is stressed when it figures as tonic, as in the tunes of the healing song and of the Christmas carol[21] (no. 4*a*).

No. 4

a) Tierra del Fuego

b) Serbia

[15] Hornbostel (5), p. 68.
[16] *E. g.* Baud—Bovy, vol. ii, p. 247 ; Moser, p. 221.
[17] *E. g.* in der Gand, p. 196, no. 3.
[18] *E. g.* Lachmann, p. 8 (Cradle Song Wedda) ; in der Gand, p. 197, no. 4.
[19] *E. g.* Launis, no. 50 ; Stoin, no. 394.
[20] *E. g.* Stoin, nos. 68, 3903, etc.
[21] Hornbostel (5), no. 40 ; Đorđević, vol. i, no. 217 (F♯...). Cf. also the Hungarian Song on Whitsuntide in Bartók—Kodály, vol. ii, p. 189.

The tonic of the trichord, both with primitive peoples[22] and in Europe, is more frequent in the lower than in the middle position, and rare in the upper.[23] The trichord is fully symmetric when the middle note is surrounded by two identical intervals, as in Ex. no. 4. This and the next example show the same movement of tune, a flat curve but with a wide and a narrow third: a herald of the later contrast between major and minor.[24]

No. 5

a) *Wedda, Ceylon*   b) *Serbia*

In Ex. no. 6a this formula-like undulation is enlarged by a small sequence and a casually touched fourth note. A European parallel to this is found in the tune of a hymn intoned in the upper bichord and bringing the two lower notes as ornamental augmentation only in the cadence.[25]

No. 6

a) *Tierra del Fuego*

b) *Bulgaria*

Tonal and structural functions in music are conditioned by each other, consequently their development must have been interdependent. Differentiation in whole and half finals means both. This is apparent in bichordic[26] and still more markedly in trichordic melodics.[27]

---

[22] Sachs, p. 42.
[23] Examples: Wiora (1), p. 38; Väisänen (2), nos. 7 and 8; Canteloube, vol. ii, p. 273; Coussemaker, no. cl.
[24] Wertheimer, p. 308; Đorđević, vol. ii, p. 232 (D'...).
[25] Hornbostel (5), no. 23; Stoin, no. 251.
[26] Sachs, p. 34 *et seq.*; and our Ex. no. 2.
[27] Bose, no. 2; Đorđević, vol. ii, no. 212 (E...). — See also Schneider (5), no. 10; Densmore (1), no. 34; cf. Stoin, no. 3939 with Rieman, p. 107.

No. 7

a) Uitoto, Columbia

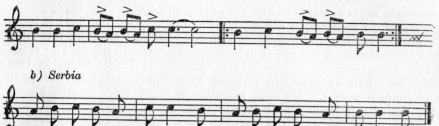

b) Serbia

The succession bichord-trichord-tetrachord is not a pure "adding up of notes one at a time", but it brings forth further primitive features of music. First of all, four notes in the same direction give the impression of a linear expansion of the compass : the *melodic line* which should be distinguished from the pre-melodic line of the sliding voice. At the same time a consonance, the fourth, appears as a support and a frame. The voice having risen to the fourth, reaches a pitch harmonically affiliated to the starting note. This relation constitutes a kind of bracket enclosing the intermediary notes and forms a kind of entity of the four notes. Our example 8a clearly shows the two levels tonally affiliated, and in bar 2 we find the bridge between them. In the French refrain the four-note descent is followed by a three-note undulation, whereas the Good-Friday Song from Gottschee interrupts and repeats the descent (C' B A—C' B A G—B A G).[28]

No. 8

a) Indian, British Columbia

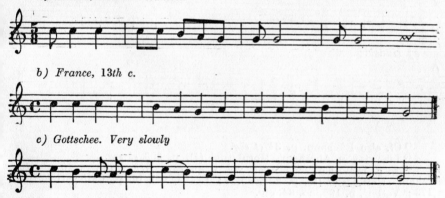

b) France, 13th c.

c) Gottschee. Very slowly

[28] Abraham—Hornbostel (5), no. 19 (159), with drum accompaniment ; Gennrich, p. 166 ; Deutsches Volksliedarchiv A 109, 576.

A far greater variety of keys is inherent in the tetrachord than in two- or three-note systems. In the possible distribution of whole and semitones we can detect the germs of the different octave types of the *do, re, mi, fa* modes.[29] In the material at my disposal the final is more frequently on the lowest note than on the second, seldom on the third and quite rarely on the upper note.[30] Tetrachords with tritone and chromatic formations are naturally also rare. Tetrachordic tunes in two lines with half or complete cadence were fundamental in Europe.[31] The frequency of tetrachordic melodies in South-East Europe makes us think of correlations with Ancient Greece.

2. From Bitony to Tetratony. Between the expressly "chordic" and "tonic" modes are those defined by the third. The small calling third, generally sung in the upper position, is current all over the world. The lower note figures as closing note in the majority of such cases. In Ex. no. 9a, a signal used for calling home the bear, this note is only superficially touched upon, while in Ex. 9b. and c. a dance and a rain song, it is accentuated. In example 9d, on the contrary, a ritual introductory and closing formula, and in example 9e, a swinging children's song, the accent and the final are in a higher pitch.[32]

No. 9

a) *Vogule, Russia*
b) *Indian, British Columbia*
c) *Spain*
d) *Pangwe*
e) *Hungary*

[29] Cf. also Riemann, p. 34 *et seq.*
[30] Likewise in Abraham—Hornbostel (1), p. 293 *et seq.*
[31] *E. g.* Deutsche Volkslieder, vol. ii, p. 237 ; Wiora (4), p. 20 *et seq;* Abraham—Hornbostel (2), p. 261, no. 8 ; Grove, vol. iv, p. 627b ; Gennrich, p. 173 ; Vetterl, p. 196, no. 84, etc.
[32] Sources : 9a. Väisänen (1), p. 219, no. 138 (the pitch is given as C#) ; b. Abraham—Hornbostel (1), no. 25 (165, D...) ; c. Schneider (3), no. 12 (C...) ; d. Hornbostel (3), vol. ii, p. 3 ; e. Bartók—Kodály, vol. i, p. 389.

The small calling third and its completion to trichord D' C' B[33] are joined by the three-note forms of steps and thirds, known to everybody from children's sing-songs. The *"Laterne, Laterne"* type, quoted by Robert Lachmann, is sung by working women *(a)* and by a chorus in canon *(b)* as done by our children *(c and d)*.[34]

No. 10

a) Indian, Brazil　　　　　　　　*b) Semang, Malacca*

c) Sardinia　　　　　　　*d) Cologne*

Forms F E C and A F E are, of course rare but G E D[35] is rather frequent. A different structure appears, however, with the same stock of notes, as soon as the third in the leap is displaced by a fourth, *e. g.* A G C' G[36]. The same applies to the later significant[37] series D' C' D' A, as against C' D' C' A. It was sung in a strikingly similar form as an independent call in Central-Africa on the Pangwe "Feast of the Soul" and in a German relict area to the beating of discs at solstice[38]. This shows that forms considered by some authors as the properties f the West, are also ancestral possessions of other continents.

No. 11

a) Pangwe　　　　　　　　*b) German, Carpathians*

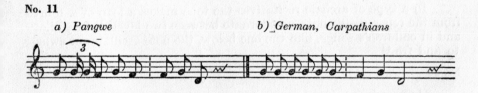

[33] *E. g.* Hornbostel (5), no. 41 ; Sušil, no. 2176 ; for Westfäl. shepherds' call see Moser, p. 94.
[34] Sources : 10*a.* Hornbostel (4), no. 19 ; *b.* Kolinski, p. 618, no. 6 (G...) ; *c.* Fara, p. 90, no. 17 (F♯...) ; *d.* Erk–Böhme, no. 1842 (D'...).
[35] *E. g.* Abraham–Hornbostel (1), p. 299, no. 9 ; Lach, vol. i/2, p. 42, no. 42 ; Väisänen (1), p. 32 ; Vetterl, p. 56 ; etc.
[36] Conform. *e, g.* in Loorits, no. 168B and Žganec, no. 1*b.*
[37] Maerker, p. 90 *et seq.*
[38] Hornbostel (3), p. 343, no. 6 ; Jungbauer–Hornstrich, no. 23.

Both here and in the following patterns, a characteristic consonance, the fourth or the fifth, has a structure-shaping value, figuring not merely as a backbone, as in the tetrachord, but also as a leap. Consonances must not be conceived as having originally been simultaneously concordant and later successive notes, but as numerically conditioned qualitative relations, which are equally original in melodics and in polyphony. They are "harmonic" tonal relations which prevail by their pregnancy against non-harmonic ones as, e. g. a right angle against angles of 80 or 100°.[39] Only in this sense, and not in the sense of disjoined or broken chords, can we speak of the principle of consonance, of sense for harmony and of triadic melodics with primitive peoples. The kind of melodics consisting exclusively or mainly of consonant leaps and melodic common chords prevails, as well known, among such primitive tribes as Pygmies in Central Africa and New Guinea; by no means is this melodics born in a roundabout way of intersecting the succession of steps by frame consonances, and still less by the indirect means of breaking originally simultaneous chords.

Singing in fourth is explicitly bitonic in the following *healing song* (a) and *wedding song* (b).[40]

No. 12

a) Indian, Tierra del Fuego

b) Bulgaria

In a type of archaic recitatives the tone makes a leap of a fourth from the repercussive note, or alternate between two levels.[41] In yodles[42] and in children's songs, like the one below, the note oscillates or swings to and fro.[43]

No. 13

a) Chuvash, Russia

[39] For basic considerations see Metzger.
[40] Hornbostel (5), no. 39; Stoin, no. 636.
[41] See Wiora (1), p. 23 *et seq.*
[42] *E. g.* Hornbostel (2), p. 53.
[43] Lach, vol. i/4, p. 62, no. xvii/7 (C instead of 2/4); Žganec, no. 1*a*.

194

b) Croatia...

Bitonic singing in fifth is found, *e.g.*, in old bear rituals of Lap-
landers and Ostyaks[44]. In sixths, like a pendulum, rings the Lapp song
To the cow, similarly to the French herdsman's air: *Va, chien, va!*
Arrête la vache![45]

In primitive "triadic melodics" fourths and fifths are similarly
frequent leaps. Here fifths were certainly not formed by building thirds
one above the other, as if these should have the precedence. Such an
air may have a broad movement[46], but it may be cosily narrow and
agreeable as in cradle songs.

Schneider distinguishes "*durchlaufende*" and oscillating fanfars[47].
The fact, that the oldest triadic melodics in the folk songs of the Western
world can be traced back far beyond the accordics of modern times is
demonstrated by such parallels, as the two shepherd's calls 14*a* and *b*,
or the two children's songs 14*c* and *e*.[48]

No. 14

In other surroundings such formations may sometimes arise that
are reminiscent of wind melodics of medieval programmatic pieces, such
as the *Kühhorn*.[49]

---

[44] See Wiora (4), p. 11, no. 5.
[45] Tirén, no. 246, Canteloube, vol. ii, p. 266.
[46] *E. g.* Kunst (1), no. 137; (3), p. 29.
[47] Schneider (1), p. 148
[48] Sources: 14*a*. Tirén, p. 179, no. 415; *b*. Deutsches Volkslied, vol. xviii,
p. 7 (yodled high G); *c*. Kunst (1), p. 105, no. 134; *d*. Hornbostel (2), no. 5;
e. Bartók—Kodály, vol. i, p. 491. Cf. also Wiora (1), p. 35 *et seq*.
[49] Kurosawa, p. 5; Mayer—Rietsch, p. 324.

No. 15

a) Formosa

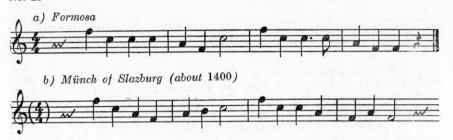

b) Münch of Slazburg (about 1400)

Remarkably rare are series of one-way consonant leaps, forming together a dissonance, *e. g.*[50] two fourths E A D', the more frequent are, on the other hand, sequences consisting of a leap and a step. As against the agreeable, smooth circling within the common chord, they often ring sharp and angular (Ex. nos. 20 and 21), in other cases they figure as a filling to the triadic movement only modifying their character (Ex. no. 18). Between these two kinds are ranged those in which fourth-accented and third- or fifth-accented motives follow each other, *e. g.*[51]

No. 16

a) Smith Sund Eskimoes

b) South Moravia

Here too, one and the same scale offers the possibility of different "modes". Thus, for instance, the scale G A B D' is not necessarily to be looked upon as a tendency toward G major; the same notes may constitute the following backbone for a melody: A B A G/A D'A[52]

It is better suited to the general character of the realm of sounds, and is more natural and frequent, that the wider intervals should be ranged deeper and the smaller ones higher; hence the distances decrease upwards and increase downwards. Thus, *e. g.* the scale C' G F E occurs seldom, while the sequence B A G D, known from the children's song,

[50] *E. g.* Stoin, no. 578; Đorđević, vol. ii, no. 534.
[51] Leden, no. 19; Hensel, p. 3 *et seq.* (B...).
[52] Stoin, no. 198.

the more frequently ; which is illustrated in a ritual dance and a pastoral call[53] :

No. 17

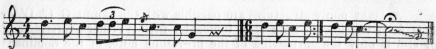

a) *Indian, British Columbia*   b) *France, Bresse. Several times*

Forms B A G and G D can also be imagined as a link between two motives. The two appear first jointly and than separately in the example[54] below :

No. 18

a) *Formosa*

b) *Gottschee*

The frame of fifths with the minor third and without second underlies further four-note formations ; these differ according to the size and weight of the fourth. Let us compare a Russian song, the famous nuptial air sung by the drunken Varlaam in Mussorgsky's *Boris Godunov*[55], with the children's song (19*b*), with a lyrical song (*c*) and with the song about the snake as regards the key.

No. 19

a) *Indian, British Columbia*   b) *Cheremiss, Russia*

c) *North-East Russia*

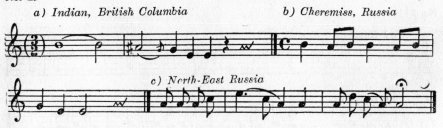

[53] Abraham—Hornbostel (1), no. 3 (142, E"...) ; Canteloube, vol. iii, p. 298.
[54] Kurosawa, p. 5 ; Deutsches Volksliedarchiv A 110,136 (Landsch. Vldr. 24, p. 74).
[55] Sources : 19*a*. Abraham—Hornbostel (1), no. 14 (E"..., with drum accompaniment) ; *b*. Lach, vol. i/3, p. 36, no. 73 ; *c*. Panóff, p. 10 ; *d*. Schneider (5), no. 9.

d) Mato Grosso Indians, Brazil

A great many structures are possible with the gamut G C' D' or
D G A. If the lowest note is a tonic, the fifth is either overstressed[56]
or else is only the surpassing of the prevailing note, of the dominant
in a broader sense.[57]

No. 20

a) Menominee Indians, Wisconsin (USA)   b) Lapland

c) Serbia

But even the uppermost[58] or the middle degree may become a
stressed final and thereby a tonic. If, in the latter case, the nethermost
note is touched but lightly, then the scale, in fact, looks like a bichordic
one with a single escapade into the lower fourth. And how different is
the impression produced by the tune of a Russian nuptial song, from
which C. Brăiloiu has drawn his conclusions! As in the collation of all
melodies similar in form, let us, here too, give the same attention to
both differences and similitudes:

No. 21

a) Russia

b) Bulgaria

[56] E. g. D' C' D' G (Tirén, no. 87).
[57] Densmore (2), no. 26 (C♯..); Tirén, p. 180, no. 416; Đorđević, vol.
ii, no. 339 (G...).
[58] E. g. Stoin, nos. 342, 967, 2177.

The octave D G A D' yields a particularly symmetric form, as *e. g.* in the following recitative from a religious play. Such a limitation to the central second and the three simplest numerical ratios or consonances (1 : 2 : 3 : 4) appear like a native rock of tones. The broadness and significance of the formation stand even more in relief in the parallel case, where the upper D is less stressed and the lower D is missing.

No. 22

3. Unessential Augmentation by Secondary and Auxiliary Notes. The forms here discussed may also be surrounded or interwoven with secondary notes. These consist of vocally uncertain incursions, such as cries and *glissandos*, and of accessory incidental notes, which neither belong to the scale in question, nor transform it into some other scale any more than *pien*-tones transform pentatony. But these are not mere filling notes, but swinging, flinging and other alien notes, as in the following example[59] :

No. 23

In this and other cases the voice leaping high may hit, instead of the desired octave, a neighbouring note; yet it seems that sometimes the concluding note is either deliberately not the tonic or is a note utterly alien to the gamut: having for some time moved within the same circle of tones, the singer finally leaps out of it. Beside the repose on the final note, the stressed cadence, the stopping at an arbitrary spot of the circling, or other cases. Such flights or deviations seem to be another basic form in concluding a tune.

[59] S toin, no. 923. See also nos. 162, 290, 577, 584, 626, 672, 903, 925, 926, etc.

If, in this manner, the occurring pitches are not only counted, but weighed, and the auxiliary notes discounted, several melodies, built apparently on five or more degrees, will turn out to be fundamentally only two- or four-note tunes. Thus, for instance, the magic dance of the Eskimoes in Brăiloiu's collection[60] is not fully pentatonic, but generally remains within a trichord and deviates only from time to time to an alien upper or lower note. The same applies to the interrelation of two- and four-note stocks. *E. g.* a long song in 68 "bars" deviates from the E G third but in three instances passing transitorily to A.[61] In his lectures von Hornbostel stressed the point that a great number of Weddan, Fuegian, and other songs were, in fact, merely bitonic though they here and there happen to touch upon two other notes.

The number of notes within a gamut is, as a matter of fact, not increased by intoning a note now somewhat higher, now somewhat lower, though the varying span of an interval may change the number of degrees within the octave[62]. If the pitches intoned are measured in cents, the number of different cent values obtained may often be very high, while the number of "degrees" conceived still remains very small.

It is a somewhat different case when a regular change, an alternation between the adjacent degrees, develops[63].

No. 24

a) Indian, British Columbia

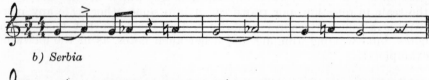

b) Serbia

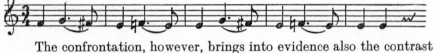

The confrontation, however, brings into evidence also the contrast between the oscillating span of certain small intervals and their subtle change, such as has developed in the middle and great civilizations of the ancient Near-East and Europe[64].

Finally, let us mention the intermediate forms of the keys discussed and the oscillation between them *(e. g.* the transposition of the tonic to another note). The primitive and early forms of modulation and of the alternation of major and minor can be detected in the melodies of few notes.

---

[60] *Collection Universelle*, 6/I.
[61] Schneider (6), no. 7.
[62] Hornbostel (1), p. 19.
[63] Abraham—Hornbostel (1), no. 33, p. 305; Đorđević, vol. ii, no. 559.
[64] Cf. also the problem raised by W. Danckert (p. 81 *et seq.)* by adopting a changing-leading note tonality in the North-European heroic lays.

4. Unessential Expansion by Transposition. In the foregoing it has been supposed that the motive and its inherent key are maintained on an absolute pitch ; each degree until the end of the song is related more or less strictly to the absolute initial pitch. In opposition to pitch-consistent melodics, in non-consistent melodics a motive is repeated, together with its tonal stucture, in another position (shifting of a motive, transposition, sequence), or two motives of different position or "key" follow each other.

In the first case of non-consistent melodics it is not the key that changes, but it is the motive, together with its tonal structure that is sung in different pitches. In what we would call "ladder melodics" the song does not consist of as many degrees as absolute pitches are heard, but a motive of a few notes is heard in a higher, or lower, or still lower pitch, until the voice rises upwards and transposes the motive again several times[65]; it is repeated in space as it is done in time. The movement of such melodics is wide, but its "compass" is actually not wide, if we mean the range of the motive. The primitive singer transposes his motive along the pre-musical, the *apeiron* of his voice, and by no means in an organized periodic system, as a European coloratura singer would do, singing a series of notes in sequences through several octaves. The former's voice would move, as on a slide, and not as on the spiral stairs of the octave system, even if this glitters through like an unrealized background. In this sense the number of actual degrees is generally small, even in wide ladder melodics.

In the second case we have a succession of two motives in different tonal orders. The song goes on for some time, *e. g.* according to the formula G A G E, and is closed with the fourth leap G C': as in the following Indian dance and the children's round: *"Nix in der Grube"*[66].

No. 25

   a) Indian, British Columbia

   b) Saxony and Silesia   *Shouting*

In case the singer has pentatony or a major scale in mind, he will first confine himself to the bottom part of this wide gamut,

---

[65] *E. g.* Hornbostel (1), p. 18 *et seq.*
[66] Sources : 25*a*. Abraham — Hornbostel (1), no. 20 (160, E...) ; *b*. Erk — Böhme, no. 1891.

leaving the completing section of flight until the end. In another interpretation, however, two motives of simple structure are joined, but no tonal connexion takes place, and the C̆, as the common fundamental note of both motives, is not felt as predominant from beginning to end. The primitive manner of joining the lines involves the joining of their keys. At the beginning the two systems of few notes stood separately, they were not yet summed up in a higher system of relations.

*

Our survey is far from being sufficient to give a definite answer to all the problems raised, but our references to other works and the considerations in this paper have helped us to arrive at some general conclusions.

It is evident that the modes here discussed cannot be deduced from pentatonic, major, minor, or ecclesiastic scales. They were widespread for a long time among primitive peoples, while the modes comprising more degrees, developed in middle and great civilizations, remained alien to them. They possess certain properties with regard to the succession of intervals, the melodic pattern and the structural features, which other scales lack.[67] But, despite this primitiveness and insignificance, they do not appear as unfinished or fragmentary, or as if could not be understood without the help of other, perfect modes. Tetrachord, fanfare-like singing on the "common chord", the joining of the central second and consonances, and other forms appear as independent, significant structures. In the *Gestaltlehre*,[68] they are "excellent" systems, possessing their own "essence". These are the elementary "ideas" of tonal order, and as such, may be compared to the elementary figures of geometry and ornamentation.

In order to be able to grasp their original meaning and value, they should be compared not only to later tonal system but also to pre-musical tones and sounds, against which they must have prevailed as the early forms of music proper. It is prejudice to allege that the primitive singer was not interested in defined steps and their system. A trend in this sense was surely evoked by those currents of the stone age, which turned toward fixing and abstraction, toward custom and rite in the different domains of the mind. It may be that historic antecedents of music were defined by stimuli similar to those that developed cubic-geometric primitive shapes in early art. Primitive forms of music have probably been discovered in the same spirit and probably often in religious rapture, like the original forms of the visible world by Promethean creators.

One of the pioneers in examining the question of the sense in which the singing of primitive peoples follows keys, was von Hornbostel, yet the

[67] Cf. Brăiloiu on tetratony etc. *loc. cit.*
[68] For basic considerations see Metzger, pp. 221, 316 *et passim*.

pages in his study on *Melody and Scale* opening up new vistas in musicology should be critically separated from those influenced by the musical conception of the age of Debussy and the impressionists. Primitive "vocal music" is not implicitly "scaleless", but is founded on scales or succession of notes ("tone-rows")[69] in a broader sense. The latter, however, are far less rationalized than scales of higher civilizations based on theory and instruments, they allow of uncertain intervals, are less self-assertive and are adhered to less consciously and strictly. The primitive singer does not regard them as given patterns, as we do. They are customs inherent in the melodic formulae; being present in the practice of melodics not as theoretically conscious scales, but rather as *customary tonalities* ; and this is the precondition without which it could not be discovered by the scholar of our days as an "empirical law". Accordingly, the successions of notes as used in a given civilization do not form a system like in ours. When we make music or listen to it, we have the keyboard, the tonal system, the totality of our scales in our minds ; these make up the area on which we move ; and of the whole tonal area which we realize in its entity, we let now one now another ring out. In ancient singing, on the contrary, the dividing line between notes and the system imagined against it existed but in the kernel. The usual systems or the "succession of notes used" in this singing are actually scales, *i. e.* keys, but in a broader sense, of which we must exclude everything that is added to it by the music of great civilizations.

Of course, it would be biased to emphasize only the differences between ancient and later forms; those carried the germs of many things that flourished only at a later period. This is why such stuctures, as *e. g.*, the patterns known from children's songs, could later be considered as sections of the major scale, pentatony, or ecclesiastical modes. These germs, however, were not only reinterpreted but also re-formed. In the majority of cases the melodies in few notes of the Balkans do not represent unaltered primitive forms, but forms that had been subject to the refining influence of later music. Though children's songs and European folk songs have preserved some traces of the ancient forms, most of these residues have not remained intact ; they have been influenced by new forces, *i. e.* the musical art of ancient and western peoples, and by the later styles of folk music itself.

The old age of scales discussed here is already evident from the distribution of their places of origin ; from their frequency, their rarity, or their absence in certain places. In Europe they have been recorded, in general, only in relict areas and in connection with children's songs, or with old texts and customs, within epic songs, for instance, only as one-line melodies and as old types of tunes covering a short stanza. They survive more vigorously in the traditions of savage peoples, partic-

[69] Hornbostel in *Samml. Vergl. Musikw.* vol. i, p. 366.

ularly among the more primitive tribes. They are, obviously, more ancient than pentatony. They belong to the most ancient kind of tonal systems known to us, and, what is more, to the most ancient that ever existed ; this can be inferred by systematical considerations, without taking into account the parallels drawn between prehistory and earliest childhood. They are evidences of the origin of music following the pre-musical sound, and this alone imparts to them a special importance in the history of music. Moreover, their influence lends them an additional importance, since they continue to live in the archaic layers of Eastern and Western ritual songs and have developed into systems of five and more degrees.

And no less essential for musicology are these successions of notes. The rudiments of music are reflected here in a more original form than in recent children's and folk songs. Ancient forms, that were to become blocks and backbones, shine here in the archaic purity of their origin. More convincingly than by generalizing the properties of modern music, can we recognize through them the nature of the tonal *Logos*.

REFERENCES

Abraham, O. and E. M. von Hornbostel, (1) *Phonographierte Indianermel. aus Brit-Columbia*, in *Sb. f. vgl. Mw.* vol. i, 1922, pp. 293 — 310.
    (2) *Phonogr. ind. Mel.*, *ibid.* pp. 251—290.
Bartók, Béla, *Volksmusik der Rumänen von Maramureş*, München 1923.
Bartók, Béla and Zoltán Kodály, *A Magyar Népzene Tára. Corpus Musicae Popularis Hungaricae*, Budapest 1951 —
Bartók Béla and A. B. Lord, *Serbo-Croatian Folk Songs*, New-York 1951.
Baud-Bovy, S., *Chansons du Dodécanèse*, vol. i, Athens 1935, vol. ii, Paris 1938.
Bose, F., *Die Musik der Uitoto*, in *Zs. f. vgl. Mw.* vol. ii, 1934.
Brăiloiu, C., *Sur une mélodie russe*, in P. Souvtchinsky's *Musique russe*, vol. ii, Paris 1953, pp. 329 — 391.
Brehmer, Fr., *Melodieauffassung u. melod. Begabung des Kindes*, in *Zs. f. angew. Psychol.* Suppl. 36, 1925.
Canteloube, J., *Anthologie des chants pop. français*, 4 vols, Paris 1951.
Collaer, P., *Les phénomènes primitifs de l'invention musicale*, in *Acta Oto-Rhino-Laryngologica Belgica*, 1954, pp. 9 — 15.
de Coussemaker, E., *Chants pop. des Flamands de France*, new ed. Lille 1930.
Danckert, W., (1) *Grundriss der Volksliedkunde*, Berlin [1939]
    (2) *A félhangnélküli pentatónia eredete* (The Origins of Anhemitonic Pentatony), in *Kodály Emlékkönyv*, pp. 9 — 18.
    (3) *Älteste Musikstile u. Kulturschichten in Ozeanien u. Indonesien*, in *Zs. f. Ethnol.* vol. 77, 1952, pp. 198 — 213.
Densmore, Fr., (1) *Papago Music*, Washington 1929 (Smithsonian Inst. Bureau of Americ. Ethnol., Bulletin 90)
    (2) *Menominee Music*, Washington 1932 (*ibid.* Bull. 102)
Đorđević, V. R., *Srpske narodne melodije* (Serbian Folk Melodies), 2 vols., Skoplje 1928 — 1931.
van Duyse, Fl., *Het oude nederl. lied*, 3 vols and reg., 's-Gravenhage and Antwerpen 1903 — 1908.
Erk, L. and F. M. Böhme, *Deutscher Liederhort*. 3 vols., Leipzig 1893.
Estreicher, Z., (1) *Tanzgesänge d. Rentiereskimos*. Diss. Freiburg, Switzerland, 1946.

(2) *Teoria dwutonowych melodii* (The Theory of Two-Note Melodies), in *Kwartalnik muzyczny*, vol. xxi, 1948, pp. 208—233.

(3) *La musique des Esquimaux-Caribous*, in *Bull. de la Soc. Neuchâteloise de Géorg.* vol. 54, 1948, pp. 1—53.

(4) *Die Musik der Eskimos*, in *Anthropos*, vol. 45, 1950 pp. 659—720.

Fara, G., *L'anima della Sardegna*, in *La musica tradiz.* Udine [1940].

Felber, E. and B. Geiger, *Die ind. Musik der vedischen u. der klass. Zeit*, in *Sitzungsber. Ak. Wien*, phil.-hist. Kl. vol. 107/7, 1912.

in der Gand, Hanns, *Scelta di canzoni popolari ticinesi*, in *Schw. Arch. f. Volkskde*, vol. xxxii, 1933, pp. 193—248.

Gennrich, Fr., *Rondeaux, Virelais und Balladen. . .* vol. ii, Göttingen 1927.

Grove, *Dictionary of Music and Musicians*, 5th ed. 1954.

Hauffen, A., *Die Deutsche Sprachinsel Gottschee*, Graz 1895.

Hensel, Walther : *Finkensteiner Blätter*, vol. x, 1933.

von Hornbostel, E. M., (1) *Melodie und Skala*, in *Jb. Peters*, 1912, pp. 11—23.

(2) *Bemerkunger üb. einige Lieder aus Bougainville*, in E. Frizzi's *Ein Beitr. z. Ethnol. in Boug. u. Buka*, in *Baessler-Arch.* Suppl. vi, 1914, pp. 53—56.

(3) *Musik*, in G. Tessmann, *Die Pangwee*, vol. ii, Berlin 1914, pp. 320—357.

(4) *Musik der Makuschi, Taulipang u. Jekuana*, in Th. Koch—Grünberg's *Vom Roroima zum Orinoco*, vol. iii, Stuttgart 1923, pp. 397 *et seq.*

(5) *The Music of the Fuegians*, in *Ethnos*, 1948, pp. 61—102.

Jungbauer, G. and A. Horntrich, *Die Volkslieder der Sudetendeutschen*, Kassel [1938].

[Kodály Emlékkönyv] *Emlékkönyv Kodály Zoltán hatvanadik születésnapjára* (Treatises in Honour of Z. Kodály's Sixtieth Birthday), Budapest 1943.

Kolinski, M., *Die Musik der Primitivstämme auf Malakka u. ihre Beziehungen zur samoanischen Musik*, in *Anthropos*, vol. 25, 1930, pp. 585—648.

Kremenliev, B. A., *Bulg.—Macedon. Folk Music*, Univ. of Calif. Press 1952.

Kunst, Jaap, (1) *Music in Flores*, in *Internat. Arch. f. Ethnogr.* Suppl. 42, Leiden 1942.

(2) *Een en ander over de Muziek en den Dans op de Kei-Eilanden* Amsterdam 1945 (Koningl. Verrenig. "Ind. Instituut", Mededeling lxiv, Afd. Volkenkunde 18).

(3) *De inheemsche muziek en de zending*, Amsterdam 1947.

Kurosawa, Takatomo, *The Musical Bow of the Yunun Tribe in Formosa and Suggestions as to the Origin of the Pentatonic Scale*, Japanese Music Institute (no yr. and pl.)

Lach, Rob., *Gesänge russ. Kriegsgef.* 3 vols. in 4, 2 and 2 sect. in *Sitzungsber. Ak. Wien*, phil.-hist. Kl., 1914—1952.

Lachmann, R., *Die Musik aussereurop. Natur- u. Kulturvölker*, Potsdam [1929] (Bücken-Handbuch).

Launis, A., *Suomen kansan sävelmiä. Neljäs jakso: Runosävelmiä. I. Inkerin runosävelmät* (Finnish Folk Tunes. Fourth series : Runo Songs. I. Ingrian Songs), Helsinki 1910.

Leden, Chr., *Über die Musik der Smith Sund Eskimos u. ihre Verwandtschaft m. d. Musik d. amerik. Indianer*, Copenhagen 1952.

Loorits, O., *Volkslieder der Liven*, Tarttu 1936.

Maerker, Br., *Gregor. Gesang u. deutsches Volkslied, einander ergänzende Quellen unserer musikalischen Vor- u. Frühgeschichte*, in *Jb. f. Volksliedf.* vol. vii, 1941, pp. 71—127.

Mayer, F. A. and H. Rietsch, *Die Mondsee-Wiener Liederhs. u. der Mönch v. Salzburg*, Berlin 1896.

Metzger, W., *Psychologie*, Dresden and Leipzig 1941

Moser, H. J., *Tönende Volksaltertümer*, Berlin [1935].

Reinhard, K., *Die Musik de Lolo*, in *Baessler-Archiv* N. F. vol. iii, 1955, pp. 195—216.

Panóff, P., *Die altslav. Volks- u. Kirchenmusik*, Potsdam [1930] (Bücken Handbuch).
Riemann, H., *Folkloristische Tonalitätsstudien*, Leipzig 1916.
Rihtman, Cvjetko, *Polifoni oblici u narodnoj muzici Bosne i Hercegovine* (Polyphonic Forms in the Folk Music of Bosnia and Herzegovina), in *Bilten Instituta za Proucavanje Folklora u Sarajevo*, vol. i, 1951, pp. 7—20.
Rimsky-Korsakov, N. D., Сборник русских народных песен. 100 chants populaires russes, St. Petersburg and Paris [1882]
Sachs, C., *The Rise of Music in the Ancient World East and West*, New-York [1943]
Schneider, Marius, (1) *Ethnologische Musikforschung*, in *Lehrbuch d. Völkerkunde*, ed. by K. Th. Preuss, Stuttgart 1937, pp. 135—171.
(2) *Die musikalischen Beziehungen zw. Urkulturen, Altpflanzern u. Hirtenvölker*, in *Zs. f. Ethnol.* vol. 70, 1938, pp. 287—306.
(3) *Los cantos de lluvia en España*, in *Anuario musical*, vol. iv, 1949, pp. 3—55.
(4) *Cancionero pop. de la Prov. de Madrid*, vol. i, Barcelona and Madrid 1951.
(5) *Contribution a la musica indigena del Matto Grosso (Brasil)*, in *Anuario musical*, vol. vii, 1952, pp. 159—165. —
(6) *Musica filipina*, in *Anuario musical*, vol. vi, 1951, pp. 91—93.
Stoin, V., *Narodni pesni ot Timok do Vita* (Folk Songs from Timok till Vita), Sofia 1928.
Stumpf, C., (1) *Lieder der Bellakula-Indianer*, in *Sb. f. vgl. Mw.* vol. i, 1922, pp. 87—103.
(2) *Phonogr. Indianermelodien*, ibid. pp. 113—126.
(3) *Die Anfänge der Musik*, Leipzig 1911.
Sušil, Fr., *Moravské národni písně* (Moravian Folk Songs),Prag [1941].
Szabolcsi, B., (1) *A primitiv dallamosság: a hanglejtéstöl az ötfokúságig* (Primitive Melodics: from Intonation to Pentatony), in *Kodály Emlékkönyv*, pp.19—31.
(2) *Five-Tone Scales and Civilization*, in *Acta Musicologica*, vol. xv, 1943, pp. 24—34.
(3) *A melódia története* (The History of Melody), [Budapest 1950].
Tampere, H., (1) *Eesti rahvaviiside antologia* (Anthology of Estonian Folklore), I. Tarttu 1935.
(2) *Kuusalu vanad rahvalaulud* (Folk Songs), I. Tallin 1938.
Tirén, K., *Die lappische Volksmusik*, Stockholm [1942].
Väisänen, A. O., (1) *Wogul. u. ostjak. Melod.* in *Mém. de la Soc. finno-ougrienne*, 73, Helsinki 1937.
(2) *Mordwinische Melodien*, ibid. 92, Helsinki 1942.
Vetterl, K., *Lidové písne a tance z valašskokloboucka* (Folk Songs and Dances), I. Prag 1955.
Volkslieder mit ihren Melodien, Deutsche — ed. by *Dtsch. Volksliedarchiv*, Berlin and Leipzig 1935.
Volkslieder, Gottscheer — ed. as above 1930 (Landschaftl. Vldr Heft 24).
Werner, Heinz, *Die melodische Erfindung im frühen Kindesalter*, in *Sitzungsber. Ak. Wien*, phil.-hist. Kl. vol. 182/4, 1917.
Wertheimer, Max, *Musik der Wedda*, in *SIMG*, vol. xi, 1909/10, pp. 300—309.
Wiora, W., (1) *Zur Frühgeschichte d. Musik in den Alpenländern*, in *Schriften d. Schweiz. Ges. f. Volkskunde*, 32, Basel 1949.
(2) *Die vergleichende Frühgeschichte der europäischen Musik als methodische Forschung*, in *Kongr.-Ber.*, Basel 1949, pp. 212—221.
(3) *Der tonale Logos*, in *Musikforschung*, vol. iv, 1951, pp. 1—35, 153—175.
(4) *Europ. Volksgesang*, in *Das Musikwerk*, ed. by K. G. Fellerer, Cologne [1952].
(5) *Schrift u. Tradition als Quellen der Musikgeschichte*, in *Kongr.-Ber.*, Bamberg 1953, pp. 159—175.
Žganec, Vinko, *Narodne popjevke hrvatskog Zagorja napjevi* (Folk Songs from the Croatian Zagorje), in *Zbornik Jugoslav. Narodnih Popjevka*, Book 4.

LAJOS BÁRDOS

NATURAL TONAL SYSTEMS

In the course of investigating the primitive forms of folk music it has long been realized that, on the most diverse parts of the globe, the same or very closely related melodic elements can be found which seem to be completely independent of either race, age or place:

No. 1

a) Vedic melody

Felber K 60, p. 30   b) Hungarian   MI 918
etc,

c) Vogule   Väis. 92

d) Finnish   KI 7   e) Russian

Rimsky 46   f) Hungarian   MI 657

and so on, almost infinitely. We find major seconds and minor thirds, and also their sum, the perfect fourth, irrespective of their different functions in the tonal system. It is this fact we have in mind when we select the final G' to connect the melodies instead of grouping them according to their common stock of notes.

But *why* are the minor third and the whole tone the basic melodic elements?

They may be interpreted as the remnants of a common melodic property originating from times immemorial, as suggested, for instance, by the Chinese—Central-Asian—Hungarian relationships (see above examples *h* and *i*). But even if this were indeed the case, we could still ask *why* this common "legacy" is restricted to *these very* elements?

And how to account for its extraordinary persistence for survival? Or would it be proper to assume a causal genetic affinity between the musical instincts of an Indian woman of Brazil, a Gregorian chanter and a German child of our days?

No. 2

Would the overtones provide the answer? True enough, we may find the minor third (5 : 6) and the major second (8 : 9, 9 : 10) among them, but the ternion of the children's songs is too high and far in the range of the overtones (15 : 18 : 20) to suggest acoustical reasons for its predominant part in primitive melodies. If natural melodies were rooted in the overtones alone — as is, indeed, the development of the

European sense for harmony,[2] — leaps of octaves, fifths, fourths and major thirds should prevail. In reality, however, we find most frequently major seconds and minor thirds. But why?

These problems I have for several decades been endeavouring to solve. And I have found the answer in the course of a long roundabout train of thoughts.

The long roundabout. It is a well known fact that the simplest and clearest way of explaining pentatony is to denote it as a five-member sequence of fifths (marked hereunder as 5°):

No. 3

Similarly, diatony is to be regarded as a seven-member sequence of fifths:

No. 4

An idea inevitably suggests itself: what if we investigate the further part of the closed series of fifths?

Hexatony (6° system). The first to be investigated in this connection is the hexatony of fifths ranging between the five-note system (5°) and the seven-note system (7°). The notes in pentatony can be completed in two ways: by adding either the lower, or the higher fifth:

No. 5

In both cases we obtain the major hexachord, as well as an explanation as to the origin of the unusual popularity and naturalness of this group. It is obvious that six notes can in no other way enter into a more natural

---

[2] Cf. Sándor Kovács, *Zeneesztétikai problémák* (Aesthetical Problems in Music), Budapest 1911, p. 11 ff.

relationship, provided we assume the criterion of this relationship to be the perfect fifth acoustically regarded as a primary phenomenon. In children's songs the major hexachord[3] is, indeed, derived from pentatony under our very eyes:

No. 6

This conception is corroborated by the historical development of European composed music as well. It is the feeling for the hexachord that — between the primitive pentatonic strata of the Gregorian chants and the more developed seven-note diatonic melodies — gives rise to the greatest number of the most diverse *modal melodies:*

No. 7

---

[3] "Part of the hexachordal melodies seem to have come from pentatony...", "... the note *fa* in our hexachordal melodies may be a late newcomer." Kodály, *Die ungarische Volksmusik*, Budapest 1956, p. 81.

210

This fact is reflected in the old theory of music as well. For a considerable length of time musical thinking moved in hexachords, and not along octave scales. Even as late as the age of harmonic-functional diatony interwoven with chromatics, the "closest related six notes" still formed a compact group. Eight out of the 24 major fugues of Bach's *Well-Tempered Clavier, i. e.* exactly a third of the total, have major hexachord themes. (It should be noted that both volumes begin with a fugue of this type).

The major hexachord, as an independent and complete tonal system, involves much more than a six-note major scale ; it has a highly variable tonal stock yielding the most diverse types of melodies according to modality, principal notes, a compass and final note (see also Ex. no. 7)

No. 8

We rarely realize that this series of notes has inversions as well which can be regarded as different modes or different "sections" of the 6° system :

No. 9

Diatony (7° system). It is a common occurrence both in Gregorian music and in the Palestrina style (where the hexachord theme is followed by a fifth-answer in another key) that while the basic musical theme is still maintained in the 6° system, the juxtaposition of two hexachords related by fifths produces full diatony. Thus, we are, so to say, half way between the 6° and 7° systems as can frequently be seen in Hungarian folk songs, even in those of the latest style :

No. 10

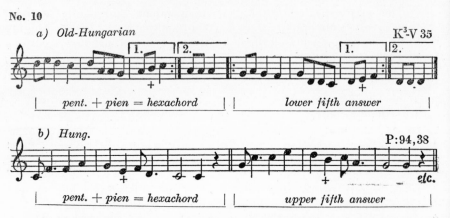

The "growth-rings" can readily be detected : the basic theme, the first line of melody essentially comprises five notes which completed by a *pien*-tone produce hexatony. The complete seven-note scale is obtained only by the *addition* of the lines. Consequently the stock of notes is the following :

No. 11

$$
\left.\begin{array}{l}
\boxed{\text{F} \mid \text{C} \mid \text{G} \mid \text{D} \mid \text{A} \mid +\text{E}} \quad 5^\circ + 1 = 6^\circ \\
\boxed{\text{C} \mid \text{G} \mid \text{D} \mid \text{A} \mid \text{E} \mid +\text{B}} \quad 5^\circ + 1 = 6^\circ
\end{array}\right\} = \boxed{\text{F} \mid \text{C} \mid \text{G} \mid \text{D} \mid \text{A} \mid \text{E} \mid \text{B}} \; 7^\circ
$$

Genuine diatony is obtained only when both *pien*-tones *(fa, ti)* are well established.

Ultradiatony. The investigation of hexatony leads to the recognition of the fact that pentatony, hexachord, and diatony represent originally successive phases in the development of the tonal stock. And we may inquire whether this will be the trend in further development as well.

Octatony (8° system). Theoretically the next step can be made in two ways again :

No. 12

ta

D i a t o n y

fi

Indeed the most natural eight-note scale is obtained by adding *ta* (B♭) or *fi* (F♯) to a diatony. *All* of the eight-note melodies of the Gregorian chant,[4] still in use, belong to this type (according to traditions they are always denoted by B♭—F—C—G—D—A—E—B). The same phenomenon is to be observed in Hungarian folk songs. When a diatonic melody is coloured by an eighth note, this is in most cases either *ta* or *fi*. Since this octatony of fifths can be considered a sum of two diatonic systems related by fifths, the notes in such melodies will consist of two coupled diatonic modes related by fifths. Instead of the many examples at our disposal, only a few characteristic types are given hereunder. For the sake of better illustration, they are quoted in the Gregorian B—B♭ system :

No. 13

a) Lydian + Major — K³-V 254

b) Major + Mixolydian — P: 94,5

c) Mixolydian + Dorian — K³-V 21

d) Dorian + Aeolian — MI 849

[4] If in the course of time further alterations cropped up in the plainsong, it is characteristic that they have always been reduced to the eight-note system by a common sense for tonality. The theory of fifths as applied in our investigations does not claim to be suitable for explaining *every* possible musical phenomenon but can be used to account for the most general and most natural ones.

213

e) *Aeolian + Phrygian*

Since we have, so far, found no Hungarian example[5] for the coupling of the Phrygian and Locrian modes, let a Gregorian melody illustrate it:

No. 14

The feeling of the octatony can, however, be traced not only in the succession of notes, *i. e.* in melody, but also in their simultaneity, *i. e.* in harmony. When the *organum in fifths* is built upon a diatonic melody, the fifths sung in accompaniment complete the stock by the fifth of *ti*, *i. e.* by *fi* to form an eight-note scale. This form still survives in the folkloric duets of Iceland:

No. 15

Enneatony (9° system). The development outlined so far follows a straight line. If B and B♭ of the basic melody alternate, the octatony described above turns into a nine-note series by means of the answer in fifth.

No. 16

---

[5] The only melody of this type (BNJ. p. 318) so far registered has come from an error committed by the singer: the last line of the melody came off one fifth higher. This is another proof of the priority of the fifth. Why does not a folk song singer slide away a semitone and why does he not switch over into a key related to the original one by a third?

Is it a mere coincidence that this type is so common among the nine-note Hungarian folk songs? Although these altered notes do have different tonal functions, they can readily be recorded with the nine-note stock B♭—F—C—G—D—A—E—B—F♯:

No. 17

Hungarian

Decatony (10° system). In medieval organums the tenth member of the column of fifths appears sporadically at first, then more and more frequently either as an E♭[6] (the upper fourth or lower fifth of B♭) or as C.[7] (as a consonant of F♯). Hungarian folk songs, preferring in their basic construction even nowadays five-, six-, and seven-note systems, do not reach this degree as a rule. Nevertheless, the above type is the most common among the few melodies known so far.

---

[6] Husman, *Die drei- und vierstimmige Notre Dame Organa*, Leipzig 1940, pp. 20 and 25.

[7] Husman, *op. cit.* note on p. 104.

No. 18

Hungarian

K³-V 262

The modal structure of this melody could be explained in two ways :

o. 19

Dorian : fa · do · so · re · la · mi · ti · ♯fi · ♯di · ♯si
Aeolian : do · so · re · la · mi · ti · ♯fi · ♯di · ♯si · ♯ri

Hendecatony (11° system). This is another important step in the development of our composed music. Palestrina's whole musical realm is based on a closed eleven-note system.[8]

No. 20

Function	♭ ta	fa	do	so	re	la	mi	ti	♯ fi	♮ di	♯ si
in the basic keys	B♭	F	C	G	D	A	E	B	F♯	C♯	G♯
transposed (1♭)	E♭	B♭	F	C	G	D	A	E	B	F♯	C♯

Hungarian folk songs do not go as far as that, except for one or two extremely intricate melodies :[9]

---

[8] Neither single *ma* (E♭) nor *ri* (D♯) causes any break in the entity and completeness of the style. See Jeppesen, *Des Palestrinastil und die Dissonanz,* Leipzig 1925, p. 23.

[9] Indebted to Béla Avasi.

No. 21

Hungarian

Muz. F. 145c

The stock of notes of this melody corresponds exactly to that of Palestrina's (transposed Dorian):

No. 22

Dorian:	ta	fa	do	so	<u>re</u>	la	mi	ti	fi	di	si
Aeolian:	fa	do	so	re	<u>la</u>	mi	ti	fi	di	si	ri

Dodecatony[10] *and Polytony.* Though the series of fifths was expanded with extraordinary audacity by Cipriano de Rore, Gesualdo, Monteverdi, and others, the prevailing "natural" musical feeling was definitely unable to perform a *saltus in natura* of this size. The basic musical feeling still preferred diatony for a long time to come, and the use of chromatics remained rather restricted. — Then the introduction of equal temperament opened up almost unlimited possibilities for enriching the stock of notes. The written notes in the *Well-Tempered Clavier* covers a series of fifths consisting of as many as 28 (!) members:

No. 23

[10] The main theme of Kodály's *Dances from Marosszék* is a twelve-note folk tune. It is not a vocal but an instrumental melody.

217

Nevertheless, — disregarding the changing notes — even the great Vienna classics, as a rule, confined themselves, in constructing their harmonies, to applying a functional fifteen-note system adding to diatony four members upwards and four members downwards:

No. 24

in C major

15°

The discovery of *sa* (G♭) and *li* (A♯) and of many others was a case for the Romanticists like Chopin, Liszt, and Wagner, and was later followed by the total dissolution of the crystal of fifths in the dodecaphony of Schönberg and others.

The great disappointment. Having found the stock of notes to have developed by the addition of fifths from pentatony into polytony both in European music and in Hungarian folk song (and certainly in other areas as well), we felt tempted to account for the prepentatonic or infrapentatonic phenomena by including them in this logical sequence. For the monotonous recitation and the first four phases our working hypothesis has yielded the following patterns:

No. 25

And here our labouriously constructed and seemingly flawless castle of fifths was suddenly shaken to its very foundation. The facts contradicted the theory.

Infrapentatony. Though perfect fourths can often be heard in two-note singsongs and folk song lines:

No. 26

218

the fifth, which can be regarded acoustically as primary, is astonishingly rare:

No. 27

In the available two-note material, instead of the above-mentioned intervals[11], it is the major second that prevails :

No. 28

as well as the minor third :

No. 29

[11] These statements are based upon the investigations of some 10,500 melodies. Valuable assistance was rendered by my pupils, Mária Katanics, Lajos Munkácsy and Margit Tóth in the investigation of the Gregorian melodies of the *Liber Usualis.*

Though among the three-note systems the tritony of fifths (3° system) is more frequent:

No. 30

even its inversion :

No. 31

and the perfect fourth construction also occurs, though less often :

No. 32

Yet, the dominating types are not these but the "ternion of children's songs", specified in the introduction (see nos. 1 and 2), and its reflection, the "psalmodic ternion":

No. 33

as well as the ancient recitative trichord:

No. 34

a) *Greg. (Gloria VII)*   LU p.35

b) *Hung. Children's Song*   MI. 92   c) *Hung.*   MI

d) *Hung.*

Járdányi 9   e) *Vogule*   Väis. 24

f) *Icelandic*   Leifs 7

g) *Rumanian*   B:RC 18

h) *Armenian*   A:Enf. p.23

Quintal tetratony (4° system) occurs quite frequently in four-note melodies:

No. 35

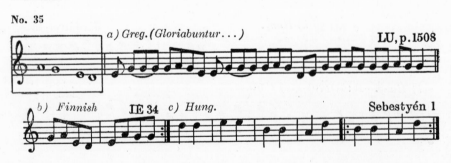

a) *Greg. (Gloriabuntur . . .)*   LU, p.1508

b) *Finnish*   IE 34   c) *Hung.*   Sebestyén 1

224

we come across even its inversions:

No. 36

nevertheless the recitative quaternion is equally frequent, if not more so :

No. 37

and here we have its symmetrical reflection, the quaternion of overtones which can still be accounted for by acoustical reasons

No. 38

as well as in inverted and extended form:

No. 39

How, then, are all these phenomena to be explained?

Why can everything *above* pentatony be so readily adapted to the law of fifths, to the Chinese *Lü* and why do all *infra*pentatonic phenomena escape it?

Let us investigate the common features of the most frequent types, and in what respect they differ from the closed fifth-groups:

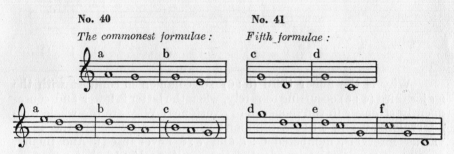

It is obvious that those having a *narrower compass* seem to be prior to the others and more natural.

Further problems. If, in this primitive stage the melody is determined by some *parlando*-like ambit and not by the acoustical relationship of the fifths, why is the trichord *do-re-mi* less frequent than the combination of the major second and the minor third (see nos. 1, 2, and 33) having a wider ambit?

In any case we must return to the starting point in this labyrinth of problems and ask: why have exactly the major second and the minor third become the commonest elements of melody formation when the *semitone* shows a much closer relationship to speech-like intonation? Why are the children's songs like the first variant in no. 42, and why are they not like the second?

No. 42

Further questions are met with: why do we never come across any other interval than those in our present tonal system? Why does not our musical instinct divide the octave into, say, seven, ten or seventeen intervals? Or should we still find the answer in the harmonics after all? But if so, why are, for instance, the 7th, 11th, and 13th notes "ekmelodic", *i. e.* excluded from the melody?

No. 43

Why is the minor third (5 : 6) so common in contrast with the major third (4 : 5) occurring so rarely, when the latter is lower and consequently stronger in the sequence of overtones? Why are the whole-tone intervals 8 : 9 and 9 : 10 a common occurrence and why are the anonymous intervals, numbered 6 : 7 and 7 : 8 never used? And finally, why have we completely adopted the semitone 15 : 16, but never assimilated the intervals 10 : 11, 11 : 12, 12 : 13, and 13 : 14? Last but not least, how do we account for the mysterious tenacity of the acoustically completely alien *la* in such formulae as these:

No. 44

Anyhow, why do we have to introduce two contradictory principles for explaining the evolution of the poorer and richer formulae: the (semitonic) *proximity* of notes in case of the 2—3—4-note melodies and the (quintal) *affinity* of notes in the 5—6—7-etc. note systems?

On the way to solution. Weighing the discrepancies of the aforesaid two principles, it suddenly occurred to me that intervals could be considered on the basis of *both* principles: to what extent does the given interval satisfy the requirements of both the semitonic proximity (S) and the quintal affinity (Q)[12]

---

[12] It is to be noted that these are intervals that form the fundamental elements of functional harmony: B—C leading-note step (S = melodic attraction) above the bass G—C (Q = harmonic attraction).

The figures above the notes indicate the smallest number of quintal steps needed to reach the required interval. These intervals occur but once on the corresponding *continua* of fifths, and can, therefore, be considered determinants and characteristic of the system in question.

230

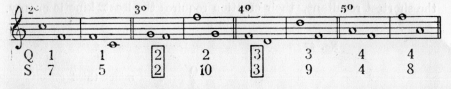

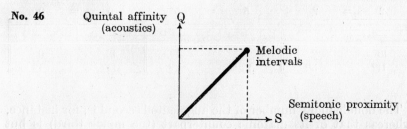

What else could better account for the obvious naturalness of the whole tone and of the minor third than the fact that by adding up their index numbers in *both* dimensions we obtain the smallest total (2,2 and 3,3)!

Consequently the selection of the intervals used in melodies seems to be governed by two factors: the *quintal affinity*[13] rooted in nature and the *semitonic proximity* derived from the intonation in speech. The actually sung common interval is thus the resultant of the two aforementioned forces

No. 46

[13] One may object to this by saying that if all intervals are deduced merely from perfect fifths, the index numbers display rather unnatural dissonances. If, for instance, the major third were to be derived from four acoustically perfect fifths, the Pythagorean interval 64 : 81 would be obtained, whereas the natural acoustic major third has the simple ratio of 64 : 80, *i. e.* 4 : 5. In this case harmonic notes are likely to play a part. It is a well-known fact that our hearing is inclined to rectify minor distunings and is able to substitute the next consonance. Without possessing an ability like this, even the tempered fifths of the pianoforte would be unbearable.

Since of all intervals the major second and the minor third have the shortest resultant, their creation requires the least kinetic energy.

No. 47

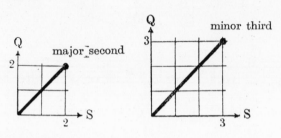

This would explain the fact why the intonation of the ultradiatonic intervals (those in systems consisting of more than seven notes) is so much more difficult than that of the enharmonic corresponding intervals in the diatonic range:

No. 48

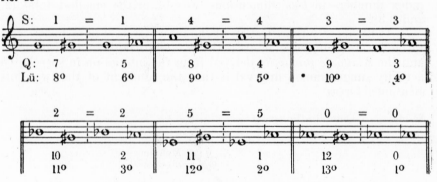

The double index number of the augmented second is, for instance, 9,3 whereas that of its diatonic counterpart (the minor third) is but 3,3, etc. These considerations clearly explain why the enharmonic change A♭—G♯ is so alien to the *a cappella* style: our sense of tonality must make a *salto mortale* of twelve fifths which can rarely be performed without a "fracture" in the intonation.

Let us now apply this new interpretation to the possible elementary ternions. The intervals of two and three semitones respectively can be arranged in four different ways (on the symmetry axis D):

232

No. 49

Q S: 2 2   2 3   3 2   3 3

Another disappointment. Our train of thoughts seems to show another gap here. If the theory of "two forces — one resultant" were correct, the above sequence would show the frequency of occurrence as well, for it is the trichord $do — re — mi$ that has the lowest QS index number $(2 + 2 = 4)$. Nevertheless the most common are the figures 49b and c. Where is the snag?

The solution. It gave me plenty of difficulty to find out the mistake. The point is that in the meantime, we deserted the starting theory, our set of fifths, the $L\ddot{u}$. It is insufficient to investigate the intervals of a melody by themselves, (this would be an inorganic study of intervals), the melody must be examined in its entirety (organic study of melodies). Let us first state the extent of the series of fifths ($L°$) represented by the complete stock of notes. :

No. 50

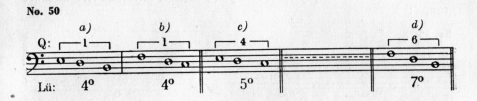

Thus everything will find its proper place. The notes in 50a and b fit into the 4° system whereas for the recitative trichord a 5° L system is required. In fact, should we neglect the $L\ddot{u}$ mesure, the perfect fourth $(1,5)$ and the semitone $(5,1)$ would obtain the same "index of naturalness":

No. 51

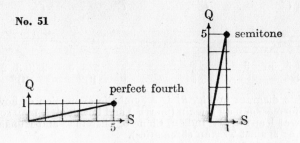

though the fourth is obviously much more elementary than the more differentiated minor second. The difference is revealed by the quintal index: for a fourth a 2° system is sufficient, whereas a semitone calls for a sense of the 6° system.[14]

Let us see whether our threefold index will stand the further tests.

Out of the specified elements eight types of quaternions can be formed. Let them be classified according to *Lü* :

No. 52

The tritone under *e* may well have a closed ambit (2, 2, 2) but it requires a highly developed sense of 7° and appears indeed embedded only in seven- or more-note systems (Gregorian chant, Slovak folk music) since it has neither perfect fourth nor perfect fifth support to rely on. The line begins with the formulae having the narrowest compass (QS = = 2 + 2 + 3 = 7) within the smallest Lü-index (4°, 5°).

Our two elementary intervals yield sixteen different five-member groups :

No. 53

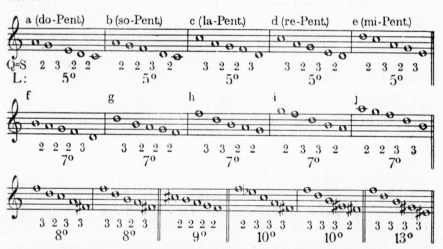

---

[14] The diagram in Fig. 51 is a symbolic expression of how close to earth a musical formation may remain (fourths) and how high it may soar up to human heights (great leaps in the Indian, Chinese, Cheremiss and Hungarian pentatonic folk songs as against Tristan chromatics).

234

It is quite natural that the dominating formulae among the different types of melodies will be those having the smallest L index number and possessing the most modest QS index number[15].

Let us experiment with other intervals too. Here are some trichord formations :

No. 54

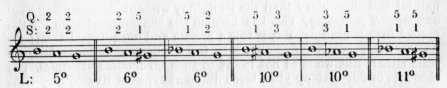

	Q. 2 2	2 5	5 2	5 3	3 5	5 5
	S: 2 2	2 1	1 2	1 3	3 1	1 1

L: 5°   6°   6°   10°   10°   11°

Multimembered formations are to be investigated by measuring all the possible intervals in them, for the melodies belonging to the given system may, in principle, cause any two members of the stock to form relevant intervals. Thus the latent, potential harmonic elements of the stock are taken for a starting point in performing the measurements. For the sake of illustration let us compare an unusual East-European anhemitonic pentatony :

No. 55

Moravian   Janáček 7

with the *so*-pentatony and with its *quasi minore* variant, a wellknown Japanese scale :

No. 56

Pentatony   *All intervals*

	Q: 2	4	1	3	2	1	1	3	1	2	$=\frac{20}{46}$ 5°
	S: 2	4	7	9	2	5	7	3	5	2	

Japan. "Kumoi"

	Q: 5	3	1	4	2	6	1	4	1	5	$=\frac{32}{46}$ 7°
	S: 1	3	7	8	2	6	7	4	5	1	

[15] It is remarkable how characteristic the remotest formations $(k - p)$ are of Béla Bartók's music. To the very important discoveries mades by Ernő Lendvai (*Bartók stilusa* [Bartók's Style], Budapest 1955) we may add that Bartók seems to have drawn the remotest and final consequences from the original elements of folk music by having applied such far-fetched fifth-groups.

| Q: | 5 | 10 | 6 | 4 | 5 | 1 | 1 | | 4 | 6 | 2 | $=\frac{44}{42}$ |
| S: | 1 | 2 | 6 | 8 | 1 | 5 | 7 | | 4 | 6 | 2 | |

The threefold indexes point to the fact that systems, in which a more important part is played by the semitone step, seem to be less natural and elementary than the pentatony without semitone. — *"The"* *anhemitonic pentatony?* This has become the conventional term for the perfect-fifth-pentatony. But is this a precise and unequivocal term? By no means. There is no semitone in the Siamese pentatonic distance scale either. But we need not resort to such far-fetched examples. The elements of our diatony yield three different types of five-note systems (naturally each having five modes)[16].

No. 57

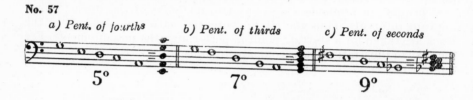

a) *Pent. of fourths*   b) *Pent. of thirds*   c) *Pent. of seconds*

5°   7°   9°

We may find a few sporadic examples to illustrate type 57*b* :

No. 58

Anhemitonic pentatony of thirds:

a) *Hebrew (Djerba)*

Lachmann 2, p. 109   b) *Rumanian*

B: Bihar 6

---

[16] A peculiar arrangement. Each system can be illustrated as a homogenous set of fourths, thirds, or seconds. Diatony has, in fact, no other intervals than these, let alone the prime, of course. The fifth, sixth and seventh are but their inversions, while the ninth, tenth, etc. are to be considered their extensions.

but type 57c has so far not been registered in folk music. Here again the system of fifths proves very instructive:

No. 59

		C	G	D	A	E		
a)		C	G	D	A	E		
b)	F	—	G	D	A	—	B	
c)	B♭	—	C	—	D	—	E	—	F♯

Although whole-tone pentatony would best meet the requirements of speech-like tonal proximity, it could by no means suit the requirements of naturalness because it is a system with scattered constituents and therefore inorganic.

No. 60

Collation of melodies. Our QSL system enables us to compare longer melodies as well, provided we measure all the intervals of a melody, neglecting, of course, the repetitions of notes (perfect primes) and the dead intervals of the caesurae. Let us test the method with a well-known parallelism in Bartók's treatise[17] between a Hungarian and a Ruthenian melody adding a remarkably analogous Icelandic tune (see no. 60).

Melody	Q total	S total	Average	Q	S	L[18]
60a	43	57	(:19)	2,2	3	4°
60b	45	59	(:18)	2,4	3,1	6°
60c	64	80	(:20)	3,2	4	7°

This is what Zoltán Kodály says of the connection between the Hungarian and the Ruthenian melodies: "It is impossible to believe the Ruthenian to be the original and the Hungarian to have been borrowed. It is much more probable that the Hungarian melody is the original : it has more vitality, sharper contoures, a structure of perfect fifths and an almost pure pentatony with a single unstressed *pien*-tone"[19].

Our threefold index raises the probability to the rank of mathematical-physical certainty. And if we feel the Icelandic melody to be less natural, our feeling is justified by the higher index numbers.

The solution of the problems. The method of the three-dimensional QSL measurement explains quite a number of questions :

A) Why does the "natural" sense for melody reject the ekmelodic intervals? The answer is : because these (for instance : G-i, i-C, F-k, etc., see no. 43.) are inaccessible by means of building up the column of fifths.

B) Why is the fifth-repercussion less common among two-note melodies than the fourth when both of these intervals are equally characterized by a first-grade quintal relation? The answer is : because under equal Q conditions the decisive factor is the S index : the ambit of the fifth covers seven semitones, whereas that of the fourth includes only five.

C) Why is the D—G—C' type (fourth above fourth, see example 32) less common among the 3° formation than G—C'—D'(wholetone above fourth, see example 30) or its reflection, the C—D—G (fourth above whole tone, see example 31)? The answer is : because, though all of them are three-note quintal formations, the ambit of the latter two is only a fifth, whereas that of the fourth-above-fourth is a seventh, *i. e.* ten semitones.

---

[17] Bartók, *Népzenénk és a szomszéd népek zenéje* (Our Folk Music and the Folk Music of our Neighbours), nos. 64a and 64b.
[18] The last figure is the index number of the basic motive (the first bar) of the melody in question.
[19] Z. Kodály, *A magyar népzene* (Hungarian Folk Music), Budapest 1952, p. 43.

D) Which is the mysterious factor that causes so many melodies of the *do-re-mi* or *do-re-mi-so* type to end in *la,* even if the latter does not appear in the melody before the final note!

No. 61

This minor keynote is completely alien to the harmonic system represented by the other notes (see also Ex. no. 43). Investigating the relationship of this acoustically alien *la* to the other notes of the melodies :

No. 62

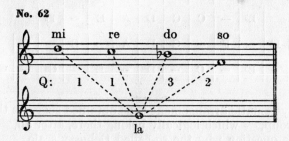

we will find that this *la* is in the closest quintal relation with *all* constituting notes taken collectively. The appearance of this final note is obviously facilitated by the descent at the end of the phrase, *i. e.* by the "cadence". Thus the quintal affinity and the speech-like character gain the upperhand over the range of overtones.

E) Why is the historical development of melody above the hexachord governed by the sole principle of adding up the fifths and why can all phenomena in this realm be readily interpreted without recurring to what we may call a second dimension, the narrow ambit of speech? The answer is : because in the six- and seven-note formations the notes are close enough to each other to keep the S index numbers low.

F) Why is diatony the most natural among the seven-note systems when the elements of diatony (two semitones and five whole tones) permit to construct two additional systems?[20]

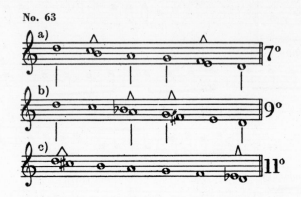

No. 63

The closeness or the dispersion of the elements in the Q structure are in direct ratio to the naturalness of these groups of notes :

No. 64

			F	C	G	D	A	E	B		
		B♭	—	C	G	D	A	E	—	F♯	
	E♭	—	F	—	G	D	A	—	B	—	C♯
A♭	—	B♭	—	C	—	D	—	E	—	G♯	—	G♯

If the systematic arrangement thus obtained suggests the addition of a fourth group, — which logically belong there, after all, — we get an answer to the question why the so-called Debussy scale

No. 65

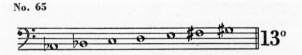

[20] With seven modes each. See *Énekszó*, Budapest, vol. viii/5, 1940—1941, p. 817.

240

is so far from being natural: not a single perfect fifth can be found in it. (This phenomemon is analogous with whole-tone pentatony; see Ex. nos. 57e and 59c.)

G) Why is pentatony in folk music completed to a seven-note system in three ways only, when in principle there is a fourth possibility too?

No. 66

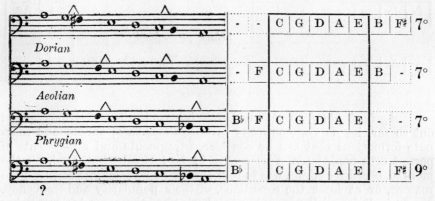

The answer is obvious: the closed 7° stocks are more natural than discontinuous systems full of gaps (cf. also nos 63c, 64c).

H) Why is the minor hexachord less frequent than the major hexachord, when the former has a narrower ambit?

No. 67

The answer is: because the closed 6° system is more natural than the discontinuous 7° system.

I) Why are the major and minor pentachords also rather common beside pentatony? The answer is: though the major and minor pentachords are characterized by a high *Lü* index number (6°), this is counterbalanced by the fuller and closer speech-like ambit. Yet the fact that pentatony is more general all over the world is a proof of the primary importance of the quintal index.

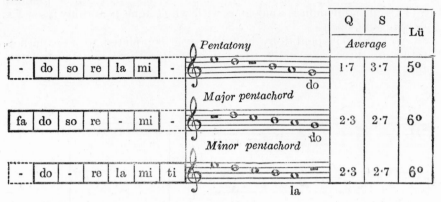

	Q	S	Lü
	Average		
Pentatony — do so re la mi — do	1·7	3·7	5°
Major pentachord — fa do so re - mi — do	2·3	2·7	6°
Minor pentachord — do - re la mi ti — la	2·3	2·7	6°

Again about infrapentatony. On the basis of the investigations carried out so far, let us systematically arrange those two-, three-, and four-note formations that can be considered fragments and antecedents of perfect-fifth pentatony. This seems to be logically indicated, all the more so, because our aim was to find out their characteristic features, the reasons, or at least the conditions, of their popularity and frequency. No. 69 includes all the possible pentatonic two-, three-, and four-member groups, and their quintal structure, their possible transpositions within pentatony, it interprets their place within the system by means of relative solmization and above all their index number in the system of fifths (Q), in the system of semitones (S), and their degrees in the set of fifths (L). Their inversions and their transpositions in octaves as well as their extentions beyond the octave have been omitted since they do not affect the Q and L values. (We tentatively suggest a terminology covering formations hitherto unnamed).

This conception as expounded above does not claim to solve all musicological problems which have arisen in folk music. Yet we tried to throw light upon, and to interpret systematically, some of the commonest features of musical manifestations the world over. We have perhaps found some *common* principles that underlie the most diverse and heterogenous melodic phenomena such as the primitive melodies consisting of but a limited number of notes, pentatony, hexachordic melodies, and diatony, Gregorian octatony, the stock of notes in Palestrina's works up to Liszt's and Debussy's systems. On the other hand, the fundamental principles here deviced may prove productive in further research for solving problems and answering questions as for instance: why have so many different styles of melodies formed within one and the same system, say pentatony, and why is *do* pentatony preferred in certain regions, as are the *la* or *so* final notes in others? Why do we find in some areas a trend toward pentatony and why do others have a preference for

	Lü	do	so	re	la	mi	Infrapentatonic groups	Q	S	L
Duals	B♭	F, F	C, C	G	G	D	**I.a.** Perfect fourth (= fifth)	1	5	2°
	B♭	—, F	C, C	G, —		D	**b.** Major second (= Minor seventh)	2	2	3°
	B♭	—, F			G	D	**c.** Minor third (= Major sixth)	3	3	4°
	B♭					D	**d.** Major third (= Minor sixth)	4	4	5°
Ternions	B♭	F, F	C, C, C	G, G		D	**II.a.** Quintal tritony	$1\frac{1}{3}$	$4\frac{2}{3}$	3°
	B♭	F, F	C	G, —		D	**b.** Psalmodic ternion	2	$3\frac{1}{3}$	4°
	B♭	—, F	C	G, G		D	**c.** Ternion of children's songs	2	$3\frac{1}{3}$	4°
	B♭	F				D	**d.** Major triad	$2\frac{2}{3}$	$4\frac{2}{3}$	5°
	B♭	—	C			D	**e.** Recitative trichord	$2\frac{2}{3}$	$2\frac{2}{3}$	5°
	B♭			G		D	**f.** Minor triad	$2\frac{2}{3}$	$4\frac{2}{3}$	5°
Quaternions	B♭	F, F	C, C	G, G		D	**III.a.** Quintal tetratony	$1\frac{2}{3}$	4	4°
	B♭	F	C	—		D	**b.** Quaternion of overtones	$2\frac{1}{6}$	$3\frac{5}{6}$	5°
	B♭	—	C	G		D	**c.** Recitative quaternion	$2\frac{1}{6}$	$3\frac{5}{6}$	5°
	B♭	F	—	G		D	**d.** Harmonic quaternion	4	4	5°

16*

pentachord? How to explain the fact that in certain cultural communities — as for instance, in Indian-Persian-Arabic-Balkan music characterized by augmented seconds — the prevailing formations are not those that have proved to be most natural, etc.?

Summing up

As soon as the melodiousness detaches itself from speech-like sliding of the voice *(vox continua)* and reaches the realm of distinctly regulated pitches *(vox concreta)*, two forces seem to become active:

a) the acoustic sense for the fifths selects from the speech-like *vox continua* the notes closest related to one another by the fifths; and

b) the sense for speech-like intonation selects, in turn, from this screen of fifths the elements that best suit it: whole tone, minor third, and, only in the third place, the perfect fourth;

c) however, the notes obtained in this way will not become a loose heap of notes, but will be connected by musical feeling into more or less closed tonal systems;

d) beside these fundamental trends, the range of overtones — apart from the primary fifth — seems to play a less important role. (For instance, the predominance of the major ternion and of the major pentachord over their minor variants showing the same QSL indexes; and the correction of the Pythagorean major third into a natural interval; etc.).

For measuring and comparing stocks of notes, intervals and melodies it seems best to use the method of measuring the distances between notes by such units as the perfect fifth and fourth, respectively, (Q), and by semitones (S). The procedure includes the following steps:

a) in abstract formations (such as tonal systems; tonal stocks) each member shall be related to the other and the Q and S distances of every potential interval between them shall be measured (see no. 56);

b) the same procedure is to be followed in the case of concrete melodies: each step of the melody shall be measured (except for repetitions and dead intervals; see no. 60);

c) in both cases the sums of Q and S shall be divided by the number of factors and the average of the latter computed. Apart from the average figures it shall be established, of how many members the set of perfect fifths should consist in order to include the complete melodic formation. The smaller this combined QSL index turns out to be, the more common and the more natural the given group of musical notes will be.

Thus the instinctive and natural melodics proves to be the common product of the acoustic relation by fifths and of the speech-like semitonic proximity, that is, of Nature and Man.

And how could it be otherwise?

244

REFERENCES

A : Appr = Arma, Paul, *Chantons pour apprendre le français*, Budapest 1949.

A : Enf = Arma, Paul, *Si tous les enfants de la terre mêlaient leurs voix...* Paris 1948.

A : Eur = Arma, Paul, *Chantons les vieilles chansons d'Europe*, Paris 1946.

B = Bartók Béla, *A magyar népdal* (The Hungarian Folk Song), Budapest 1924.

B : Bihar — Bartók Béla, *Cântece poporale românești din comitatul Bihor* (Rumanian Folk Airs from County Bihor), București 1913.

B : Gy = Bartók Béla, *Népzenénk és a szomszéd népek népzenéje* (Our Folk Music and that of the Neighbouring Peoples), Budapest 1934, in German : Berlin 1935, *Ung. Jahrb.* vol. xv, 2—3.

B : RC = Bartók Béla, *Melodien der rumänischen Colinde*, Wien 1935.

BK = Bartók & Kodály, *Erdélyi magyarság*, *Népdalok* (Hungarians of Transylvania, Folk Songs), Budapest 1921.

Bálint Sándor, *Szeged népe* (The people of Szeged), Szeged 1933.

BNJ = Berze Nagy János, *Baranyai magyar néphagyományok* (Folk Traditions in County Baranya), Pécs 1940.

Botsford Collection of Folk Songs, New York 1931.

Breazul, G., *Die Musikerziehung in Rumänien*, București 1936.

Car = Caranica, Ioan, *130 de melodii populare aromânești* (One Hundred and Thirty Arumanian Folk Songs), București 1937.

Curtis, N., *The Indian's Book*, 1923.

D : 96 = Domokos Pál Péter, *96 csángómagyar népdal* (Ninty-six Csángó-Hungarian Folk Songs), Budapest 1953.

Fabó Bertalan, *A magyar népdal zenei fejlődése* (The Musical Evolution of the Hungarian Folk Song), Budapest 1908.

Felber, E., *Die indische Musik der vedischen und der klassischen Zeit* in *Sitzungsberichte d. Akad. d. Wiss.*, Wien 1912.

H—CH = Haslund & Christensen, *Zajagan, Menschen und Götter in der Mongolei*, Stuttgart 1940?

HS = Bárdos Lajos & Kertész Gyula, *Harmonia Sacra*, Budapest 1934.

Janáček, Leoš, *Moravská lidova poesie v písních* (Moravian Folk Poetry in Songs), Praha, 1947.

Járdányi Pál, *A kidei magyarság világi zenéje* (Hungarian Secular Music in Kide), Kolozsvár 1943.

K : Bic = Kodály Zoltán, *Bicinia Hungarica* vols. i—iv, Budapest 1941—42.

K : 5 = Kodály Zoltán, *Ötfokú zene I—IV* (Pentatonic Music, vols. i—iv), Budapest 1943—47.

K I II = Kodály Zoltán, *Iskolai énekgyűjtemény I—II* (Collection of Songs for Schools, vols. i—ii), Budapest 1943—44.

K³-V = Kodály Zoltán, *A magyar népzene* (Hungarian Folk Music), 3rd ed., Budapest 1952. Melodies compiled by L. Vargyas.

K 60 = Gunda Béla, *Emlékkönyv Kodály Zoltán 60. születésnapjára* (Treatises in Honour of the 60th Birthday of Z. Kodály), Budapest 1943.

K 70 = Szabolcsi Bence & Bartha Dénes, *Emlékkönyv Kodály Zoltán 70. születésnapjára* (Treatises in Honour of the 70th Birthday of Z. Kodály), Budapest 1953.

KG : Orm = Kiss Géza, *Ormányság* (The Region Ormányság), Budapest 1937.

KL : LL = Kiss Lajos, *A Lengyel László játék* (The Play Lengyel László), see. K 70, p. 373.

KL : 108 = Kiss Lajos, *108 magyar népdal* (Hundred-and-eight Hungarian Folk Songs), Budapest 1943.

K-Sz = Káldi László & Szabolcsi Bence, *Daloskönyv* (Book of Songs), Budapest 1942

Kishonti Barna & Bárdos Lajos, *Száll az ének I—IV* (Singing Songs, vols. i—iv), Budapest 1939—42.

Lach, Robert, *Die Musik der Natur- und orientalischen Kulturvölker*, see in G. Adler, *Handbuch der Musikgeschichte*, 1924.

Lachmann, Robert, *Musik der aussereuropäischen Völker*, see in Bücken, *Handbuch der Musikwissenschaft*, Wildpark, Potsdam 1928.

Lajtha László, *Ujra megtalált magyar népdalstílus* (An Early Type of Hungarian Folk Song Detected), see in K 60, p. 219.

Leifs, Jón, *Isländische Volkslieder*, Wolfenbüttel, Berlin 1929.

Lewalter, Johann, *Deutsches Kinderlied und Kinderspiel*, Kassel 1911.

LU = *Liber usualis missae et officii*, Tournai 1941, no. 780.

MI = Bartók & Kodály, *A magyar népzene tára. I. Gyermekjátékok* (Gy. Kerényi). *Corpus Musicae Popularis Hungaricae* (vol. i, Children's Plays), Budapest 1951. Muz. F. = Phonographic records in the Ethnographic Department of the Hungarian National Museum, Budapest.

P : 94 = Péczely Attila, *Rózsa. 94 magyar népdal* (Rose. Ninty-four Hungarian Folk Songs), Budapest 1953.

P : 107 = Péczely Attila, *107 magyar népdal* (One Hundred-and-seven Hungarian Folk Songs), Budapest 1947.

R : 111 = Rajeczky Benjamin & Gönyey Sándor, *111 táncdal* (One Hundred-and-eleven Dance Tunes), Budapest 1949.

Rimsky-Korssakoff : *100 russische Volkslieder*, Wien 1925.

Schn = Schneider, Marius, *Die Geschichte der Mehrstimmigkeit*, vol. i, Berlin 1934.

Sebestyén Gyula, *Regös-énekek* (Regös Lays), Budapest 1902.

Sharp, C., *English Folk Songs from the Southern Appalachians*, London 1932.

Sz : Ch = Szabolcsi Bence, *Uj kínai népdalgyüjteményekről. Dallamtörténeti kérdések, IV* (About New Collections of Chinese Songs. From the History of Melody), see in K 70, p. 758.

Sz : E = *Egyetemes művelődéstörténet és ötfokú hangsorok* (The Universal History of Civilization and Pentatonic Scales), in *Ethnographia — Népélet*, Budapest 1936.

Sz : Mel = Szabolcsi Bence, *A melódia története* (The History of Melody), Budapest 1950.

V : Áj = Vargyas Lajos, *Áj falu zenei élete* (Musical Life in the Village of Áj), Budapest 1941.

V : K = Vargyas Lajos, *Régi népdalok Kiskunhalasról* (Old Folk Songs from Kiskunhalas), Budapest 1954.

Väis = Väisänen, A. O., *Wogulische und Ostjakische Melodien*, Helsinki 1937.

ZL = Szabolcsi Bence & Tóth Aladár, *Zenei lexikon, I — II* (Encyclopedia of Music, vols. i — ii), Budapest 1930.

BÉLA AVAS

TONAL SYSTEMS DERIVED FROM PERMUTATING INTERVALS*

The constantly growing collection of musical folklore has brought to light melodies having the most diverse stocks of notes. The tonal system and scale categories used up to now have proved inadequate to designate every feature even in the melodic realm of modern composed music. The theoretical designations and experiments in classification are falling behind the heights attained by music. There are, however, certain constant, unchanging factors in the creation of melodies, which may enable us to draw conclusions as to the unexploited possibilities.

The method used in the theory of music has up to now been an inductive one : it has derived certain regularities from given melodies and set up classification systems. In the following we shall attempt to apply the principle of deduction to certain fields in the theory of melody, and to evolve theoretically a system in which all the melodic possibilities will have their places assigned to them according to mathematical considerations. In proceeding, however, we shall select a condition which imposes certain limits to the sphere of possibilities. This condition is tempered dodecatony and the free interpretation of enharmony within it. We are not concerned, therefore, with various "untuned" tonal systems (without perfect fourths, fifths, octaves, etc.) which we often come across in various kinds of primitive music. We regard them as acoustical variants of the series of intervals discussed here and have therefore excluded from our discussion all problems (as well as the literature) relating to them.

The determining of a melody's stock of notes is the result of theoretical abstraction. The tonal stock reveals, on the one hand, the number

* The author wishes to point our that Professor Lajos Bárdos has for several years been studying problems running parallel to the questions raised in this paper. The method of arranging the tonal systems by the sequence of fifths originates from him. He has always been ready to give the author friendly advice and assistance.

of the different notes that constitute the melody and, on the other, the intervals between them. But two or three different notes may constitute the material of any melody however long, moreover, most melodies do not contain every interval that otherwise exists between the members of the stock of notes.

If we place the members of any tonal stock in an endless row, disregarding the height of their register, then the intervals of the consecutive notes show a certain regularity. The reason for this is the identifying force of the perfect octave. Such an abstraction of the tonal stock yields the tonal system of a melody.

The tonal system arrays all the notes of a melody differing from each other (tonal stock) within an octave, though it may well be that they occur over two or three octaves of the melody. Thus what is a contiguous interval in the tonal system, may not be contiguous within the stock of notes unless shifted an octave or two.

The tonal system has no starting or ending note. It is characterized, on the one hand, by the number of notes within an octave (quantitative factor), and, on the other, by the regular succession of the intervals (structural factor). The scales or modes of a tonal system are obtained by starting or ending a series of notes on an arbitrary but definite note. The number of modes most frequently depends on the quantitative factor (that is, there are as many modes as there are notes within an octave), yet a certain peculiarity of the structure of the tonal system (as we shall see later) may reduce this number (for example, the whole-tone system consists of six different notes, yet it makes no difference on which note we start to build the scale).

Our investigations refer to the melodic substance. The tonality question, over and above this, deals with the dominating and subordinating relations of the notes within a given melody.

Let us attempt a survey of tonal systems (and in connection with these: scales) having one to twelve degrees. Let our smallest structural element be the (tempered) semitone dividing the octave into twelve equal parts. Thus we proceed from the monotonous chant, sounded on one note, to the upper limit which is a differentiated melody consisting of twelve semitones.

The natural groups of tonal systems are determined by the quantitative factor. They are shown in column I of our first table. The number of the structural elements again depends on the quantitative factor: there are as many intervals as there are degrees in the tonal system. The computation of the possible permutation of the intervals is a mathematical task. If we assume the half-distance to be the unit, we must designate the intervals with the following number: unison = 0, minor second (chromatic semitone) = 1, major second = 2, minor third = 3, major third = 4, perfect fourth = 5, augmented fourth (diminished fifth) = 6, perfect fifth = 7, minor sixth = 8, major sixth = 9, minor seventh = 10, major seventh = 11, and perfect octave = 12.

It follows from the definition of the tonal system that the sum of the intervals of a scale system is always 12. The mathematical formulation of the calculation of the possibilities is as follows : let us write down the 12, whole-number addable sums ! By substituting these numbers for the above corresponding intervals, we obtain all the interval groups constituting the tonal systems. We find these in column II of the first table.

The intervals of each group (in most cases) may be written down in many different sequences. All the possible sequences constitute the structure of all the possible modes. We obtain this mathematically by the permutation of the 12 sums to be added and the substitution of the proper intervals for the number values. If we write down the sequence possibilities of the interval groups not only within an octave but through several octaves, then the modes belonging to a common tonal system show an identical structure. The structural factor of the tonal system (in most instances), therefore, may be designated not only by a permutating formula, but by any one of the permutating groups that contain a definite sequence of the permutating elements. Since the computation of the permutating groups of interval possibilities is identical in a great number of instances, we indicate these with algebraic formulae in column III of our first table.

Column IV shows the number of permutating groups, $i.\,e.$, of tonal systems, whereas in column V the results of full permutation, the number of modes are listed. These latter are usually equal to the product of the numbers found in columns I and IV, that is, the number of notes multiplied by the number of tonal systems. There are, however, tonal systems of exceptional structure (as we have pointed out above), in which a scale of independent construction may not begin on every note. These have been marked in columns III and V with an asterisk.

Let us illustrate with examples what we have said about our table. The intervals of pentatony without semitones are 32232 (three major seconds and two minor thirds). The algebraic formula of the five numbers is aaabb. The following permutating groups may be formed from them : aaabb and aabab. The complete permutation is : aaabb, aabba, abbaa, bbaaa, baaab, aabab, ababa, babaa, abaab, and baaba, that is, two tonal systems, each with five modes. In the table of pentatonic systems, column II, we may find another interval group without a semitone, having the structure 22224, which designates the five modes of a tonal system.

In the melodic world of primitive peoples it frequently happens that certain notes differ in pitch from the pitches of notes used in European music. For example, the interval of 171 cents is somewhat smaller than a small whole tone (182 C.), and the tempered *pelog* system based upon it cannot be fitted exactly into our table. But if we round off the cent values to the nearest round number (the European tempered semitone is 100 C.), then we obtain a system of which the *pelog* is a tuned variant :

171 343 514 686 875 1028 1200 approach the
200 300 500 700 900 1000 1200 cent values therefore according to our table it is the acoustical variant of the diatony indicated with the interval values 1221222.

If we substitute the numerical values of column II for the algebraic symbols of column III, we obtain the interval structures of all the tonal systems. Our next task is to imagine living notes in the place of these rows of lifeless numbers. Since, however, these numbers may represent also any enharmonic variant of the suitable intervals (for instance, 3 = minor third, and 3 = also an augmented second, etc.), and the intervals may be reckoned arbitrarily from any one note (for example, D—F and A♭—C♭ are equally minor thirds), we need standardizing principles for making comparisons and groupings.

The independence of the notes of the tonal systems calls for an independent name and interpretation of each note. But our musical notation knows of only seven fundamental notes, consequently the notes can have individual names each only in tonal systems having one to seven degrees. In tonal systems having eight to twelve notes, one, two . . . to five derived notes are added to the seven independently named notes. These considerations enable us to determine precisely which enharmonic variants of a certain tonal system should be included in our comparisons.

Our next question is in which transposition should the given enharmonic variant be included. The basis of European musical thinking is the seven-note, diatonic tonal system (the system of fundamental notes). All musical manifestations of a different kind are either measured against it or derived from it. Among the possible transpositions of diatony those indicated with the fundamental notes are the most natural (one mode of which is, for instance, D—E—F—G—A—B—C). This serves as a point of departure in the theory of music too. Hence, among the transpositions of our tonal systems we select the possibility in which the notes most closely approach these notes.

The sequence of perfect fifths is the only possible succession of the seven fundamental notes which shows a regular connection. (It was Lajos Bárdos who called my attention to this phenomenon which had earlier been known in Chinese music theory. The illustration of tonal systems on a column of fifths was also his idea.)

B
E
A
D
G
C
F

The centre of the column of fifths is the note D, and the marginal note of the diatony in the direction of the dominant is B, and in the direction of the subdominant it is F. We obtain the uniform portrayal of the tonal systems by arranging their notes on the column of fifths so that the two marginal notes are at equal distances from the centre D. If the two marginal members of the tonal system encompass an even number of fifths, then this may be solved with one transposition, but in case an uneven number of fifths two transpositions are required for the tonal system.

The portrayal of tonal systems on the column of fifths may serve as a basis for determining the sequence of tonal systems with identical quantitative factors (see column I of the second table). The notes of diatony form a close series round the centre D. The further the members of a tonal system are from the centre D, the more alien the system is to diatony. We can exactly determine this distance by calculating the number of fifths separating each note of the tonal system from D. Thus we obtain the index of fifths (which we may also call the "quintal index") characteristic of a given transposition of the system. Since, however, the various transpositions of the tonal systems lead as a rule to different results, and since the index of fifths is often not characteristic, in order to determine the index of the sequence, all the transpositions of the tonal systems including the D centre are necessary. Therefore an extreme transposition will be the one whose most dominant member is D, and the other extreme transposition will be the one whose most subdominant member is D. The sum of the indexes of fifths of all the transpositions determined in this way yields the index characterizing the tone system on the column of fifths. The smaller this number is, the closer the tonal system is related to diatony, and the lower its position will be in the sequence, and vice versa. The tonal systems defined in keeping with our aim are on this basis included in the second table.

The interval numbers of the structural factor determining the tonal system may be found in column I of the second table. The numbers indicate a mode from which we may readily build the rest of the modes. Among the interval-indicating number groups the one with the smallest arithmetical value is included in the table.

For example, the structural formulae of the modes frequently occurring in the pentatonic system of Hungarian folk music are: 22323 (ending in *do*), 23223 (ending in *so*), 23232 (ending in *re*), 32232 (ending in *la*), and 32322 (ending in *mi*). From among these we have thus included in our table the 22323 interval group indicating the mode ending in *do*.

The notes of the transposition (or transpositions) of the tonal system centrally placed on the column of fifths may be found in column II of the second table. (The tonal system is always represented by the mode the structure of which is given in column II of the second table).

The number in parentheses after the notes indicates the index of fifths
of the transposition.

For example, among the transpositions of Hungarian pentatony,
C—D—E—G—A is central:

E

A

D

G

C

its index is 6, because A and G are each one fifth away, and E and C
are each two fifths away from the centre D.

Not in every tonal system does central transposition yield the
smallest index. The transpositions, having the lowest index number, of
these exceptional tonal systems and the indexes themselves are given
in column III. (In case of more transpositions of identical lowest index
number the one lying closest to the centre was chosen).

For example, the index of the central transposition B—C—D—
—F—G of the 12324 pentatonic system is 9 (B=3, C=2, D=0, F=3,
G=1), whereas the numerical value of F#—G—A—C—D is 8 (F# = 4,
C = 1, A = 1, C = 2, D = 0), which, therefore, is the minimal trans-
position.

In column IV are the indexes of the tonal systems, that is, the
sums of the indexes of transpositions including D.

For example, the transpositions of Hungarian pentatony have the
following indexes : the one in which the dominant marginal note is D,
i.e., B♭—C—D—F—G, has 10 ; the one in which the subdominant
marginal note is D, i. e., D—E—F#—A—B, has again the same value,
10 ; the transpositions and their indexes in between are: F—G—A—C—D
having 7 ; C—D—E—G—A having 6, and G—A—B—D—E having 7.
The index of the tonal system itself, is, therefore 10—7—6—7—
—10 = 40.

On the basis of the indexes obtained for column IV we may set up
the order of the tonal systems. In quite a number of instances, however,
we find that the indexes of two tonal systems are identical. The structural
factors, the features on the column of fifths, and the indexes of the
transpositions of such pairs are each other's inversions.

For example, the formula of the interval group of the harmonic
minor tonal system is 1212213, (C#—D—E—F—G—A—B♭), the reverse
of this number is characteristic of another tonal system 1213122 (F#—G—
A—B♭—C#—D—E). The illustrations of the pairs of tonal systems on
the column of fifths are :

C#   F#
—   B
—   —
E   A
A   D
D   G
G   C
—   —
F   —
B♭   E♭
—

The sets of the indexes of the transpositions containing D are:

28—23—20—17—16—17—20—25—30—35

35—30—25—20—17—16—17—20—23—28

The indexes of both tonal systems are thus **231** each.

In column V of the second table the Roman numerals are the ordinal numbers of the tonal systems, with two numbers for the pair of them. Very rarely it happens that the indexes of three or four tonal systems are identical. In such cases the sequences will be determined by the index of the minimal (and at the same time often central) transposition.

Our investigations have so far been focused on the structural factor of the tonal systems, and we have treated the quantitative factor only as a natural group-forming principle. The quantitative factor, however, not only determines the number of notes in the tonal systems, but also indicates the number of the twelve notes of dodecatony that do not occur in the system. For instance, the white keys of the piano form a seven-note, diatonic system, while the black keys form a pentatonic system. To any "n"-member system there belongs a complementary "12—n" member system. (Compare with the "total" figures in column IV of the first table.)

In our Supplements we have arranged all the tonal systems, illustrated in fifths, so as to have the complementary systems placed beside their counterparts.

Let us, for example, turn to the columns of fifths of the pentatonic and heptatonic systems. Our first diagram is the pentatonic system no. I. The black circles indicate notes, their names may be read at the beginning of the row on the column of fifths. The notes of the complementary heptatonic system are marked ×, which naturally, are, not centred round D. The complement to the pentatonic system according to the diagram, therefore, is the heptatonic system no. I. This is shown by the two diagrams indicating the heptatonic system no I and its complementary system.

Often the complementary system, consisting of notes marked ×, is the enharmonic variant of some system already determined. This can be seen from the identity of the structural factor.

253

For example, the pair of the pentatonic systems nos. II and III are complemented by the enharmonic variants of the pair of heptatonic systems nos. XXXI and XXXII.

As a complementary system on the column of fifths we have given the diagram of the enharmonic variant with the smallest index of fifths. We have included their transposition (transpositions) centered round D and the indexes of the transposition in column VI of the second table. The numbers to be found in column VII are the indexes of this system of enharmonic variants.

If the tonal systems are classified according to the index of the system of enharmonic variants, their order of sequence will but rarely correspond to the ordinal numbers given in column V. Thus the sequence of the tonal systems that may be called chromatic is shown in column VIII.

As to which "12—n"tonal system is complemented by the ordinal-numbered system in column V, is shown by the Roman numeral of column IX. (This latter makes orientation in the supplement easier.)

For example, the central transpositions of the heptatonic systems nos. XXXI and XXXII mentioned above are:

XXXI   XXXII

A♯—B—C—D♭—E♭—F—G♯,   A♯—B—C—D♭—E♭—F♯—G♯,

D♯—E—F—G♭—A♭—B♭—C♯,   D♯—E—F—G♭—A♭—B—C♯.

The transpositions centered round D of the pair of heptatonic systems originated as a complement to the pair of the pentatonic systems nos. II and III are:

E—F—F♯—G—A—B—D,   E—F—F♯—G—A—C—D,

A—B♭—B—C—D—E—G,   A—B♭—B—C—D—F—G.

The examples show that they are each other's transposed enharmonic variants.

The inversion of the structural factor of any unpaired tonal system yields itself: its diagram on the column of fifths is symmetrical to D (if it encompasses an uneven number of fifths), or to the D—A-axis (if it constitues an even number of fifths), and the index numbers of its transpositions increase from the centre proportionally.

For example, the formula of the intervals in the heptatonic system no. I. (diatony) is 1221222, its inversion starting from the fourth number (this is arbitrary) is 1221222. Its diagram on the column of fifths is symmetrical to D (see Supplement), the sequence of the indexes of its transpositions is 21—16—13—12—13—16—21.

The diagrams of some systems standing by themselves do not yield a symmetrical shape. In this case the diagram and its inversion indicate different enharmonic variants of one and the same system. Yet these tonal systems always have an enharmonic variant, the notes of which are symmetrical to D.

For example, see the diagram, in the Supplement, of the hexatonic system no. XXXV, which complements the hexatonic system no. XII.

We have come to the end of our discussion. Our tonal systems, arrived at deductively, as a result of mathematical and musical consideration, exhaust all the possibilities of tempered semitonal dodecatony. A noteworthy parallel may be drawn between the sequence of the systems and the living melodies known so far. Our experiences will verify the fact that most melodies belong to the tonal systems with lower indexes. We cannot, however, find any melody that could not (with regard to enharmony and the tempered semitone) be fitted into one of our systems.

We may note, incidentally, that our tonal-system tables exhaust not only the possibilities of the melodic stocks, but also those of harmony. Thus, for example, three different notes constitute not only 19 tonal systems but also 19 different kinds of chords. (The modes being the inversions of the chord.) The productive interpretation of enharmonic variants is possible here too ; the enharmony of the dominant seventh chord and the German sixth, for example, etc. are well known.

At the end of our study we quote a few melodic examples selected from the works of Bartók to illustrate some infrequent tonal systems. (Since Lajos Bárdos' treatise, which is related to our theme, carries abundant folk-music examples, we have dispensed with them. A full collection of examples cannot be compiled either from folk music or from composed music. Living music may never exhaust all the possibilities.) We must not think, however, that our classifying work is completed. The two conditions imposed by our aim : tempered dodecatony and the free interpretation of enharmony, are theoretical stipulations. Progress has led from melodies of two or three notes to pentatony. The introduction of *pien* tones (a phenomenon not commonly known all over the world) has brought heptatony into existence. Chromatic notes have been introduced among the whole tones and have in living music achieved a status of independence, while theory only derives their names ; in fact, tempering permits their enharmonic interchange. In composed music it occurs more and more frequently that within a melody, the enharmonic notes each play an individual part. If we add the experiments aimed at obtaining intervals a great deal smaller than the tempered semitone, then we can understand that our dodecatonic systems do not provide satisfactory answers to everything, but serve as a starting point for further investigations.

Table I

Number of notes in the tonal system	Possible intervals	Mathematic formulae of the permutating groups of the possible intervals	Number of tonal systems	Number of modes
One-note tonal system	0 12	a	1	1
		total	1	1
Two-note tonal system	1 11	ab	1	2
	2 10	ab	1	2
	3 9	ab	1	2
	4 8	ab	1	2
	5 7	ab	1	2
	6 6	aa*	1	1*
		total	6	11
Three-note tonal system	1 1 10	aab	1	3
	1 2 9	abc, acb	2	6
	1 3 8	abc ...	2	6
	2 2 8	aab	1	3
	1 4 7	abc ...	2	6
	2 3 7	abc ...	2	6
	1 5 6	abc ...	2	6
	2 4 6	abc ...	2	6
	3 3 6	aab	1	3
	2 5 5	aab	1	3
	3 4 5	abc ...	2	6
	4 4 4	aaa*	1	1*
		total	19	55
Four-note tonal system	1 1 1 9	aaab	1	4
	1 1 2 8	aabc, aacb, abac	3	12
	1 1 3 7	aabc ...	3	12
	1 2 2 7	aabc ...	3	12
	1 1 4 6	aabc ...	3	12
	1 2 3 6	abcd, abdc, acbd, acdb, adbc, adcb	6	24
	2 2 2 6	aaab	1	4
	1 1 5 5	aabb, abab*	2	6*
	1 2 4 5	abcd ...	6	24
	1 3 3 5	aabc ...	3	12
	2 2 3 5	aabc ...	3	12
	1 3 4 4	aabc ...	3	12
	2 2 4 4	aabb*...	2	6*
	2 3 3 4	aabc ...	3	12
	3 3 3 3	aaaa*	1	1*
		total	43	165

Number of notes in the tonal system	Possible intervals	Mathematic formulae of the permutating groups of the possible intervals	Number of tonal systems	Number of modes
Five-note tonal system	1 1 1 1 8	aaaab	1	5
	1 1 1 2 7	aaabc, aaacb, aabac, aacab	4	20
	1 1 1 3 6	aaabc ...	4	20
	1 1 2 2 6	aabbc, aabcb, aacbb, ababc, abacb, abbac	6	30
	1 1 1 4 5	aaabc ...	4	20
	1 1 2 3 5	aabcd, aabdc, aacbd, aacdb, aadbc, aadcb, abacd, abadc, abcad, abdac, acadb, acbad	12	60
	1 2 2 2 5	aaabc ...	4	20
	1 1 2 4 4	aabbc ...	6	30
	1 1 3 3 4	aabbc ...	6	30
	1 2 2 3 4	aabcd ...	12	60
	2 2 2 2 4	aaaab	1	5
	1 2 3 3 3	aaabc ...	4	20
	2 2 2 3 3	aaabb, aabab	2	10
		total	66	330
Six-note tonal system	1 1 1 1 1 7	aaaaab	1	6
	1 1 1 1 2 6	aaaabc, aaaacb, aaabac, aaacab, aabaac	5	30
	1 1 1 1 3 5	aaaabc ...	5	30
	1 1 1 2 2 5	aaabbc, aaabcb, aaacbb, aababc, aabacb, aabbac, aabcab, aacabb, aacbab, ababac	10	60
	1 1 1 1 4 4	aaaabb, aaabab, aabaab*	3	15*
	1 1 1 2 3 4	aaabcd, aaabdc, aaacbd, aaacdb, aaadbc, aaadcb, aabacd, aabadc, aabcad, aabdac, aacabd, aacadb, aacbad, aacdab, aadabc, aadacb, aadbac, aadcab, abacad, abadac	20	120
	1 1 2 2 2 4	aaabbc ...	10	60
	1 1 1 3 3 3	aaabbb, aababb, aabbab, ababab*	4	20*
	1 1 2 2 3 3	aabbcc, aabcbc, aabccb, aacbbc, aacbcb, aaccbb, abbacc, abbcac ababcc, abacbc, abaccb, abcabc*, abcacb, abcbac, acacbb, acbacb*	16	90*
	1 2 2 2 2 3	aaaabc ...	5	30
	2 2 2 2 2 2	aaaaaa*	1	1*
		total	80	462
Seven-note tonal system	1 1 1 1 1 1 6	aaaaaab	1	7
	1 1 1 1 1 2 5	aaaaabc, aaaaacb, aaaabac, aaaacab, aaabaac, aaacaab	6	42
	1 1 1 1 1 3 4	aaaaabc ...	6	42
	1 1 1 1 2 2 4	aaaabbc, aaaabcb, aaaacbb, aaababc, aaabacb, aaabbac, aaabcab, aaacabb, aaacbab, aabaabc, aabaacb, aababac, aabacab, aabbaac, aacabab	15	105
	1 1 1 1 2 3 3	aaaabbc ...	15	105
	1 1 1 2 2 2 3	aaabbbc, aaabbcb, aaabcbb, aaacbbb, aababbc, aababcb, aabacbb, aabbabc, aabbacb, aabbbac, aabbbac,		

Number of nodes in the tonal system	Possible intervals	Mathematic formulae of the permutating groups of the possible intervals	Number of tonal systems	Number of modes
Seven-note tonal system	1 1 2 2 2 2 2	aabbcab, aabcabb, aabcbab, aacabbb, aacbbab aacbabb, abababc, ababacb, ababbac, abacabb	20	140
		aaaaabb, aaaabab, aaabaab	3	21
		total	66	462
Eight-note tonal system	11111115	aaaaaaab	1	8
	11111124	aaaaaabc, aaaaaacb, aaaaabac, aaaaacab, aaaabaac, aaaacaab, aaabaaac	7	56
	11111133	aaaaaabb, aaaaabab, aaabaab, aaabaaab*	4	28*
	11111223	aaaaaabbc, aaaaaabcb, aaaaacbb, aaaababc, aaaabacb, aaaabbac, aaaabcab, aaaacabb, aaaacbab, aaabaabc, aaabaacb, aaababac, aaabacab, aaabbaac, aaabcaab, aaacaabc, aaacabab, aaacbaab, aabaaabac, aabaaacab, aababaac	21	168
	11112222	aaaabbbb, aaababbb, aaabbabb, aaabbbab, aabaabbb, aababbabb, aababbab, aabbaabb*, aabbabab, abababab*	10	70*
		total	43	330
Nine-note tonal system	111111114	aaaaaaaab	1	9
	111111123	aaaaaaabc, aaaaaacb, aaaaaabac, aaaaaacab, aaaaabaac, aaaaacaab, aaaabaaac, aaaacaaab	8	72
	111111222	aaaaaabbb, aaaaababb, aaaaabbab, aaaababaabb, aaaababab, aaaabbaab, aaabaaabb, aaabaaabab, aaababaab, aabaabaab*	10	84*
		total	19	165
Ten-note tonal system	1111111113	aaaaaaaaab	1	10
	1111111122	aaaaaaaabb, aaaaaaabab, aaaaaabaab, aaaaabaaab, aaaabaaab*	5	45
		total	6	55
Eleven-n. tonal sys.	11111111112	aaaaaaaaaab	1	11
		total	1	11
Twelwe-n. ton. sys.	111111111111	aaaaaaaaaaaa*	1	1*
		total	1	1

Table II

I	II	III	IV	V	VI	VII	VIII	IX
Interval group characteristics of the tonal system	Central transposition(s) of the tonal system	Transposition(s) with lowest quintal index	Quintal index of the tonal system	Ordinal number of the tonal system	Central and minimal transposition(s) of the enharmonic variant with the lowest index in the tonal system	Quintal index of the enharm. var.	Ordinal number of the tonal system with respect to the enharm. v.	Ordinal number of the 12—n member, complementary tonal system
ONE-NOTE TONAL SYSTEM								
0-12	D	(0)	0	I				I
TWO-NOTE TONAL SYSTEM								
5-7	A D D G	(1) (1)	2	I				I
2-10	G A	(2)	6	II				II
3-9	E G A C	(3) (3)	12	III				III
4-8	C E	(4)	20	IV				IV
1-11	B C E F	(5) (5)	30	V				VI enh. v.
6-6	F B	(6)	42	VI				V enh. v.
THREE-NOTE TONAL SYSTEM								
2-5-5	G A D	(2)	6	I			1	I
2-3-7	D E G G A C	(3) (3)	16 16	II— III			2—3	II— III
2-7-3	G A E C D A	(3) (3)						

I — Interval group characterising the tonal system	II — Central transposition(s) of the tonal system	III — Transposition(s) with lowest quintal index	IV — Quintal index of the tonal system	V — Ordinal number of the tonal system	VI — Central and minimal transposition(s) of the enharmonic variant with the lowest index in the tonal system	VII — Quintal index of the enharm. var.	VIII — Ordinal number of the tonal system with respect to the enharm. v.	IX — Ordinal number of the $12-n$ member, complementary tonal system
2-2- 8	C D E (4)		26	IV			4	VI enh. v.
3-5-4	E G C (5)	B D G (4)	27	V—			5—6	IV—
3-4-5	A C E (5)	D F A (4)	27	VI				V
1-2-9	B C D (5) E F G (6)		39	VII—			7—8	XVII—
1-9-2	B C A (6) E F D (5)		39	VIII				XVIII enh. v.
1-7-4	B C G (6) E F C (7)	F# G D (5)	41	IX—			9—10	XV—
1-4-7	B C E (7) E F A (6)	A B♭ D (5)	41	X				XVI enh. v.
3-3-6	B D F (6)		54	XI			11	IX
2-4-6	F G B (7)	C D F# (6)	55	XII—			12—13	VII—
2-6-4	A B F (7)	D E B♭ (6)	55	XIII				VIII
1-5-6	B C F (8)	C# D G (6)	58	XIV—			14—15	XIII—
1-6-5	E F B (8)	B♭ E♭ A (6)	58	XV				XIV enh. v.
4-4-4	B D F# (8)		92	XVI			19	XII
1-3-8	F# G B♭ (9)	C# D F (8)	93	XVII—	F F# A (8) B♭ B D (7)	72	16—17	X—
1-8-3	A B♭ F# (9)	D E♭ B (8)	93	XVIII	F F# D (7) B♭ B G (8)	72		XI

260

I	II	III	IV	V	VI	VII	VIII	IX
Interval group characterising the tonal system	Central transposition(s) of the tonal system	Transposition(s) with lowest quintal index	Quintal index of the tonal system	Ordinal number of the tonal system	Central and minimal transposition(s) of the enharmonic variant with the lowest index in the tonal system	Quintal index of the enharm. var.	Ordinal number of the tonal system with respect to the enharm. v.	Ordinal number of the 12-n member, complementary tonal system
1-1-10	C♯ D E♭ (10)		140	XIX	F F♯ G (8) B♭ B C (9) C♯ D (7) E F F♯ (9) A B♭ B (8) D E♭ E (7)	74 74	18	XIX enh. v.

FOUR-NOTE TONAL SYSTEM

I	II	III	IV	V	VI	VII	VIII	IX
2325	D E G A (4) G A C D (4)		20	I			1	I
2235	C D E G (5)		33	II–III			2–3	II–III
2253	C D E A (5)		33					
2343	G A C E (6)		34	IV			4	IV
1272	B C D A (6) E F G D (6)		48	V			5	XXXIII enh. v.
1254	B C D G (6) E F G C (8)		50	VI–VII			6–7	XXV–XXVI enh. v.
1452	B C E A (8) C F A D (6)		50					
1722	B C G A (7) E F C D (7)		50	VIII–IX			8–9	XXXI–XXXII enh. v.
1227	B C D E (7) E F G A (7)		50					

I Interval group characterising the tonal system	II Central transposition(s) of the tonal system	III Transposition(s) with lowest quintal index	IV Quintal index of the tonal system	V Ordinal number of the tonal system	VI Central and minimal transposition(s) of the enharmonic variant with the lowest index in the tonal system	VII Quintal index of the enharm. var.	VIII Ordinal number of the tonal system with respect to the enharm. v.	IX Ordinal number of the 12-n member, complementary tonal system
1434	B C E G (8)		52	X			10	XXIX enh. v.
	E F A C (8)							
2433	F G B D (7)		67	XI–XII			11–12	V–VI
2334	A B D F (7)		67					
2226	F G A B (8)		68	XIII			13	VIII
1236	B C D F (8)		70	XIV–XV			14–15	XVIII–XIX enh. v.
1632	E F B D (8)		70					
1524	B C F G (9)	F♯ G C D (7)	71	XVI–XVII			16–17	XXIII–XXIV enh. v.
1425	E F A B (9)	A♭ B D E (7)	71					
1542	B C F A (9)		71	XVIII–XIX			18–19	XXVII–XXVIII enh. v.
1245	E F G B (9)		71					
1416	B C E F (10)		74	XX			20	XXII enh. v.
1344	F♯ G B♭ D (9)		113	XXI–XXII			36–37	XIV–XV
1443	A♭ D F♯ (9)		113					
1218	F♯ G A B♭ (10)		114	XXIII			38	XL enh. v.
2244	B♭ C D F♯ (10)		116	XXIV			39	XIX enh. v.
	D E F♯ B♭ (10)		116					

I	II	III	IV	V	VI	VII	VIII	IX
Interval group characterising the tonal system	Central transposition(s) of the tonal system	Transposition(s) with lowest quintal index	Quintal index of the tonal system	Ordinal number of the tonal system	Central and minimal transposition(s) of the enharmonic variant with the lowest index in the tonal symste	Quintal index of the enharm. var.	Ordinal number of the tonal system with respect to the enharm. v.	Ordinal number of the 12-n member, complementary tonal system
1623	(11) A B♭ E F♯	(11) D E♭ A B	117	XXV—			30—31	IX—X enh. v.
1326	(11) F♯ G B♭ C	(11) C♯ D F G	117	XXVI				
1263	(11) A B♭ C F♯		117 117	XXVII— XXVIII			40—41	XX—XXI enh. v.
1362	(11) F♯ G B♭ E							XVII enh. v.
2424	(12) B♭ C E F♯		120	XXIX			41	XVII enh. v.
1533	(10) C♯ D G B♭ (12) F♯ G C E♭		136 136	XXX— XXXI	(10) F♯ F♯ B D (10) B♭ B E G	88 88	22—23	XII— XIII enh. v.
1335	(12) A B♭ C♯ E (10) D E♭ F♯ A				(10) F♯ F♯ A C (10) B♭ B D F	88 88		
1317	(10) A B♭ C♯ D (10) D E♭ F♯ G		140	XXXII	(12) F♯ F♯ A B♭ (12) F♯ G B♭ B	122 122	42	XXX enh. v.
3333	(12) C♯ E G B♭ (12) F♯ A C E♭		144	XXXIII			43	XVI enh. v.
1353	(12) C♯ D F B♭ (14) F♯ G B♭ E♭ (14) A B♭ C♯ F♯ (12) D E♭ F♯ B		152 152	XXXIV	(8) F♯ F♯ A D (8) B♭ B D G	88	21	VII

Table rotated 90°. Columns I–IX as labelled in the header.

I — Interval group characterising the tonal system	II — Central transposition(s) of the tonal system	III — Transposition(s) with lowest quintal index	IV — Quintal index of the tonal system	V — Ordinal number of the tonal system	VI — Central and minimal transposition(s) of the enharmonic variant with the lowest index in the tonal system	VII — Quintal index of the enharm. var.	VIII — Ordinal number of the tonal system with respect to the enharm. v.	IX — Ordinal number of the 12-n member, complementary tonal system
1146	C♯ D E♭ G (11)		171	XXXV—	F F♯ G B (11)	96	34—35	XXXV—
					B♭ B C E (11)	96		XXXVI enh. v.
1164	C♯ D E♭ A (11)		171	XXXVI	E F F♯ C (11)	96		
					A B♭ B F (11)	96		
1128	C♯ D E♭ F (13)		179	XXXVII—	F F♯ G A (8)	90	25—26	XLI—
					B♭ B C D (10)	90		XLII enh. v.
1182	C♯ D E♭ B (13)		179	XXXVIII	D E F F♯ (10)	90		
					G A B♭ B (8)	90		
1173	C♯ D E♭ B♭ (14)		186	XXXIX—	F F♯ G D (8)	90	27—28	XXXVII—
					B♭ B C G (10)	90		XXXVIII enh. v.
1137	C♯ D E♭ F♯ (14)		186	XL	E F F♯ A (10)	90		
					A B♭ B D (8)	90		
1515	D E♭ G♯ A (12)		204	XLI	B C F F♯ (12)	88	24	XXXIV
	G A♭ C♯ D (12)				E F B♭ B (12)	88		enh. v.
1155	G♯ A B♭ E♭ (16)		224	XLII	F F♯ G C (10)	96	32—33	XXXIX
	C♯ D E♭ A♭ (16)				B♭ B C F (12)	96		enh. v.
					C C♯ D G (8)			
					E F F♯ B (12)			
					A B♭ B E (10)			
					D E♭ E A (8)			
1119	A♯ B C D♭ (20)		380	XLIII	E F F♯ G (10)	92	29	XLIII
	D♯ D E♭ G♭ (20)				A B♭ B C (10)			enh. v.

FIVE-NOTE TONAL SYSTEM

I — Interval group characterising the tonal system	II — Central transposition(s) of the tonal system	III — Transposition(s) with lowest quintal index	IV — Quintal index of the tonal system	V — Ordinal number of the tonal system	VI — Central and minimal transposition(s) of the enharmonic variant with the lowest index in the tonal system	VII — Quintal index of the enharm. var.	VIII — Ordinal number of the tonal system with respect to the enharm. v.	IX — Ordinal number of the 12–n member, complementary tonal system
22323	C D E G A (6)		40	I			1	I
12522	B C D G A (7) / E F G C D (8)		59	II			2—3	XXXI—XXXII enh. v.
12252	B C D E A (8) / E F G A D (7)		59	III				
12234	B C D E G (8) / E F G A C (9)		61	IV			4—5	XIX—XX enh. v.
14322	B C E G A (9) / E F A C D (8)		61	V				
22233	F G A B D (8)		80	VI			6	II
12324	B C D F G (9)	F# G A C D (8)	83	VII			7—8	XI—XII enh. v.
14232	E F A B D (9)	A B♭ D E G (8)	83	VIII				
12342	B C D F A (9)		83	IX			9—10	XXIII—XXIV enh. v.
12432	E F G B D (9)		83	X				
15222	B C F G A (10)	F# G C D E (9)	84	XI			11—12	XXVII—XXVIII enh. v.
12225	E F G A B (10)	A B♭ C D E (9)	84	XII				

I Interval group characteris-ing the tonal system	II Central transposition(s) of the tonal system		III Transposition(s) with lowest quintal index		IV Quintal index of the tonal system	V Ordinal number of the tonal system	VI Central and minimal transposition(s) of the enharmonic variant with the lowest index in the tonal system		VII Quintal index of the enharm. var.	VIII Ordinal number of the tonal system with respect to the enharm. v.	IX Ordinal number of the 12-n member, complementary tonal system
12216	B C D E F	(10)			86	XIII				13	L enh. v.
12414	E F G B♭ C	(11)	B C D F♯ G	(10)	88	XIV—				14—15	XV— XVI enh. v.
14142	B C E F A	(11)	E F A B♭ D	(10)	88	XV					
12144	F♯ G A B♭ D	(10)			134	XVI				34	XLI enh. v.
13224	F♯ G B♭ C D	(11)	C♯ D F G A	(10)	134	XVII—				35—36	VI— VII enh. v.
14223	A B♭ D E F♯	(11)	D E♭ G A B	(10)	134	XVIII					
12243	A B♭ C D F♯	(11)			137	XIX—				37—38	XXI— XXII enh. v.
13422	F♯ G B♭ D E	(11)			137	XX					
12126	F♯ G A B♭ C	(12)	C♯ D E F G	(11)	138	XXI—				39—40	LIII— LIV enh. v.
12162	F♯ G A B♭ E	(12)	B C D E♭ A	(11)	138	XXII					
22224	B♭ C D E F♯	(12)			138	XXIII				41	V
13242	F♯ G B C E	(13)	C♯ D F G B	(12)	141	XXIV—				42—43	XIII— XIV enh. v.
12423	A B♭ C E F♯	(13)	D E♭ F A B	(12)	141	XXV					
13152	A B♭ C♯ D G D E♭ F♯ G C	(11) (12)			167	XXVI—	F♯ G B♭ B E E F A♭ A D	(14) (12)	146	53—54	XXIX— XXX enh. v.
13125	A B♭ C♯ D E D E♭ F♯ G A	(12) (11)			167	XXVII	F F♯ A B♭ C G G♯ B C D	(14) (12)	146		

I — Interval group characteristics of the tonal system	II — Central transposition(s) of the tonal system	III — Transposition(s) with lowest quintal index	IV — Quintal index of the tonal system	V — Ordinal number of the tonal system	VI — Central and minimal transposition(s) of the enharmonic variant with the lowest index in the tonal system	VII — Quintal index of the enharm. var.	VIII — Ordinal number of the tonal system with respect to the enharm. v.	IX — Ordinal number of the 12−n member, complementary tonal system
12333	C# D E G Bb (12) F# G A C Eb (13)		169	XXVIII			60	IX
13332	A Bb C# E G (13) D Eb F# A C (12)		169	XXIX			61	X — enh. v.
13134	A Bb C# D F (13) D Eb F# G Bb (14)		177	XXX	F# G Bb B D (12)	142	45	XVII
13143	A Bb C# D F# (14) D Eb F# G B (13)		177	XXXI	F F# A Bb D (12)	142	46	XVIII — enh. v.
13233	C# D F G Bb (13) F# G Bb C Eb (16)	G# A C D F (12)	179	XXXII	F F# A B D (11) Bb B D E G (10)	110	22	III
13323	A Bb C# E F# (16) D Eb F# A B (13)	G Ab B D E (12)	179	XXXIII	F F# A C D (10) C C# E G A (11)	110	23	IV
13314	D Eb F# A Bb (14) A Bb C# E F (15)		179	XXXIV			66	VIII — enh. v.
12153	C# D E F Bb (14) F# G A Bb Eb (15)		179	XXXV	Bb B C# D G (13) Eb E F# G C (14)	173	62	XLII
12135	F# G A Bb C# (15) B C D Eb F# (14)		179	XXXVI	A Bb C C# E (14) D Eb F F# A (13)	173	63	XLIII — enh. v.

I	II	III	IV	V	VI	VII	VIII	IX
Interval group characterising the tonal system	Central transposition(s) of the tonal system	Transposition(s) with lowest quintal index	Quintal index of the tonal system	Ordinal number of the tonal system	Central and minimal transposition(s) of the enharmonic variant with the lowest index in the tonal system	Quintal index of the enharm. var.	Ordinal number of the tonal system with respect to the enharm. v.	Ordinal number of the 12—n member, complementary tonal system
11424	C# D Eb G A (12)		202	XXXVII	E F F# Bb C (15) F# G G# C D (13) Bb B C E F# (15) Ab A Bb D E (13)	149 149	58	XXXIII enh. v.
11226	C# D Eb F G (14)	G# A Bb C D (13)	210	XXXVIII	F F# G A B (11) Bb B C D E (10)	104	16—17	LV—LVI
11622	C# D Eb A B (14)	F# G Ab D E (13)	210	XXXIX	E F F# C D (10) Ab Bb B F G (11)	104		
11244	C# D Eb F A (14)		210	XL	Bb B C D F# (13)	145	51—52	XLIV—XLV enh. v.
11442	C# D Eb G B (14)		210	XLI	Ab Bb B F G (13)	145		
11433	C# D Eb G B (15)	G# A Bb D F (14)	217	XLII	F F# G B D (11) Bb B C E G (12)	112	28—29	XXXIV—XXXV enh. v.
11334	C# D Eb F# A (15)	F# G Ab B D (14)	217	XLIII	E F F# A C (12) Ab Bb B D F (11)	112		
11613	C# D Eb A Bb (15)		218	XLIV	Bb B C F# G (14) F F# G C# D (13)	146	55—56	LI—LII enh. v.
11316	C# D Eb F# G (15)		218	XLV	E F F# A Bb (14) Ab Bb B D Eb (13)	146		
11262	C# D Eb F B (16)		218	XLVI	C C# D Eb Bb (13) F F# G A Eb (14) Ab Bb B C# G (14) D Eb E F# C (13)	173 173	64	LVII enh. v.

I — Interval group characterising the tonal system	II — Central transposition(s) of the tonal system	III — Transposition(s) with lowest quintal index	IV — Quintal index of the tonal system	V — Ordinal number of the tonal system	VI — Central and minimal transposition(s) of the enharmonic variant with the lowest index in the tonal system	VII — Quintal index of the enharm. var	VIII — Ordinal number of the tonal system with respect to the enharm. v.	IX — Ordinal number of the 12−n member, complementary tonal system
11253	C# D Eb F Bb (17)	A# B C D G (14)	225	XLVII—	F F# G A D (9) / Bb B C D G (10)	106	18—19	XLVIII—XLIX enh. v.
11352	C# D Eb F# B (17)	E F G# A D (14)	225	XLVIII	E F F# A D (10) / A Bb B D G (9)	106		
11343	C# D Eb F# Bb (18)		232	XLIX	F F# G Bb D (12) / C C# D F A (11) / A Bb B D F# (12) / D Eb E G B (11)	142 / 142	44	XXXVI enh. v.
12315	D Eb F G# A (15) / G Ab Bb C# D (16)		252	L—	B C D F F# (12) / E F G Bb B (13)	145	49—50	XXV—XXVI enh. v.
15132	G# A D Eb F# (16) / C# D G Ab B (15)		252	LI	B C F# A (13) / E F Bb B D (12)	145		
11415	G# A Bb D Eb (16) / C# D Eb G Ab (17)		260	LII—	F F# G B C (13) / Bb B C E F (14) / C C# D F# G (12)	118	32—33	XXXVII—XXXVIII enh. v.
11514	C# D Eb G# A (17) / F# G Ab C# D (16)		260	LIII	E F F# B C (14) / A Bb B E F (13) / D Eb E A Bb (12)	118		
11235	G# A Bb C Eb (18) / C# D Eb F Ab (19)	A# B C D F (16)	260	LIV—	Bb B C D F (11) / F F# G A C (12) / C C# D E G (10)	112	26—27	XLVI—XLVII enh. v.
11532	C# D Eb G# B (19) / F# G Ab C# E (18)	E F G# B D (16)	260	LV	E F F# B D (12) / A Bb B E G (11) / D Eb E A C (10)	112		

I	II		III		IV	V	VI		VII	VIII	IX
Interval group characterising the tonal system	Central transposition(s) of the tonal system		Transposition(s) with lowest quintal index		Quintal index of the tonal system	Ordinal number of the tonal system	Central and minimal transposition(s) of the enharmonic variant with the lowest index in the tonal sytem		Quintal index of the enharm. var.	Ordinal number of the tonal system with respect to the enharm. v.	Ordinal number of the 12−n member, complementary tonal system
11523	C♯ D E♭ G♯ B♭ (20) F♯ G A♭ C♯ E♭ (21)				280	LVI—	F♯ G C D (10) B♭ B C F G (13) C C♯ D G A (9) E F♯ A B (13) A B♭ B D E (10) D E♭ E G A (9)		112 112	24—25	XXXIX—XL enh. v.
11325	G♯ A B♭ C♯ E♭ (21) C♯ D E♭ F♯ A♭ (20)				280	LVII					
11217	D♯ E F G A♭ (19) G♯ A B C D♭ (20)		A♯ B C D E♭ (18)		345	LVIII—	F♯ G A B♭ (13) C C♯ D E F (12)		143 143	47—48	LXII—LXIII
11712	F♯ G A♭ D♯ E (20) B C D♭ G♯ A (19)		E F G♭ C♯ D (18)		345	LIX	A B♭ B F♯ G (13) D E♭ E B C (12)				
11163	A♯ B C D♭ G (21) D♯ E F G♭ C (22)		E♯ F♯ G A♭ D (20)		446	LX—	A B♭ B C F♯ (14) D E♭ E F B (13)		146 146	57—58	LX—LXI enh. v.
11136	A♯ B C D E (22) D♯ E F G♭ A (21)		G♯ A B♭ C♭ D (20)		446	LXI	E F F♯ G B♭ (14) B C C♯ D F (13)				
11145	A♯ B C D♭ F (23) D♯ E F G♭ B (24)		H♯ C♯ D E♭ G (21)		456	LXII—	E F F♯ G B (13) A B♭ B C E (12) E F F♯ G C (11) A B♭ B C F (12) B C C♯ D G (11)		114 114	30—31	LVIII—LIX enh. v.
11154	A♯ B C D♭ F♯ (24) D♯ E F G♭ B (23)		C♯ D E♭ F♭ A (21)		456	LXIII					

270

I	II	III	IV	V	VI	VII	VIII	IX
Interval group characteristics of the tonal system	Central transposition(s) of the tonal system	Transposition(s) with lowest quintal index	Quintal index of the tonal system	Ordinal number of the tonal system	Central and minimal transposition(s) of the enharmonic variant with the lowest index in the tonal system	Quintal index of the enharm. var.	Ordinal number of the tonal system with respect to the enharm. v.	Ordinal number of the 12—n member, complementary tonal system
11127	A♯ B C D♭ E♭ (25) D♭ E F G♭ A♭ (26)	H♯C♯D E♭ F (23)	474 474	LXIV— LXV	E F F♯ G A (11) A♭ B♭ B C D (10)	108 108	20—21	LXIV—LXV enh. v.
11172	D♯ E F G♭ C♯ (26) A♯ B C D♭ G♯ (25)	C♯ D E♭ F♭ B (23)	474 474	LXIV— LXV	E F F♯ G D (11) A♭ B♭ B C G (10)	108 108		
11118	H♯ C♯ D E♭ F♭ (30)		800	LXVI	B♭ B C C♯ D (14) E♭ E F F♯ G (15) A♭ B C C♯ (15) D♭ E♭ E F F♯ (14)	177 177	65	LXVI enh. v.

SIX-NOTE TONAL SYSTEM

I	II	III	IV	V	VI	VII	VIII	IX
122322	B C D E G A (9) E F G A C D (9)		70	I			1	I
123222	B C D F G A (10)		96	II—			2—3	II—
122232	E F G A B D (10)		96	III				III
122124	B C D E F G (11)		99	IV—			4—5	XLIV—XLV enh. v.
122142	B C D E F A (11)		99	V				XLV
122214	E F G A B C (12)		100	VI			6	XLVIII enh. v.
121224	F♯ G A B♭ C D (12)		158	VII—			22—23	XXVII—
121422	F♯ G A B♭ D E (12)		158	VIII				XXVIII enh. v.

271

I	II	III	IV	V	VI	VII	VIII	IX
Interval group characterising the tonal system	Central transposition(s) of the tonal system	Transposition(s) with lowest quintal index	Quintal index of the tonal system	Ordinal number of the tonal system	Central and minimal transposition(s) of the enharmonic variant with the lowest index in the tonal system	Quintal index of the enharm. var.	Ordinal number of the tonal system with respect to the enharm. v.	Ordinal number of the 12—n member, complementary tonal system
132222	F# G Bb C D E (13)		161	IX			24—25	IX—X
122223	A Bb C D E F# (13)		161	X				
121242	F# G A Bb C E (14)		162	XI			26	XLVI enh. v.
131232	A Bb C# D E G (13) / D Eb F# G A C (13)		194	XII			54	XXXV enh. v.
122133	E F G Ab C# (16) / A Bb C D Eb F# (16)		196	XIII			55	XXXIII enh. v.
131322	A Bb C# D F G (14) / D Eb F# G Bb C (16)		204	XIV	F#G Bb B D E (14)	166	30—31	XIV—XV enh. v.
122313	C# D E F# A Bb (16) / F# G A B D Eb (14)		204	XV	A Bb C D F F# (14)	166		
121413	C# D E F A Bb (14) / F# G A Bb D Eb (15)		204	XVI			62—63	XXXI—XXXII enh. v.
121314	F# G A Bb C# D (15) / B C D Eb F# G (14)		204	XVII				
121233	C# D E F G Bb (15) / F# G A Bb C Eb (17)		206	XVIII	Eb E F# G A C (15) / Bb B C# D E G (15)	200	58—59	XVIII—XIX enh. v.
121332	F# G A Bb C# E (17) / B C D Eb F# A (15)		206	XIX	A Bb C C# E G (15) / D Eb F F# A C (15)	200		

I	II	III	IV	V	VI	VII	VIII	IX
Interval group characterising the tonal system	Central transposition(s) of the tonal system	Transposition(s) with lowest quintal index	Quintal index of the tonal system	Ordinal number of the tonal system	Central and minimal transposition(s) of the enharmonic variant with the lowest index in the tonal system	Quintal index of the enharm. var.	Ordinal number of the tonal system with respect to the enharm. v.	Ordinal number of the 12−n member, complementary tonal system
112224	C# D Eb F G A (15)		241	XX	Bb B C D E F# (15)	169	40	XX—XXI enh. v.
114222	C# D Eb G A B (15)		241	XXI	E F F# Bb C D (15)	169	41	
114213	C# D Eb G A Bb (16)		248	XXII	Bb B C E F# G (16)	170	44	XLII—XLIII enh. v.
113124	C# D Eb F# G A (16)		248		E F F#A Bb C (16)	170	45	
112224	C# D Eb F G A (17)		249	XXIV			78	XXIV—XXV enh. v.
114222	C# D Eb G A B (17)		249	XXV			79	
222222	Eb F G A B C# (18)		250	XXVI			80	XXVI
112233	C# D Eb F G Bb (18)	G# A Bb C D F (16)	256	XXVII	F F#G A Bb D (12) / Bb B C D E G (12)	128	10	VII—VIII
113322	C# D Eb F# A B (18)	F# G Ab B D E (16)	256	XXVIII	E F F#A C D (12) / Ab Bb D F G (12)	128	11	
113142	C# D Eb F# G B (18)		256	XXIX	E F F# A Bb D (14)	166	32	XXIX—XXX enh. v.
112413	C# D Eb F A Bb (18)		256	XXX	Bb B C D F#G (14)	166	33	
113133	C# D Eb F# G Bb (19)		263	XXXI	F F#G Bb B D (15)	171	45	XVI—XVII
113313	C# D Eb F# A Bb (19)		263	XXXII	A Bb B D F F# (15)	171	46	
121323	F# G A Bb C# Eb (20)		264	XXXIII	Bb B C#D F G (16) / Eb E F#G Bb C (18) / A Bb C C#E F# (18) / D Eb F F#A B (16)	210	70	XIII

I	II		III	IV	V	VI		VII	VIII	IX
Interval group characterising the tonal system	Central transposition(s) of the tonal system		Transposition(s) with lowest quintal index	Quintal index of the tonal system	Ordinal number of the tonal system	Central and minimal transposition(s) of the enharmonic variant with the lowest index in the tonal system		Quintal index of the enharm. var.	Ordinal number of the tonal system with respect to the enharm. v.	Ordinal number of the 12−n member, complementary tonal system
121215	G♯ A B♭ C D E♭ C♯ D E F G A♭	(17) (17)		288	XXXIV	F♯G A♭ B♭ C C♯ B C D E♭ F F♯ B♭ B C♯ D E F E E F♯ G A B♭	(17) (17) (17) (17)	210 210	17	LVIII enh. v.
123132	D E♭ F G♯ A C G A♭ B♭ C♯ D F G♯ A B D E♭ F♯ C♯ D E G A♭ B	(17) (19) (19) (17)		294 294	XXXV	B C D F F♯ A E F G♭ B♭ B D	(13) (13)	132	16	XII
123123	D E♭ F G♯ A B G A♭ B♭ C♯ D E	(18) (18)		294 294	XXXVI–XXXVII	E F G♭ B♭ B C♯ A B♭ C E♭ E F♯	(18) (18)	212 212	72–73	XXXVI–XXXVII enh. v.
132132	D E♭ F♯ G♯ A C G A♭ B C♯ D F	(18) (18)				F♯ G B♭ C C♯ E B C E♭ F F♯ A	(18) (18)			
112215	G♯ A B♭ C D E♭ C♯ D E♭ F G A♭	(18) (20)		302 302	XXXVIII–XXXIX	F F♯ G A B C B♭ B C D E F	(18) (18)	134 134	17–18	LIX–LX enh. v.
115122	C♯ D E♭ G♯ A B F♯ G A♭ C♯ D E	(20) (18)				E F F♯ B C D A♭ B♭ B E F G	(18) (18)			
114123	G♯ A B♭ D E♭ F C♯ D E G A♭ B♭	(19) (21)		308 308	XL–XLI	F F♯ G B C D B♭ B C D E F	(13) (15)	134 134	19–20	XL–XLI enh. v.
113214	C♯ D E♭ F G♯ A F♯ G A B♭ C♯ D	(21) (19)				E F F♯ A B C A B♭ B D E F	(15) (13)			

I	II	III	IV	V	VI	VII	VIII	IX
Interval group characteris-ing the tonal system	Central transposition(s) of the tonal system	Transposition(s) with lowest quintal index	Quintal index of the tonal system	Ordinal number of the tonal system	Central and minimal transposition(s) of the enharmonic variant with the lowest index in the tonal system	Quintal index of the enharm. var.	Ordinal number of the tonal system with respect to the enharm. v.	Ordinal number of the 12-n member, complementary tonal system
114132	G# A B♭ D E♭ F# (20) C# D E♭ G A♭ B (20)		308 308	XLII– XLIII	E F F# B♭ B D (16)	174 174	48—49	XXII–XXIII enh. v.
112314	C# D E♭ F G# A (20) F# G A♭ B♭ C# D (20)				B♭ B C D F F# (16)			
112323	G# A B♭ C E♭ F (21) C# D E♭ F A♭ B♭ (23)	A# B C D F G (17)	314 314	XLIV– XLV	F F# G A C D (11) B♭ B C D F G (13)	128 128	8—9	IV–V
113232	C# D E♭ F# G# B (23) F# G A♭ B C# E (21)	E F G# A B D (17)	314 314		E F F# A B D (13) A♭ B♭ D E G (11)			
112332	G# A B♭ C E♭ F# (22) C# D E♭ F A♭ B (22) C# D E♭ F G# B (22) F# G A♭ B♭ C# E (22)			XLVI	C C# D E G B (14) F F# G A C E♭ (16) A♭ B♭ B C# E G (16) D E♭ E F# A C (14)	200 200	60	XI
113115	G# A B♭ C# D E♭ (21) C# D E♭ F# G A♭ (21)		316	XLVII	F F# G♭ B♭ B C (17) C C D F F# G (15) E F F# A B♭ B (17) B C C# E F F# (15)	175 175	50	LXXI enh. v.
113223	G# A B♭ C# E♭ F (24) C# D E♭ F# A♭ B♭ (24) F# G A♭ B♭ C# E♭ (24) C# D E♭ F# G# B♭ (24)		328 328	XLVIII	D E♭ E G A B (12) C C# D F G A (12)	100 100	29	VI
131313	G A♭ B C D# E (21) C D♭ E F G# A (21)		394	XLIX	A B C# D F F# (17) D E♭ F F# G B♭ B (17)	214	76	XLIX enh. v.

I	II	III	IV	V	VI	VII	VIII	IX
Interval group characterising the tonal system	Central transposition(s) of the tonal system	Transposition(s) with lowest quintal index	Quintal index of the tonal system	Ordinal number of the tonal system	Central and minimal transposition(s) of the enharmonic variant with the lowest index in the tonal system	Quintal index of the enharm. var.	Ordinal number of the tonal system with respect to the enharm. v.	Ordinal number of the 12—n member, complementary tonal system
112134	D# E F G Ab C (21) G# A Bb C Db F (23)	A# B C D Eb G (19)	400 400	L— LI	F F#G A Bb D (13)	163 163	27—28	L— LI enh. v.
113412	F# G Ab B D# E (23) B C Db E G# A (21)	E F Gb A C# D (19)			A Bb B D F# G (13)			
112134	D# E F G Ab B (22) G# A Bb C Db E (22)		400 400	LII— LIII	A Bb B C# D F (16) D Eb F# Gb Bb (16)	208 208	68—69	LII— LIII enh. v.
114312	F# G Ab C D# E (22) B C Db F G# A (22)				C C#D F# Ab Bb (16) F F# G B Db Eb (16)			
112125	D# E F G Ab Bb (23) G# A Bb C Db Eb (25)	A# B C D Eb F (21)	414 414	LIV— LV	F F#G A Bb C (15) C C# D E F G (13)	130 130	14—15	LXVII— LXVIII enh. v.
115212	F# G Ab C# D# E (25) B C Db F# G# A (23)	E F Gb B C# D (21)			A Bb B E F# G (15) D Eb E A B C (13)			
112512	F# G Ab Bb D# E (24) B C Db Eb G# A (24)		414 414	LVI— LVII	C C#D E A Bb (14) F F# G A D Eb (14)	198 198	56—57	LXIII— LXIV enh. v.
112152	D# E F G Ab C# (24) G# A Bb C Db F# (24)				A Bb B C#D G (14) D Eb E F# G C(14)			
111333	A# B C D Eb G (23) D# E F G# A C (23)		512	LVIII	E F F# G BbC# (19) A Bb C Eb F# (19)	218	77	XXXIV enh. v.

276

I	II	III	IV	V	VI	VII	VIII	IX
Interval group characterising the tonal system	Central transposition(s) of the tonal system	Transposition(s) with lowest quintal index	Quintal index of the tonal system	Ordinal number of the tonal system	Central and minimal transposition(s) of the enharmonic variant with the lowest index in the tonal system	Quintal index of the enharm. var.	Ordinal number of the tonal system with respect to the enharm. v.	Ordinal number of the 12-n member, complementary tonal system
111423	A♯ B C D♭ F G (24) D♯ E F G♭ B♭ C (26)	E♯ F♯ G A♭ C D (22)	522 522	LIX— LX	E F F♯ G B♭ C (16) B C C♯ D F G (14)	170 170	42—43	XXXVIII— XXXIX enh. v.
111324	A♯ B C D♭ E F♯ (26) D♯ E F G♭ A B (24)	G♯ A B♭ C♭ D E♭ (22)	522 522		A B♭ B C E F♯ (16) D E♭ E F A B (14)			
111315	A♯ B C D♭ E F (25) D♯ E F G♭ A B♭ (25)		522 522	LXI— LXII	E F F♯ G B♭ B (17)	175 175	51—52	LXI— LXII enh. v.
111513	D♯ E F G♭ B C (25) G♯ A B♭ C♭ E F (25)				A B♭ B C F F♯ (17)			
111243	A♯ B C D♭ E♭ G (26) D♯ E F G♭ A♭ C (28)	E♯ F♯ G A♭ B D (24)	540 540	LXIII— LXIV	A B♭ B C D F♯ (14)	166 166	34—35	LVI— LVII enh. v.
111342	A♯ B C D♭ E G♯ (28) D♯ E F G♭ A C♯ (26)	G♯ A B♭ C♭ D F♯ (24)	540 540		E F F♯ G B♭ D (14)			
111225	A♯ B C D♭ E♭ F (28) D♯ E F G♭ A♭ B♭ (30)	H♯ C♯ D E♭ F G (24)	550 550	LXV— LXVI	E F F♯ G A B (14) A B♭ B C D E (12)	130 130	12—13	LXV— LXVI enh. v.
111522	A♯ B C D♭ F♭ G♯ (30) D♯ E F G♭ B C♯ (28)	C♯ D E♭ F♭ A B (24)	550 550		E F F♯ G C D (12) A B♭ B C F G (14)			
111234	A♯ B C D♭ E♭ F♯ (29) D♯ E F G♭ A♭ B (29)		550 550	LXVII— LXVIII	E F F♯ G A C (13) A B♭ B C D F (13)	167 167	36—37	LIV— LV enh. v.
111432	D♯ E F G♭ B♭ C♯ (29) G♯ A B♭ C♭ E♭ F♯ (29)				E F F♯ G B♭ D (13) A B♭ B C E G (13)			

I	II	III	IV	V	VI	VII	VIII	IX
Interval group characterising the tonal system	Central transposition(s) of the tonal system	Transposition(s) with lowest quintal index	Quintal index of the tonal system	Ordinal number of the tonal system	Central and minimal transposition(s) of the enharmonic variant with the lowest index in the tonal system	Quintal index of the enharm. var.	Ordinal number of the tonal system Aith respect to the enharm. v.	Ordinal number of the 12—n member, complementary tonal system
111252	A♯ B C D♭ E♭ G♯ (31) D♯ E F G♭ A♭ C♯ (31)		568	LXIX	E F F♯ G A D (11) A B♭ B C D G (11)	124	7	LXIX enh. v.
114114	A♯ B C E F G♭ (26)		586	LXX	B♭ B C E F F♯ (18)	178	53	LXX enh. v.
111414	A♯ B C D♭ F G♭ (31) D♯ E F G♭ A♯ B (31)	H♯ C♯ D E♭ G A♭ (27) C♯ D E♭ F♭ G♯ A (27)	631 631	LXXI	E F F♯ G B C (15) A B♭ B C E F (15)	136	21	XLVII enh. v.
112116	E♯ F♯ G A B♭ C♭ (28)		736	LXXII	F F♯ G A B♭ B (16)	172	47	LXXV enh.v.
111216	E♯ F♯ G A♭ B♭ C♭ (34)	H♯ C♯ D E♭ F G♭ (32)	785	LXXIII LXXIV	E F F♯ G A B♭ (15)	167 167	38—39	LXXVI LXXVII enh. v.
111612	G♯ A B♭ C♭ E♭ F♯ (34)	C♯ D E♭ F♭ A♯ B (32)	785		A B♭ B C F♯ G (15)			
111144	H♯ C♯ D E♭ F♭ A♭ (28)		838	LXXV	A B♭ B C C♯ F (18) D E♭ E F F♯ B♭ (18) B♭ B C C♯ D F♯ (18) E♭ E F F♯ G B (18)	214 214	74—75	LXXII enh. v.
111135	H♯ C♯ D E♭ F♭ G (31)		911	LXXVI	A♭ B C C♯ E (17) D E♭ E F F♯ A (15) B♭ B C C♯ D G (15) E♭ E F F♯ G C (17)	204	64—65	LXXIII LXXIV enh. v.
111153	H♯ C♯ D E♭ F♭ A (31)		911	LXXVII		204		
111126	H♯ C♯ D E♭ F♭ G♭ (38)		974	LXXVIII	B B♭ C♯ D E (16) E♭ E F F♯ G A (16) A♭ B C C♯ G♯ (16) D E♭ E F F♯ C (16)	204	66—67	LXXVIII LXXIX enh. v.
111162	H♯ C♯ D E♭ F♭ A♯ (38)		974	LXXIX		204		

SEVEN-NOTE TONAL SYSTEM

I	II	III	IV	V	VI	VII	VIII	IX
Interval group characterising the tonal system	Central transposition(s) of the tonal system	Transposition(s) with lowest quintal index	Quintal index of the tonal system	Ordinal number of the tonal system	Central and minimal transposition(s) of the enharmonic variant with the lowest index in the tonal system	Quintal index of the enharm. var.	Ordinal number of the tonal system with respect to the enharm. v.	Ordinal number of the 12–n member, complementary tonal system
111117	G♯♯ A♯ B C D♭ E♭ (45) C♯ D♯ E F G♭ A♭ (45)		1450	LXXX	A B♭ B C C♯ D (15) D E♭ E F F♯ G (15)	202	61	LXXX enh. v.
1221222	B C D E F G A (12)		108	I			1	I
1212222	F♯ G A B♭ C D E (14)		182	II			8	VI
1212213	C♯ D E F G A B♭ (16) F♯ G A B♭ C D E♭ (17)		231 231	III IV			29—30	XXXII—XXXIII enh. v.
1213122	F♯ G A B♭ C♯ D E (17) B C D E F♯ G A (16)							
1122222	C♯ D E♭ F G A B (18)		280	V			55	XXIII
1122213	C♯ D E♭ F G A B♭ (19)	G♯ A B C D E F (18)	287	VI	B♭ B C D E F♯ G (16)	237	38—39	XVII—XVIII enh. v.
1131222	C♯ D E♭ F♯ G A B (19)	F♯ G A♭ B C D E (18)	287	VII	E F F♯ A B C D (16)	237		
1131213	C♯ D E♭ F♯ G A B♭ (20)		294	VIII	F F♯ G B♭ B C♯ G (20) B♭ B C E♭ E F♯ D (21) E F F♯ A B C C♯ (21) A♭ B♭ B D E♭ F F♯ (20)	247 247	52	XXXII
1212123	G♯ A B C D E♭ F (20) C♯ D E F G A♭ B (21)		336 336	IX X	F♯ G A B♭ C C♯ E♭ (22) C♯ D E F G G♯ B♭ (21)	298 298	64—65	XXVIII—XXIX
1212132	G♯ A B C D E♭ F♯ (21) C♯ D E F G A♭ B (20)				E♭ E F F♯ G A♭ B♭ C♯ (22) A♭ A B C D E♭ F♯ (21)			

279

I Interval group characteris-ing the tonal system	II Central transposition(s) of the tonal system	III Transposition(s) with lowest quintal index	IV Quintal index of the tonal system	V Ordinal number of the tonal system	VI Central and minimal transposition(s) of the enharmonic variant with the lowest index in the tonal system	VII Quintal index of the enharm. var.	VIII Ordinal number of the tonal system with respect to the enharm. v.	IX Ordinal number of the 12−n member, complementary tonal system
1122123	G♯ A B♭ C D E♭ F (21) C♯ D E♭ F G A♭ B♭ (24)	A♯ B C D E F G (19)	350 350	XI XII	F♯ G A B C D (14) B♭ B C D E F G (15)	150 150	4—5	VII—VIII
1132122	C♯ D E♭ F♯ G♯ A B (24) F♯ G A♭ B C♯ D E (21)	E F G♭ A B C D (19)			E F F♯ A B C D (15) A♭ B D E F G (14)			
1122132	G♯ A B♭ C D E♭ F♯ (22) C♯ D E♭ F G A♭ B (23)		350 350	XIII XIV	C C♯ D F♯ G B♭ (18) F F♯ G A B C E♭ (19)	237 237	40—41	XXIV—XXV
1123122	C♯ D E♭ F G A B (23) F♯ G A♭ B♭ C♯ D E (22)				A B♭ B C♯ E F G (19) D E♭ E F♯ A B♭ C (18)			
1123113	C♯ D E♭ F G♯ A B♭ (24) F♯ G A♭ B♭ C♯ D E♭ (25)		364 364	XV XVI	F F♯ G B♭ B C D (17) C C♯ D F F♯ G A (16)	195 195	19—20	XIV—XV
1131132	G♯ A B♭ C♯ D E♭ F♯ (25) C♯ D E♭ F♯ G A♭ B (24)				E F F♯ A B♭ D (17) A♭ B D E♭ E G (16)			

280

I	II		III		IV	V	VI		VII	VIII	IX
Interval group characterising the tonal system	Central transposition(s) of the tonal system		Transposition(s) with lowest quintal index		Quintal index of the tonal system	Ordinal number of the tonal system	Central and minimal transposition(s) of the enharmonic variant, with the lowest index in the tonal system		Quintal index of the enharm. var.	Ordinal number of the tonal system with respect to the enharm. v.	Ordinal number of the 12−n member, complementary tonal system
1121313	D♯ E F G A♭ B C	(24)	A♯ B C D E♭ F G	(23)	455	XVII—	F F♯ G A B♭ C♯ D (18)		241	44—45	XXX—XXXI enh. v.
	G♯ A B♭ C D♭ E F	(25)			455	XVIII	B♭ B C D E♭ F♯ G (19)		241		
1131312	F♯ G A♭ B C D♯ E	(25)	E F G♭ A B♭ C♯ D	(23)			E F F♯ A B♭ C♯ D (19)				
	B C D♭ E F G♯ A	(24)					A B♭ B D E♭ F♯ G (18)				
1121223	D♯ E F G A♭ B♭ C	(25)	E♯ F♯ G A B♭ C D	(21)	469	XIX—	F F♯ G A B♭ C♯ D (15)		187	9—10	IV—V
	G♯ A B♭ C D♭ E♭ F	(28)			469	XX			187		
1132212	F♯ G A♭ B C♯ D♯ E	(28)	A B♭ C♭ D E F♯ G	(21)			A B♭ B D E F♯ G (15)				
	B C D♭ E F♯ G♯ A	(25)									
1122312	F♯ G A♭ B♭ C D♯ E	(26)	C♯ D E♭ F G A♯ B	(25)	469	XXI—	C C♯ D E♭ F♯ A♭ (18)		235	33—34	XIX—XX
	B C D♭ E♭ F♯ G♯ A	(27)			469	XXII	F F♯ G A B D E♭ (17)		235		
1121322	D♯ E F G A♭ B♭ C♯	(27)	C♯ D E♭ F G♭ B	(25)			A B♭ B C♯ D F G (17)				
	G♯ A B♭ C D♭ E♭ F♯	(26)					D E♭ E F♯ G B♭ C (18)				

I	II	III	IV	V	VI	VII	VIII	IX
Interval group characterising the tonal system	Central transposition(s) of the tonal system	Transposition(s) with lowest quintal index	Quintal index of the tonal system	Ordinal number of the tonal system	Central and minimal transposition(s) of the enharmonic variant with the lowest index in the tonal system	Quintal index of the enharm. var.	Ordinal number of the tonal system with respect to the enharm. v.	Ordinal number of the 12−n member, complementary tonal system
1121232	D♯ E F G A♭ B♭ C♯ (28)	A♯ B C D E♭ F G♯ (27)	483	XXIII	A B♭ B C♯ D E G (16)	225	25	IX
	G♯ A B♭ C D♭ E♭ F♯ (29)	E F G♭ A♭ B C♯ D (27)	483	XXIV	D E♭ E F♯ G A C (15)	225	26	X
1123212	F♯ G A♭ B♭ C♯ D♯ E (29)				C C♯ D E G A B♭ (15)			
	B C D♭ E♭ F♯ G♯ A (28)				F F♯ G A C D E♭ (16)			
1113123	A♯ B C D♭ E F G (26)	E♯ F♯ G A♭ B C D (25)			B♭ B C C♯ E F G (20)			
	D♯ E F G♭ A B♭ C (27)				E♭ E F F♯ G B♭ C (21)			
1113213	A♯ B C D♭ E F♯ G (27)	G♯ A B♭ C♭ D E F (25)	588	XXV	F F♯ G G♯ B C D (19)	243	48	L
	D♯ E F G A B C (26)		588	XXVI	B♭ B C C♯ E F♯ G (21)	243	49	LI enh. v.
					E♭ E F F♯ A B C (20)			
					A♭ A B♭ B D E F (19)			
1112223	D♯ E F G♭ A♭ B♭ C (29)	B♯ C♯ D E♭ F G A (25)	616	XXVII	A B♭ B C D E F♯ (16)	190	13	XI
	A♯ B C D♭ E♭ F G (32)		616	XXVIII	D E♭ E F G A B (15)	190	14	XII
1113222	A♯ B C D♭ E F♯ G♯ (32)	C♯ D E♭ F♭ G A B (25)			E F F♯ G B♭ C D (16)			
	D♯ E F G♭ A B C♯ (29)				B C C♯ D F G A (15)			

282

This table is rotated 90°. Columns are numbered I–IX.

I	II	III	IV	V	VI	VII	VIII	IX
Interval group characterising the tonal system	Central transposition(s) of the tonal system	Transposition(s) with lowest quintal index	Quintal index of the tonal system	Ordinal number of the tonal system	Central and minimal transposition(s) of the enharmonic variant with the lowest index in the tonal system	Quintal index of the enharm. var.	Ordinal number of the tonal system with respect to the enharm. v.	Ordinal number of the 12–n member, complementary tonal system
1112313	D# E F G♭ A♭ B C (30) A# B C D♭ E♭ F# G (31)	E# F# G A♭ B♭ C D (29)	616	XXIX–XXX	A B♭ B C D F F# (17)	195	21–22	XXVI–XXVII enh. v.
1113132	A# B C D E F G# (31) D# E F G♭ A B♭ C# (30)	G# A B C♭ D E♭ F# (31)	616		E F F# G B♭ B D (17)	195		
1112232	A# B C D♭ E♭ F G# (34) D# E F G♭ A♭ B♭ C# (35)	H# C# D E♭ F G A# (32)	644	XXXI–XXXII	E F F# G A B D (14) A B♭ B C D E G (13)	146	2–3	II–III
1112322	A# B C D♭ E♭ F# G# (35) D# E F G♭ A♭ B C# (34)	C# D E♭ F♭ G♭ A B (32)	644		E F F# G A C D (13) A B♭ B C D F G (14)	146		
1122114	A# B C D E F G♭ (26)		658	XXXIII	B♭ B C D E F F# (25)	317	66	XXXVII enh. v.
1121214	A# B C D E♭ F G♭ (29)	H# C# D E F G A♭ (27)	679	XXXIV–XXXV	A B♭ B C# D E F (18) D E♭ E F# G A B♭ (17)	235	35–36	XLII–XLIII enh. v.
1141212	E F G♭ A# B C# D (29)	D E♭ F♭ G# A B C (27)	679		C C# D F# G A B♭ (17) F F# G B C D E♭ (18)	235		

I Interval group characteristics of the tonal system	II Central transposition(s) of the tonal system	III Transposition(s) with lowest quintal index	IV Quintal index of the tonal system	V Ordinal number of the tonal system	VI Central and minimal transposition(s) of the enharmonic variant with the lowest index in the tonal system	VII Quintal index of the enharm. var.	VIII Ordinal number of the tonal system with respect to the enharm. v.	IX Ordinal number of the 12−n member, complementary tonal system
1121412	C♯ D E♭ F G♭ A♮ B (32)		700	XXXVI	C C♯ D E F A B♭ (17) F♯ G A B♭ D E♭ (18) A B♭ B C♯ D E F (18) D E♭ E F♯ G B C (17)	235 235	37	XLIX enh. v.
1113114	A♯ B C D♭ E F G♭ (33)	B♯ C♯ D E♭ F♯ G A♭ (31)	707	XXXVII–XXXVIII	E F F♯ G B♭ B C (19) B C C♯ D F F♯ G (19) A B♭ B C E F F♯ (18) D E E♭ F A B♭ B (19) (18)	199 199	23–24	LII enh. v.
1114113	D♯ E F G♭ A♮ B C (33)	C♯ D E♭ F♭ G♯ A B♭ (31)	707					
1112214	A♯ B C D♭ E♭ F G♭ (36)	F♯♯ G♯ A B♭ C D E♭ (29)	728	XXXIX–XL	E F F♯ G A B C (16) A B♭ B C D E F (15) E F F♯ G B C D (15) A B♭ B C E F G (16)	152 152	6–7	LVI–LVII enh. v.
1114122	D♯ E F G♭ A♮ B C♯ (36)	F♯ G A♭ B♭ C♯ D E (29)	728					
1121133	E♯ F♯ G A B♭ C♭ D (28)		826	XLI	F F♯ G A B♭ B D (16)	192	17	XVI

I	II	III	IV	V	VI	VII	VIII	IX
Interval group characterising the tonal system	Central transposition(s) of the tonal system	Transposition(s) with lowest quintal index	Quintal index of the tonal system	Ordinal number of the tonal system	Central and minimal transposition(s) of the enharmonic variant with the lowest index in the tonal system	Quintal index of the enharm. var.	Ordinal number of the tonal system with respect to the enharm. v.	Ordinal number of the 12—n member, complementary tonal system
1112133	E# F# G A♭ B♭ C♭ D (33)	B# C# D E♭ F G♭ A (32)	861	XLII	E F F# G A B♭ C# (20) / A B♭ B C D E♭ F# (19)	243	**50**—61	XXXV—XXXVI
1113312	G# A B♭ C♭ D E# F# (33)	C# D E♭ F♭ G A# B (32)	861	XLIII	E F F# G B♭ C# D (19) / A B♭ C E♭ F# G (20)	243		
1121124	E# F# G A B♭ C♭ D♭ (35)	B# C# D E F G♭ A♭ (34)	875	XLIV	B C C# E♭ E F G (21) / F# G G# B♭ B C D (20)	287	**60**—61	XL—XLI enh. v.
1121142	E# F# G A B♭ C♭ D# (35)	A# B C D E♭ F♭ G# (34)	875	XLV	B C C# E♭ E F A (20) / E F F# A♭ A B♭ D (21)	287		
1112124	E# F# G A♭ B♭ C♭ D♭ (40)	G## A# B C D♭ F (34)	910	XLVI	E F F# G A B♭ C (17) / B C C# D E F G (16)	191	**15**—16	LIV—LV enh. v.
1114212	G# A B♭ C♭ D# E# F# (40)	E F G♭ A♭ B C# D (34)	910	XLVII	A B♭ B C E F# G (17) / D E♭ E F A B C (16)	191		
1112142	E# F# G A♭ B♭ C♭ D# (40)	B# C# D E♭ F G♭ A# (39)	910	XLVIII	E F F# G A B♭ D (15)	187	**11**—12	XLVII—XLVIII enh. v.
1112412	G# A B♭ C♭ D♭ E# F# (40)	C# D E♭ F♭ G A# B (39)	910	XLIX	A B♭ B C D F# G (15)	187		

I	II	III	IV	V	VI	VII	VIII	IX
Interval group characterising the tonal system	Central transposition(s) of the tonal system	Transposition(s) with lowest quintal index	Quintal index of the tonal system	Ordinal number of the tonal system	Central and minimal transposition(s) of the enharmonic variant with the lowest index in the tonal system	Quintal index of the enharm. var.	Ordinal number of the tonal system with respect to the enharm. v.	Ordinal number of the $12-n$ member, complementary tonal system
1111323	B♯ C♯ D E♭ F♭ G A (32)		1022	L	C C♯ D E♭ E G A (16)	195	18	XIII
1111314	B♯ C♯ D E♭ F♭ G A♭ (37)	F♯♯ G♯ A B♭ C♭ D E♭ (36)			A B♭ B C C♯ E F (21) D E♭ E F F♯ A B♭ (21)	252 252	53—54	XLIV—XLV enh. v.
1111413	B♯ C♯ D E♭ F♭ G♯ A (37)	E♯ F♯ G A♭ B♭♭ C♯ D (36)	1057 1057	LI—LII	B♭ B C C♯ D F♯ G (21) E♭ E F F♯ G B C (21)			
1111233	B♯ C♯ D E♭ F♭ G♭ A (39)				B♭ B C♯ D E G (17) E♭ E F F♯ G A C (18)	231 231	31—32	XXI—XXII
1111332	B♯ C♯ D E♭ F♭ G A♯ (39)		1085 1085	LIII—LIV	A B♭ B C C♯ E G (18) D E♭ E F F♯ A C (17)			
1111224	B♯ C♯ D E♭ F♭ G♭ A♭ (44)	A♯♯ B♯ C♯ D E♭ F G (39)			B C C♯ D E♭ F G (19) F♯ G G♯ A B♭ C D (18)	283 283	56—57	XXXVIII—XXXIX
1111422	B♯ C♯ D E♭ F♭ G♯ A♯ (44)	C♯ D E♭ F♭ G♭ A B (39)	1120 1120	LV—LVI	C♯ D E♭ E F A B (18) G♯ A B♭ B C E F♯ (19)			

Table (rotated 90°; columns I–IX read as in the column headers):

I — Interval group characterising the tonal system	II — Central transposition(s) of the tonal system	III — Transposition(s) with lowest quintal index	IV — Quintal index of the tonal system	V — Ordinal number of the tonal system	VI — Central and minimal transposition(s) of the enharmonic variant with the lowest index in the tonal system	VII — Quintal index of the enharm. var.	VIII — Ordinal number of the tonal system with respect to the enharm. v.	IX — Ordinal number of the 12—n member, complementary tonal system
1111242	B♯ C♯ D E♭ F♭ G♭ A♯ (46)		1148	LVII	B C C♯ D E♭ F A (19)	283	58	XLVI enh. v.
					C♯ D E♭ E F G B (19)	283		
1112115	C♯ D♯ E F G A♭ B♭ (42)	G♯♯ A♯ B C D♭ E♭ F♭ (41)	1372	LVIII	C C♯ D E♭ F F♯ G (20)	290	62—63	LXII
	F♯ G♯ A B♭ C D♭ E♭♭ (43)				G G♯ A B♭ C C♯ D (19)	290		LXIII enh. v.
1115112	F♯ G A♭ B♭ C♯ D♯ E (43)	E F G A♭ B♯ C♯ D (41)	1372	LIX	C♯ D E♭ E A B♭ B (20)			
	B C D♭ E♭♭ F♯♯ G♯ A (42)				F♯ G A♭ A D E♭ E (19)			
1111215	C♯ D♯ E F G A♭ B♭ (49)	A♯♯ B♯ C♯ D E♭ F G♭ (46)	1442	LX	B♭ B C C♯ D E F (19)	241	46—47	LX
	F♯♯ G♯ A B♭ C♭ D♭ E♭ (50)				E♭ E F F♯ G A B♭ (20)	241		LXI enh. v.
1111512	E♯ F♯ G A B♭ C♯ D♯ (50)	C♯ D E♭ F♭ G♭ A♯ B (46)	1442	LXI	A B♭ B C C♯ F♯ G (20)			
	A♯ B C D♭ E♭♭ F♯♯ G♯ (49)				E F F♯ G G♯ C♯ D (19)			
1111134	G♯♯ A♯ B C D♭ E♭ F (48)	A♯♯ B♯ C♯ D E♭ F♭ G (46)	1631	LXII	A B♭ B C♯ D F (18)	239	42—43	LVIII
	C♯ D♯ E F G♭ A♭ B♭ (49)				D E♭ E F F♯ G B♭ (19)	239		LIX enh. v.
1111143	G♯♯ A♯ B C D♭ E♭ F♯ (49)	B♯ C♯ D E♭ F♭ G♭ A (46)	1631	LXIII	A B♭ B C C♯ D F♯ (19)			
	C♯ D♯ E F G♭ A♭ B (48)				D E♭ E F F♯ G B (18)			

I	II	III	IV	V	VI	VII	VIII	IX
Interval group characteristics of the tonal system	Central transposition(s) of the tonal system	Transposition(s) with lowest quintal index	Quintal index of the tonal system	Ordinal number of the tonal system	Central and minimal transposition(s) of the enharmonic variant with the lowest index in the tonal system	Quintal index of the enharm. var.	Ordinal number of the tonal system with respect to the enharm. v.	Ordinal number of the $12-n$ member, complementary tonal system
1111125	G𝄪 A♯ B C D E♭♭ F♭ (55) C♯ D♯ E F G♭ A♭♭ B♭♭ (56)	A𝄪 B♯ C♯ D E♭ F♭ G♭ (53)	1729	LXIV— LXV	A B♭ B C♯ D E (17) D E♭ E F F♯ G A (16)	229	27—28	LXIV— LXV enh. v.
1111152	G𝄪 A♯ B C D♭ E♭♭ F♯𝄪 (56) C♯ D♯ E F G♭ A♭♭ B♯ (55)	B♯ C♯ D E♭ F♭ G♭♭ A𝄪 (53)	1729		A B♭ B C♯ D G (16) D E♭ E F F♯ G C (17)	229		
1111116	A♯ B♯ C♯ D E♭ F♭ G♭ (60)		2380	LXVI	B C C♯ D E♭ E F (20)	286	59	LXVI enh. v.

EIGHT-NOTE TONAL SYSTEM

I	II	III	IV	V	VI	VII	VIII	IX
11122122	E F F♯ G A B C D (16) A B♭ B C D E F G (16)		168	I			1	I
11121222	E F F♯ G A B♭ C D (17)		208	II— III			2—3	II— III
11122212	A♭ B C D E F♯ G (17)		208					
11212212	C C♯ D E F G A B♭ (18) F F♯ G A B♭ C D E♭ (20)		262 262	IV			10	IV
11212122	A B♭ B C♯ D E F♯ G (20) D E♭ E F♯ G A B C (18)							
11212122	A B♭ B C D E F G (19) D E♭ E F♯ G A B C (19)		262 262	V— VI			11—12	XI— XII
11221212	C C♯ D E F♯ G A B♭ (19) F F♯ G A B C D E♭ (19)							

I	II	III	IV	V	VI	VII	VIII	IX
Interval group characterising the tonal system	Central transposition(s) of the tonal system	Transposition(s) with lowest quintal index	Quintal index of the tonal system	Ordinal number of the tonal system	Central and minimal transposition(s) of the enharmonic variant with the lowest index in the tonal system	Quintal index of the enharm. var.	Ordinal number of the tonal system with respect to the enharm. v.	Ordinal number of the 12—n member, complementary tonal system
11121312	E F F# G A Bb C#D (20) A Bb B C D Eb F#G (20)		268	VII			16	XXXIII
11112222	B C C# Eb F G A (20) C# D Eb E F G A B (20)		314 314	VIII			30	XIII
11112213	C# D Eb E F G A Bb (21)		325 325	IX X	Bb B C C# D E F# G (21) Eb E F F# G A B C (21) A Bb B C C# E F G (21) D Eb E F F# A Bb C (21)	268 268	26—27	XXV—XXVI
11113122	B C C# D Eb F# G A (21)							
11211222	A Bb B C# D Eb F G (22) C# D Eb F F# G A B (22)		326 326	XI	B C C# Eb E F G A (22)	238	9	XXIV
11131212	C C# D Eb F# G A Bb (22)		328 328	XII XIII	E F F# Gb B C D (22) A Bb B C E Eb F# G (22) E F F# G A Bb C C# (22) A Bb B C D Eb F F# (22)	274 274	24—25	XXIX—XXX enh. v.
11121213	C# D Eb E F# G A Bb (22)							

I	II	III	IV	V	VI	VII	VIII	IX
Interval group characterising the tonal system	Central transposition(s) of the tonal system	Transposition(s) with lowest quintal index	Quintal index of the tonal system	Ordinal number of the tonal system	Central and minimal transposition(s) of the enharmonic variant with the lowest index in the tonal system	Quintal index of the enharm. var.	Ordinal number of the tonal system with respect to the enharm. v.	Ordinal number of the 12-n member, complementary tonal system
11211213	C# D Eb F F# G A Bb (23)		333	XIV–XV			41–42	XXI–XXII
11211312	A Bb B C# D Eb F# G (23)		333					
12121212	D Eb F F# G# A B C (24)		384	XVI	C C# Eb E F# G A Bb (24)	332	40	XXXII
11221122	D Eb E F# G# A Bb C (24)		388	XVII	A Bb B C# Eb E F G (24)	330	39	XXXVI enh. v.
	G Ab A B C# Eb F (24)		388					
	C# D E F G G# A B (24)							
	F# G Ab Bb B C C# D E (24)							
11112123	G# A Bb B C D Eb F (24)		392	XVIII–XIX	Bb B C C# D E F G (20)		19–20	XIV–XV
	C# D Eb E F G Ab Bb (26)		392		Eb E F F# G Ab A B C (22)			
11113212	B C C# D Eb F# G# A (26)		392		A Bb B C C# Eb E F# G (22)	268		
	E F F# G Ab Bb B C# D (24)		392		D Eb E F F# G# A Bb C (20)	268		
11112132	G# A Bb B C D Eb F# (25)		392	XX–XXI	A Bb B C C# Eb E G (23)	325	35–36	XXVII–XXVIII
	C# D Eb E F G Ab B (25)		392			325		
11112312	B C C# D Eb F G# A (25)				Eb E F F# G A C C# (23)			
	E F F# G Ab Bb B C# D (25)							

I	II	III	IV	V	VI	VII	VIII	IX
Interval group characterising the tonal system	Central transposition(s) of the tonal system	Transposition(s) with lowest quintal index	Quintal index of the tonal system	Ordinal number of the tonal system	Central and minimal transposition(s) of the enharmonic variant with the lowest index in the tonal system	Quintal index of the enharm. var.	Ordinal number of the tonal system with respect to the enharm. system T.	Ordinal number of the 12—n member, complementary tonal system
11113113	C♯ D E♭ E F G♯ A B♭ (26)		400	XXII	B♭ B C C♯ D F F♯ G (22)	284	29	XX
	F♯ G A♭ A B♭ C♯ D E♭ (26)		400		E♭ E F F♯ G B♭ B C (24)	284		
	F♯ G G♯ A B♭ C♯ D E♭ (26)				A♭ B C C♯ E F F♯ (24)			
	B C C♯ D E♭ F♯ G A♭ (26)				D♭ E♭ E F F♯ A B♭ B (22)			
11131122	G G♯ A B♭ C♯ D E♭ F (25)		402	XXIII—XXIV	E F F♯ G B♭ B C D (19)	219	6—7	XVI—XVII
	C C♯ D E♭ F♯ G A♭ B♭ (27)		402		A♭ B C D E F F♯ (19)	219		
11122113	C♯ D E♭ E F♯ G♯ A B♭ (27)							
	F♯ G A♭ A B C♯ D E♭ (25)							
11123112	C C♯ D E♭ F G♯ A B♭ (26)		406	XXV—XXVI	A B♭ B C D F F♯ G (18)	212	4—5	VI—VII
	F F♯ G A♭ B♭ C♯ D E♭ (28)		406		E F F♯ G A B♭ B D (18)	212		
11121132	G♯ A B♭ B C♯ D E♭ F♯ (28)							
	C♯ D E♭ E F♯ G A♭ B (26)							

291

I	II	III	IV	V	VI	VII	VIII	IX
Interval group characterising the tonal system	Central transposition(s) of the tonal system	Transposition(s) with lowest quintal index	Quintal index of the tonal system	Ordinal number of the tonal system	Central and minimal transposition(s) of the enharmonic variant with the lowest index in the tonal system	Quintal index of the enharm. var.	Ordinal number of the tonal system with respect to the enharm. v.	Ordinal number of the 12-n member, complementary tonal system
11121123	G♯ A B♭ B C♯ D E♭ F (27)				E F F♯ G A B♭ B C♯ (23)	274	22—23	XVIII—XIX
	C♯ D E♭ E F♯ G A♭ B♭ (27)				A B♭ C D E♭ E F♯ (21)	274		
11132112	C C♯ D E♭ F♯ G♯ A B♭ (27)		406	XXVII—XXVIII	E F F♯ G B♭ C♯ D (21)			
	F F♯ G A♭ B C♯ D E♭ (27)		406		A B♭ C E♭ E F♯ G (23)			
11212113	C♯ D E♭ F F♯ G♯ A B♭ (28)				F♯ G A B♭ C C♯ D (20)		21	X
	F♯ G A♭ B♭ B C♯ D E♭ (28)		412	XXIX	B♭ B C D E♭ F F♯ G (22)	272		
					A B♭ B C♯ D E F F♯ (22)	272		
					D E♭ E F F♯ G A B♭ B (20)			
11111313	D♯ E F F♯ G A♭ B C (28)		516	XXX	E♭ E F F♯ G G♯ B C (28)	412	43	XXXI enh. v.
	G A♭ B♭ C D♭ E F (28)				A♭ A B♭ B C♯ E F (28)			
11111223	D♯ E F F♯ G A♭ B♭ C (29)		530	XXXI—XXXII	A B♭ B C C♯ D E F♯ (21)	268	18—19	VIII—IX
	G♯ A B♭ B C D♭ E♭ F (31)		530		D E♭ E F F♯ G A B (20)	268		
11111322	D♯ E F♯ G A♭ D F G (31)				A B♭ B C C♯ D F G (20)			
	G♯ A B♭ B C D♭ E F♯ (29)				D E♭ E F F♯ G B♭ C (21)			

I	II	III	IV	V	VI	VII	VIII	IX
Interval group characterising the tonal system	Central transposition(s) of the tonal system	Transposition(s) with lowest quintal index	Quintal index of the tonal system	Ordinal number of the tonal system	Central and minimal transposition(s) of the enharmonic variant with the lowest index in the tonal system	Quintal index of the enharm. var.	Ordinal number of the tonal system with respect to the enharm. v.	Ordinal number of the 12—n member, complementary tonal system
11111232	D♭ E F F♯ G A♭ B♭ C♯ (32) G♯ A B♭ C D♭ E♭ F♯ (32)		544	XXXIII	A♭ B C C♯ D E G (18) D E♭ F F♯ G A C (18)	256	13	V
11131113	A♯ B C D♭ E F F♯ G (30) D♭ E F G♭ A B♭ C (30)		644	XXXIV	E F F♯ G B♭ B C C♯ (24) A B♭ C E♭ E F F♯ (24)	280	28	XLI enh. v.
11114112	D E♭ E F G♭ A♮ B C (31) A♯ B C C♯ D E F G♭ (31)		755 755	XXXV–XXXVI	E♭ E F♯ G G♭ C C♯ (25) A♭ B♭ B C C♯ E♭ E F (25)	329 329	37—38	XXXIV–XXXV enh. v.
11111214	A♯ B C C♯ D E♭ F G♭ (34) C♯ D♭ E F G♭ A♯ B (34)		776 776	XXXVII–XXXVIII	A♭ B C C♯ D E F (20) D E♭ F F♯ G A B♭ (20) A♭ B C C♯ D F♯ G (20) D E♭ F F♯ G B C (20)	266 266	14—15	XXXIX–XL enh. v.
11121114	A♯ B C D♭ E♭ E F G♭ (38) A♯ B C C♯ D♯ E F G♭ (38)	B♯ C♯ D E♭ F F♯ G A♭ (34) G♯ A B♭ C D♭ E♭ F♭ (34)	804 804	XXXIX	E F F♯ G A B♭ B C (20)	220	8	XLII enh. v.
11111133	E♯ F♯ G A♭ A B♭ C♭ D (34) E♭ F♯ G G♯ A B♭ C♭ D (34)		952 952	XL	B♭ B C C♯ D E♭ E G (22) C C♯ D E♭ E F F♯ A (22)	324 324	33	XXIII

I	II	III	IV	V	VI	VII	VIII	IX
Interval group characterising the tonal system	Central transposition(s) of the tonal system	Transposition(s) with lowest quintal index	Quintal index of the tonal system	Ordinal number of the tonal system	Central and minimal transposition(s) of the enharmonic variant with the lowest index in the tonal system	Quintal index of the enharm. var.	Ordinal number of the tonal system with respect to the enharm. v	Ordinal number of the $12-n$ member, complementary tonal system
11111124	E# F# G A♭ A B♭ C♭ D♭ (41)	E# C# D E♭ E♭ F G♭ A♭ (39)	1001	XLI— XLII	A B♭ B C C# D E♭ F (21)	315	31—32	XXXVII— XXXVIII enh. v.
11111142	E# F# G G# A B♭ C♭ D♭ (41)	A# B C C# D♭ E♭ F♭ G# (39)	1001		B C C# D E♭ E F A (21)	315		
11111115	C# D# E F F# G A♭ B♭♭ (46)		1528	XLIII	A B♭ B C C# D E♭ E (22)	324	34	XLIII enh. v.

NINE-NOTE TONAL SYSTEM

I	II	III	IV	V	VI	VII	VIII	IX
11121122	E F F# G A B♭ B C D (20)		240	I			1	I
11112122	A B♭ B C C# D E F G (21) / D E♭ E F G A B♭ C (22)		293 / 293	II— III			2—3	II— III
11112212	A B♭ B C C# D E F# G (22) / D E♭ E F F# G A B C (21)							
11121212	E F F# G A B♭ C C# D (22) / A B♭ C D E♭ F F# G (23)		299 / 299	IV— V			4—5	V— VI
11121212	E F F# G A B♭ B C# D (23) / A B♭ C D E♭ E F# G (22)							
11111222	A B♭ B C C# D E♭ F G (24) / C# D E♭ E F F# G A B (24)	E F F# G G# A B♭ C D (23) / F# G A♭ A B♭ B C D E (23)	360 / 360	VI	B C C# D E♭ E F G A (22)	348	10	IV

I	II	III	IV	V	VI	VII	VIII	IX
Interval group characterising the tonal system	Central transposition(s) of the tonal system	Transposition(s) with lowest quintal index	Quintal index of the tonal system	Ordinal number of the tonal system	Central and minimal transposition(s) of the enharmonic variant with the lowest index in the tonal system	Quintal index of the enharm. var.	Ordinal number of the tonal system with respect to the enharm. v.	Ordinal number of the 12–n member, complementary tonal system
111122112	C♯ D E♭ E F G A B♭ B (24)		360	VII–VIII			13–14	XII–XIII
111121122	B C C♯ D E♭ F F♯ G A (24)		360					
111121212	C C♯ D E♭ E F♯ G A B♭ (24)		362	IX			15	XI
111111213	C♯ D E♭ E F F♯ G A B♭ (25)		367	X–XI			16–17	XVII–XVIII enh. v.
111111312	A B♭ B C C♯ D E♭ F♯ G (25)		367					
112112112	A B♭ B C♯ D E♭ F F♯ G (26)		370	XII			18	XVI
111121113	G♯ A B♭ B C D E♭ E F (26)		430	XIII–XIV	B♭ B C C♯ D E F F♯ G (24)	305	8–9	XIV–XV
	C♯ D E♭ E F G A♭ A B♭ (27)		430		E♭ E F F♯ G A♭ B♭ B C (25)	305		
111131112	B C C♯ D E♭ F♯ G G♯ A (27)				A B♭ B C C♯ E♭ E F♯ G (25)			
	E F F♯ G A♭ B C C♯ D (26)				D E♭ E F F♯ A♭ A B♭ B C (24)			
111113112	C C♯ D E♭ E F G♯ A B♭ (28)		444	XV–XVI	A B♭ B C♯ D F F♯ G♯ B♭ (23)	303	6–7	IX–X
	F F♯ G A♭ A B♭ C♯ D E♭ (29)				D E♭ E F♯ G B♭ B C (24)	303		
111112113	C♯ D E♭ E F F♯ G♯ A B♭ (29)		444		A B♭ B C♯ D E F F♯ (24)			
	F♯ G A♭ A B♭ B C♯ D E♭ (28)				D E♭ E F F♯ G A♭ B♭ B (23)			

I	II	III	IV	V	VI	VII	VIII	IX
Interval group characterising the tonal system	Central transposition(s) of the tonal system	Transposition(s) with lowest quintal index	Quintal index of the tonal system	Ordinal number of the tonal system	Central and minimal transposition(s) of the enharmonic variant with the lowest index in the tonal system	Quintal index of the enharm. var.	Ordinal number of the tonal system with respect to the enharm. v.	Ordinal number of the 12−n member, complementary tonal system
11111123	G♯ A B♭ B C C♯ D E♭ F (29) C♯ D E♭ E F F♯ G A♭ B♭ (30)		448 448	XVII— XVIII	C C♯ D E♭ E F F♯ G A (23)	355 355	11—12	VII— VIII
11111132	G♯ A B♭ B C C♯ D E♭ F♯ (30) C♯ D E♭ E F F♯ G A♭ B (29)				A B♭ B C C♯ D E♭ E G (23)			
11111114	A♯ B C C♯ D E♭ E F G♭ (36)		852	XIX	B♭ B C C♯ D E♭ E F F♯ (28)	370	19	XIX enh. v.

TEN-NOTE TONAL SYSTEM

I	II	III	IV	V	VI	VII	VIII	IX
11111121112	A B♭ B C C♯ D E F F♯ G (25) D E♭ E F F♯ G A B♭ B C (25)		330	I			1	I
11111111122	A B♭ B C C♯ D E♭ E F G (26) B C C♯ D E♭ E F F♯ G A (26)		394 394	II			3	II
11111111212	C C♯ D E♭ E F F♯ G A B♭ (27) A B♭ B C C♯ D E♭ E F♯ G (27)		401 401	III			3	III
11111112112	A B♭ B C C♯ D E♭ E F♯ G (28) C♯ D E♭ E F F♯ G A B♭ B (28)		406 406	IV			4	IV

I	II	III	IV	V	VI	VII	VIII	IX
Interval group characterising the tonal system	Central transposition(s) of the tonal system	Transposition(s) with lowest quintal index	Quintal index of the tonal system	Ordinal number of the tonal system	Central and minimal transposition(s) of the enharmonic variant with the lowest index in the tonal system	Quintal index of the enharm. var.	Ordinal number of the tonal system with respect to the enharm. v.	Ordinal number of the 12–n member, complementary tonal system
111121111112	G# A Bb B C D Eb E F F# (30) C# D Eb E F G Ab A Bb B (30) B C C# D Eb E F F# G G# A (30) E F F# G Ab A Bb B C C# D (30)		478 478	V	A Bb B C C# Eb E F F# G (32)	380	6	VI
111111113	G# A Bb B C C# D Eb E F (31) C# D Eb E F F# G Ab A Bb (31) F# G G# A Bb B C C# D Eb (31) B C C# D Eb E F F# G Ab (31)		486 486	VI	Bb B C C# D Eb E F (29) F# G Ab A Bb B C C# D Eb E (29) F F#	409 409	5	V

ELEVEN-NOTE TONAL SYSTEM

I	II	III	IV	V	VI	VII	VIII	IX
11111111112	Ab Bb B C C# D Eb E F F# G (30)		440	I				I

TWELVE-NOTE TONAL SYSTEM

I	II	III	IV	V	VI	VII	VIII	IX
111111111111	Db Eb E F F# G G# A Bb B C C# (36) G A Ab Bb B C C# D Eb E F F# (36)		572	I				—

Forty-four Duos for Violin
No. 42

Violin 1: four-note scale, **XXVII**
Violins 1 and 2 together: eight-note scale, **XII**

Microcosmos
No. 109

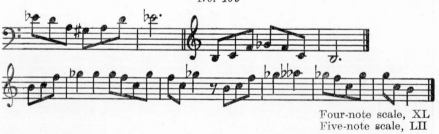

Four-note scale, **XL**
Five-note scale, **LII**

Concerto
Fourth Movement, First Subject, Oboe

Five-note scale, VII

Sketches
No. II

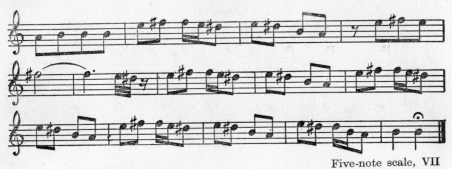

Five-note scale, VII

Microcosmos
No. 136

Five-note scale, XXIII

Forty-four Duos for Violin
No. 8

Five-note scale, XXVI

299

The Wooden Prince

The Playful Gestures of the Princess

Five-note scale, XXXIX

Concerto

Third Movement, from Tenth Bar, Oboe

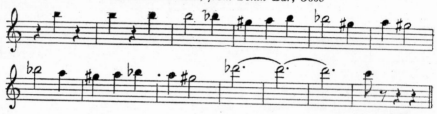

Six-note scale, LXXX

The Miraculous Mandarin

The Mandarin Tries to Seize the Girl

Six-note scale, LI

Two Pictures

Second Movement, First Subject

Seven-note scale, II

First Sonata for Violin and Pianoforte

Third Movement, First Subject, Violin

Seven-note scale, II

Suite for Piano

Third Movement, Subject

Seven-note scale, X

Third Concerto for Pianoforte

Third Movement, First Subject

Eight-note scale, V

Music for String Instruments

First Movement, First Subject

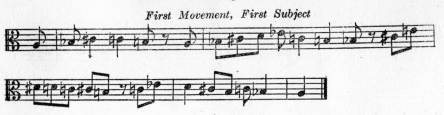

Eight-note scale, XLIII

Sonata for Violin Solo
Subject of the Fugue

Eight-note scale, XLIII

The Wooden Prince
Dance of the Forest

Nine-note scale, I

Second String Quartet
First Movement, First Subject

Ten-note scale, VI

Sonata for Violin Solo

Melody

Eleven-note scale

Concerto for Violin

First Movement, Second Subject

Twelve-note scale

PÁL JÁRDÁNYI

THE DETERMINING OF SCALES AND SOLMIZATION IN HUNGARIAN MUSICAL FOLKLORE

The method of relative solmization (at all times the tonic in major is *do*, and in minor *la*) may be credited with unparalleled success in music pedagogy. It has proved to be the most excellent means for sight-singing and ear training. It seems, however, that in addition to pedagogy science, too, can make use of it. We must not forget that if something is practical, usually it is also true. If it is easier for a music student to sing a tune by means of solmization than without, then it may be assumed that the solmization syllables are "true", that they illuminate the melody, they denote, and express its scale characteristics.

Owing to the discoveries of Zoltán Kodály on scales in Hungarian folk music, we have known for some 40 years that pentatony is their oldest and most important characteristic. Kodály has also pointed out that the pentatonic root can be found in many melodies which at first glance appear to be diatonic. In these, together with the transposition of the melody sections to the interval of a fifth, the scale, too, is transposed. For example, no. 61 of the Vargyas' *Collection* in Z. Kodály : *A magyar népzene* (Hungarian Folk Music)*, 1952.

The scale character and scale transposition of this and similar melodies are denoted most simply and clearly by solmization. Is the

* All examples are taken from this work.

upper stratum of this melody pentatonic? Obviously it is, for the notes C^2-D^2-F^2-G^2-A^2 give a clear anhemitonic pentatonic scale. Its solmization is *so-la-do-re-mi*. (N.B. A constant rule for the solmization of the anhemitonic pentatonic scale is that only the syllables *do-re-mi-so-la* may be included in it!) But if we examine the second half of the melody in the lower stratum we again find a pentatonic scale: G^1-B^{b1}-C^2-D^2-F^2. Its solmization is *la-do-re-mi-so*. Hence, in the upper stratum $D^2 = la$, and in the lower stratum $G^1 = la$. In other words there are two *la* scales, two pentatonic systems in the melody. Solmization clearly shows the presence of the two pentatonic systems. Should we try to sing the foregoing melody within one system of solmization, we would have to resort to the use of alien syllables (*fa* or *ti*) which are not present in pentatony. If we continued the solmization of the upper stratum ($D^2 = la$) in the lower section, the solmization syllable *fa* would fall on the B^{b1} note of the lower stratum. And the other way around: should we impose the syllables of the lower stratum ($G^1 = la$) upon the upper stratum, the highest note (A) in the melody would be *ti*. Both solmizations would be falsifications because we would be attaching syllables not included in the pentatonic system to some notes which belong to the pentatonic system.

The presence of two systems, the transposition of the scale, is characteristic not only of *pentatonic* melodies. We find it also in *diatonic* melodies constructed on the interval of the fifth. For example, no. 430:

The scale of the foregoing melody — for want of a better name — used to be called Dorian. It would appear that this conclusion tells

almost nothing about the scale character of the melody. By mechanic-
ally placing the notes of the melody in a row we do, indeed, get a Dorian
scale, but we have failed to show that this so-called Dorian scale stems
from the transposition of a minor tetrachord melody section to the
interval of a fifth. Solmization, on the other hand, (if we sing the lower
stratum with $G^1 = la$, and the upper stratum with $D^2 = la$) reveals the
scale essence of the melody, and leaves no need for further explanation
and arguments. Without a doubt the substitution of "two-system diatonic
melody with a *la* ending" for the technical term "Dorian" would be more
to the point.

Belonging also to this scale category are the so-called Dorian
melodies in which, although there is hardly any or no fifth relationship
between the melody sections, the two layers of the tune are so clearly
and distinctly divided that we can hear and feel the presence of two
separate minor tetrachord or minor pentachord scales. For example,
no. 264:

All melodies with *la* endings, in which there is no transposition of
scale, are built on a single system. For example, no. 120:

The above example proves that a melody showing traces of a stratifying fifth structure is *not* necessarily of two systems. If in the upper stratum in place of the major sixth of the melody's basic note we hear a *minor* sixth, we do not hear any scale transposition whatever. In the upper stratum as well as in the lower the $G^1 = la$ solmization appears to be the most natural.

Beside the great mass of one- and two-system, pentatonic and diatonic melodies with *la* endings, there are fewer with *do* endings (that is, of a major character) in Hungarian folk music. Outside of them the groups with *so* and *mi* endings are important. Hungarian folk songs may be divided into four main scale groups on the basis of our researches up to now — *la* ending, *do* ending, *mi* ending and *so* ending. We may characterize the four groups most simply with four variants of one and the same melody. Examples nos. 293—296:

Tempo giusto

Vet-tem ma - ru - já - nát, Vá-rom ki - ke - lé - sit.

Az én é - dö - sem - nek Meg visz-sza - té - ré - sit.

Tempo giusto

Most jöt - tem Er - déĺy - bőlə Hat ló - val, hin - tó - val,

Hat ló - val, hin - tó - val S ëgy ron-gyos szol - gá - val.

Tempo giusto

Hess pá - va, hess pá - va, Csá-szár-né pá - vá - ja!

Ha én pá - va vol - nék, Jobb rëg-gel föl - kel - nék.

Tempo giusto

Hess pá-va, hess pá - va, Csá-szár-né pá - vá - ja!

Ha jén pá - va vol - nék, Jobb rög-gel föl - kel - nék.

The main notes of the *la* ending variant, in addition to the final note, are the *minor third* and the *fifth,* of the *do* ending the *major third* and the *fifth,* of the *mi* ending the *fourth* and the *minor sixth,* and of the *so* ending the *fourth* and the *major sixth.* The connection between the *la* and *mi* ending variants is clear : the two melodies are almost identical note for note, the one essential difference being that one ends on *la* and the other on *mi.* This same relationship exists between the *do* and *so* ending variants.

In our opinion, the uncommonly important role of the fourth and sixth above the final note is most marked in the tunes ending on *mi* and *so.* And although most *mi* ending melodies meet the criterion of the *Phrygian* scale (and most *so* ending ones of the *Mixolydian*), it appears to be more proper and correct to group the melodies here again on the basis of the closing note, in place of the old, modal scale categories (Phrygian, Mixolydian). After all, even the foregoing *mi* and *so* ending examples (together with many other melodies) indicate that the minor second above the final is no essential requisite for *mi* ending melodies (though it is a primary characteristic of the Phrygian scale), nor is the minor seventh indispensable in *so* ending melodies (Mixolydian character).

*

It is not the purpose of our paper to present an exhaustive, complete study of the scale types of Hungarian folk music. It only proposes to give information on a method of determining scales. This method (the method of relative solmization) is young, and is far from being able to boast of final, conclusive results. But the present results already prove that its use in place of the generally used categories of scales (Dorian Phrygian, Mixolydian, etc.) is more precise and authentic. It determines scales not from a series of notes abstracted from the notes of the melody, but on the basis of the main notes of the melody. It illuminates the hidden scale characteristics of a melody more clearly than all earlier methods. The advantage of the method in the analysis of complex melodies from the standpoint of scales is particularly obvious. For example, no. 416:

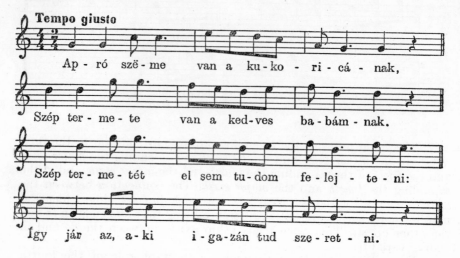

Ap - ró szë - me van a ku - ko - ri - cá - nak,

Szép ter - me - te van a ked - ves ba - bám - nak.

Szép ter - me - tét el sem tu - dom fe - lej - te - ni:

Így jár az, a - ki i - ga - zán tud sze - ret - ni.

Sections 1 and 4 of the foregoing melody are unequivocally *so* endings. If we examine the two middle sections separately, we gain a melodic pattern that is characteristic of the upper stratum of two-system *la* ending melodies. The correct solmization would be : sections 1 and 4 : $G^1 = so$; and sections 2 and 3 : $D^2 = la$. It is clear, therefore, that our melody is a cross between a *so* and a *la* ending scale type. What did the old terminology say about the scale of such a melody? Simply that it was Mixolydian. Yet, this is obviously something *else* than a typical Mixolydian.

Melodies with "mixed" scales similar to the above are not rare in Hungarian folk music. In addition to a crossing of the *la* and *so* types, we have examples of the crossing of *la* and *mi* types too. And outside of these, a meticulous examination by means of solmization throws light on the existence of many extremely complex scale structures. It is certain that the introduction of relative solmization in Hungary is a great gain not only for music pedagogy, but also for musicology.

VIKTOR BELIAEV

EARLY RUSSIAN POLYPHONY

The present paper is a short survey of the characteristics of the early forms of the Russian *written vocal* polyphony as documented in the Russian non-linear (neumatic) manuscripts.

These documents have never been adequately studied. This accounts for the considerable contradictions that are involved in the interpretations of this form of Old-Russian musical art, offered by the different scholars. One of the pre-eminent researchers of Russian liturgical chant D. V. Razumovsky in his *Tserkovnoie penie v Rossii* (Liturgical Chant in Russia), published in 1867 in Moscow, describing the earliest form of Russian polyphony called *strochny* chant and for the first time publishing, in order to illustrate his description, *strochny* three-voice polyphony after the pattern of the *"trekh-strochny* linear demestic chant of the end of the 17th century" from the library of V. F. Odoevsky, found it sufficient to characterize this type of Old-Russian polyphony with the following : *"trekh-strochny* demestic chants contained, in fact, not many harmonic perfections : intervals such as seconds occur very frequently in it".

At the turn of the century one of the greatest scholars studying Russian ecclesiastical chant was A. V. Preobrazhensky who in his work *Ocherki istorii tserkovnogo penia v Rossii* (Essay on the History of Liturgical Chant in Russia), published in a second edition in 1910, and carrying photostatic copies of a number of pages from the original manuscripts of *strochny* polyphony, writes as follows : "the original form of polyphonic singing in Russia is the so-called *strochny* chant which serves as a sort of link between the old and the new chant as far as it *comprises the non-linear kriukovoi notation* (of homophonic compositions, *V. B.*) *and the new polyphony"*. Incorrectly characterizing *strochny* polyphony and ascribing to it features that belong to a later form of the *znamenny* polyphony, he writes :. "the harmonic accompaniment to the basic melody consisted of triads in different positions and inversions ; the position of the accompanying voices corresponded to the concept of the chord

311

at that time in Russia and was far from being correct... In general, harmony was rather imperfect, noisy, vague, blurring the basic melody sung by the middle voice".

If such outstanding experts in the field of Russian liturgical chant as Razumovsky and Preobrazhensky characterized *strochny* polyphony so superficially and inexactly, then it is no wonder that the great historian of Russian musical culture N. F. Findeisen, who wrote later than Razumovsky and Preobrazhensky and was no expert of Old-Russian chant, in his *Ocherki po istorii muzyki v Rossii* (Essays on the History of Music in Russia) published in 1928, altogether refuses to characterize *strochny* polyphony, stating that the Khazan notation, with which the works of this polyphony had been recorded, "has remained unstudied up till now".

In stating that the Khazan notation has been left unstudied, Findeisen is at the same time both right and wrong. He is wrong insofar as one of the great many manuscript alphabets of this notation, called also *demestvenny* ("demestic ") or *putevoi*, was published — although in a somewhat crude and unelaborate form — by Razumovsky in his above-quoted work. He is right insofar as the works of *strochny* polyphony recorded in this notation have, with the exception of occasional patterns, not been deciphered, though they number several hundreds and include also *stikhera* from the *"Oktoikh"* sung during the vigil and the liturgy.

The recent access to new material concerning the different forms of Old-Russian polyphony enables us to examine more closely their characteristic features. This is the task of the present paper which, therefore, is necessarily only a preliminary study of Old-Russian polyphony.

*

The principal feature of early Russian written vocal polyphony is that this polyphony *arose through a change that had come about in the homophonic ecclesiastical melodies and principally in those of the basic raspev of the Russian Church—the znamenny raspev* on the basis of combining these melodies with the contrapuntal voices accompanying them. Hence, since Russian written polyphony arose as a result of the complication of the original homophonic chant of the Russian Church, the melodic patterns of which served as *canti firmi* for the early Russian polyphonic compositions, by no means could the origins of this polyphony be dated back earlier than the 11th century, that is, by no means earlier than the introduction into Russia of Christian chant, the principal Russian form of which was the *znamenny raspev*. Insofar as the style of *strochny* polyphony reached its full development in the 16th century, as seen from the manuscripts that have come down to us, the emergence of Russian

312

written polyphony will have to be placed somewhere between the 11th and the 16th centuries, most likely closer to the 11th than to the 16th.

The earliest form of Russian written polyphony was the two-voice polyphony that arose from the unison singing of liturgical melodies with sporadically improvised divergences of the voices at close intervals. Let us take an example of this temporary two-voice polyphony from the beginning of the Psalm *Na retse vavilonstei* quoted in S. V. Smolensky's paper *Znachenie XVII veka i ego kantov i psalmov v oblasti sovremennogo tserkovnogo penia, tak naz. prostogo penia* (The Importance of the 17th Century, its Psalms and Chants in Contemporary Liturgical Singing, the So-called Simple Melodic Pattern), where it had been taken over from the lithographed repertory of the historic concerts given by the Moscow Synodal Academy of Liturgical Chant in 1895. This example has been deciphered from non-linear notation by A. D. Kastalsky:

Owing to a lack of documented material we are unable to date the rise of this and of the following form of *strochny* two-voice polyphony, but we assume it highly probable that, in the two-part performance of liturgical chants, the custom of deviating from the basic melody had been borrowed from the polyphonic singing of Russian folk songs, that is, from cases when underlying voices were sung to the basic melodic pattern. In assuming this we must, naturally, allow for the practice of the polyphonic performance of Russian folk songs prior to the introduction of the polyphonic execution of Russian liturgical chants. Examples of two-voice folk singing of the kind we have just seen in liturgical two-voice polyphony are numerous. Let us, for instance, take the song *Chto zhe ty da cheremuskha* from the *Pesni Pinezhia* recorded by E. V. Hippius and Z. V. Evald in which two-voice polyphony originates in the variational deviation of one of the voices from the basic melodic pattern of the song :

In addition to this form of Russian written two-voice polyphony
we can cite an even more developed form of this same two-voice polyphony. One example we can quote is the beginning of the *Kheruvimskaia
pesnia* (to be referred to as the "Cherub Song") from the MS no. 233,
dating from the end of the 17th or the beginning of the 18th century,
of the Synodal Academy, others being contained in several other MMS
of this Institute, preserved in the State Historical Museum, Moscow:

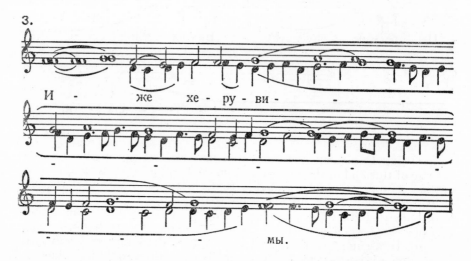

In this example the basic melody, otherwise called the "*put*", is
sung by the upper voice which is accompanied by the contrapuntal
lower voice called "*niz*". Some features of this carefully elaborated
form of early Russian two-voice polyphony require elucidation.

All compositions written in the two-voice style begin in the unison
of the two voices that diverge at the accented sections by no more than
a fourth, which is the basic interval of this two-voice polyphony. The

basic interval is used both in alternation with other intervals and in successions of parallel fourths.

Let us examine a few typical cases of voice-leading used in this form of two-voice polyphony.

As a first example let us take the motion from a fourth to a unison with a sustained upper voice, a motion not represented in previous examples in its pure form but extremely frequent in this type of two-voice polyphony:

In our examples we have the following variants of the above combination of voices :

1. The motion of the lower auxiliary note to the level of the upper voice :

2. The complication of the motion of the lower voice by starting at an interval of a third leading to the upper voice :

3. The introduction into the above combination of a lower auxiliary note leading to the sustained note of the upper voice which sometimes, as in this case, produces an interval of a second between the two moving voices :

4. A further combination of this passage in one of the following forms :

8.

or

9.

where the upper voice is complicated by the introduction of an auxiliary note leading to the basic note, without which the above passage would appear as follows :

10.

But in the following motion of the lower voice the G of the upper voice, to which a fourth is sung in the lower, should be regarded not as an auxiliary note to A but as an independent note in the progression of the upper voice :

11.

It should be noted that the melodic motion which we look upon as the succession of the lower auxiliary note and the following basic note of the melodic progression :

12.

or:

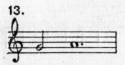

13.

is recorded in the non-linear notation of *strochny* chant by a single sign, a fact that supports the correctness of our interpretation of the above melodic succession.

If the rising fourth of the melody we are discussing

14.

begins not on the lower third but on the lower fourth under the sustained note of the upper voice, it results in the following combination of voices in which the interval of a fifth occurs in relation to the upper voice as an unaccented auxiliary note in the course of the progression of the lower voice:

15.

The second the lower voice thus forms with the upper voice is regarded in this type of two-voice polyphony as an independent harmonic interval and is used in many instances as such, as can be seen from the following examples:

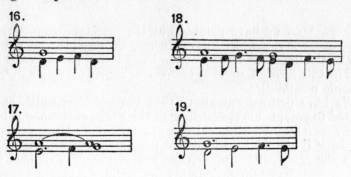

16.

18.

17.

19.

20.

and so on.

In some instances the second even plays the role of a cadential interval that closes not only one of the inner sections of the composition but the whole composition as, for instance, in the "Cherub Song" the beginning of which we have cited above and which is concluded in the following manner:

21.

If, in addition, we consider motions in parallel fourth such as these:

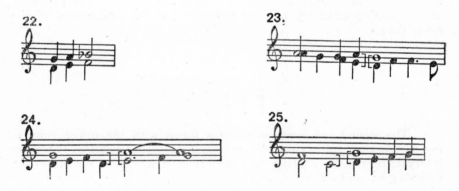

22.   **23.**

24.   **25.**

and others, then we have pointed out the principal characteristics of this two-voice style, which, nevertheless, do not give an exhaustive picture of the immense variety of the basic techniques of voice-leading as used in this form of *strochny* two-voice singing exceptionally rich in polyphonic possibilities.

We have pointed out above that the melodies which had been submitted to polyphonic remodelling in the works of *strochny* polyphony are the generally used liturgical ones, preferentially those of *znamenny raspev*. Now it should be added that these melodies, when used as *canti firmi* in the compositions of *strochny* polyphony, are extended twofold and sometimes carry a few melodic ornamentations as opposed to ordinary (so-called *obychny*) chant. When these melodies are performed in one voice they are no longer called *znamenny* but *putevoi* or *putny raspev*. As an example of such a transformation from *znamenny* into *putevoi* we can cite the eulogy of the Virgin's Birth, written in the 5th *echos* (*glas*) in two variants — *znamenny* and *putevoi* — according to the 1772 edition of the *Obikhod* (daily round of services):

26.

Знаменный распев

Ве - ли - ча - ем тя

Путевой распев

пре - свя - та - я де - во

и чтем свя - тых тво - их ро - ди - те - лей

и все - слав - но - е сла - вим

Such an extension of the basic melody in *strochny* polyphony is a perfectly natural means of joining to it the mobile lower voice which displays more developed passages in contrast to the protracted notes of the basic melody. This circumstance required the elaboration (for *strochny* polyphony) of a special kind of non-linear notation which originated in the generally used *znamenny* notation and was adapted to the requirements of recording more complicated melodic passages and patterns.

In the new notation, called *demestvenny*, *putevoi* or *khazansky*, the basic signs of *znamenny* notation came to be used as signs denoting double length or sometimes even other melodic-metrical values. A number of new signs were added and the number of auxiliary signs enhanced in order to modify the value of the basic ones. In addition to this they came to be used in ligatures resulting in a large number of complicated signs.

Let us quote a few examples.

The sign of the hook

27.

$\swarrow$

which in *znamenny* notation has the value of a semitone was used in *putevoi* notation to denote a whole tone. Whereas in *znamenny* notation its use was confined to the following variants

28.

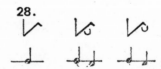

in *putevoi* notation it acquired even a larger number of values:

29.

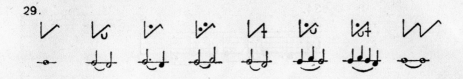

and so on.

The signs

30.

denoting in *znamenny* notation a gradually falling and/or rising motion by fourths, shows the following development in *putevoi* notation in different variants

31.

and so on.

The uniting of the following basic signs

32.

into one combined sign

33.

in connection with the mark placed nearby (the letter M) indicates the following complicated melodic motion

34.

which is the amalgamation and the abbreviation of the following

35.

The reading of the *putevoi* notation, though very complicated, involves no special difficulties in homophonic compositions, but presents considerable obstacles in polyphonic ones because of the difficulties of co-ordinating the voices of these compositions inasmuch as the metrical values of the different signs, which can be read both in their normal values and in their protracted or shortened values, are conditioned by the relation of the signs of one voice to those of the others.

The earliest documents of *strochny* polyphony known to us, as we have already pointed out, date from the 16th century and belong to the so-called signless, non-linear notational documents that contain no definite indication as to the pitch of the notational signs. At the end of the 16th century the signless notational text of these documents was provided with marks, that is, letters that precisely indicated the pitch of every single *znamia*. This enables us now to read the non-linear scores of *strochny* polyphony. By the second half or toward the end of the 17th century, a part of these scores was deciphered and transcribed into linear notation by singers who were well acquainted with the style of performance of *strochny* polyphonic compositions. The collation of non-linear originals with their transcriptions into notes on lines enables us to fully acquaint ourselves with the idiom of *strochny* polyphony thus ensuring the possibility of an exact and correct reading of the documents of this polyphony which, as we have already seen, is notable for the peculiarity of its style.

Returning to the two forms of *strochny* polyphony we have already studied, we perceive that in the first of them the basic melody is carried by the lower voice, the underlying counter-melody being sung by the upper voice, whereas, in the second case it is the other way round, that is, the basic melody is found in the upper voice and the counter-melody in the lower. Though of underlying origin, this counterpoint has a very elaborate character which speaks of the high degree of development of this kind of *strochny* two-voice polyphony. Which of these two forms of two-voice polyphony is of earlier origin we cannot tell as yet but we can and must turn the attention of our readers to the fact that by uniting these two forms of *strochny* two-voice polyphony through the line of the basic melody common to both forms, we obtain a three-voice combination of *strochny* polyphony which is the widest known and most elaborate type of this polyphony, called *troestrochie* or *troestrochnoe penie*.

The compositions of *strochny* three-voice polyphony, in which the upper voice is called "*verkh*" the middle one "*put*" and the lower one "*niz*" begin, as a rule, either in the unison of all voices or by a solo intonation by the lower voice. This technique, common to both *strochny* polyphony and Russian folk song polyphony, is extremely suitable for the intonation of polyphonic vocal compositions executed without any instrumental accompaniment or prelude. By this intonation the vocal ensemble is given the starting note or the starting line of the melodic progression which would gradually and sometimes imperceptibly go over into the lines of the contrapuntal progression of the voices. It is highly probable that here, when applying the technique of unison or solo intonation in polyphonic compositions and when applying the technique of underlying accompaniment in order to form a polyphonic musical texture, *strochny* polyphony must have been influenced by Russian folksong polyphony.

Embarking upon the relation of contrapuntal voices in *strochny* three-voice polyphony, it must be stressed that both lower voices in this three-voice polyphony are in the same relationship to one another as they are in the *strochny* two-voice polyphony of the second type, and can be performed independently of the third voice, because they form with one another a totally accomplished combination of voices. As far as the upper voice, the *verkh* is concerned, its design follows closely the upper voice of the first type of *strochny* two-voice polyphony and, being more mobile in the three-voice combination than the principal (middle) voice and less so than the other lower voice, forms with the two lower voices a fourth-fifth consonance in the basic harmonic points:

36.

which consists of the simultaneous singing of two perfect consonances from the bass and is regarded in the *strochny* polyphonic idiom as a harmonious consonance analogous to the triad in European and Russian liturgical polyphony of a later type which in the present paper we call *znamenny* polyphony.

As a first example of the *strochny* three-voice polyphony it will be best to quote the beginning of the Cherub Song known to us from its two-voice form but given here in its second version, that is, in its three-voice form according to the manuscript of the late 17th century or the early 18th century, no. 220 of the Synodal Academy:

Both lower voices in the above-quoted fragment from the three-voice version of the Cherub Song as expounded in the "big" *raspev*, except for a few consonances at the end of this fragment, are identical with the two voices of the two-voice version of this song, called the "small" (shortened) *raspev*. In the main we have already come to the end of the analysis of this two-voice polyphony. As far as the analysis of the *strochny* three-voice polyphony is concerned as a whole and in its details, that is, the analysis of the progression of the upper voice in the *strochny* three-voice polyphony, which voice is bound to go into contra-puntal and harmonic combination not only with the main (middle) but also with the lower voice, this involves considerable difficulties. But even in this case the fourth-fifth harmonic base is clearly perceptible behind the interweaving of the voices of this three-voice polyphony which is often rather complicated. This can be seen, for instance, from the analysis of the closing passage of our example, given in the following notational table where, beside the basic type of this fragment (line no. 1) we have (in lines nos. 2 and 3) its harmonic extract in a lesser (line no. 2) and in a greater (line no. 3) degree of concentration :

Figures 1—4 in the above table give us the melodic progression of all the three voices on a fourth-fifth consonance :

The progression of the upper voice is based here on the steps between the "chord" notes G and A, with the introduction, in two cases, of the auxiliary note F added to G, whereas the centre of this progression is A. However, F in certain respects can be regarded as potentially belonging to the basic fourth-fifth consonance which in this case acquires the following structure :

40.

The fact that we can regard in this case the note F as a potential note of the basic consonance is due, in the first place, to the frequent use in *strochny* three-voice polyphony of the following combinations of voices and the like :

where F is felt as a chord note rather than an "occasional" note and, in the second place, to the use in *strochny* three-voice polyphony of the cadence of double second (second-third) consonance :

43.

which, in this case, is a substitute for a fourth-fifth consonance :

44.

This same potentional inclusion of the note F in the chord notes in the above consonance and that of analogous notes in other consonances, explains the frequent use in the upper voice of the following motion in relation to the middle voice:

which we can observe in figures nos. 3 and 4 of our table.

As to figures 5 and 6 of this table, in the progression of the upper voice, A is sung with lower and upper auxiliary notes.

Thus the basic note of the upper voice in our fragment taken from the Cherub Song is A, which at the beginning participates in the formation of the fourth-fifth consonance, then in that of simple fourth consonances and, finally, in that of the unison consonance of all the three voices as well as of cadence-consonances of this whole fragment.

While characterizing, in general outlines, the function of the upper voice in *strochny* three-voice polyphony, we can notice that, as a rule, it never deviates from the middle voice more than by a fourth upward, that sometimes it crosses the middle voice and quite frequently follows it in seconds as in the parallel progression of all three voices with fourth-fifth consonances, as well as in the different motions at intervals of seconds.

This short survey of *strochny* three-voice polyphony is, naturally, by no means exhaustive. For such an analysis neither the material nor the observations made on the characteristics of the style of this three-voice polyphony are sufficient. The fact, however, that we know of it enables us to talk of *the national character of this polyphonic style and of the high degree of its evolution on Russian soil unaffected by any foreign influences*.

This is where the development of *strochny* polyphony comes to an end, yielding to the development of another kind of Russian written polyphony that arose on another basis and to which, in the present paper, we have assigned the name *znamenny polyphony* because its compositions are recorded generally in the ordinary *kriukovoi* notation used for recording the singing of the *znamenny raspev* and are no longer recorded in *khazansky, demestvenny* or *putevoi* notation.

We shall now cite an example of *znamenny* polyphony written in the ordinary *kriukovoi (stolpovoi)* notation. Our example will be an Antiphone, written in the fourth *echos, Ot iunosti moeia* from V. M. Metalov's *Ocherk istorii pravoslavnogo tserkovnogo penia v Russii* (Essay on the History of the Pravoslav Liturgical Chant in Russia):

46.

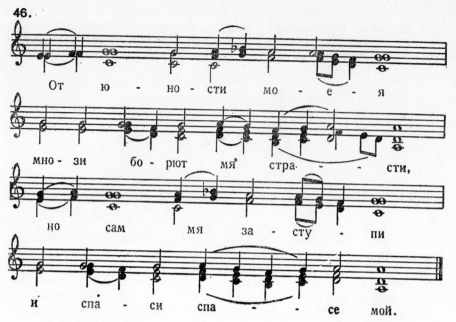

От ю — но-сти мо — е — я мно — зи бо-рют мя стра — сти, но сам мя за-сту — пи и спа — си спа — — се мой.

In the fine style in which the melody of this antiphone is harmonized we can see, first, the frequent use of incomplete or "empty" triads (without the third), especially in cadences and, secondly, the use of the technique of the parallel progression of triads. This technique is widely used, among others, for the harmonization of great jubilant passages and of vocalization in chanting the word "Alleluia" and in similar cases.

*

We have gone through the principal phases in the evolution of early Russian polyphony the records of which are written in non-linear notation and which is prominent because of the peculiarities of its style. Thanks to these we consider them as the two fundamental forms of early Russian polyphony.

Both these polyphonic forms undoubtedly influenced the later form of the *partesny* chant, that is, singing by notational parts written in linear notation and forming the parts of liturgical compositions, written by composers in the new harmonic style. The time when the style of the *partesny* chant emerged, presumably the second half of the 17th century, coincides with the years when the earlier forms of Russian polyphony ceased to develop. Nevertheless the *strochny* chant, the oldest form of Russian polyphony, survived till the 18th century and, what is more, the compositions of *znamenny* polyphony, a transitional form leading from *strochny* to *partesny* polyphony, survived in its different patterns in the church till the end of the 19th century if not till the beginnings of the 20th. In general these forms of early Russian polyphony were superseded comparatively early by the compositions of *partesny* chant, the development of which, from the very outset, made great strides forward, preparing the appearance of such great creative talents as D. S. Bortniansky (1751—1825), whose compositions created a whole epoch in the development of the new Russian liturgical polyphony, playing an enormous part in the evolution of musical culture in Russia not only in the field of Church music but also on a much larger scale by producing a new Russian musical idiom. This was the soil on which, in a certain sense, flourished the talent of the founder of the Russian national musical school M. I. Glinka, after whom Russian music soon reached the importance of a potential factor in the development of the musical culture of the world.

BENJAMIN RAJECZKY

PARALLELS OF LATE–GREGORIAN ORNAMENTS IN HUNGARIAN FOLK SONGS

An illuminating chapter of B. Szabolcsi's *History of Melody*[1] deals with the musical ornaments in Europe. Proceeding from Lach's statement according to which ornamentation can be considered as an elementary factor of melody-shaping, a compendium of musical formation, Szabolcsi arrives at the following thesis : the ornaments indicate various types of European musical thinking, they determine ornament- and melody-forming principles operating simultaneously side by side within the different cultural spheres (as stated by Besseler of the Italo-Burgundian and English territories with reference to the 15th century).

Thus Szabolcsi examines four domains of style of European ornamentation : 1. the Mediterranean region with embellishments constituting an extension of the melodic line, 2. the Atlantic region with ornaments promoting movement, 3. the Baltic region (Central Europe) with ornaments having variation force, and 4. Eastern Europe where an old monodic musical culture concentrates on ornamentation all forces that elsewhere have lead to polyphony or to the extension of structure (as, according to P. Wagner's interpretation, in the case of the Gregorian melismata) and thereby giving the melody a far stricter unity of motive (or as Hornbostel says of the ornamentation of Western Asia, much sharper outlines).[2] The ornamental elements of the North-European group seem to him insignificant.[3] — But beyond all these components, the author assumes a common basis without which it would be hard to understand the Gregorian influence throughout Europe.[4]

It is at this juncture that we start our essay and direct the attention to some elementary forms of this "common basis". The indi-

---

[1] Szabolcsi Bence, *A melódia története*, Budapest 1950, pp. 135—145.
[2] See *op. cit.* p. 140 and note 11 ; p. 145 with bibliography.
[3] The peculiar Swedish melismata mean something more.
[4] See *op. cit.* p. 143.

vidual grace notes or groups of them serve to give prominence to the melodic line, but have no form-building effect. We do not wish to reach back, as may be expected, to the early "punctuation melismatics", but restrict ourselves to the comparison of late Gregorian music with the Hungarian folk song. With this restriction we wish, on the other hand, to avoid the choral style in which the ornamentation, as a melody-forming factor, covers or transforms these elementary forms, and on the other, to exclude polyphonic music in which the role of these formulae is too well known. By "late Gregorian" we mean the variants of hymn and sequence of the 15th and 16th centuries. We have chosen this group for two reasons : 1. as syllabic or only sporadically and slightly melismatic pieces, their melody lines throw into relief the ornamental groups at first sight and lend themselves for a comparison with the *parlando-rubato* melodies of our folk-music ; 2. it poses the *question of rhythm*.

Since Idelsohn's parallels[5] it is evident that the kinds of folk-music flourishing today possess significant reserves of evidence concerning the question of Gregorian rhythmics, the substantial exploitation of which has just been started by musicology in our days.[6] Though it was more than half a century ago that O. Fleischer pointed to the significance of contemporary folk music for the history of music,[7] the venture of a too far-reaching conclusion seemed too ambitious, especially because of the erroneous supposition that in the field of chant every comparison touching a certain group of style had to be referred to the whole store of melody. Thus the rhythmisation of Riemann, Fleischer and Houdard, inspired by folk music could never convince contemporary chant-practice to think of a serious analysis of their "division of unity-value". The general distrust with which every theory of Gregorian rhythm is received today, refers, first of all, to its total application, and in so far as it does, justly so, but it also affects partial solutions to such an extent that, e. g., in spite of possessing considerable material for comparison, the drawing of the real rhythmic picture of the simple choral psalmody has not been achieved.[8]

[5] *Parallelen zwischen gregorianischen und hebräisch-orientalischen Gesangsweisen,* in *Zs. f. Mw.* vol. 4, 1922, pp. 515—524.
[6] Unfortunately we are not informed about the particulars of the Intern. Congress for Mediterranean Music in Palermo, 1954. — Di Salvo's comparison of Byzantine notations with Sicilian liturgical practice (Intern. Congress for Church-music, 1950) are only known to us from a review *(Riv. Mus. Ital.* vols. iv—vi, pp. 182—185). — About the venture of De Van see H. Engel, *Der dritte Kongress d. Internat. Gesellschaft f. Musikwissenschaft in Barcelona,* in *Zs. f. Mw.* 1936.
[7] O. Fleischer, *Ein Kapitel vergleichender Musikgeschichte* in *SIMg* vol. i, 1899—1900 pp., 1—53. — *Cf.* the principles concerning plainsong and folk songs by B. Maerker in : *Greg. Gesang u. Deutsches Volkslied,* in *Jhb. f. Volksliedfor-schung.* vol. vii, 1941, pp. 71—73.
[8] For instance, also Besseler who in his *Musik des Mittelalters u. der Renaissance,* pp. 34—41, evaluates the Syrian and Hebrew examples, like P. Wagner before him, from the point of view of common style and common origin.

The preliminary condition for a solution of the problem of Gregorian rhythm is the strict demarcation of the particular style groups (or even smaller subdivisions) and often also the exclusion of particular factors of style : since it is the question of comprehending a thousand-year old, ever changing art.

So we should like to investigate, in the last phase of plainsong history, those groups of notes which (already registered in the use of diminution of the Renaissance-age) are still extant in present Hungarian folk music, and which raise the question : *what rhythmical form they may have possessed?* In doing so, we could, of course, not think of an exhaustive presentation, having at our disposal neither the ornament system of the plainsong, nor that of the Hungarian folk song.[9] It will be a matter of further careful studies to trace the change of embellishments from the 16th century back as far as possible.

Our *examples* are taken from Hungarian and foreign sources of Hungarian libraries[10] and we also refer to Moberg's work.[11] The examples of folk songs originate from Transylvania and Moldavia where ornamentation still flourishes.

What is to be mentioned in the first place is the slide of different length which is crystallized from the *portamento* into a conscious grace, from a narrow-ranged form into a broken chord (nos. 1—6 and passim). It is used inconsistently as are all other ornaments, in the same way as a folk singer follows his momentary impulses (nos. 7—8). The frame role of the upper and lower changing note gives impulse to conscious flourishes from the mordent to the simple, reversed, and extended form of the turn and *cambiata* (nos. 3—5, 9 *et seq.*). Measured rhythm facilitates the repetition of certain ornaments or the succession of sequences (nos. 13, 14*b*). It is remarkable how a group of ornaments retains its place, even after many years (nos. 14*c-d*). The intonation supported from below,which often occurs in Hungarian folk music as well as in that of others peoples, is to be met only rarely in the manuscripts (nos. 14*c-d*, 15).[12] The placing of the ornament at the beginning or end of the words is often strikingly arbitrary (nos. 16—17), as is the choice of the form of embellishment (nos. 18—20).

The melody-shaping grace tending to become an independent melodic section, restricts itself to a single turn (nos. 22—23), which

[9] D. Johner *(Wort u. Ton im Choral*, 2nd ed. pp. 178, 188, 216—219, 150—168) and P. Ferretti *(Estetica gregoriana*, 1934, pp. 96—127) give a clear survey of the punctuation melismatics, as well as an analysis of the variation technique, yet also without reference to the ornament idea. — Unfortunately, we did not have access to R. Fasano's work: *Storia degli abbellimenti musicali del canto gregoriano al Verdi.*

[10] Published in B. Rajeczky's *Melodiarium Hungariae Medii Aevi*. vol. i, Budapest 1957.

[11] C. A., Moberg, *Über die schwedischen Sequenzen*, Uppsala 1927.

[12] S. A. Beischlag, *Die Ornamentik der Musik*, 2nd ed. 1953, p. 33.

most frequently unfolds completely at the end of the line or strophe (nos. 24—26).

Ornaments that more or less modify rhythm can be found at the present only in folk music (nos. 27—28).

From our examples it can be clearly seen that the ornaments recurring at every step originate from a common source : we come across conformities not only in their form but also in their treatment. Therefore it will not be without significance for the rhythmical interpretation of the Gregorian examples to emphasize the common feature of all the Hungarian ornaments presented as illustration : *apart from the initial and final melismata, they all signify the division of the melody-forming note into smaller values.* Should a group of notes of the Gregorian melody prove to play the role of embellishment, it will also have to be considered as having a dividing influence on duration.

*

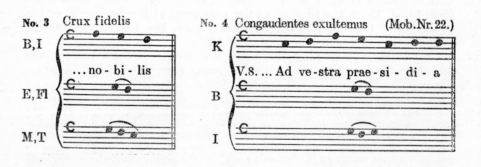

No. 1 Victimae paschali   (Mob.Nr.5a)   No. 2 Exultent filiae Sion

No. 3 Crux fidelis   No. 4 Congaudentes exultemus   (Mob.Nr.22.)

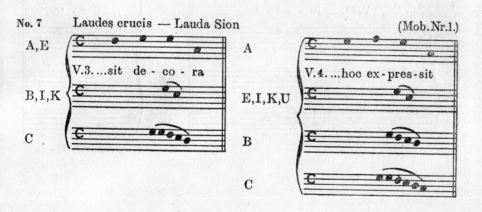

No. 9 Plausu chorus laetabundo

BC written one fourth lower

No. 10 Ave praeclara m. st.   (Mob. Nr. 36.)   **No. 11** Ave maris st.

No. 12 Verbum bonum   (Mob. Nr. 7.)

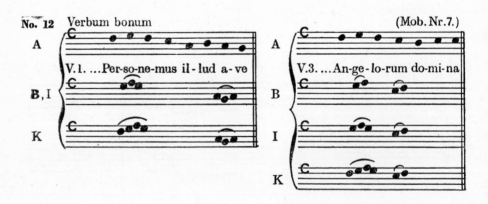

No. 13 Virginalis turma sexus   (Mob.Nr.66.)

V.6. Hic ma - nus foe - mi - ne - a

No. 14 Giusto

a   Vet tem ma ru já nát

♪=138   ♪=144

b   Lu - da - sim, paj - tá - sim

♪=126

c   Më - nyecs - ke, më nyecs - ke

♪=160   ♪=104

d   Hej pá - vo, he - jə pá - va [!]

♪=112

a = Sz. Nd. no. 72
b = F 141/A/d
Same singer ⎰c = Domokos, no. 9. (1932, not. Bartók)
⎱d = Népm. Int. 234/B/b (1952)

No. 15 Sancti Spiritus (Mob.Nr.14.)

No. 16 Veni Sancte Sp. (Mob.Nr.6.)

No. 17 Giusto ♩=168

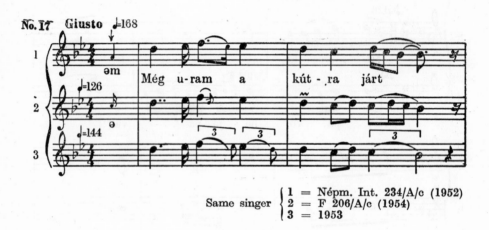

Mèg u-ram a kút-ra járt

Same singer
1 = Népm. Int. 234/A/c (1952)
2 = F 206/A/c (1954)
3 = 1953

No. 18 Laetabundus (Mob.Nr.4.)

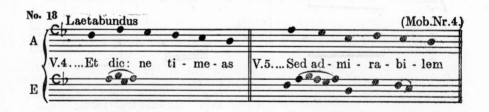

V.4....Et dic: ne ti-me-as   V.5....Sed ad-mi-ra-bi-lem

No. 19   Regis regum civis ave

H

...Re - gni con-sors glo - ri - ae

D,Fg

M

No. 20 ♩=92   F 199/B/a

1.Str. Ej,   haj

2.Str.   ha - jə

3.Str.

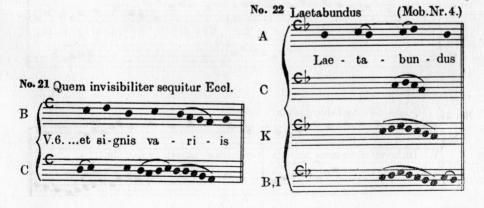

No. 22 Laetabundus   (Mob.Nr.4.)

A

Lae - ta - bun - dus

C

No. 21 Quem invisibiliter sequitur Eccl.

B

K

V.6. ...et si - gnis va - ri - is

C

B,I

No. 23 Parlando ♩=66

1. s A pün-kös-di ró-zsa Ki-haj-latt az

2. út-ra Ne-kём

ёs ki-haj-latt Szё-ke-rem-nek rúd-ja.

Same singer { 1 = F 202/A (1954)
2 = 1953

No. 24 Corde, voce, mente pura

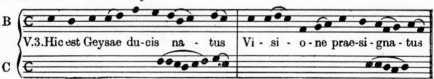

V.3.Hic est Geysae du-cis na-tus   Vi-si-o-ne prae-si-gna-tus

No. 25 Quam dilecta tabernacula

V,7.In bi-vi-o te-gens nu-da Ge-mi-nos pa-rit ex Ju-da

No. 26

Rubato ♩=66

1.Str.

csə
Mó-nár An-na szép më - nyecs-ke, csə

2.Str. ♩=132

csə
— Je - re ve-lem Mó - nár An - na sə

1.Str.

Mó - nár An - na szépə më - nyecs-ke

2.Str.

Je - re **rit.** ve - lem sə Mó - nár An-na! sən

1.Str. ♩=132 **a tempo** ♩=84

s O - da - më - ne Saj - gó Má - rə-toɲ,

2.Str. ♩=100

— Nem më - nyëk én, Saj - gó Má - rə - ton, sə

1.Str. ♩=60

rit. s O - da - më - ne **al** Saj - gó Már-ton.

2.Str. ♩=60

Nem më-nyëk én, Saj gó Már-ton !

No. 27

♪=286

a

Sə Hë - gyën - fül-dön já - ro - ga-tok

♪=160

b

Hë - gyën s fő-dö-nə já-ro - go - ta-kə

a = F 47/A (Not. by Bartók)
b = F 206/B

No. 28

a = Sz. Nd. no. 73.
b = F 213/A/a

SIGNS OF MANUSCRIPTS

A = Esztergom, Christian Museum, Cantionale of the Dominican Nuns, 15th c·
B = *Ibid.* Metropolitan Library, Gradual of King Vladislas (1490—1516).
C = *Ibid.* Gradual of Cardinal Bakócz (1487—1500).
D = *Ibid.* Psaltery, 15th c.
E = Simlău—Csiksomlyó (Rumania) Bibl. O. F. M. Gradual of Fr. Clemens de Hunyad, 1524.
F = *Ibid.* Psaltery, 15th c. Fg : Gothic Characters, Fl : Latin characters.
G = Košice—Kassa (Czechoslovakia), National Library, Psaltery, 15th c.
H = Budapest, National Museum, *c. l. m. ae.* 128. Psalterium Blasii, before 1419.
I = *Ibid. c. l. m. ae.* 172 a—b, *Graduale Cassoviense,* beginning of the 16th c.
K = *Ibid., c. l. m. ae.* 259. Gradual of the Collegiate Chapter St. Martin in Bonn. (Marg. Scheiffartz, between 1456—1482).
L = *Ibid. c. l. m. ae.* 243. Czech Cantional, 15th c.
M = Jaszov—Jászó (Czechoslovakia), Antiphonary of the hermits of St. Paul, 15th c.
N = Budapest, National Museum, *c. l. m. ae.* 317. Pontifical, 14th c.

ABBREVIATIONS OF SOURCES

Sz. Nd. = Bartók—Kodály : *Népdalok, Erdélyi Magyarság* (Folk songs. Hungarians of Transylvania), Budapest, 1921.
F. = Gramophone Records of the Hungarian Etnographic Museum.
Népm. Int.= Gramophone Records of the Institute for Popular Art.
Dates = Tape-recording.
Domokos = Domokos P. Péter : *A moldvai magyarság* (The Hungarians of Moldavia), 3rd ed. Kolozsvár 1941.

VINKO ŽGANEC

THE ELEMENTS OF THE YUGOSLAV FOLKLORIC SCALES IN SERBIAN LITURGICAL CHANT

The Serbian composer St. St. Mokranjac noted the majority of Serbian chants and published part of them in print under the title *Osmoglasnik*[1]. In this book the liturgical chants are arranged according to "tones" (modes) of which there are eight. That is why the collection is called *Osmoglasnik (Oktoekhos)*. The rest of the material noted by Mokranjac was edited by Kosta Manojlović[2].

Besides Mokranjac also other melographers noted and published liturgical chants.[3] None of these notations dates back earlier than the second half of the 19th century.

Up to now very few old neumatic manuscripts have been discovered. Kosta Manojlović believes that such codexes could be found in the Hilander monastery on Mount Athos. Of the known manuscripts he mentions the *stikhirs* of the 5th tone, written in hagiopolitic (round, Middle Byzantine) neumes from Hilander, published by the archimandrite Nićifor Dučić in the fifth volume of his literary works (1895) ; further those from the National Library in Belgrade, no. 93, and some other minor manuscripts. These, however, have not been deciphered and no attempt has been made to carry out a comparison between the present liturgical melodies and the notations of the oldest liturgical chants.

For the study of such melodies only the contemporary material is at our disposal, as it exists in practice, and therefore we have to rely solely on this source for our inferences.

The liturgical chant in the Serbo-Orthodox Church of Jugoslavia is derived from Byzantine church music. The connection between Serbian

---

[1] *Oktoekhos* (The Eight Tones), Belgrade 1908.
[2] Stevan St. Mokranjac, *Pravoslavsko srpsko narodno crkveno pojanje. Opšte pojanje* (Pravoslav Serbian Liturgical Folk Songs. Common Singing), ed. and compl. by Kosta P. Manojlović, Belgrade 1935. XV + 495 pages.
[3] Kornelije Stanković (1862/63), Gavrilo Boljarić i Nikola Tajšanović (1887/91), Tihomir Ostojić (1887/96), Petar Kostić i Jefta Petrović (1899), Jovan Kozobarić (1893), Joco Pajkanović (1906), Tanasi pop Teodorov (1896), Dimitrije Stojačić, Lazar Terzin, Branko Cvejić, Laza K. Lera, Nenad Barački.

and Byzantine music is clearly reflected in the way the melodies of the
eight modes of Byzantine and Serbian liturgical chants are distinguished.
Just as each mode in the Byzantine liturgical chant has its typical
melodic formulae, so are the melodies of each "*glas*" (there are altogether eight of them) in the Serbian liturgical chant built according
to the same principle. To which of the eight "*tones*" a melody belongs
is determined, first of all, not by the type of its scales, but by a definite
melodic formula that has always been attached to this "*tone*", although
according to musical principles it should fall within another "*glas*"
(tone).

The first glas. The melodies belonging to *glas* I are divided into
four types. Their scales and compass are as follows:

No. 1

All melodies belonging to this first *glas* end on D[1]. On closer in-
spection of their melodic line, we find the final note D[1] to be the tonic
of the *re* mode. This is what their melodic cadences indicate, of course
only on the condition that we consider these melodies in their mono-
phonic version without the accompaniment of the second voice. At one
time they were, in fact, sung in unison.

But today most of these melodies are sung in two voices, especially
those sung by the people. We do not know when the practice of two-
voice singing arose in liturgical chant. It probably occurred very early,
certainly soon after two-voice singing of the present type cropped up
in secular Jugoslav musical folklore.

What is the singing in two voices like? It is a singing in thirds
with the final note D[1] accompanied by the lower fifth. In this way the
melody ends with a half-cadence on the dominant harmony. Through
this kind of accompaniment some important changes occurred in these
melodies. This happened in the following manner:

a) the function of the final note D[1], which originally was the
tonic, changed and became, in the two-voice version, the second degree to
in the scale;

b) the tonality of the melody changed, *i. e.* the melody was transferred from the original D-tonality to the C-tonality, with C as tonic;

346

c) the Dorian major sixth (D—B) changed into the minor sixth (D—B♭) ;

d) while in the original authentic Dorian scale the first tetrachord (D—G) was separated from the second tetrachord (A—D²) by a *diazeuxis*, in the new scale, which looks like a Mixolydian one, the tetrachords (C—F) and (F—B♭) are now connected by a *synaphe*.

The former Dorian tonality looks now as follows (melody and accompaniment) :

No. 2

These four types of scales of the first *glas* can be reduced to one scale which is known in Jugoslav musical folklore as "fifth major". In its whole compass it looks like this :

No. 3

This is a specific scale in Jugoslav folk song which ends on the second degree of the scale with a dominant harmony. This scale was discovered by the Jugoslav folklorist M. A. Vasiljević on analyzing 400 songs in one of his printed collections of folk songs. The melodies of these songs move, for the most part, within the frame of a larger or smaller section of the scale shown above; none of the songs covers the whole compass. Each ends on the same final note (D¹). Hardly any of them have a larger range than 8 notes. One or two melodies reach the maximum[4] height : E♭².

The melodic structure of the songs from Vasiljević' collection, which belong to this scale, is such that the particular melodic groups move within one, two, or three tetrachords (bound by a slur). Until now no song moving within all four tatrachords has been discovered.

[4] With Vasiljević this scale is transposed one fourth higher, having, consequently, the final note G¹.

All tetrachords are alike, of an Ionian character, and all are harmonized according to the same harmonic formula. The transition from one into another is achieved by modulatory means. There is no false relation between E^1—$E^{\flat 2}$; B—$B^{\flat 1}$; $F^{\sharp}$—F^1 in the sense of classical harmonics. The central tetrachord is : C D E F and the final phrase of the melody always moves in its compass and has the final note D^1.

The liturgical melodies of the first *glas* have assumed all the characteristics of this Jugoslav folkloric scale, the above-mentioned "fifth major", also called "antique major".

Thus, the liturgical scale of the Serbian church chant, called first *glas, has been completely folklorized.*

Second glas. The melodies of *glas* II have two types of scales. 1. In the first type the initial and the final notes are always E^1.

No. 4

On comparing this scale with the old church scales, we find that it resembles the Hypophrygian scale the closest. The most striking deviation from the Hypophrygian scale consists in the note $A^{\flat}$. This note is at the same time one of the most important characteristics of the Jugoslav folkloric scale called "major-minor scale" : it has the major-third and the minor-sixth.

This scale has also been folklorized, which came about in two ways :

a) first the intonation of A became probably lower and lower until the major third yielded to the minor third. The lowering of the perfect fourth is exemplified in Jugoslav musical folklore in several regions. The most important phenomenon in this respect is to be found in the Istrian scale, in which the Phrygian cadence has been preserved to the present day, but the fourth degree of the scale has been lowered, as also here in the second *glas* ;

b) when the melodies of the second *glas* began to be sung in two voices, the final note was no longer sung in unison, but the contralto-accompaniment in major third (C^1) was joined to it. By the addition of the major third in its accompaniment, the function of this note changed: the tonic became the third degree of this scale, and, at the same time, the function of the tonic was taken over by the accompanying tone. Thus the melodies of *glas* II were transferred from the E-tonality to the C-tonality.

Thereby the liturgical melodies of the first type of *glas* II assumed important characteristics of the Jugoslav folkloric scale, called "major-minor scale". But the folklorization of this scale has not been completely carried through in all its consequences. The secular songs composed in the major-minor scale also end in "fifth major" as above, *i. e.* on the second note of the scale. On the other hand, the liturgical chants of the second *glas* end on the major third of the tonic harmony.

In consequence, the form of this scale, sung, as it is today, in two voices, looks as follows (*a*) :

No. 5

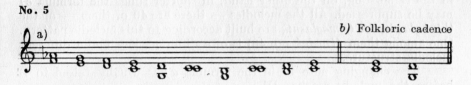

The folkloric cadence of the major-minor scale (*b*) has not yet penetrated liturgical singing.

2. The scale of the second type of *glas* II is the following :

No. 6

and probably comes from the Lydian scale in which the tritone, through continued practice, changed into the perfect fourth. In the chants of this type of scale there are no striking characteristics peculiar to secular folklore melodies.

Third glas. The melodies of *glas* III move in a scale possessing a complex tonal material :

No. 7

The songs of the third *glas* exhibit a rather complicated musical architectonic structure. Their first part moves in the section of the scale F-major within the range of a pentachord, in the case of long melodies within the hexachord *7a*, and ends with a final cadence on F. The second part of the melody is cadenced by means of the melodic formula *7b* to D^1. The third part of the melody *7c* moves within the frame of the pentachord C—G and can be enlarged to B^{b1}. This part ends with the melodic formula *c)* by means of which it modulates into the dominant. These songs close with a new melodic material in the frame of the range *a)* and with the final on F. The formulas *b)* and *c)* can be repeated in the same song, on the other hand, in shorter songs the formula *c)* may be suppressed. All the melodies — there are 40 of them — of the third *glas* in the *Osmoglasnik* are built according to this melodic pattern. One among them *(kondak* no. 40) is of a different key and a different melodic structure.

The changing note B^b in the formula *a)* is usually raised to B before the melody reaches D^2.

Here is a shorter melody[5] in the same *glas*.

No. 8

The melodies of this *glas* could, on the strength of their structure, have some remote relation to the Hypolydian scale.

Although the architectonic structure of this *glas* deviates from the general structural types of our folk melodies, yet traces of folklorization can be observed in the succession of diatonic steps of the melody, the pentachordal and hexachordal frame of the melodic range,

[5] Mokranjac, *op. cit.* p. 76.

350

the chromatization of the fourth degree of the scale, the two-part singing in thirds, etc.

Fourth glas. The melodies of *glas* IV move within two scales.
1. The first scale is this:

No. 9

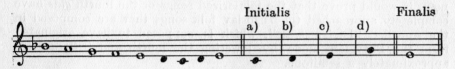

According to compass it is the same scale as that of type *b)* of the first *glas;* but they differ in the final note. There the final note is D^1, here it is E^1.

If we suppose that the note E is the tonic — and probably that was the case at one time — we have here the rests of the Phrygian or Hypophrygian scale.

Also this scale was folklorized when they began to sing the melodies of *glas* IV in two voices. Folklorizing produced the following results:

a) the final note became the third degree of the C-tonality;

b) the fifth degree (B) was intoned always lower and lower until it became B♭. This lowering of the fifth degree probably began before the change of the final note from the first to the third degree occurred. We have a proof of this hypothesis in the Jugoslav so-called "Istrian scale", which has the character of the Phrygian scale with lowered fifth, but in which the function of the final note has not changed even today, *i. e.* the tonic has not become the third degree.

Today the note B♭ is felt as a Mixolydian seventh.

2. The second kind of melodies of the fourth *glas* have the following scale:

No. 10

It is similar to the scale of *glas* II/1 but without B♭.

This scale has been folklorized in the same way as *glas* II/1. Hence all holds good for this scale what has been said about the other.

The difference between the two melodies of these two *glas* does not lie in the key or the tonal characteristics, but rather in the specific melodic figures displaying different features in *glas* IV/1.

In both types of *glas* IV we have two deviations from the diatonic scale of the Phrygian mode:

a) in the first type we have the lowered fifth degree;

b) in the second type we have the lowered fourth degree.

The pitch of the notes has not yet been examined by exact measuring to ascertain whether in *glas* IV/1 the note A^1 is not somewhat lower than the tempered A^1. In case such measuring would really reveal a lower note, it would prove that the folklorized songs of the fourth *glas* have completely approached the Jugoslav folk songs that are composed in the so-called "Istrian scale", which is supposed to have originated from the Phrygian mode by lowering the fourth and fifth degrees approximately a semitone.

Fifth glas. The melodies composed in *glas* V have the following scale:

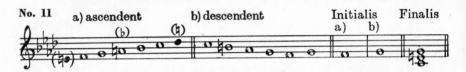

In type 1, the ascending melodic phrases have the scale marked *a)*, the pattern for descending ones is *b)*.

With ascending phrases the prevailing melodic succession of notes is F—G—A, and with the descending ones A^b—G—F. In the ascending phrases the oriental tetrachord hardly ever occurs, but in the descending ones the oriental tetrachord is the rule.

Each melody ends on the second degree of the scale (on the dominant-harmony), like in the melodies of the first *glas*.

The range of the melodies very rarely reaches the sixth (D^2). In the *Osmoglasnik* this case occurs only once, and in one melody[6] we find a D^{b2}.

2. The second type of this *glas* produces melodies of larger pattern moving within the following framework of notes:

No. 12

[6] Mokranjac, *op. cit.* p. 165.

This formula also fixes the four melodic cadences of each part (sentence) of the melody; as can be seen, the melody modulates into the dominant at about the centre. As a rule, we do not find such modulations in Jugoslav folklore. On the other hand, a constant phenomenon in our profane musical folklore is that the melodies and some of their phrases end on the second degree of the scale.

In the songs of the fifth *glas* we find hardly any traces of the Lydian scale of the old church. The melodies of this *glas* are folklorized in the following sense:

a) their scale is almost the same as that of the folk songs in the "fifth major".

b) in a great number of songs the oriental tetrachord occurs in the same position as in the Jugoslav secular musical folklore.

Sixth glas. The melodies of *glas* VI are composed in three types of scales.

1. In the system of St. St. Mokranjac who transposed all songs of the *Osmoglasnik* into F-tonality, the scale of the first type has the following compass:

No. 13

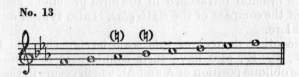

All the melodies of the first type are arranged in a way that the particular parts of these melodies move in the following sections of this main compass:

No. 14

Judging by the final note of the melody (C²), the songs of this type were transposed by Mokranjac into C-tonality and not into F-tonality. This opinion of ours is supported by the fact that the cadence on C² is found not only in the final cadence of these melodies, but also in the majority of other conclusions. See the formulae *c)* and *d)* of the above-mentioned compass of this *glas!*

If Mokranjac had been consistent in transposing all melodies into F-tonality, the compass of his sixth *glas* would have looked like this:

No. 15

This form stands also visually much nearer to the *fa* mode (plagal) than the first.

This type of *glas* VI has, of course, greatly deviated from the F mode, *i. e.* from the Hypolydian scale, precisely through the penetration of the folkloric elements of the vernacular profane folklore.

a) The Lydian fourth (F—B) has completely disappeared from Jugoslav folklore. This is reflected in *glas* VI from where it has also disappeared. The note B has changed into B♭.

b) The oriental tetrachord in the form presented above as parts 14*a) e) f)* of the compass of the sixth *glas*, is also typical of the profane musical folklore.

c) The other degrees of this scale having changed their pitch, *i. e.* D—D♭, E—E♭, also have their counterpart in profane folklore.

d) The oblique position of A and A♭, which occurs in these melodies, is to be found in the same form also in secular Jugoslav songs which belong to the type of songs composed in "fifth major" (see explanation above concerning *glas* I).

2. The second scale-type of the songs of the sixth *glas* has the following compass:

No. 16

The historical development of the melodies of this scale type has not yet been sufficiently examined, but its folklorization has produced the same or at least similar results, as can be seen:

354

a) in the melodies of *glas* II type 1, and
b) in the melodies of *glas* IV type 2.

3. The third scale type of the songs of the sixth *glas* looks as follows :

No. 17

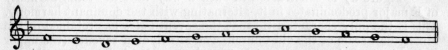

This scale type is related to the *fa* mode (plagal).

The liturgical songs composed in this scale have a characteristic feature that has not been observed until now in our profane musical folklore. This is how St. St. Mokranjac describes it : "Some singers are inclined to sing also these melodies, as well as those of the second *glas*, in 'major minori, *i. e.* in the scale with major third and minor sixth, which prompted us to put the signature of D major for these melodies in this book. Yet the singers never manage to raise the major third in these melodies to such sufficient height as demanded by the third degree of the major scale. They sing it somewhat lower — not as if they could not reach the major third vocally, but because it is inconsistent with the character of the melody." Whether this characteristic is a trace of ancient times, a vestige of the way in which these liturgical melodies were sung in the time of their formation, or whether it constitutes a remnant of folkloric usage which has today become extinct in the profane melodies — are questions which only further studies will be able to answer.

Seventh glas. The melodies of *glas* VII move within the following compass :

No. 18

The first part of most melodies is based on the tonal range shown under *a)*. Before the final figure *b)* the phrase *e)* occurs, next comes another phrase of the melody on the following tonal basis *f)* followed by the final figures *b)*.

The scale of these melodies of the seventh *glas* comprehends the notes C, D, E, F, G, A, B^b, C. The tonic is always F. Consequently, the scale of the seventh *glas* is plagal. The majority of the melodic material of the songs moves, however, in the pentachord F^1—C^2. The figures *b)* and *e)* are rare. In longer songs sometimes both occur together, in shorter ones, however, none of them appears.

Figure *a)* is constructed in such a way that the tonic harmony of F major predominates in it, alternating with the dominant harmony. This is the only characteristic that the seventh *glas* has retained of the Mixolydian scale of the old Church. The Mixolydian seventh (the upper E^b ^{2}) has not been preserved. The lower Mixolydian seventh was changed into the *subsemitonium modi* with which a great number of melodies begin. In this respect we have here the same case as in a great many secular folk songs in fifth major, where besides the upper Mixolydian also the lower one in the lower octave appears changed into the *subsemitonium modi*.

Whoever wishes to compare the seventh *glas* with the Mixolydian scale, should conceive all musical examples a whole tone higher. Here they are given in F tonality in which Mokranjac printed his notations. Whether the seventh *glas* has developed from the Mixolydian scale of the old church can no longer be ascertained from the present form of the songs. In any case many of its elements have their root in Jugoslav musical folklore.

Eighth glas. The melodies of *glas]* VIII are composed in several scale-types. They move within the following types of compass. Type 1 :

No. 19

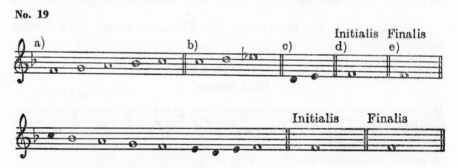

The main part of the melody *a)* is constructed in pentachord. In some places the melody is amplified in the frame of further notes *b)* and ends in F. It occurs only exceptionally that the melody is augmented with a motive below the tonic *c)*.

In the material of the melody the tonic triad F A C predominates which, with the augmented motive *b)*, is more reminiscent of the Mixolydian scale of the old Church than of the Hypomixolydian scale.

356

2. The melodies of the second type have the compass of the hexachord :

No. 20

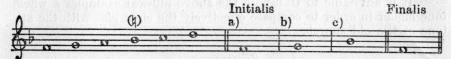

There are several cases in this type where the melody leaps from the tonic to the upper fourth degree which reminds us of the 8th tone of the old Church (Hypomixolydian scale). Some melodies even begin on the fourth degree. In this type the fourth is often augmented (as changing note) ; such alterations often occur in our profane folklore.

3. Then follow the melodies of the third type within this range:

No. 21

In the course of the melody the cadences of the particular melodic phrases change from G to F ; one passage ends on G, the other on F, thus alternating till the last cadence which ends on F.

4. The melodies of the fourth type have the following range :

No. 22

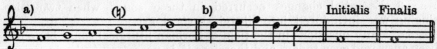

The melodies of this type are based, in the first part, on the material of scale-section *a)* and, in the second part, on the scale formula *b)*.

5. The fifth type is the amplified second type *a)* with a new melodic motive *b)* which cancels the Mixolydian seventh and regularly appears in the melody before the final phrase. The melody ends on the tonic.

From this detailed synthesis of the various scale-types of the liturgical melodies of *glas* VIII it can be seen that also in this *glas* few traces of the Hypomixolydian scale of the old church have remained. What has remained of it appears also in Jugoslav profane musical folklore. These are : in the first, second and fifth type, pentachordal and hexachordal scale systems ; in the third type, the periodical alternation of the cadences on the first and second degree of the scale. The melodies of the fourth type are alien to Jugoslav musical folklore. In the same way, the motive *b)* of the fifth type, as shown above, is also rather foreign, though not unknown. It is rather unorganically grafted into these melodies.

It is advisable to transpose the above musical examples a whole tone higher in order to compare effectively the eight *glas* with the 8th tone of the old church.

Summary

From the above presentations of the scale formulae of the Serbian orthodox liturgical songs in the notation of St. St. Mokranjać' *Osmoglasnik*, the following conclusions may be drawn:

1. The names "first, second, third . . . eighth *glas*", by which the particular melody groups are called in the *Osmoglasnik*, do not correspond to what these, or the corresponding names of the Byzantine *ekhoi*, or Gregorian tones of the old Church, designate. Only here and there can some unimportant traces of resemblance or similarity be found between them.

2. The dissimilarity has arisen from the fact that Serbian church singing had been continually subject to the influence and development of folk music, and that is why in all these melodies, traces of present Jugoslav musical folklore are to be found (not only of Serbian folklore proper), and probably also survivals of older forms which today have disappeared from profane folklore. In addition to this it must be realized that there existed no written notations at all of these songs — expecially of these forms which prevailed in the oldest times — until recently when the melographers of modern times began to note them (end of the 19th century).

3. Essential changes occurred in these songs when two-voice singing was introduced into liturgical vocal art.

4. Many questions in the field of Serbian liturgical songs have not been answered even today, and therefore it is necessary to begin serious studies concerning this important cultural legacy, first of all to preserve the entire material by tape recording after the performance of the best traditional singers.

SAMUEL BAUD-BOVY

THE STROPHE OF RHYMED DISTICHS IN GREEK SONGS

Πολιτικὸς στίχος

A fifteen-syllable "great verse" with a caesura, the πολιτικὸς στίχος or "vulgar verse" has been the most general form of Greek song ever since the Byzantine period.

Its first hemistich consisting of eight syllables is either oxytone or proparoxytone ; the second, seven-syllable hemistich is always paroxytone. The number of syllables is invariable and only paired syllables or initial ones may carry tonic accent.[1]

> Ἄκου καὶ νὰ σὲ φίλουνα   εἰς τὸλ λαιμὸ 'ποκάτω
> ἐκεῖ ποὺ παίτζει καὶ χτυπᾶ   τ' ἅγιο Κωστανινᾶτο[2].

Underlining the stressed syllables of the above distich, the following scheme can be obtained :

1	2	3	4	5	6	7	8		9	10	11	12	13	14	15
1	2	3	4	5	6	7	8		9	10	11	12	13	14	15

The analysis of dance songs composed in great verse reveals that the strong part of the measure or bar equally coincides either with the paired syllables or with the initial of the hemistich, or else, if the penultimate syllable is prolonged, with the final syllable of the line.

The Strophes of the Great Verse

The simplest and most frequent strophic system is the one in which a single great verse corresponds to each musical strophe, either in

---

[1] For further details see : S. Baud-Bovy, *La chanson populaire grecque du Dodécanèse. I. Les Textes*, Paris 1936, pp. 39—62.

[2] Μ. Γ. Μιχαηλίδου Νουάρου, *Δημοτικὰ Τραγούδια Καρπάθου*, Athens, 1928, p. 288, no. 35.

its original form or with repetition of syllables or hemistichs, or accompanied by refrains.

Another system, rather unexpected but nearly as current as the one mentioned above, is the one in which each strophe comprises *one line and a half:* thus the first hemistich of each line, except the first, is sung twice, *viz.* at the end of the strophe and at the beginning of the next. In an earlier paper of mine[3] I have attempted to explain the origin of this strange type.

Finally a strophe may, though less frequently, embrace a *couplet of great verses.* It will suffice to skim over any collection of Greek folk songs to find that this strophic system is applicable only to rhymed distichs or poems with couplet rhymes. Consequently, we may conclude that the appearance of this strophic system is closely connected with the appearance of rhyming.

Rhymes in Greek Folk Songs

"The origin of rhyme in Greek versification has been a frequently investigated and much-debated question. Research has, however, led to the conclusion that, except for a few attempts at rhyming found sporadically in both Greek prose and verse, rhyme in modern Greek literature is the result of the contact of Hellenic civilization with that of the West. These cultural relations were first established in a systematic way and continued on the Greek islands near the shores of Asia Minor."[4]

Two manuscripts, both containing love songs from the islands, one dating from the 15th century[5] and the other from the beginning of the 16th century,[6] give us an idea about the approximate date of the introduction of rhymes in Greek poetry. They are rare in the first manuscript but occur more frequently in the second, where the number of distichs is also greater.

Is it possible to fix the time and the place when and where the ancient songs in unrhymed great verse came to be supplanted by rhymed distichs and other polystichal songs with couplet rhymes? Where — to go back to our first question — and when did the type of musical strophe appear which was to combine the earlier independent great verses into groups two by two according to both meaning and form?

---

[3] *Sur la strophe de la chanson cleftique,* in *Annuaire de l'Institut de Philologie et d'Histoire orientales et slaves,* vol. x, 1950, *Mélanges Henri Grégoire,* vol. ii, pp. 53—78.

[4] Κ. Θ. Δημαρᾶ, ῾Ιστορία τῆς νεοελληνικῆς λογοτεχνίας, Athens 1948, vol. i, p. 69.

[5] D. C. Hesseling and H. Pernot, ᾽Ερωτοπαίγνια (Love Songs), Paris—Athens 1913, p. viii.

[6] H. Pernot, *Chansons populaires grecques des XV et XVIe siècles,* Paris 1931, p. 7.

In order to answer this question we must first consider whether or not this strophe exists in the folk poetry of the two great western civilizations with which at that time the Greek world was in contact : *i. e.*, in Italian and French folk poetry.

The Fifteen-Syllable Paroxytone Line in Italian and French Poetry

The rhythmical pattern of the fifteen-syllable great verse is one of the commonest in folk poetry. Though being aware of the difference between versification based on the length of syllables and versification based on tonic accent, *i. e.*, between *metrum* and *rythmus*, one will unfailingly be amazed at the striking resemblance of the rhythmical pattern of great verses to the catalectic iambic tetrameter of Aristophanes : 'Ὡς ἥδομαι καὶ τέρπομαι καὶ βούλομαι χορεῦσαι (Plutos 288), or to the catalectic iambic septenary of Plautus : Domum redimus clanculum, dormimus incenati (Rudens 302).[7]

Frequent as it is in French folk poetry, this pattern can scarcely be found in Italian verse. The reason seems to be that, except for Piedmont where the French influence is noticeable, the first hemistich is considered by the Italians to be a proparoxytone line, a *settenario sdrucciolo*, and hence likely to be replaced by the *settenario piano* or *trunco* in which the number of syllables is reduced to seven or six.[8] Anyhow, as far as I am aware, it does not appear in any of the Italian folk songs, save in some of Piedmont.

One of them, a rather wide-spread song, is nothing but a translation[9] of an ancient French song, *La Brebis sauvée du loup*. The first hemistich of both original and translation is in octosyllabic oxytone verse :

La bargera larga i mutun	al lung de la rivera
ël sul levà l'era tant cáud	la s'è setà a l'umbreta.
Entre Paris et Saint-Denis	z'y avait une bergère
qui faisait paître son troupeau	le long d'une lisière.[10]

Mr. P. Verrier has clearly proved the ancient origin of these verses which were popular before the 12th century[11], and this makes it superfluous to come back to that question. Moreover, he has shown with a number of examples its diffusion not only to the South, but, first of

---

[7] Quoted by P. Verrier, *Le vers français*, Didier, Paris 1931—1932, vol. ii, p. 249.

[8] Fr. d'Ovidio, *Versificazione italiana e Arte poetica medioevale*, Milan 1910, p. 190.

[9] Cost. Nigra, *Canti Popolari del Piemonte*, Turin, 1888, p. 372.

[10] P. Verrier, *op. cit.* vol. i, p. 139.

[11] *Op. cit.* vol. ii, pp. 223—224.

all, to the North, *i. e.*, to Germany, England and Scandinavia.[12] The strophe of the narrative songs always comprises a pair of these great verses, thus forming, properly speaking, a "couplet".[13]

Thus it will seem quite natural to attribute simply to French influence the establishment in Greek poetry not of a verse which had been known there for centuries, but of a strophic system which grouped the lines of that type by twos.

French Influence in Cyprus

We must search for the place of this innovation on one of the Greek islands, *i. e.*, on Cyprus where a French dynasty reigned for three centuries.

During the 14th century, relations between the Greek and the French, which formerly had been characterized by a certain tension, gradually improved. In 1368 Pope Urbane V was obliged to take measures against Catholic women who attended orthodox services.[14] Some years later, during a plague, in 1393, King James I took the initiative of a procession, the character of which, as rightly stressed, was clearly "Greek"[15]. On the other hand, certain Greeks came to be gallicized to such an extent that the chronicler Leonce Macheras could rightly state that, after the conquest of the island by the Lusignans, the Cypriots had begun to learn French and corrupt Greek, so that by his time (the first half of the 15th century) the inhabitants of the island wrote in a hybrid language which no one in the world could understand.[16]

In Cyprus, Greek aborigines and their French masters had a similar taste for music and song. Estienne de Lusignan in his *Description de toute l'isle de Chypre* (1580) says that the great landowners "amused themselves with fencing and tournaments, with playing the lute ; they loved music, and every nobleman was perfect in singing or playing the lute". As to "common folk and burghers and others of moderate excellence", they were people "endowed with a natural inclination to poetry, who composed by themselves with grace and elegance without following precepts or old patterns. They also sang beautifully"[17].

Thus every condition seemed to be given for the establishment of a fruitful contact between French and Cyprian poetry.

[12] *Op. cit.* vol. iii, pp. 292—316.
[13] *Op. cit.* vol. i, p. 173.
[14] G. Hill, *History of Cyprus*, Cambridge 1940—1952, vol. iii, p. 1082.
[15] Θ. Α. Σοφοκλέους, Ἐνδείξεις περὶ ἐπιδράσεως τοῦ ὀρθοδόξου ἑλληνισμοῦ ἐπὶ τῶν Φράγκων ἐν Κύπρῳ ἐπὶ Φραγκοκρατίας, in Κυπριακαὶ Σπουδαί, vol. xvi, 1953, pp. 11—23.
[16] Ed. Miller and Sathas, vol. i, p. 85.
[17] Quoted after Th. Siapkaras-Pitsillidès, *Poèmes d'amour en dialecte chypriote*, Athens 1952, p. 18.

And I think I have found in contemporary French and Cyprian folklore the traces at least of one of the airs which were borrowed by the Cypriots from the French.

The Air of Cyprian "Laments"

There is, indeed, a tune which with its variants is used today for singing nearly all rhymed laments in Cyprus, both profane and religious : *The Dirge of the Blessed Virgin, Saint George killing the Dragon,* and *The Resurrection of Lazarus.* In the latter we have to do with a "begging song" *(chanson de quête)* sung by children on their way to ask for eggs.[18]

Here is a version of this tune recorded in 1946 in the village of Saint-Epictète by Mr. Th. Kallinikos, protopsalt of the Archbishop of Cyprus :[19]

Ex. 1.

Ἄ - δε μαν-τά - το σκο-τει-νὸν κ'ἠ - μέ - ρα λυ - πη - μέ - νη

Πού ἦλ- θεν σή - με - ρον σὲ μέν, τὴν πολ-λο - πι - κραμ-μέ - νην.

N. B. We have reduced all our examples to the same unit of duration and to the same pitch in order to facilitate comparison. We have dispensed with the use of bars requiring much precaution, but we indicate the beginning of lines and hemistichs.

It is obvious that we have to do with a strophe embracing a distich of rhymed great verse.

There is in France, too, an air of religious lament on the Passion of Christ, which at the beginning of the 17th century appears as a "begging" song[20], and at present is sung by the peasantry of Low Normandy on the last fasting days to solicit butter and eggs.[21]

We are illustrating three variants of it. The first (no. 2) is from Normandy and its musical strophe comprises a single line, whereas the second variant (no. 3) from the French Alps[22] and the third (no. 4) from Provence[23] have two melodic lines in the same strophe.

[18] Θ. Καλλινίκου, Κυπριακὴ λαϊκὴ Μοῦσα, Nicosia 1951, p. 198.
[19] *Op. cit.* p. 191, no. 81.
[20] Verrier, *op. cit.* vol. i, p. 125.
[21] J. Fleury, *Littérature orale de la Basse-Normandie,* Paris 1883, p. 219.
[22] J. Tiersol, *Chansons populaires recueillies dans les Alpes françaises,* Grenoble 1903, p. 91.
[23] D. Arbaud, *Chants populaires de la Provence,* vol. ii, Aix 1864, p. 1.

Ex. 2.

Or ap-pro-chez, pe-tits et grands, et ve-nez pour en-ten-dre
La Pas-si-on de Jé-sus-Christ, qui fut triste et san-glan-te.

Ex. 3.

La Pas-si-on de Jé-sus-Christ, vous plaît-il de l'en-ten-dre ?

E-cou-tez-la, pe-tits et grands, a-vec grand ré-vé-ren-ce.

Ex. 4.

La Pas-si-on de Jé-sus-Christ, que fait tant bon en-ten-dre,

La Pas-si-on ·de Jé-sus-Christ, que fait tant bon en-ten-dre.

We can ascertain, at first glance, the striking resemblance between the French and Greek songs. They have the same syllabic division, the same caesura and, moreover, one can notice the almost total identity of the first phrase of the Norman and Cyprian versions. Their modes alone seem to differ. If we examine more closely these French songs, especially the beginning of the Provençal version, we can easily ascertain that they belong to the *re* mode, *do* being nothing but a subtonic sound serving to link a subsequent verse, as is usual in begging songs where no pause is made in singing until the singers feel entitled to a generous reward for the performance of a sufficient number of couplets. The collector of the Norman version explicitly remarks that "the tune is performed without any interruption or lingering on the tonic sound".

The Greek variants of this air are numerous, as one can easily see, because it has spread all over the Aegean Sea up to the shores of the Black Sea. If it were possible to arrange all of them in a comparative table, it would be just as easy to find equivalents for almost each of the phrases of the French song.

We can compare, for instance, the second phrase of the Alpine version (no. 5) with the second phrase of a version from the Black Sea (no. 6)[24]

Ex.5.

vous plaît-il de l'en-ten-dre?

Ex.6.

βάλ' ἕ - να'ς σὸ πο - τή - ρι.

or the third phrase of the Alpine version with the third phrase of a version from Chalki (Dodecanese)[25]

Ex.7.

E - cou-tez-la, pe - tits et grands...

Ex.8.

Χρι - στοῦ τὴ Θεί - α Γέν - νη - ση...

or its last phrase with that of two variants of a Rhodian New Year begging song sung by the same informant (nos. 10 and 11)[26-27].

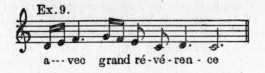

Ex.9.

a --- vec grand ré - vé - ren - ce

[24] Ἀρχεῖον Πόντου, vol. ii, 1929, p. 198, no. 20 bis.
[25] S. Baud-Bovy, *Chansons du Dodécanèse*, Athens 1935; vol. i; p. 271, no. 5.
[26] *Op. cit.* p. 65, no. 17.
[27] *Loc. cit.* variant.

Ex. 10.

ὁ Κύ - ρι - ος στὸν κό - σμο

Ex. 11.

ὁ Κύ - ρι - ος στὸν κό - σμο.

Summing up we can rightly state that the difference between a Greek and a French variant is not greater than between two Greek or two French variants. As this strophic form was frequent in France before the 12th century and appeared considerably later in Greece, it is impossible to presume a Greek influence upon French versification. On the contrary, it seems evident that this song was imported to Cyprus under the Lusignans, and that the identity of the traditional Greek verse and the verse of the newly imported song contributed to the quick adoption of the new strophic system. Moreover, the existence of semi-professional minstrels who probably served French and Greek masters at the same time, just as later Greek and Turkish patrons, must have speeded up the time of borrowing.

There is, however, a difficulty which I do not want to conceal. As in the case of so many genuine French folk songs, the song on the Passion of Christ is also based on a single rhyme or assonance *(entendre, sanglante, soutenance, prendre*, etc.). That means that its poetic form does not involve a two-line strophe. Indeed, while the Alpine version unites the lines by two, the Provençal version repeats the same line twice, whereas the Norman version has but one line per strophe. Anyhow, as Mr. Verrier has remarked, "the unity of the couplet is attested and maintained by the unity of meaning".[28]

At any rate, each strophe of the version introduced to Cyprus must have contained two assonant or rhyming lines constituting a semantic unity. As it would be impossible to compose in Greek a song of some length on a single rhyme or assonance, it is perfectly natural that in the Dirge of the Blessed Virgin (no. 1), for instance, a couplet rhyming in *eni* (λυπημένη — πολλοπικραμένην, ἀρφανεμένη — σκοτεινιασμένη) is followed by an assonant couplet in *oss* ... *ou* (λογισμός μου — δικός μου, Θάνατός σου — δικός μου) and by a succession of varied rhymes (ἥλιον — σπήλιον, ῾Υιός μου — κόσμον, φωλιεύκαν — ἐφεύκαν, etc.).

What the Greek song borrowed from the French was the pattern of strophe containing two great verses united by rhyme and sense.

[28] *Op. cit.* vol. i, p. 198.

As to the date of borrowing, it must have taken place anterior to 1489, because in that year the island was taken by the Venetians, whose influence was to become predominant on the island in the 16th century. The date may go back to the first part of the 15th century, a period when the relations between Greece and France were close. We may quote, for example, the life of Macheras himself, the principal chronicler of Cyprus (he died before 1458) who, being a true servant of the French kings of Cyprus, remained, notwithstanding, a good orthodox Greek.

Cyprian Variants

The same way of using this air for a religious lament, either "begging" or not, both in France and Cyprus, makes us think that this was the type introduced into Cyprus.

This air must have gained wide popularity over this large island. The tunes to which the ποιητάρηδες, the semi-professional minstrels already mentioned, rhymed either the formerly unrhymed ballads or their new compositions on contemporary events, are nothing else but variants of this very same air :[29]

Ex. 12.

Ἀ - κού - στε ἴν - ταν νὰ σᾶς πῶ τζιαὶ Γρι - σκα - νοὶ τζιαὶ Τοῦρ-τζιοι,

Ἐ - λᾶ - τε, σο - ρευ - τῆ - τε μου, τζιαὶ μὲν κά - μνε - τε κού- τζιν.

The marked difference of the *incipit* is very likely due to its contamination with the beginning of another tune. From the fact that its rhythmical structure is based almost exclusively on quavers we must not draw any further conclusion, because in another version,[30] closely related to that one, we can find the rhythm of religious songs.

[29] Καλλίνικος,, *op. cit.* p. 131, no. 56 Γ'. It is worth while translating the words of this version. They attest that the ποιητάρηδες sang to orthodox Greeks and Mussulman Turks as well, just as their ancestors had to court the favour of the Catholic French as well as of their correligionists :
Mon récit, Turcs et Chrétiens, s'il vous plaît de l'entendre,
Venez, groupez-vous près de moi sans davantage attendre
[30] *Op. cit.* p. 179, no. 75.

Ex. 13.

Νῆ - εν ἠ - στρά - ψη ὁ Θε - ός, νῆ - εν κα - ῆ ἡ ὤ - ρα,

ὁ κα - η - μέ - νος ὁ Σπα - σηῆς ἐ - πή - αιν - νεν τήχ Χώ - ρα.

When the subject of the song is particularly dramatic, the *ποιητάρης* employs chromatic scales. This is the case with the song of *Hadjiargyris*, a Cypriot who during the Ottoman occupation was a collector of taxes and secretary of the Turkish rulers. His extorsions and cruelty made him hateful to his compatriots. Having been found guilty of the murder of a Greek and his little child, he was denounced to the Vali and hanged on a mulberry tree. The singer invites Turks and Greeks to listen to the performance :

> Turcs et Grecs qui êtes présents,   et rassemblés ici,
> approchez-vous pour écouter   un bien triste récit.[31]

Ex. 14.

Τοῦρ - τζιοι Ρω - μιοὶ 'πού βρέ - χε - - στε τζι' ὅσ' εἶ - στε συ - να - μέ - νοι — ,

Ἐ - λᾶ - τε ν' ἀ - γροι - τζιή - σε - τε μιαὶ λί - την λυ - πη - - μέ - νην.

Its compass is wide, its mode is different ; but a comparison of the first and last phrases of this song with the corresponding phrases of the first song we have seen (no. 1) will suffice to prove their close relationship.

*

This type of strophic system is not limited in Cyprus to narrative songs, religious, or profane. It must have been applied also to lyrical songs especially to the type sung during fasting days by young girls balancing on a swing and improvising tunes. (The swing is called *σοῦσα*, from the verb *σειῶ* 'to swing', in Cyprian). Some of the "swing" songs are similar to the French songs of the Passion of Christ ; this time, however, we have to do with independent distichs[32] and not with polystychal songs :

[31] *Op. cit.* p. 157, no. 67.
[32] Chr. Apostolides, *Cyprus Songs and Dances*, Limassol 1910, p. 13, no. 5. Each line is repeated, the repetion of the second varies.

368

Θε - έ μου, νᾶρ - ταν σή - κω - σες, νὰ κρε - μα - στοῦν οἱ σοῦ - σες,

τζιαὶ νὰ γε - μώ - σουν τὰ στε - νὰ οὖλ - λο μαυ - ρομ - μα - τοῦ - σες.

We can notice here, as we have seen already in no. 14, a tendency
to protract not the paired syllables, the stressed ones, but the odd syllables. This tendency appears more markedly in other versions.[33]

Ex. 16.

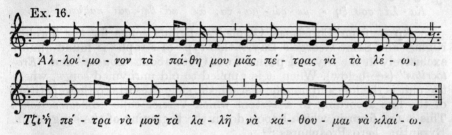

Ἀλ - λοί - μο - νον τὰ πά - θη μου μιᾶς πέ - τρας νὰ τὰ λέ - ω,

Τζι'ἡ πέ - τρα νὰ μοῦ τὰ λα - λῆ νὰ κά - θου - μαι νὰ κλαί - ω.

These few examples — one could easily multiply them — bear
witness to the fecundity of this strophic system in Cyprus and to the
diversity of the songs it generated.

The Propagation of the Two-Line Strophe in the Greek World

Outside Cyprus this diversity is considerably less, though we can
find in other places each type sung on the island of the Lusignans.

Thus, for instance, in the small seaport of Castellorizo lying half-
way between Cyprus and Rhodes, rhymed historical poems are sung to
a chromatic air[34] which has undoubtedly some analogy with one of the
Cyprus airs (no. 14) :

Ex. 17.

Στὰ χί - λια ἐν - νια - κό - σι - α, τὸ ἔ - τος δε - κα - έ -- ξι,

Ἀ - κού - σα - τέ μου νὰ σᾶς πῶ τί ἔ - μελ - λε νὰ τρέ - ξη.

[33] Κλ. Ἀρτεμίδου, Ἀπὸ τὰ Κυπριακὰ δημοτικὰ τραγούδια, in Κυπριακαὶ Σπουδαί,
vol. xvi, 1952, Nicosia 1953, p. μδ', no. 9.
[34] Baud-Bovy, op. cit. p. 353, no. 14.

In Rhodes all songs of this strophic type I gathered are narratives, mainly religious and begging songs. One of these songs, for Saint Basil's Day[35] (January the 1st), is similar to the song of the Passion of Christ from Provence (no. 4):

Ex. 18.

Apart from Christmas Carols,[36] religious songs for the Twelfth Night[37] and Saint George's Day,[38] this type of strophe is found almost exclusively in the rhymed poems from Crete about *"Soussa"* and *"Erotocritos"* (see below). When it is applied to old unrhymed songs, where the unit is the line and not the distich, the singer resorts to the repetition of the line according to a system which Verrier calls *"concatenation"*. This is the form in which I took down the beginning of the song of the Byzantine hero Prosphoros :[39]

Ex. 19.

Translation:

At the extreme end of the land near the morass the savage
Once an old woman bore a child and he was called Prosphore
Once an old woman bore a child and he was called Prosphore
He came into the world on Saturday and was baptized on Sunday.

In Crete, as well as in Castellorizo and Rhodes, this type of tune can be found only with rhymed narrative songs, mostly profane but

[35] *Op. cit.* p. 62, no. 16b.
[36] *Op. cit.* p. 65, no. 18.
[37] *Op. cit.* p. 68, no. 19.
[38] Unpublished version recorded in the village of Soroni.
[39] *Op. cit.* p. 84, no. 24.

sometimes religious *(The Dirge of the Blessed Virgin* and *The Song of Saint George)*. One of the most widespread ones is the *Song of Soussa* :

> Every morning as it's dawning   when the flowers blossom
> Listen to me, and I'll tell you   the mournful song of Soussa

of wonderful Soussa who came to be stabbed by her brother for letting herself be seduced by valiant Sari Bahri.

Soussa, I am afraid, owes her short existence to a misunderstanding. *The Song of Soussa*, τῆς Σούσας τὸ τραγούδι, is nothing but simply the 'swing" song τῆς σούσας τὸ τραγούδι as in Cyprus they call the tune of improvised distichs usually sung at Easter by young girls. When τῆς σούσας τὸ τραγούδι was introduced to Crete, where the swing is called κούνια, σούσα was interpreted as a first name, a variant of Σουσάνα Susanna, and, as it often happens in hagiography, once the heroine was baptized, an adventure had to be attributed to her.

Be that as it may with this hypothesis, the song itself was very popular; it passed from Crete to Chios,[40] to Rhodes, to Castellorizo, and as far as Sinassos, Cappadocia[41] to quote only the regions where its air was recorded. As to its text it was found all over the Aegean Sea, in Peloponnesus, and in the ports of the Black Sea. Its Cretan origin is nearly always confirmed by references to Soussa having been the "pride of Crete", the "flower of Crete".[42] The fact that the song did not spread on the islands of the Ionian Sea to which so many inhabitants of Crete escaped when the Venetians evacuated their land proves that the song was composed after the conquest of the island by the Turks (1669). Soussa's lover Saribali or Sarbey seems to have been an important Turkish personality.

The Sinassos version will prove how little the peregrinations have changed the song :

Ex. 20.

Τὰ δε-κα-πέν-τε τοῦ Μαϊ-οῦ ἀ-νοί-γει τὸ ζεμ-πού-λι,

Ἀ-κού-σα-τε νὰ σᾶς εἰ-πῶ τοὺς Σού-σας τὸ τρα-γού--δι

[40] H. Pernot, *Rapport sur une mission scientifique en Turquie* in *Nouvelles Archives des Missions scientifiques*, vol. xi, p. 118, no. 109.
[41] Γ. Δ. Παχτίκου, *260 Δημώδη Ἑλληνικὰ Ἄσματα*, Athens 1905, p. 31, no. 25.
[42] The present paper was in page-proofs when I received Mr. Emm. I.Doulgerakis' monograph *La chanson populaire crétoise de Soussanna* published in *Κρητικὰ χρονικά* vol. Θ', 1955, pp. 334—376. Mr. Doulgerakis remarks that the song was particularly popular with seamen and must have originated among the Moslem inhabitants of Crete, probably before 1679.

In Crete this air is sung with all rhymed songs on historical subjects. Today it is best known, however, as the *Air of Rotocritos*.
The novel in verse bearing the same title was written by Vizenzos Cor-
naros in the first half of the 17th century. It was not primarily meant
for singing ; it is full of enjambments from one hemistich to the other,
from one line to the other, and even from one distich to the next. But,
greatly refined as it is, its versification still relies upon the distichs of the
great verse. The peasants of Crete instead of reciting long fragments
of the poem they have learnt by heart often prefer to sing it, accompanied or not by the *lyra*. I quote two lines to show the form in which I
recorded it in 1954 in the village of Kritsa :[43]

Ex. 21.

Ὡς μπῆ-κεν ὁ — Ρω-τό-κρι-τος στὴ φυ-λα-κήν ἀρ-χί-ζει —

Νὰ τῆς μι-λῆ καὶ σπλα-χνι-κὰ νὰ τήν ἀ-ναν-τρα-νί-ζη.

The resemblance of this version to the Cyprian versions and
mainly to those of Rhodes is obvious.

*

We have so far found this air outside Cyprus only in rhymed
polystichal songs. Independent distichs in Dodecanese and in Crete are
either sung to dance tunes or have preserved their one-line strophe.

Yet on the shores of the Black Sea and in the ports of Pontus this
air has been recorded only with distich. Just as in the case of the Cyprian
swing songs with texts in self-contained distichs, here too, we can notice
the tendency to protract the odd syllables and not the paired ones.
In spite of the distance between Cyprus and the Black Sea there is a
striking resemblance between the rhythmical structure of the swing
song (no. 16) and the following air[44] though the melody of the latter
comes closer to the air of the ποιητάρης in no. 13 :

[43] Tape recording, Crete I r, from the *Folklore Music Archives of Mrs
Merlier* in Athens.
[44] Δημ. Κουτσογιαννοπούλου, Τραγούδια, in Ἀρχεῖου Πόντου vol. ii, Athens
1929, p. 198, no. 20.

Ex. 22.

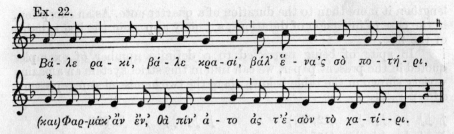

Βά - λε ϱα - κί, βά - λε κϱα - σί, βάλ' ἔ - να'ς σὸ πο - τή - ϱι,

(καὶ)Φαϱ-μάκ'ἂν ἔν,' Θὰ πίν' ἀ - το ἁς τ'ἐ - σὸν τὸ χα - τί - - ϱι.

At first glance there is nothing left in common between this song and the French lament on the Passion of Christ. But I could have quoted a variant from Trebizond [45] the first phrase of which coincides almost literally with the first phrase of the version from Low-Normandy (no. 2):

Ex. 23.

Α - γιὰ Σο - φιὰ μυ - ϱο - λο - - γᾷ —

There is obviously no direct relation between them. But the scope of the present paper has been to prove that their resemblance, nevertheless, is not merely accidental.

Appendix
The Rhythmical System of the Greek Versions and the French Songs

The observant reader might have been struck by the fact that two signs of duration, the crotchet (♩) and the quaver (♪)[46], were sufficient for the notation of all Greek songs quoted. And indeed, all of them belong to a system called *syllabic giusto* by Constantin Brăiloiu. The characteristics of this system are : "1. Exclusive use of two invariable durations, their relation being either 1 : 2 or 2 : 1. 2. Free alternation of elementary rhythmical groups formed of two or three such durations."[47]

In the Greek songs here analyzed the rhythmical groups, as a rule, do not comprise more than two of these durations, except when the initial syllable of a hemistich is stressed, and the only distortion of the system is due to the fact that sometimes the sixth syllable of the second hemistich is regarded as a contraction of two syllables (the sixth and seventh of the first hemistich). Moreover in most instances the singer does not

---

* An additional syllable as it often occurs in songs from Pontus.
[45] Παχτίκος, *op. cit.* p. 50, no. 38.
[46] The only exception occurs in no. 16 where we can find the rhythm ♩ ♩ ♪
[47] C. Brăiloiu, *Le giusto syllabique, Un système rhythmique populaire roumain* in *Annuario musical del Instituto Español de Musicologia* vol. vii, 1952, pp. 117—158, see p. 118.

lengthen it more than to the duration of a quarter note. As an exception, in the case of inversion of durations, a ♩. may appear in the last syllable of the line.

In spite of being restricted to a definite number of examples quoted in the present paper, we can find in this strict system an amazing variety shown in the table below, where the two hemistichs are represented separately :

♪ ♪♪ ♪♪ ♪♪ ♪ (12, 17)   ♪ ♪♪ ♪♪ ♩ ♪ (18)

♪ ♪♪ ♪♪ ♪♪ ♩ (17)   ♪ ♪♪ ♪♪ ♪ ♩ (12, 17)

♪ ♪♪ ♩♪ ♪♪ ♩ (1, 13, 19, 21, 23)   ♪ ♪♪ ♩♪ ♩ ♩ (1, 19, 21)

     ♪ ♪♪ ♩♪ ♪ ♩(.) (6, 13, 19, 21)

♪ ♩♪ ♩♪ ♪♪ ♩ (20)   ♪ ♩♪ ♩♪ ♩. ♩ (20)

♪ ♪♪ ♩♩ ♪♪ ♩ (18)

♩ ♪♪ ♪♪ ♪♪ ♩ (8, 17)   ♩ ♪♪ ♪♪ ♩ ♩ (10, 11, 17, 18)

♪ ♪♪ ♪♩ ♪♪ ♩ (15)   ♪ ♪♪ ♪♩ ♪ ♩ (15)

♪ ♪♪ ♪♩ ♪♩ ♩ (14)   ♪ ♪♪ ♪♩ ♩ ♩ (14)

     ♪ ♪♪ ♪♩ ♪ ♩. (14)

♪ ♪♩ ♪♪ ♪♩ ♩ (16, 22)   ♪ ♪♩ ♪♪ ♪ ♩ (16, 22)

In certain cases this metrical system gives the impression of regular measures in the sense of the traditional theory of music : certain types could be understood as $\frac{2}{4}$, $\frac{5}{8}$, $\frac{6}{8}$ measures. But the theory advanced by Brăiloiu on Rumanian syllabic songs accounts for all forms of the variants.

Is this a system exclusively applicable to the folk music of Eastern Europe ? I do not think so. On the contrary, I should think that some of our French songs written usually in $\frac{6}{8}$ — a border case of *"giusto"* as we have just seen — complied with this system whenever they were not sung to dances, and showed the characteristics of a musical recital, as in the instance of the begging songs. I am convinced that in the Alpine and Provençal versions of the Passion of Christ (nos. 3 and 4) the ♩. notes are replaced by ♩ which imparts suppleness to the tune and intelligibility to the text. I am also inclined to attribute to the Alpine version the most frequent rhythmical pattern of Greek songs, such as no. 24.

Ex. 24.

La Pas-si-on de Jé-sus-Christ

where the musical rhythm breaks the hemistich into two equal parts, as happens so often with internal rhymes (rime *"batelée"*)[48] in songs of this rhythmical type, whether they are French or Latin, German or Greek, ancient or modern :

L'âne est tombé   dans un fossé,   la pauvre bête est morte[49]

Nunc comprimas   hac lacrimas   et luctum qui te urget[50]

Vil reine wip,   din schoner lip   wil mih ze sere schiezen[51]

Ὡς ἥδομαι   καὶ τέρπομαι   καὶ βούλομαι χορεῦσαι[52]

Ταχειὰ ταχειὰ   'ν'ἀρχιμενιὰ,   πρώτη ἀρχὴ τοῦ χρόνου[53]

In order to prove that our hypothesis is not so adventurous as it may seem at first glance, we present a ballad sung by an old woman in the district of Saargemünd.[54] It is about a count who disguises himself in order to win the favour of his beloved. This ballad, like many German and Northern ballads, has a rhythmical pattern very similar to that of the great verse, but procedes in places, as is usual in German versification, by "coinages" of syllables.

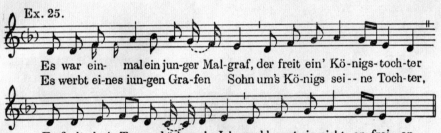

Ex. 25.

Es war ein-   mal ein jun-ger Mal-graf, der freit ein' Kö-nigs-toch-ter
Es werbt ei-nes iun-gen Gra-fen   Sohn um's Kö-nigs sei - - ne Toch-ter,

Er freit drei Tag und ü-ber ein Jahr und konnt sie nicht er-frei - en.
Er werbt drey Tag und sie - ben Jahr und konnt sie nicht er - wer-ben.

---

[48] Verrier, *op. cit.* vol. ii, p. 224.
[49] *Loc. cit.*
[50] *Loc. cit.* p. 225, extract from *Suscitatio Lazari* by Hilarius, disciple of Abelardus.
[51] *Op. cit.* vol. iii, p. 301 (*Carmina Burana*, no. 116a).]
[52] Aristophanes, Plutos, *v.* p. 288.
[53] A begging song from Crete, see *50 Δημώδη ᾄσματα Πελοποννήσου καὶ Κρήτης, Συλλογὴ Ὠδείου Ἀθηνῶν*, Athens 1930, p. 66.
[54] Louis Pinck, *Volkslieder von Goethe in Elsass gesammelt mit Melodien und Varianten aus Lotharingen*, Metz 1932. p. 82. The tune is given here in a pitch one degree lower, the key signature has two sharps for the first line and one for the second, so that the alteration of the sixth degree is doubtful. Under the words of the informant are given those noted by Goethe, featuring a single "coinage" of syllables.

I think we can rightly state that if, instead of putting down our French songs by ear, with all prejudices of our musical culture, we had taken them down from the records as the one above, we could have noticed that a number of them (ballads not sung to dances, laments, begging songs) belong, as a matter of fact, to the "syllabic *giusto*". It happened also to me that, during my first voyages to the Greek islands, I put down certain tunes in *"giusto"* as if they were in $\frac{6}{8}$ and in $\frac{5}{8}$ rhythms, ready to use a *fermata* ($\frown$) whenever durations occurred that seemed irrational, — whereas they simply fitted into a system different from the one I was familiar with.

*

Summing up : if present-day Greek song with a strophe consisting of a couplet of two rhymed "great verses" seems to have originated from French songs, the examination of Greek songs, in their turn, will help us to form a notion of the rhythm and mode of French songs at the end of the Middle Ages.

376

CONSTANTIN BRĂILOIU

PENTATONY IN DEBUSSY'S MUSIC

The present paper neither raises nor solves any new problem. Its scope is limited to prepare, but from a single aspect, the solution of an old unresolved problem which could be formulated as follows : Being of very different origin and character, how could the material used by Debussy be blended, as it has been, into such a homogenous unity ? Or, to put it more simply : what does his art consist in ?

It is needless to say that any answer would require a thorough-going analysis not only of the tonality (or, as it is here, of one of its components), but also of the resulting melodic characteristics ; of the harmony considered in a closer relation to melody than was done in the past ; of the rhythm; of the form itself and, finally, of all that is involved in the composition of music. It would require not only that the composite character of the substance handled by Debussy be recognized (as it has been for long), but also that, before any attempt at definition and the recognition of certain proportions, the scholars should agree as to the origin and relative importance of the elements used by the composer. Unfortunately this agreement does not seem to have been reached. Léon Vallas[1], for instance, thinks that the "ecclesiastic modes" were discovered by Debussy "in the Russian music of the Five rather than in the Gregorian chant which *does not seem to have caught his attention*". Julia d'Almendra[2], on the other hand, published an entire volume on the ecclesiastic modes in Debussy's oeuvre (mentioning, moreover, his visit to Solesmes which undoubtedly must have taken place), and A. Gastoué[3] wrote in explicit terms : "Did not we see Claude Debussy devoutly attend the services in Saint Gervais Church, a pencil in hand, taking down in his book, the melodies which struck him the most among the Gregorian chants and the motets of Palestrina ?"

---

[1] L. Vallas, *Achille-Claude Debussy*, Paris 1944, p. 72.

[2] Julia d'Almendra, *Les modes grégoriens dans l'oeuvre de Claude Debussy*, Paris 1950.

[3] A. Gastoué, *L'église et la musique*, Paris 1935, p. 60.

As far as tonality is concerned, we must remind the reader that already the first interpreters spoke of defective scales, of diatonic scales, of a series of exceptional intervals, recalling sometimes the Far East on the whole, other times Spain, and then sometimes China and sometimes the Gipsies. The use of pentatony (by the way implicitly included in this enumeration) has been similarly signaled several times, though the allusions made to it have been rarely based on examples. Critics have not tried to indicate the places featuring the "five-note scale" in the tonality of Debussy, nor to show the way in which it determines his invention of melodies. Hence, we believe that some remarks concerning the above questions will not be superfluous and we hope they will stimulate a general investigation so much needed.[4]

*

Debussy was, to all appearances, perfectly aware of his own devices even if he did not like to exhibit them or let anybody into the secret of handling them. Pentatony in his composition is not an unconscious or reflex-like reminiscence. He proves it himself by referring to it whenever he wants to evoke something "not from here" : *Pagodes* ; the exotic herdsman and the English soldier of *La Boîte à joujoux;* the honourable S. Pickwick ; *La Fille aux cheveux de lin* (conveying a kind of mysteriousness). This admitted pentatony aiming at *couleur locale* serves in a way as a screen for all that emerges from his works, if not always dissimulated but, at least, very often intimately associated with other components which suddenly evoke or shroud it.

On the other hand, we must remember, right at the outset, that the majority of pentatonic features characteristic of Debussy's idiom appear as early as his first works and persist up to the last ones, especially those ample processions ascending by seconds, which surprise us in his early melodies, for instance in *La belle au bois dormant* or in the *Fleur des blés:*

[4] In the following it will be inevitable, first of all, to transpose each example to the same key to facilitate comparison ; then sometimes to reduce the quoted passages to their musical pattern ; and finally to refer to two books : *Sur une chanson russe* in *Musique russe*, vol. ii, Paris 1952, and *La métabole pentatonique*, in *Mélanges d'histoire et d'esthétique musicale offerts à Paul-Marie Masson*, vol. i, Paris 1955, because it has not been possible to consider each problem duly dealt with in these two works. The reading at first will appear somewhat difficult and the author apologizes for it. Yet any other way would have been detrimental to the clarity of this study. The examples quoted can be re-established in their entirety by anybody who knows them or wants to look them up at their original sources. Let us mention here that Mr. Jacques Chailley has undertaken an inquiry, similar to this one, but covering, the whole modern period.

Le long des blés que la bri-se fait on - du - (ler)

or in the *Romance*:

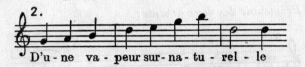

D'u - ne va - peur sur - na - tu - rel - le

and which have their counterparts also in the falls of similar amplitude:

Sem - blaient re - ver - dir les feuil-les fa-(nées)

(Les cloches)

Rise and fall are occasionally linked together:

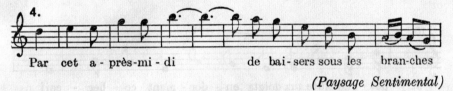

Par cet a - près-mi - di de bai - sers sous les bran-ches

(Paysage Sentimental)

This is to be found in the second song of *Ariettes oubliées*:

Qui pé - né - tre mon coeur

in *La mort des Amants*:

(réfléchi-)ront leurs dou-bles lu - miè - res Dans nos deux es-prits, ces (miroirs)

379

in the *Spleen* of the *Paysages belges*:

Et   de la   cam-pagne in - fi - nie   et   de tout

then in *Le Promenoir des deux amants*:

Se   re - po-sent dans ce   vi - vier

and also in the second of the *Three Poems* by Stéphane Mallarmé *(Placet futile)*:

Blon - de dont les coif - feurs di - vins   sont les or - (fèvres)

or

M'y   pei - gne flûte aux doigts en - dor - mant ce   ber - cail

and

J'u - se mes feux et   n'ai   rang dis - cret que d'ab - (bé)

just as in *Le Martyre de Saint Sébastien* (a version for voice and piano, p. 90):

Tu   es lou-é,   L'é - toi - le   de loin parle   à l'é-toi - le

380

or

Je fau-chais l'É-pi de fro-ment ou-bli-eu-se de l'as-pho-dè-le

(p. 39)

and also in the *Noël des enfants qui n'ont plus de maisons:*

Mais don-nez la vic-toire aux en-fants de Fran-ce

Locutions of that kind often preserve their clearly vocalic feature even when played on instruments :

(Ballad for piano)

or

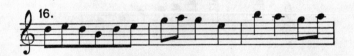

(Fantasy for piano and orchestra, red., p. 10)

or

(Suite bergamasque: Clair de lune)

or

(ibid.: Menuet)

or

(Tarantelle-Styrienne)

and also

(La mer, p. 19 of the score)

and

(Hommage à Rameau)

or

(ibid.)

We find, however, that these inflexions take, at an early stage, a more openly instrumental turn, sometimes by extending over a compass rather unusual for the voice :

(Rêverie)

which seems to predict the first of the *Epigraphes antiques (Pour invoquer Pan)* :

as well as *La Cathédrale engloutie* where the crest of the chords shows, at a given moment, this ample curve :

The adaptation to instruments is achieved by the agility and the capricious pattern of the line : let us recall the *Hommage à S. Pickwick*, and also :

(...D'un Cahier d'esquisses)

383

or, however, that these inflexions take at an early stage
a more nearly instrumental pace, sometimes by extending over a compass rather unusual for the voice:

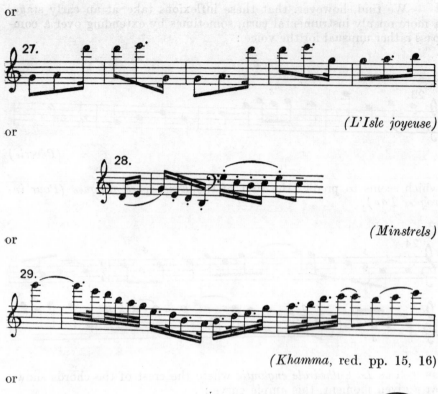

27.

(*L'Isle joyeuse*)

or

28.

(*Minstrels*)

or

29.

(*Khamma*, red. pp. 15, 16)

or

30.

(*Sonata* for violin and piano, pp. 4, 5)

or the theme of *Les Collines d'Anacapri* (first disturbed by a transitional
note which forthwith disappears):

31.

It often happens that these figures without detaching themselves from the melodic substance turn into flourishes or "traits":

(2nd Arabesque)

In *La Damoiselle élue* (red., p. 18) this conjunction :

points far ahead, to the short dialogue of the flute and the hautboy in the *Jeux* (score, p. 25) :

Akin to these are the long volutes of the first *Etude* for piano (*Pour les "cinq doigts"*) :

those in the *Reflets dans l'eau:*

in the *Sonata* for violin and piano:

and

or this *ostinato* of the violoncellos in *La mer* (score, pp. 5, 6, 7, **11, 15**):

and, long before that, in *Pelléas et Mélisande* (red., p. 245):

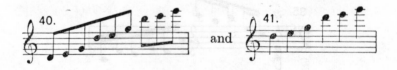

The pseudo-decorative nature of such melodic expressions renders them suitable for various adaptations, whenever an opportunity arises. Also the motive in *Les Collines d'Anacapri:*

accelerates, while fading away :

and later being reduced to accompaniment only.

Similarly, a kind of pentatonic *arpeggio* on the first violin develops in the slow movement of the *Quartet*

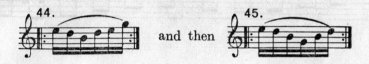

and then

These "*traits*" can be found almost everywhere, such as the *Fantasy* nding in this gamut :

then in

(red., p. 20)

down till :

(red., p. 19)

25*

The *Quartet* presents a number of them:

49.

or

50.

or

51.

or

52.

which undoubtedly reminds us of:

53.

(1st Arabesque)

In *Pelléas* (red., p. 103) we have :

which will recur, in a slightly modified form, in *La Mer* (score., pp. 132—133, 134) :

We would not say for sure that nothing of what has been exposed refers directly to the large undulations of the flute and the harp in the *Nuages* (score., p. 12) :

or to these lively successions of forths and fifths sometimes mixed with thirds and seconds, used in some places of *La Mer* (pp. 6, 15, 16, 17, 30, 31) :

or in the *Etude Pour les quartes* :

and

59.
Stretto

at the end of *La Fille aux cheveux de lin:*

60.

and in this episodic passage of *Ibéria:*

61.

8va

not to speak of the striking ascension of pentatonic chords in the *Martyre* (red., pp. 29 et sq.):

62.

8va

All that seems to characterize a distinct category generated in the atmosphere of the World Exhibition of 1889.

One can notice that when an organized melodic fragment does not exceed the ambit of a sixth or a seventh, it assumes sometimes the form

of one of the five first pentatonic modes. This appears for the 1st mode
(1—2—3—5—6 = *so la si re mi*) already in *Fleurs des blés*, where

J'ai trou-vé de bon-ne pri - se

points ahead to

Le gars en noir et la fille en ro - se

(Chevaux de bois)

or to

tou-tes les é - toi - les tom - bent

(Pelléas, red., p. 249)

and also to

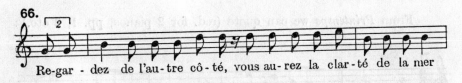

Re-gar - dez de l'au-tre cô - té, vous au-rez la clar-té de la mer

(Pelléas, red., p. 41)

and to the utterances of Golaud pulling Mélisande by her hair :

Vous al - lez me suivre à ge - noux, A ge-noux de-vant moi

(Pelléas, red., pp. 2 14—215

391

The inverse melodic movement yields for instance :

(Suite bergamasque: Passepied)

or

Je viens sou-vent m'as-seoir i - ci vers mi - di

(Pelléas, red., p. 56)

but also :

...le ciel er - rant de ton oeil an - gé - li - que mon - te

(Three Poems by Mallarmé, I: Soupir)

From *Printemps* we can quote (red. for 2 pianos, pp. 1, 2 etc.) :

from *Ibéria* (score, p. 98) :

from *Pantomime* (in the *Quatre mélodies* published in the supplement of the *Revue Musicale*, May 1926) :

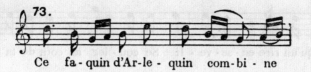

Ce fa-quin d'Ar-le-quin com-bi-ne

from *Pelléas* (red., p. 249) :

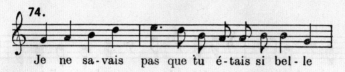

Je ne sa-vais pas que tu é-tais si bel-le

from the third of the *Trois Chansons de France (Rondel)*:

Pour ce que Plai-sance est mor-te, Ce may suis ves-tu de noir

and, above all, the second of the *Three Ballads by François Villon*:

Les biens de vous, ma da-me et ma maî-tres-se

It is probably not worth while dealing with the melodies in the 2nd and 3nd mode (by the way both comparatively rare), since the vocal impulses that suggest them should be ranged rather among the extended segments of the scale discussed above. Besides, only a few of them yield the entire series of their two scales.

See for the second mode (2—3—5—6—1 = *la si re mi so*) :

Dans ce va-gue d'un Di-man-che, Voi-ci

(L'Echelonnement des haies)

393

and then

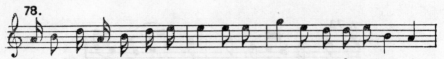

Ain-si qu'un rire en - se - ve - li   Se cou - ler au coin de ta bou - che

(Three Poems by Mallarmé, III: Eventail)

and

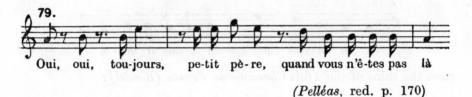

Oui, oui, tou-jours,   pe-tit pè - re, quand vous n'ê-tes pas   là

(Pelléas, red. p. 170)

and also

Pel-lé - as   et pe - ti - te   mè - re ne par-lent-ils ja - mais de (moi)

(Pelléas, red., p. 160)

For the 3rd mode $(3-5-6-1-2 = si\ re\ mi\ so\ la)$, we quote the *cantabile* of *Pelléas* (red., p. 248) :

On di - rait de l'eau pu - re sur mes mains

and in *Villon's Ballad* to his mother :

ne peult me - rir n'a - voir les cieulx

The rest is fragmentary :

Voi-ci que le prin-temps

or

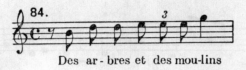

Des ar - bres et des mou-lins

(L'Echelonnement des haies)

or

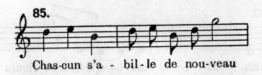

Chas-cun s'a - bil-le de nou-veau

(Trois Chansons de France, I)

The 4th pentatonic mode $(V - VI - 1 - 2 - 3 = re\,mi\,so\,la\,si)$ has only a secondary role in Debussy's music. Its scale appearing in joint descending degrees imparts an enchanting sweetness to the first bars of Fauré's *La bonne Chanson*. In *La Damoiselle élue* we can hear the echo of this Faurian suavity (red., p. 13) :

Je le pren-drai par la main

and, even more so, at the end of the *Promenoir des deux amants* :

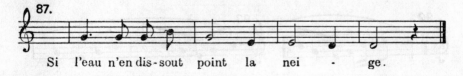

Si l'eau n'en dis-sout point la nei - ge.

395

of what *Les Angélus* have given already a foretaste :

We can find, besides :

(Aquarelles, II : Spleen)

and also

(Trois Chansons de France, II)

or

(Chansons de Bilitis, III:
Le tombeau des Naïades)

It is different with the 5th mode (VI — 1 — 2 — 3 — 5 = *mi so la si re)*, the scale of which contains the melodic kernel which can be detected at the beginning of *La Fille aux cheveux de lin* and from which Debussy's idiom derives, more than once, a specific coloration :

396

This germ did not wait until 1913 to burst into bloom. It is adumbrated already in the *Fantasy* (red., p. 13):

and in the *Proses lyriques* (I):

...d'or main-te - nant ter-nis

in *L'Echelonnement des haies:*

(l'onde) rou - lé - e en vo - lu - (tes)

Golaud sings *(Pelléas, red., p. 66):*

A-t-il vu quel-que cho- se d'ex-tra - or - di - nai - re

Pelleas (p. 109):

...(la) voûte est cou - ver - te d'é - toi - les

and Melisande (p. 282):

Oui, oui, je te par- don-ne... que faut-il par-don-ner?

Or other examples :

100.

Ma dou - leur, don - ne - moi la main, viens par i - ci

(Recueillement)

or

101.

il me re - gar - da d'un re - gard si ten - dre

*(Chansons de Bilitis, II :
La Chevelure)*

We find, here and there, several "saw-toothed" lines characteristic of some, mainly northern, folk songs and also of certain Wagnerian passages which might have been inspired by them. In spite of its playful features the first *Arabesque* has a slight touch of the Tetralogy :

102.

just as the trimming of the *Etude Pour les "cinq doigts"* :

103.

and, as it seems, also those in *Pour les sonorités opposées* :

104.

whereas vague reminiscences of *Parsifal* hover about the *Chevaux de bois:*

105.

Tour - nez, tour-nez, bons che-vaux de bois

and, one would say in :

106.

Où vont-ils dor - mir cet - te nuit ?

(Pelléas, red., p. 231)

An artist as ingenious and as rebellious to coercion as Debussy was unable to employ methodically the same means for the same purposes. It would be a temerarious attempt to connect these "crenelated profiles" with :

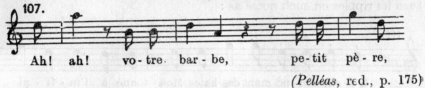

107.

Ah! ah! vo-tre bar - be, pe-tit pè - re,

(Pelléas, red., p. 175)

or with

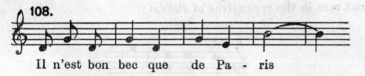

108.

Il n'est bon bec que de Pa - ris

(Ballade des femmes de Paris)

or even with

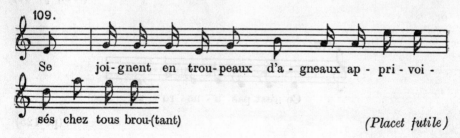

109.

Se joi-gnent en trou-peaux d'a - gneaux ap - pri-voi -

sés chez tous brou-(tant)

(Placet futile)

399

or

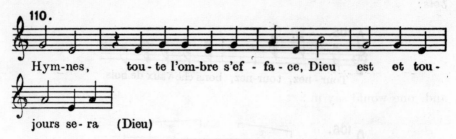

Hym-nes,   tou-te l'om-bre s'ef - fa - ce, Dieu   est   et tou-
jours se-ra   (Dieu)

(*Martyre*, pp. 20, 21)

and, what is more, to suppose that they might have a common source.

The two trichords, wholetone+minor third and minor third+ whole tone ("trichordal *incipits*" 1 and 2), known from psalmodic recitation and recurring, especially the second, continuously in Debussy's oeuvre, seem to have particular importance. The first, having often the function of introducing or closing a longer musical sentence, is not always as conspicuous as the second. Nevertheless in the *Paysage sentimental* it is used for an accompanying *ostinato* and *L'Echelonnement des haies* runs its ripples on such notes as :

L'é-che-lon-ne-ment des haies Mou-tonne à l'in-fi-ni

It is not rare in the recitatives of *Pelléas:*

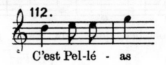

C'est Pel-lé - as

(red., p. 34)

or

Ce n'est pas u-ne ro-se

(p. 125)

or

(p. 278)

or

(p. 113)

or

(p. 67)

or

(p. 232)

And in one of Debussy's later works we find :

(*La Mer*, score, pp. 136—137 : horns)

or

(ibid., p. 25: English horn and trump.)

or

Cé - lé - brez son nom   par le   feu

(Martyre, red., pp. 20, 21)

and, which comes to the same :

Al - le - luï - a

(ibid., pp. 98—101)

The *"incipit 2"* emerges even more persistently from Debussy's melodic texture. *Les Angélus* sigh to the first beats:

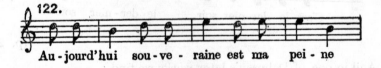

Au - jourd'hui   sou - ve - raine est ma   pei - ne

and in *Romance* we have:

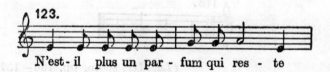

N'est - il   plus un par - fum qui res - te

402

with many replicas elsewhere. From *Proses lyriques* (I):

La nuit a des dou-ceurs de fem - me

and

Et c'est au fond vrai-ment trop gra - ve

From *Pelléas*:

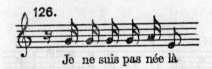

Je ne suis pas née là

(red., p. 10)

or

Voi - cì ce qu'il é - crit

(p. 25)

or

Je suis ma- la- de i-ci

(p. 82)

or

nous n'a-vons pas é - té cou-pa - bles

(p. 289)

or

Pour-quoi n'ai - je pas dit la vé - ri - té ?

(ibid.)

or

la vieil - le ser-van-te de la mort

(p. 198)

or

Il faut par-ler à voix bas-se

(p. 304)

or

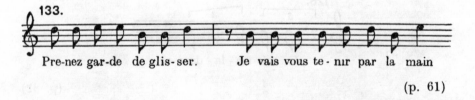

Pre-nez gar-de de glis-ser. Je vais vous te - nir par la main

(p. 61)

or

il y en a d'au-tres que nons ne pou-vons voir en-   co-   re

(p. 47)

or

Tu   ne sais   pas pour-quoi il faut que je m'é-   loi-   gne

(pp. 243—244)

The *Nuages* allots a prominent melodic function to the "*incipit 2*": the English horn lingers on it for a long time (score : p. 10) :

In *La Mer* it recurs several times. First on page 11 and 15 of the score (horns) :

then on page 29 :

finally the peroration of the third movement :

The refrain of *Noël des enfants qui n'ont plus de maisons* owes its desolate accent to this formula (pp., 1, 2, 6) :

Nous n'a-vons plus de mai- son.

And we do not stray far from the above by quoting :

la seu- le veu- ve de tout es - poir

(*Les Angélus*)

or

Je chas- sais tran-quil-le-ment dans la fo - rêt

(*Pelléas*, red, p 76)

or

At - ten-dons que la lune ait dé-chi - ré ce grand nua - ge

(*ibid.*, p. 106)

144.

Il sait mieux que moi son a - ve - nir

(ibid., p. 32)

145.

que je voie tes che-veux dé - noü - és

(ibid., p. 120)

146.

Je sais que ma mè - re me par-don-ne-ra vo - lon - tiers

(ibid., p. 28)

or the unforgettable :

147.

Vous a - vez mai-gri et vieil - li·

(ibid., p. 279)

Nothing is more surprising then to see Debussy not only "think pentatonically" without any effort, but rely ever more on the pre-pentatonic (bi-, tri-, and tetratonic) modes. It is true that one could regard these examples as fortuitous strokes of pen :

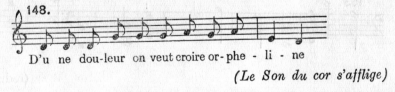

148.

D'u ne dou-leur on veut croire or - phe - li - ne

(Le Son du cor s'afflige)

or

149.

Sur - pri - se de sen - tir un coeur dans la bri - se

(Quatre mélodies: Pantomime)

or the monologue of Pelleas (red., p. 249):

150.

Je fe - rais mieux de m'en al - ler sans la re - voir

or else

151.

Je n'a - vais ja - mais rien vu d'aus - si beau a - vant toi

(Pelléas, red., p. 249)

or even, if necessary, the theme of the *Tarantelle-Styrienne:*

152.

On the other hand, there is no doubt, that he, himself, was consciously and deliberately in search for tetratony, for instance, in the interlude of *Pelléas:*

153.

(red., p. 23)

just as well as towards the end of *Jeux de vagues (La Mer*, score, p. 80 : harp) :

and also in the first idea of the score (p. 1 : violas)

which will re-echo in the fourfold alleluias of the *Martyre* (red., pp. 102—103) :

Al - le - lu - ia

and in their insrumental doublet :

as well as in the *Reflets dans l'eau:*

and in the first of the Poems by Mallarmé :

The "sign of the cross" in the *Martyre* is tritonic (red., pp. 1, 4, 16, 27, 28) :

Its amplification is also tritonic (and bitonic at the end) (red., pp. 26—27) :

just like this melody of the *Proses lyriques*:

Di - man - che sur les vil - les. Di - man - che dans les coeurs

or this intervention of the piano :

or, in *Hommage à Rameau*:

in *Jeux* (score, p. 26):

and, earlier, in the *Prelude* of the *Suite Bergamasque:*

finally on pages 28 and 29 of the *Martyre* this bitonic sequence:

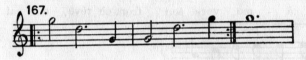

Let us consider now, on the other hand, a peculiar detail: the more or less developed melodic sections sometimes pass from one pentatonic system to another. This is a customary course in the traditional five-note music, both composed and folkloric (metabolism). And one is rather uncertain as to the intentions of the composer in passages where the change is cursory, as *e. g.*, at the beginning of *Fêtes galantes (I: En sourdine):*

or where the alternating systems are liable to discussion for their defective character or for some other reasons[5] (for instance: *Proses lyriques*, III: the passages "Dimanche, chez les petites filles", pp. 22—23, and "dévorés par d'insatiables tunnels...", pp. 24—25). But the transposition is obvious in the first piece of the *Trois Chansons de France*, pp. 3—4:

[5] Thus in our last example, if we regard *ti* of the second bar as an ornament, we can consider this piece to be written in a *"do* system" from the very beginning.

169.

Ne scay da - me ne da - moi - sel - le Qui soit en tous biens par-fais tel - le

and also in *Soupir:*

170.

Mon â - me vers ton front où rêve, o cal - me soeur Un au-tom-ne jon-ché ...

and on pages 40 and 41 of the *Cathédrale engloutie,* where the tune flutter-ing above the chords turns from the system *so* towards the system *do:*

171.

Moreover, in one instance we come across an entire musical sen-tence composed symmetrically, as sometimes in folk music, and consist-ing of two parts, each belonging to a different system : in this case to tetratonic mode and to the 1st pentatonic mode (*Jimbo's Lullaby* in *Children's Corner):*

172.

It follows, we believe, from this survey, inevitably sketchy, that Debussy borrowed from archaic tonality a number of essential assets which define his style, and that the primitive modes play a more important part in his oeuvre than is generally thought.

Yet it would be impossible to specify the extent of this part, and there seems to be no means of compiling any accurate statistics of frequency. Such an analysis should be the scope of a particular research. It will suffice to state that the pentatonic "tenure" varies considerably from one composition to the other and that (except for some picturesque pieces of the *Pagodes* type) the use of the "defective" scales, wrongly called so, does not assume a dogmatic character in any of the compositions, nor does it yield any "system" of composing, at least not in the sense the word is used today. A number of very significant works of his are saturated with pentatony and pre-pentatony *(Fantasie; Printemps; Quartet; Pelléas et Mélisande; La Mer; Trois Poèmes de Stéphane Mallarmé;* a number of his compositions for piano, especially *Hommage à Rameau);* in other pieces pentatony, floating under the surface, emerges in more than one passage *(Ballade; Première Rhapsodie* for clarinet and orchestra ; *Syrènes* from *Trois Nocturnes*[6]*; Gigues,*[7] etc.) ; finally in others we find but short manifestations *(Jeux; Ibéria;* different melodies) or insignificant traces *(Pour le piano,* etc.) ; and there are works unaffected by it altogether.

We must also remember that the experience of the ancient scales goes very far back in the career of the composer (as is made sufficiently clear by our examples). Even if we allow for an exotic influx (which is not unlikely and to which he alluded himself in some sort due to the Exhibition of 1889), we must not forget that his pentatonic vocabulary had been entirely elaborated by the time of the composition of the *Nuages,* and this might account, among other factors, for the striking unity of his oeuvre, in spite of the diversity of its objectives.

Even if the sources, from which Debussy's music derives its pentatonic features, remain (except for the Javanese inspirations) partially enigmatic we do not doubt that, in spite of the opinion of one of his

---

[6] Especially : score, pp. 91—93.
[7] Especially : score, pp. 4—5, 9 etc.

biographers[8], it was not among the Gypsies that he had the opportunity to acquaint himself with the "curious sonorities of the Greek and Chinese gamut", even if he spent "entire hours" with them. One will certainly remember that since Weber, Chopin and Liszt a number of modes totally ignored in *solfeggio* took root in the musical idiom of the West; that pentatony is used for distinct purposes in the Wagnerian theatre;[9] that Russian music is deeply imbued with it, and finally that it was not neglected by some of Debussy's predecessors and contemporaries. We may possibly also remember Debussy's erudite friend Chausson, proprietor of a library of folklore, whose books might have passed through the composer's hands.

*

There is, finally, a paramount question with which we can but deal briefly, expecting an expert to answer it in a meticulous study it undeniably deserves. The point is to reveal the personal principles underlying the handling of the material in question, and to find the ways and means Debussy employed to incorporate it in his music.

Certain evident facts which even a cursory survey seems to reveal capture our attention.

1. Even in the domain of pure melody and in parts dominated by a deliberately archaic atmosphere, long uninterrupted pentatonic passages are rare. After a segment, undeniably pentatonic, the melody shades into heptatony or is carried toward a "strange" finale which renders the tonality equivocal or, at least, effaces the memory of the mode in which the melody began:

173.

(*Prélude à l'après-midi d'un faune,* score, pp. 16—17)[10]

or:

174.

(*Tarantelle-Styrienne*)

[8] Jean Lépine: *La vie de Claude Debussy*, Paris 1930, p. 26.
[9] V. F. A. Gevaert: *Traité d'harmonie théorique et pratique*, Paris—Bruxelles 1905, p. 24.
[10] Edition Jouber, 1925.

414

This is a customary device of Debussy, one we came across in *Noël des enfants qui n'ont plus de maisons* (no. 14), and which often recurs in his works.

Hence one must regard as exceptional the beginning of the *Hommage à Rameau* (v. no. 22) and the beginning of the first piece of *Epigraphes Antiques* (v. no. 24) and also the consolation of Pelleas to Melisande :

175.

Il ne faut pas s'in-quié-ter ain - si pour u - ne ba - gue.

Ce n'est rien, nous la re - trou - ve - rons peut -

ê - tre ! Ou bien nous en re - trou - ve - rons une au - tre

2. Except for the episodes showing marked Javanese influence (as *Nuages*, score, pp. 12—13; *La Mer*, part I, score, pp. 6, 11, 15, 30 and the last bars of the part II, etc.), polyphony is not based exclusively on pentatonic components ; only sporadically do we find the association of a melody and a harmonic support, as for instance, at the beginning of the *Collines d'Anacapri;* the bars 6, 7—8 etc. of *La Mer;* on pp. 29, 98—99, 100, 101 of the *Martyre* (red.); on p. 38 of *La Cathédrale engloutie*, or in *Masques* where :

176.

is supported by :

177.

And one will remember Péter's words in connection with a lullaby for his *Tragédie de la mort* which Debussy was to set to music : "Claude ... pretended to look for the idea of this naive melody in the folklore..."[11]

More often the pentatonic melody — then regarded, to all appearances, as built on a series of defective heptatonic scales — is based on a consonant and "modal" harmony, in which the degrees of the complete series, that were supposed to underlie it, yield the fundamental sounds. This device occurs very frequently in the compositions of 19th century masters as, for instance, with Moussorgsky :

and Debussy :

(Canope)

With Debussy this style persits up to the end, but it is only one of the many thousand other sources. The procedure very soon becomes more refined by the original interpretation of the functions.

In *Pelléas* an „*incipit 2*" appears in this disguise :

je ne te dé - li - vre pas cet - te nuit

[11] René Péter : *Claude Debussy*, 4th edition, Paris 1931.

416

A similar reflexion in the *Etude Pour les "cinq doigts"* (exceptionally quoted in the original pitch) :[12]

Finally, when chromatic features interfere, the virtuosity of the composer, in some places, welds the two allegedly incompatible bodies so successfully that their fusion brings into existence a new idiom which is neither atonal nor polytonal, but rather, so to speak, "supra-tonal" :

(Des pas sur la neige)

*

If these considerations require a conclusion, we can say that the most striking of all things we have seen beside an unanticipated knowledge and an unparalelled *"savoir-faire"*, is a supreme liberty of choice and an unfailing aesthetic judgement, which is commonly called genius.

[12] Pentatonic series : *do re mi so la.*

MARGARET FAY SHAW

GAELIC FOLK SONGS FROM SOUTH UIST

The last stronghold of Gaelic folk tradition in Scotland today is the Outer Hebrides and the Island of Skye. These have not yet succumbed entirely to the influence of English education, press, and radio. The Hebrideans are people of independent spirit, loyal to their native islands, with a great love of their language, poetry, and music. They are mostly crofters or crofter fishermen. A croft is a smallholding held on hereditary tenure; it consists of a small amount of arable ground and, usually, the right to have a certain amount of cattle or sheep on the common mountain pasture. The crops raised are potatoes, oats, and barley, for human and animal food, and fishing is mostly done for lobsters and herring. An important industry is the hand-spinning and weaving of "Harris tweed" which is well known throughout much of the world; some very interesting songs are associated with this form of work.

The Hebrides were inhabited in the Stone Age and were known to the peoples of the Mediterranean in classical times as is proved by the reference in Ptolemy's *Geographical Tables*. There has always been a connection with Ireland, particularly in the Early Christian and Mediaeval periods. Although the Norsemen occupied the islands from the tenth until the thirteenth century, and left many traces in archeology, personal and place names, and loan-words in Gaelic, the Gaelic folkmusic of the Hebrides appears to be largely independent of Irish or Norse influence. But there is still scope for research here.

Publication of objective transcriptions of Gaelic folk songs only began in the present century, although volumes containing arrangements of them had appeared as early as the latter half of the seventeenth century. One of the most interesting collections was that made by Miss Frances Tolmie, a native of Skye, in her own district and, in a few cases, from people belonging to Eigg and Barra. This collection of one hundred and five songs was published in 1911 in the *Journal of the Folk Song Society* (vol. iv, part 3).

27*

In the summer of 1905 Miss Amy Murray, an American, visited the Island of Eriskay and with the help of the well known folklorist the Rev. Allan McDonald, parish priest of Eriskay, took down about a hundred airs, of which six were printed in the *Celtic Review*, vol. ii, p. 314, and twenty-six, including these six, in her book *Father Allan's Island*, published in 1920. Another fourteen were discovered by J. L. Campbell in one of Fr. Allan McDonald's notebooks. The premature death of Fr. Allan McDonald in the autumn of 1905 ended what might have been a most fruitful collaboration. The remainder of Miss Amy Murray's collection appears to be lost beyond hope of recovery in America. This is very unfortunate because she was a sensitive and accurate transcriber of folk music, and there were excellent folk of singers living in Eriskay in 1905.

A third collector was the late Mrs Kennedy Fraser who also first visited Eriskay in 1905, and later published, with the help of the late Rev. Dr Kenneth MacLeod, four volumes of Hebridean folksongs arranged for voice and piano. Great liberties were taken with the original airs and words in these volumes, which are internationally known. For serious students of folk music, the airs which she printed unarranged in the introductions to her books are of more value, though she was handicapped by ignorance of the Gaelic language and by the primitive type of recording apparatus then available.

In 1950 the Linguaphone Institute published for the Folklore Institute of Scotland a set of recordings of folksongs, made on the Isle of Barra by J. L. Campbell in 1938, together with a book of words; and the same year Mr. K. C. Craig published a small but very useful book of the words of over a hundred and forty folk songs from South Uist called *Òrain Luaidh le Màiri Nighean Alasdair*.

In 1938 Professor Otto Andersson of Åbo, Finland, visited the Isle of Lewis and took down a number of songs which he printed in 1952 with an analysis of the modes and chorus structures in his article *On Gaelic Folk-Music from the Isle of Lewis* (Budkavlen, Åbo 1952, Finland).

I went to South Uist in 1929 and made my collection while living on a croft with Miss Peigi and Miss Màiri MacRae at North Glendale between that date and 1935. Later my husband and I recorded Gaelic songs and stories with ediphone, disc, wire, and lastly tape machines in South Uist and Barra, and in the Gaelic-speaking part of Nova Scotia, Canada, where the descendants of many Hebridean emigrants live. Part of my collection, one hundred and ten songs, was published in 1955 along with other folklore under the title of *Folksongs and Folklore of South Uist* by Messrs Routledge & Kegan Paul.

In 1951 the School of Scottish Studies was founded at Edinburgh University, one of its objects being the recording of Gaelic and Scots folk song. Many recordings have been made since, which are being transcribed by Mr. Francis Collinson. So far none of this material has been published, nor has any catalogue of recordings been issued.

The style of traditional singing varies from island to island, and some songs exist in a large number of slightly differing versions. I am most familiar with the songs of North Glendale in South Uist. In this out-of-the-way settlement there were (and still are) some excellent folksingers, mostly women, with good memories unimpaired by the English education which became compulsory in the Islands in 1872, who were willing and anxious that their songs should be preserved. I am greatly indebted to their patience and encouragement.

The number of songs extant in the Hebrides, or until recently extant, must be very large indeed. These may be classified as follows :

1. Ossianic ballads, of four-line verses, usually dealing with the wars between the Gaels and the Norsemen. These contain many difficult words and expressions, and have mostly gone out of fashion. They were sung to a kind of chant,[1] without chorus.

2. *Òrain Mhóra* or "Great Songs", usually describing an important event, such as a battle or eulogizing an important person. These are usually of eight-line verses and are made to traditional airs of which the time signature is often irregular. These songs are going out of fashion.

3. *Luinneagan* or lays, *i. e.* love songs, songs of the sea or of war, humorous songs, etc. These are still very popular. They are usually of four-line verses sung with a chorus.

4. Children's songs, such as lullabies, and other little songs sung to amuse children. These are seldom sung formally and can be easily overlooked, but some have great beauty.

5. Milking songs, sung to cattle, to keep the cows quiet while being milked.

6. Songs ascribed to fairies. These often have an unusual quality which is not easy to analyse. They are often love-songs or lullabies.

7. *Puirt-a-bial* or vocal dance tunes, sung for dancing when musical instruments were not available, or for amusement. There are scores if not hundreds of these in existence.

8. Labour songs, for work which needs a rhythmic background. These were the songs which most impressed early visitors to the Highlands and Islands of Scotland, such as Pennant and Dr. Johnson. They were sung for rowing, reaping, grinding meal in the quern, churning, spinning, or waulking the cloth. The first three types are practically obsolete today, but waulking songs *(òrain luadhaidh)*, many of which have very archaic airs and words dating from the early seventeenth century, are still very much alive, as hand-made cloth is still waulked in the traditional fashion, there never having been waulking mills in the Highlands and Islands. Otherwise they seem to be unknown in Western Europe and are therefore of great interest.

The process of waulking the cloth has been described by several authors, from Pennant to Professor Otto Andersson, and I have explained

[1] See Dr Reidar Christiansen, *The Vikings in Gaelic Tradition*, Oslo 1831.

it in *Folksongs and Folklore of South Uist*, so it is not necessary to do more than describe it briefly here. When the new-made cloth is taken from the loom it requires to be shrunk and thickened before use, and the waulking or *luadhadh* is the method of shrinking it. An even number of women face each other across a narrow table. The ends of the cloth are sewn together to make a circle and it is soaked in a tub of urine, a liquid which will keep the threads soft and set the colour. It is worked back and forth with a kneading motion and passed around the table sun-wise. One of the company will be chosen to sing the song and as the hands beat the slow rhythm on the table she will sing either the verse line, or chorus and then the verse line, and the company will join in the chorus ; she will continue to sing the verses, or verse and first line of chorus, alone. The chorus is called the *fonn* or "ground" and the words are usually meaningless, but they have a mnemonic significance and must always be sung correctly, for it is the means by which the songs are identified ; different versions of a song may begin with different lines, but the chorus is always the same.

There are various forms of waulking songs and their analysis is still a matter of discussion.[2] Their verses are usually of one or two lines, and each verse line is followed by the chorus and then repeated to lengthen the song for the purpose of the labour. In the case of single-line verses the line is often sung to a different phrase when it is repeated. Such a song may last as long as twenty minutes. The process of waulking a piece of cloth was never measured in time but by the number of songs that had to be sung to waulk it. The tempo of these songs usually quickens as the song progresses, and many of them consist of sections on entirely different subjects added together to make the song long enough for the work. The chorus is always repeated three times between such sections, and the rhyme usually (but not always) changes. In certain cases ballads have been adapted for waulking.[3]

Gaelic traditional folk songs are always sung in unison and without accompaniment. The singing of part-songs by Gaelic choirs which compete at musical festivals (called *mods*) are a recent innovation, as is the competing by solo singers in singing standardized versions of songs. In folk music, words and tunes are inseparable. A traditional Gaelic singer must be given the words to the air, or at least the chorus, before he or she can recognise the song. I was once told, when 1 said that a certain singer had the air but not the words, "How could she have the song without the words?".

[2] See *The Sub-Literary Tradition in Scottish Gaelic Song-Poetry*, by James Ross in *Eigse*, vol. vii, p. 217 ; also *Folksongs and Folklore of South Uist*, p. 73.

[3] See J. L. Campbell, *Gaelic Folksongs from the Isle of Barra*, pp. 42, 55 ; George Henderson, *Arthurian Motifs in Gadhelic Literature*, in *Miscellany Presented to Kuno Meyer*, p. 27.

Out of two hundred songs I have transcribed, seventy are hexatonic; thirty-five are pentatonic, the most common modes being the 4 : 7, 3 : 7, 2 : 6, and 2 : 5. Twenty-five of the tunes are within the six-note compass and there are also several in five- and four-note compass. Irregular scales occur, the most prevalent being without 4th, and 6th notes, also (without) 4th, 6th, and 7th ; 2nd, 3rd and 5th ; 5th and 6th ; 6th and 7th ; 2nd and 7th. The Mixolydian is the most common of the complete scales, then come the Dorian, Aeolian, Ionian, Lydian, Dorian-Mixolydian, and Ionian-Mixolydian. Phrygian and Lydian are rare. The labour songs are the most frequently pentatonic ; many of them are circular.

Latha mór a ghàbhadh

Òran Mór

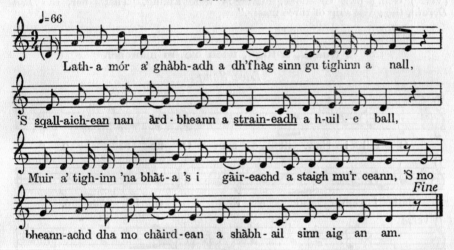

Lath-a mór a' ghàbh-adh a dh'fhàg sinn gu tighinn a nall,
'S sgall-aich-ean nan àrd-bheann a strain-eadh a h-uil e ball,
Muir a' tigh-inn 'na bhàt-a 's i gàir-eachd a staigh mu'r ceann, 'S mo bheann-achd dha mo chàird-ean a shàbh-ail sinn aig an am.

Sung by Peigi MacRae, Glendale.
Translation: The great day of danger, we left to sail across, with squalls of the high hills straining every rope, the sea coming aboard and laughing around our heads ; my blessing on my friends who saved us at the time.
Song composed to a traditional tune by Calum Ruadh MacKinnon, Barra, who died around 1933.

A' dol seachad Port Grianaig

Sailing Song

Bheir mi ó 's na hì ù à, Bheir mi ó, 's na ho gheall-adh,

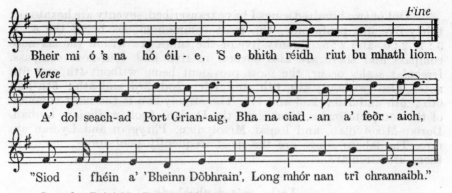

Bheir mi ó's na hó éil-e, 'S e bhith réidh riut bu mhath liom.

A' dol seach-ad Port Grian-aig, Bha na ciad-an a' feòr-aich,

"Siod i fhéin a' 'Bheinn Dòbhrain', Long mhór nan trì chrannaibh."

Sung by Peigi MacRae, in Glendale.
Translation: (Chorus) Bheir mi ó, *etc.*, I would prefer to be friend with thee. (Verse) Going past Greenock, hundreds were asking, "That's her, the *Ben Dorain*, the great ship of three masts."

'S truagh, a Rìgh, nach b'e 'm màireach

Love Song

Ó fail i rinn, ill e rinn O ho ró i o é

Fail i rinn ill e rinn Ó ho rinn ó.

'S truagh, a Rìgh, nach b'e 'm màireach An latha dh'fhal(a)bhadh mo bràthair,

Gheobh-ainn leisg-eul no dhà air A ghràidh, bhith 'gad thùirs'

Ó fail i rinn ill e rinn, ó ho rinn ó

Sung by Agnes Currie, Lochboisdale.
Translation: Sad, o Lord, 'twas not tomorrow, the day my brother would depart. I would get an excuse or two, my love, to lament you.
Cp. *Òranaiche*, 176, 178.

424

An cluinn thu mi, mo chailin donn?

Love Song

An cluinn thu mi, mo chail-in donn? Teann nall is
thoir an air-e dhomh! Tha mór-an ann am
bar ail dhiù Gur òg an leann-an dhòmhs' thu.

Sung by Mrs. John Currie, Glendale.
Translation: Will you hear me, my brown-haired girl? Come over and pay
attention to me! Many of them are of the opinion that you are (too) young a
sweetheart for me.
Cp. *Eilean Fraoich*, p. 13. Mrs. Currie first learned this song in Eriskay.

'S i nighean mo ghaoil

Love Song

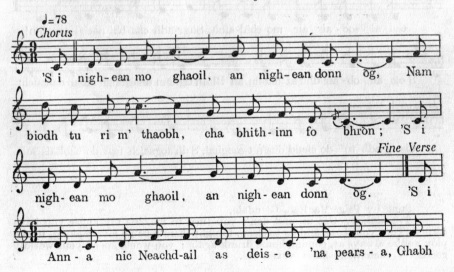

'S i nigh-ean mo ghaoil, an nigh-ean donn òg, Nam
biodh tu ri m' thaobh, cha bhith-inn fo bhròn; 'S i
nigh-ean mo ghaoil, an nigh-ean donn òg. 'S i
Ann-a nic Neachd-ail as deis-e 'na pears-a, Ghabh

425

mis' ur - ad beachd oirr' ri neach a tha beo,

Sung by Peigi MacRae, Glendale.
Translation: (Chorus) The lass that I love is the young brown-haired girl ; if you were beside me I would not be sad ; the lass that I love is the young brown-haired girl. (Verse) 'Tis Annie MacNicol who is neatest of person, I took as great a notion to her as to anyone alive.
Cp. *Orain a' Mhoid*, II, p, 9 : Angus MacLeod, *The Songs of Duncan Ban MacIntyre*, p. 102. The words of the chorus and opening verse are practically the same as in Duncan Ban's song, but the other verses Peigi MacRae sang, though on a similar subject, were different.

Éirich 's na dean tionndadh rium

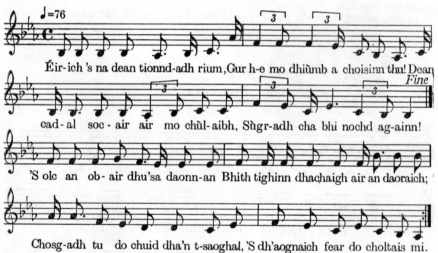

Éir-ich 's na dean tionnd-adh rium, Gur h-e mo dhiùmb a choisinn thu! Dean

cad - al soc - air air mo chùl - aibh, Sùgr-adh cha bhi nochd ag-ainn!

'S olc an ob- air dhu'sa daonn-an Bhith tighinn dhachaigh air an daoraich;

Chosg-adh tu do chuid dha'n t-saoghal, 'S dh'aognaich fear do choltais mi.

Sung by Peigi MacRae, Glendale.
Translation: Get up and don't you turn to me, 'tis my anger you have earned. Turn your back and go to sleep, tonight there'll be no love-making. Ill the ploy you're always at, coming home drunk again ; you would spend your worldly goods — such a husband vexes me.

426

Cha bhi mi 'gad thàladh
Lullaby

O bà, o bà, o bà, o ì, O bà, o
bà, o bà, o ì, O bà, o bà, o bà, o ì, Cha
bhi mi 'gad thàl-adh Bho'n shàr-aich thu mi. O

Sung by Peigi MacRae, Glendale.
Translation: O bà, o bà, o bà, o ì, I will not rock you to sleep, since you
have worn me out.

A Bhólagan, a bhó chiùin
Milking Song

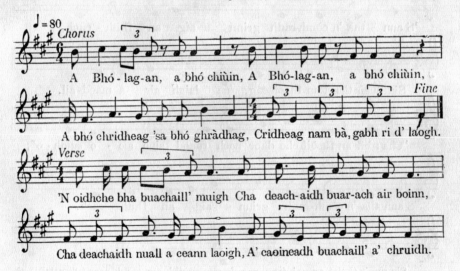

A Bhó-lag-an, a bhó chiùin, A Bhó-lag-an, a bhó chiùin,

A bhó chridheag 'sa bhó ghràdhag, Cridheag nam bà, gabh ri d' laogh.

'N oidhche bha buachaill' muigh Cha deach-aidh buar-ach air boinn,

Cha deachaidh nuall a ceann laoigh, A' caoineadh buachaill' a' chruidh.

Sung by Agnes Currie, Lochboisdale.
Translation: (Chorus) Bólagan, gentle cow, Bólagan, gentle cow, dear
little cow, beloved little cow, dearest of cows, take to your calf. (Verse) The night
(the) herdsman was outside no fetter was put on a cow, no calf uttered a low,
lamenting the herdsman of the cattle.

427

Hó Mhàiri, hó bheag

Children's Song

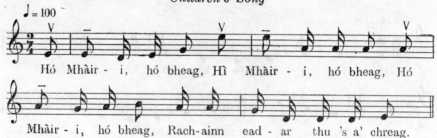

Hó Mhàir - i, hó bheag, Hì Mhàir - i, hó bheag, Hó
Mhàir - i, hó bheag, Rach-ainn ead - ar thu 's a' chreag.

Sung by Agnes Currie, Lochboisdale.
Translation: Hó Mary, hó bheag, I would go between you and the crag.
Children's Song of a type often heard — "I would go between you and the
wind, I would go between you and death, where the raven would make a cry."
Cp. *Tolmie Collection*, no. 23.

'S ann tha 'n còmhradh grinn aig an fhitheach

Children's Song

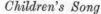

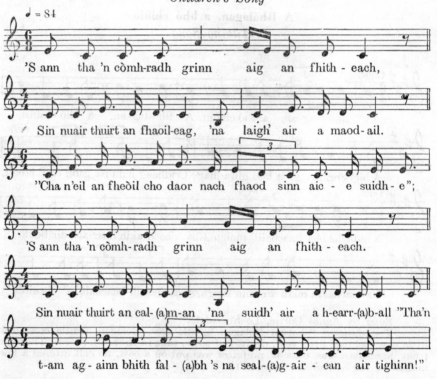

'S ann tha 'n còmh-radh grinn aig an fhith - each,

Sin nuair thuirt an fhaoil-eag, 'na laigh' air a maod-ail.

"Cha n'eil an fheòil cho daor nach fhaod sinn aic - e suidh-e";

'S ann tha 'n còmh-radh grinn aig an fhith - each.

Sin nuair thuirt an cal- (a)m-an 'na suidh' air a h-earr-(a)b-all "Tha'n

t-am ag - ainn bhith fal - (a)bh 's na seal-(a)g-air - ean air tighinn!"

428

'S ann tha 'n còmh-radh grinn aig an fhith-each.

Sung by Peigi MacRae, Glendale.
Translation: The raven has pleasant talk: then the seagull, lying on her belly, said, "Meat is not so dear that we can't sit down at it." The raven has pleasant talk. Then the dove, sitting on her tail, said, "It is time for us to be going, the hunters are coming!" The raven has pleasant talk.

A rì a ró a, cailleach a' bhreabadair

Dance Song

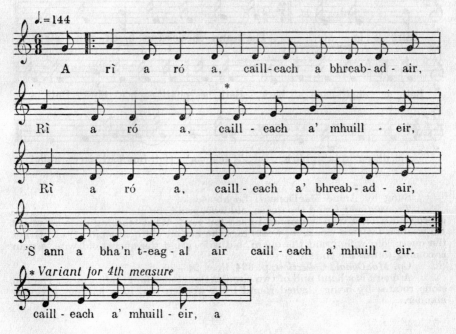

A rì a ró a, caill-each a bhreab-ad-air,

Rì a ró a, caill-each a' mhuill-eir,

Rì a ró a, caill-each a' bhreab-ad-air,

'S ann a bha'n t-eag-al air caill-each a' mhuill-eir.

Variant for 4th measure

caill-each a' mhuill-eir, a

Sung by Peigi MacRae, Glendale.
Translation: A rì a ró a, the weaver's old wife, rì a ró a, the miller's old wife, rì a ró a, the weaver's old wife, the miller's old wife had the fright of her life.

429

Beil, a chailleach, a' bhrà

Quern Song

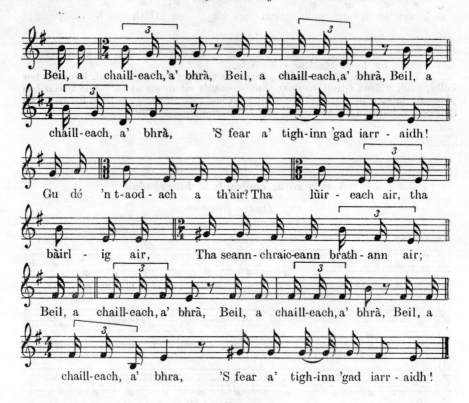

Beil, a chaill-each,'a' bhrà, Beil, a chaill-each,a' bhrà, Beil, a chaill-each, a' bhrà, 'S fear a' tigh-inn 'gad iarr - aidh! Gu dé 'n t-aod - ach a th'air? Tha lùir - each air, tha bàirl - ig air, Tha seann-chraic-eann brath-ann air; Beil, a chaill-each,a' bhrà, Beil, a chaill-each,a' bhrà, Beil, a chaill-each, a' bhra, 'S fear a' tigh-inn 'gad iarr - aidh!

Sung by Annie MacDonald, Lochboisdale.

Translation: Grind the quern, old wife, grind the quern, old wife, grind the quern, old wife, a man is coming to ask for you! What clothing does he wear? He wears a tattered cloak, he wears rags, he has an old quernskin (?) on! Grind the quern, old wife, grind the quern, old wife, grind the quern, old wife, a man is coming to ask for you!

Cp. *MacDonald Collection*, p. 334, lines 24—26.

A quern is a hand mill of two circular flat stones for grinding meal. The top stone rotates by being pushed round by a wooden pin, in a jerking, irregular manner.

430

'S gura mise tà làn airteil

Waulking Song

Fail iù ill ò ho ro éil - e, Fail
iù ill ò ro hù a hó Fail iù ill ò ho ro éil - e.
'S gur-a mis - e tà làn airt-eil Dìr-eadh 's a' teàrnadh na leach-aich.

Variant: Chorus.

Fail iù ill ò ho ro éil - e, Fail iù ill ò ro hù a ho a

* Variants for second line of verse

1.
'S math tha fios a'm dé chum bhuam thu,

2.
Bha té eil' aig bail - e 'gad bhuann-achd.

3.
Gun mhart dubh ann, gun mhart ruadh ann.

Sung by Annie MacDonald, Lochboisdale.
Translation: I am full of sorrow, climbing and descending the hillside.
Cp. K. C. Craig, p. 59.

431

Hó a, hù a, nighean dubh

Love Song

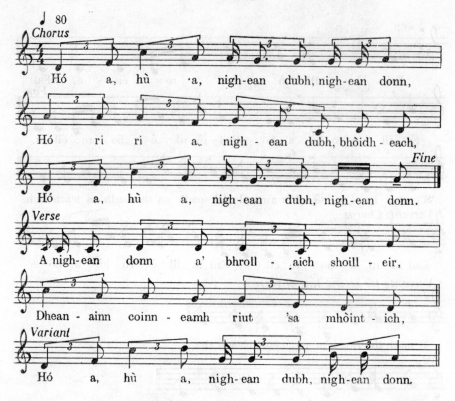

Sung by Agnes Currie, Lochboisdale.

Translation: (Chorus) Hó a, hù a, black-haired lass, brown-haired lass,
hó ri ri a, pretty black-haired lass, hó a, hù a, black-haired lass, brown-haired
lass. (Verse) Brown-haired lass of bright bosom, I wuld meet you on the
moorland.

Thug mi gaol do dh'Iain

Waulking Song

Ó hoir-eann, hoir-eann, Ho gù hoir-eann éil-e, Ó hoir-eann, hoir-eann.

Thug mi gaol do dh'Iain A miadh-ain nan ceud-an.

* B of 2ⁿᵈ measure sometimes C.

Sung by Peigi MacRae, Glendale.
Translation: (Verse) I gave love to Iain, from amongst hundreds.
This may not be the usual first line. The singer only remembered a fragment.

Ill iù, ó cha d'fhuair mi 'n cadal

Waulking Song

Ill iù, ill eó, ill-ean is ó, Ill iù, ó, chá

d'fhuair mi 'n cad-al, Ill iù, ill eó, ill-ean is ó.

Dh'fhiadh-aich an sgiob-air air bòrd mi,

'S rinn an ròg-air-e mo ghlac-adh.

Sung by Peigi MacRae, Glendale.
Translation: (Chorus) Ill iù, *etc.*, I did not get sleep. (Verse) The skipper invited me on board, and the rascal seized me.
Fragment of waulking song. Cp. K. C. Craig, p. 86.

Chì mi 'm bàta seach an rubha

Waulking Song

♩ = 76

Chorus

Hoir-eann ó ho ì ù a, Hi ù ra bhó ró hug éil - e,

Hoir - eann ó ho ì ù a. Chì mi 'm bàt - a

seach an rubh-a, 'S i 'na siubh - al fo làn éid - eadh.

Sung by Peigi MacRae, Glendale.
Translation: 1 see the boat go past the point, moving under full sail.
Cp. K. C. Craig, p. 114.

434

MAUD KARPELES

CECIL SHARP
COLLECTOR OF ENGLISH FOLK MUSIC

Cecil Sharp had only one meeting with Béla Bartók. It was at the house of a mutual acquaintance in London a few years after the end of the first World War. At that time, Bartók's folk music researches were not widely known and Sharp was only slightly acquainted with his work, but he returned home from the meeting filled with admiration, and one might almost say envy, of a man who, although considerably younger than himself, had collected a much greater quantity of material.

Sharp was born in 1859, twenty-two years before Bartók, but in folk song research he preceded him only by a couple of years. He started collecting in 1903 and his first collection, *Folk Songs from Somerset*, vol. i, was published a year later. Like Bartók, he had had a wide musical experience before he turned his attention to folk music, although, unlike him, he never achieved distinction as a composer or executant.

Fifty years ago, the contrast between the musical scene in Hungary and England was very great. England at that time was content to accept her reputation as an unmusical country ; the art of music appeared to be of interest only to a small proportion of the public ; and native music, whether in the form of art music or folk music, was almost completely ignored. In fact, English folk music was regarded not only by the uninformed public but by the musical profession as being either non-existent or worthless. As some wit of the day put it : "English folk song is either bad or Irish." What are the actual facts?

At the beginning of the century, England, unlike Hungary, had no peasant population and the continuity of her rural life had been greatly disturbed by the drift from the villages to the towns which, together with the introduction of universal elementary education, had induced a turning away from the traditional modes of life. The folk songs and dances never completely disappeared but they went underground and for the most part it was only the older people who remembered them. Only a small proportion had been noted and in another generation the bulk of the material would probably have been lost for ever, had it not been for Cecil Sharp's work in salvaging it. Although not the first collector of English folk songs, he exceeded all his predecessors and contemporaries in the magnitude of his collection and in the energy and devotion with which he applied himself to the task. He noted in all nearly 5000 songs and tunes, including variants, and many hundreds of dances. He received no offical or financial support and for many years collecting could be done only at week-ends or in the vacations when he was free from teaching engagements.

He was not a good linguist, as was Bartók, and he did not collect outside his own country, except for the expeditions he made during the years 1916—1918 to the Appalachian Mountains of North America. There he found a community whose ancestors had emigrated from Great Britain some two hundred years earlier, who were living in a state of self-contained seclusion to which Europe can offer but few parallels. Cecil Sharp's work in America may be considered not only as a supplement to his English collection, but as its crowning glory, for the tunes that he noted in the Appalachian Mountains represent a purer folk tradition than those he gathered in England: they are largely pentatonic.

Sharp did not pre-occupy himself with the scientific study of folk music to the same extent as did Bartók. Had he lived longer — he died in 1924 at the age of 64 — he would no doubt have devoted more attention to the analysis of the material he had gathered, but the first necessity was to accumulate it whilst there was yet time. His approach to the subject was in any case that of the artist or humanist rather than that of the pure scientist. He believed with passionate conviction that the songs and dances had a vitality which would enable them to be transplanted without damage from one section of the community to the whole nation provided that the task was undertaken with artistic and scholarly integrity. He therefore concerned himself with the revival of the songs and dances side by side with their preservation. The difficulties were many. It was necessary to guard against the exploitation of the material and the lowering of artistic standards and, above all, to educate the public to distinguish between what was authentic and what was bogus. Sharp's efforts to persuade the education authorities and others that old English songs such as *Sally in our Alley* and *Drink to me only with thine Eyes* are not folk songs provides a certain analogy to Bartók's dissociation of genuine Hungarian folk tradition from gypsy music.

Sharp's great treatise on English folk music[1] was published in 1907 and, considering the lapse of time that separates it from Bartók's *Hungarian Folk Music* and the different conditions of the two countries, there is a marked agreement between the two writers on the definition and nature of folk music.

[1] *English Folk Song: Some Conclusions*, 1st edition, 1907. Revised and edited by Maud Karpeles, Methuen, London 1954.

Sharp left no mechanical recordings except for a few badly deteriorated wax cylinders. He used an old Edison phonograph on a few isolated occasions, but did not persevere with it because he found that it had a somewhat deterrent effect on his informants. We must regret the scarcity of records demonstrating the old traditional style of singing, but generally speaking the transmissible essence of English folk song can be conveyed by the written notation to a degree that would be impossible in many of the folk songs of Hungary.

The bulk of the American material has been published in scientific form without accompaniment.[2] The cream of the English material has also been published, but it has not as yet been assembled in scientific form as has the Appalachian collection, and it is scattered among many different volumes. Over 400 songs and dances from the English collection have been published with pianoforte accompaniment and about half that number of songs and tunes (including variants) are to be found without accompaniment in the *Journal of the Folk Song Society* (nos. 6, 18, 20 and 31).

The following unpublished variants have been selected from Cecil Sharp's note-books. It cannot be said that they throw new light on the subject, but they may be found useful as respresenting a few of the different types of melody used in English folk song.

No. 1   **The Cuckoo**

Collected in Somerset in 1904.
A simple and typical Aeolian melody.
For full version see *Som.* iii, 48 ; *Sel.* i, 48 ; *Sch.* Set 7, no. 1321

---

[2] *English Folk Songs from the Southern Appalachians*, 2 vols. Collected by Cecil J. Sharp, edited by Maud Karpeles, Oxford University Press, London 1932, reprinted 1954.

No. 2   **The Shooting of his Dear**

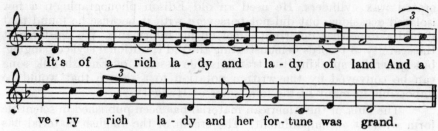

It's of a rich la-dy and la-dy of land And a
ve-ry rich la-dy and her for-tune was grand.

Collected in Somerset in 1907.
A slightly elaborated version of the melody of no. 1.
For full version see *Som.* i, 32.

No. 3   **Still Growing**

The trees they do grow high and the leaves they do grow
green; The time is gone and past, my love, when
you and I had seen; One cold win-ter's night my
love, when you and I a - lone had been. The
bon - ny lad is young, but he's grow-ing, The
bon - ny lad is young, but he's grow - ing.

Collected in Somerset in 1908.
This beautiful Dorian melody is a great favourite with English folk sing-
ers. The rise of the octave occurs in many songs.
For full version see *Som.* i, 30 ; *Sel.* ii, 40,

No. 4   **Betsy Williams**

O Bet - sy Wil - liams it is my name, O I
brought my - self un - to grief and shame By
lo - ving a young man who ne - ver loved me. It is
sor - row now then I plain - ly see.

Collected in Gloucestershire in 1921 from a gypsy woman.
The second phrase of this Dorian melody with its ascending scale of over one octave is a feature of many English folk songs.
For full version see *Sel.* ii, 40.

No. 5   **Green Bushes**

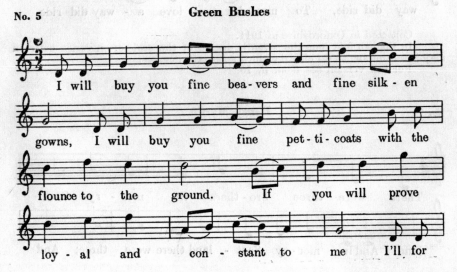

I will buy you fine bea - vers and fine silk - en
gowns, I will buy you fine pet - ti - coats with the
flounce to the ground. If you will prove
loy - al and con - stant to me I'll for

439

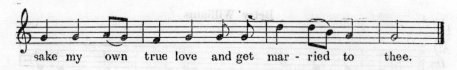

sake my own true love and get mar - ried to thee.

Collected in Somerset in 1904.
This fine Mixolydian tune is a great favourite and is often used in connection with other texts. R. Vaugham Williams has used a version of this melody and of no 9. in his *Folksong Suite*.
For full version see *Som.* ii, 16 ; *Sel.* i, 58.

No. 6   **The Female Highwayman**

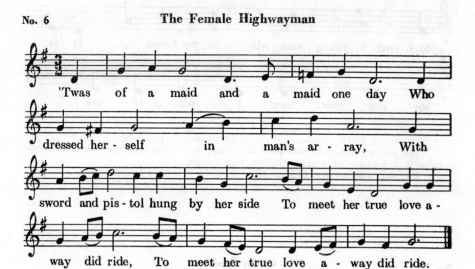

'Twas of a maid and a maid one day Who
dressed her - self in man's ar - ray, With
sword and pis - tol hung by her side To meet her true love a -
way did ride, To meet her true love a - way did ride.

Collected in Oxfordshire in 1911.
In English folk song the seventh degree of the scale often varies between major and minor, as do also the third and sixth degrees.
For full version see *Som.* ii, 10.

No. 7   **Henry Martin**

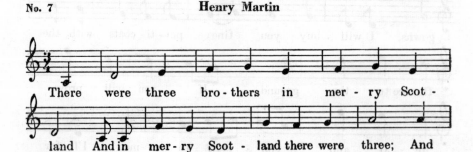

There were three bro - thers in mer - ry Scot -
land And in mer - ry Scot - land there were three; And

440

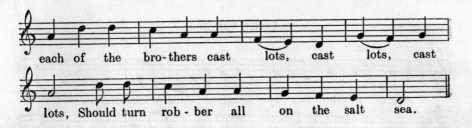

each of the bro-thers cast lots, cast lots, cast

lots, Should turn rob-ber all on the salt sea.

Collected in Somerset in 1906.
This melody like no. 5 is often pressed into the service of other songs.
The absence of the sixth degree of the scale is a common feature.
For full version see *Som.* ii, 6 ; *Sel.* i, 1.

No. 8   **The Bold Fisherman**

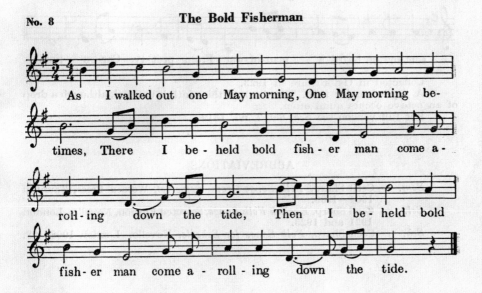

As I walked out one May morning, One May morning be-

times, There I be-held bold fish-er man come a-

roll-ing down the tide, Then I be-held bold

fish-er man come a - roll-ing down the tide.

Collected in Somerset in 1904.
A pentatonic tendency is seen in this melody, in which the fourth and
seventh are introduced only as auxiliary notes. 5-time is fairly frequent, but
not 7-time and other forms of *rhythm aksak* or what Curt Sachs calls additive
rhythm.
For full version see *Som.* iii, 42 ; *Sel.* ii, 32 ; *Sch.* Set 9, no. 1412.

Pretty Caroline

'Twas in the mer-ry month of June When bright-ly shone the

sun, 'Twas on the banks of dai-sies gay Where there

sat-en a love-lie one, And the song she sang so

mer-ri-ly It grieved this heart of mine. They

sent me on board a man-of-war From pret-ty Car-o-line.

Collected in Oxfordshire in 1923.

A typical major tune. The drop of the ninth is unusual, although a drop of an octave occurs quite often.

For full version see *Sch.* Set 7, no. 1319.

ABBREVIATIONS

Som. = Cecil Sharp, *Folk Songs from Somerset*, Wessex Press, Taunton 1904—1909.

Sel. = Cecil Sharp, *English Folk Songs*, Selected Edition, Novello, London 1921 and 1923.

Sch. = Cecil Sharp, *Folk Songs for Schools*, Novello, London 1908—22.

GYÖRGY KERÉNYI

ON CLASSIFYING FOLK SONGS AND THE CORPUS MUSICAE POPULARIS HUNGARICAE

Ever since Zoltán Kodály (1905) and Béla Bartók (1906) started collecting Hungarian folk music, among the chief problems (what, where, and how to collect?) there has emerged a question of equal rank, or sometimes even greater prominence: the "what, where, and how?" of arranging, storing and publishing the songs.

The two scholars felt the need to arrange the collected material not so much for publishing, but rather to enable them to continue their own scientific work. For this purpose they copied the songs from the notebooks, used during collecting trips, on separate leaves, to this material each added the songs of his fellow collector, later even collectors, copied in a similar way. In addition Bartók augmented his collection with variants from the neighbouring peoples, while Kodály increased his treasury with published songs and manuscripts of ancient collections.

These two roughly identical collections, comprising several thousand leaves already at the beginning, were arranged differently by the two collectors. The basic principle of Kodály's system of classification remained the same (a uniform, lexical order) from the beginning until the *Corpus Musicae Popularis Hungaricae*. Bartók, always allowing more free play to hypotheses, altered his system more than once. One of the points of crystallization in the evolution of his system is shown by the order in his work *Hungarian Folk Music*[1] : Class A (old style), Class B (new style) and Class C (miscellaneous). Later (1930—1940) he considerably modified this conception.

The manner in which these two systems, supporting each other, are realized in the *Corpus Musicae Popularis Hungaricae*, denotes the culmination point of a long development. Has anybody ever written the history of arranging musical collections? We have no knowledge of it. The chief data have been collected by Kodály[2], and the following is a review of them.

---

[1] London, 1931.
[2] *Magyar zenei folklór 110 év előtt* ('Hungarian Musical Folklore 110 Years ago), Budapest 1943.

443

Kodály found the earliest attempts at classification in the bibliography of Zahn's great work[3] which not only enumerates but also gives a thorough review of several hundred German hymn books. The first hymn book, a review of which gives information on some sort of classification, is: *824 Geistliche Psalmen*, etc. (A. Wagenmann), Nürnberg 1622[4]. This classification is not purely musical for it refers to metrical structure, *i. e.* equally to text and melody. The next hymn books continue this initiative a good century later : *Geistreiches Gesangbuch*, etc. (J. A. Freylinghausen), Halle 1733[5], and *Harmonischer Liederschatz*, etc. (J. B. König), Frankfurt a. M. 1738[6]. The system adopted in these collections is neither based on purely musical considerations, nor is it revealed in the succession of the hymns, but appears only in the index appended to the volume.

The first collection of songs, in which the musical material itself is classified according to versification, is a French hymn book : *Recueil de la musique*, etc. (C. Schmidt), Strasbourg 1758[7] ; its 68 melodies are arranged according to 45 different metrical forms. This method is applied to the vast material in Ch. Gregor's hymn book *Choralbuch*, etc. (Breitkopf), Leipzig 1784[8] containing 472 hymns in a systematized order.

In the 19th century systematization according to metrical structure was broadened by fresh viewpoints. In 1811, P. Capelle issued the songs of a musical circle of friends, under the title *La Clé du Caveau.* He published the melodies (the number of which increased to 2350 in the fifth edition) without text and musical classification. The tunes are classified according to the number of lines in the stanzas of the text ; Chapter I comprises the "regular" stanzas having 12 to 4 lines, and Chapter II the "irregular" ones. In the subsequent chapters Capelle discarded this principle and classified the material according to the genre of the text. We are not familiar with the previous editions of this collection and do not know whether they had reached Hungary at that time. The fourth and fifth editions are in Z. Kodály's possession.

At about the same time a forgotten Hungarian folklorist, János Udvardy Cserna, prepared a plan somewhat similar to the French system, yet superior to it. (To our present knowledge, "we must regard it as one of the many ideas that first flashed through a Hungarian mind", said Kodály.) The musical part of the work has not yet been located, but we are enlightened about its arrangement and the principles

---

[3] Zahn, *Die Melodien der deutschen evangelischen Kirchenlieder*, vols. i—vi, 1889—1893.
[4] Zahn, *op. cit.* vol. vi, p. 136 (467).
[5] Zahn, *op. cit.* vol. vi, p. 296 (873).
[6] Zahn, *op. cit.* vol. vi, p. 318 (916).
[7] Zahn, *op. cit.* vol. vi, p. 343 (955).
[8] Zahn, *op. cit.* vol. vi, p. 358 (994).

of classification thanks to the preface of the collection of texts which has survived in separate copybooks.[9] In this preface Udvardy Cserna proposes two different principles of classification.

I. "It would be best to classify these songs by their metre or syllables." He divides the verses of 4 to 15 syllables into eleven classes according to the first line. Hence the songs having a formula of *5. 8. 5. 8.* and *5. 5. 6. 5. 5. 6.* fall within the group of five-syllable songs. He proposes to form further groups for those with heterometric lines, but fails to expound this suggestion and to arrange these melodies seperately : the numerical order of syllables evidently refers to them too.

II. In the manuscript itself which is ready for printing we find the texts in a different order. They are grouped according to "their natural virtues", in terms of today, their genre : sorrowful, narrative, recruiting, farewell, pastoral, marching, drinking songs, drolleries, allegories, and airs. In this version of his plan the melodies are not associated one by one with the words, but follow the chapter of texts as an appendix, "according to the previously given system built on the metre of syllables".

Udvardy was the first to consider it useful to have two systems in a collection. He divines the way to the final solution of the problem by uniting several methodical arrangements and by taking into account as many characteristics as possible. Thus, in fact, he made a good guess at the final solution of the problem of classifying musical folkloric material.

Udvardy's work has remained in manuscript. The great systematizing work of the 19th century is the above-mentioned German collection of Zahn : *Die Melodien der deutschen evangelischen Kirchenlieder*. Its material surpasses anything up to then, it contains 8806 hymns, but in their classification the author ignored the characteristics of melody. His chief systematizing principle is based on the number of lines (from 2 to 26), within this on metrical structure (iamb, trochee, etc.), further on the number of syllables, and date of appearance.

The 20th century opened a new era in musical folklore, in collecting and systemizing.

Every large collection, being the thesaurus of a people's melodies, with all their archaisms and intricate interconnections in time and space, covers such a vast realm of music, that its systematic survey raises the question of classifying melodies in general.

Every simple realm of melodies, the "shapeless" tunes of a primitive society may require several principles of classification such as, *e. g.*, 1. stock of notes (later on scale, range), 2. the initial notes of a melody (dictionary order), 3. certain prominent sounds (recitative

[9] *Eredeti Nemzeti Danlok' Gyüjteménnye, leginkább a' pór ifjuság szájjából. Feljegyezgetve Udvardy János által.* (Collection of Original National Songs, Mostly from the Young Peasants' Own Lips. Noted by J. Udvardy). Hungarian Academy of Sciences, Manuscripts, 1832.

melodies), 4. the nuclei of melodies (Hungarian children's songs),
5. rhythmic formulae, etc. These principles, when applied, may bring
about further variants.[10]

The higher our melodies reach into the realm of musical forms, the
more points of view present themselves as principles for classifying.
At the beginning of the 20th century when Kodály and Bartók started
collecting, they found rich, flourishing folk music in the Carpathian
Basin. In this musical abundance the realm of primitive melodies makes
up only a small fraction (the melodies of some folk customs at spring time),
the overwhelming majority of the melodies being of regular, rounded
forms. The dominating type is the four-line song with identical or
regularly alternating number of syllables.

It was the Finn Ilmari Krohn, who pointed out the significance
of melodic lines in classification.[11] Up to his time lines had only a numerical role in classification (number of syllables). Now attention was
drawn from quantity to quality, to the significance of melodic lines.
The number of notes undoubtedly determines the melodic line to a
certain degree. But the note, towards which the line of the melody
tends, determines it at least to the same extent. The variants of the
song scarcely modify the number of syllables which is a pivotal point for
classification just like the final notes. The last of the four lines always
hastens to the final note. But what about the other three lines? What
a wealth of relationship may exist between them? The use of these
manifold relationships in classification has, indeed, widened the horizon
almost to infinity, even in the realm of Finnish folk songs to which
Ilmari Krohn has applied them. He was content with indicating the
functions the line endings have in Finnish folk songs which are so close
to harmony : tonic, dominant, in perfect and imperfect cadences, etc.
The great Finnish folk song collection *Suomen Kansan Sävelmiä*, vols.
ii--v, 1904—1928, is published (except for the first volume) according
to this system.

[10] For instance Oswald Koller recommends a classifying principle based
on the first notes of the tune, but he does not take them all into consideration,
only the stressed ones. He marks the degrees of the tune with numbers.

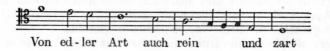

Von ed - ler Art auch rein   und zart

His marking of this tune is : 7 5 3 III. (The first note falls out, because of its
unstressed word ; III means the third note under the tonic. We have no knowledge
of this order having been realized anywhere. *Sammelbände der Intern. Musikgesellschaft*, 4. Jahrg. (1902—1903).

[11] Welche ist die beste Methode um Volks- und volksmässige Lieder nach
ihrer melodischen (nicht textlichen) Beschaffenheiten lexikalisch zu ordnen.
See the previously mentioned work *(Sammelbände*, etc.) p. 643.

446

Krohn's discovery enriched Kodály's and Bartók's imagination.[12] Hungarian music is much too manysided to be compressed into the Finnish system. The most valuable, the pentatonic music preserved through the centuries and brought to light by Kodály and Bartók, would have been excluded from it. They had to go beyond this none too elastic system. With hard work and many years of experimentation they created an almost new version of it. The scientific world was informed in 1913 of the newly created Hungarian system. "The arrangement of a song collection must be solely a musical one, purely from the point of view of the characteristics of the melody, of a dictionary order, so that the related songs, when placed next to each other, will show the main types clearly. This is the only possible way to look over the collection quickly and to compare it with other ones. In this way any tune will be found easily. The essence of the system in brief is the following: We have reduced every tune to a common final, that is, we have written down all of them to end on G^1. As the number of melody lines is four, almost without exception, we had to consider three line endings. The most important line ending is the second one, in the middle of the melody, at the end of the first period. All those songs to which this note is common, come together. In the groups formed in this way, subgroups come into existence according to the final note of the first, and within these, to the third melody line. This division is traversed by a rhythmical one; each group begins with the shortest tunes, those consisting of longer lines follow in succession. Finally within these groups the tunes are aligned according to the range: starting with those of a smaller range and increasing in size."[13] Tonic and dominant, the pillars of the Finnish system, are not mentioned here. The final notes, like the letters of the alphabet in a dictionary, are of equal rank.

The first Hungarian collection[14], a publication of folk songs in the newly devised system, was issued jointly by Bartók and Kodály: *Erdélyi Magyarság, Népdalok*, 1921 (Hungarians of Transylvania, Folksongs). It contains 150 songs. Its "Index of melodies" gives an explanation of their succession. The preface says "in this way the related types are found next to each other". The limited number of songs in the book does not fully illustrate the use of this method. Even tunes with different line endings may be related to one another. At the end of the book a synoptical table shows the arranging of tunes: it is here we perceive

[12] Ph. Kolessa, too, experimented with Krohn's system: *Melodies of Ukrainian Recitative Songs (dumy)*, Lemberg 1910, vols. i — ii. The musical material of the Lapps was collected and classified — corresponding to their special character, according to the length and content of the lines — by Armas Launis: *Lappische Juoigos-Melodien*, Helsingfors 1908.

[13] *Ethnographia* 1913, p. 313.

[14] Bartók tried to apply the system to Rumanian tunes, adapting it to the material: *Chansons populaires roumaines du département Bihar (Hongrie)*, Bucureşti 1913, and *Volksmusik der Rumänen von Maramureş*, München 1923.

447

for the first time the formulae of three figures marking the line endings and determining the tune (*e. g. 4 5* VII $= C^2 D^2 F^1$).

Hardly a few years after this publication, Bartók's great work, *Hungarian Folk Music* (with 320 examples of melodies)[15] was published. In the Transylvanian volume, the newness of melodies rescued from oblivion almost diverted attention from the novelty of classification. In the latter work it was a new classifying system, introduced in the frame of a monumental essay, illustrated by many examples, that occasioned great surprise.

This principal work of Bartók introduced a new concept into the classifying of tunes : that of style. The aim of his book was to point out "the outsanding styles in Hungarian peasant music" and their interrelations.

He describes with utmost accuracy the characteristics of the new style generally used today : "a rounded, architectural structure, represented by four different formulae : AA^5BA, AA^5A^5A (older), ABBA (newer), AABA (newest). The rhythm is a variable *giusto*[16]. The strophes are built prevailingly of isometric lines of 6 to 25 syllables". Bartók considers this style as "generally known in the first half of the past century". Within this group the examples of tunes are arranged according to the number of syllables of the melodic lines.

The old Hungarian style is not so distinct. Its chief characteristics are the pentatonic scale ending on *la* ($F^2 D^2 C^2 B^1 G^1$) and a negative feature, the lack of architectural structure. Bartók mentions, in marginal notes, the descending structure built on "changing fifths"[17] — which has since proved to be one of the criterions of this style.

The remaining tunes, *i. e.* about half of them, do not belong to either of these two styles (though some tunes were later included among those of the old styles). In this group, marked miscellaneous, we find also "popular songs" bearing urban traces and others showing the influence of foreign folk music. We take the liberty of assuming that Bartók, who raised the idea of classifying by styles, would, in the course of time, surely have taken these songs out of the miscellaneous class and — determining their marks of style — formed, beside the two independent (old and new) groups, one for *songs of urban, composed origin* (art music) and another for *songs related to other peoples' songs*. This task was left to Kodály and the *Corpus Musicae Popularis Hungaricae*.[18]

*

[15] *A Magyar Népdal*, Budapest 1924.

[16] Alternating according to the length of the syllables.

[17] „The whole original structure being repeated a fifth lower" (A^5A^5AA or A^5B^5AB). Bartók, *Hungarian Folk Music*, p. 22.

[18] From Bartók's book — for unknown reasons — there are two indices missing : those of cadence order and of initial words. The variants with different line endings had got next to each other, but we find no reference to this at the place designated by the system. (*János bácsi heged je*, 151*b*). Anyone seeking the well-known *Erdő, erdő, erdő* on the principle of the given system, will not be able to find it in Bartók's book (299 *c*, see also 233).

Volume I of the *Corpus*, the *Children's Games* (1951), contains the "primitive" strata of Hungarian folk music which comes closest to the beginnings of human singing. In the first place it deals with the specific "pure" material, later with children's songs derived from the world of adults, finally with those related to other peoples' songs. The children's tunes, long held to be pure Hungarian and ancient traditional, are built up of two kinds of melodic motives : *mi re do* and *so la so mi* (their extensions included). In both groups they are assembled around characteristic melodic nuclei: *mi re | do re, mi re | do mi do*, etc. The length of each melodic nucleus extends to two bars in $^2/_4$ time. Generally they are to be found at the beginning of the songs. The melodic nuclei of the second division, known best are *so la so* (an independent group within *so la so mi*), *so fa mi, so mi do*, etc. [19]

These "twin bars" of Hungarian popular children's songs are remarkable for being greatly inclined to cling together. The richer the action of the play, the more possibility there is for a round dance, the more voluminous the melody becomes. At such times the twin bars are not only repeated *ad libitum*, but new twin bars are connected to the chief ones (the melodic nuclei). Children's songs consisting of 10 to 12 kinds of twin bars are not rare. The listing of such combined material may obviously not be attempted until the constituting elements have been systematized. Consequently, the musical index of the volume is a *twin-bar catalogue* which, like a dictionary, includes in a system all occurring twin bars in the order of their initial notes,

from the lowest notes  V—1—| VII#—VI—|

to the highest notes 8—88 | 7#—6—|

as well as the twin-bar melodies of *non-major hexachordal* character and those extending *to three bars*.

This catalogue, containing over two thousand twin bars, among which some 1200 occur several times, is planned to be an independent appendix to the *Children's Games* volume,[20] though in the volume itself we may find a chapter referring to this : "The Relationship

[19] See *Folk Music: Hungarian* in *Grove's Dictionary of Music*, 1954, vol. iii, p. 280.

[20] According to another plan, this catalogue will be augmented with the parallel listing of the twin-bar material of other peoples' children's songs. This comparative collection may reveal — by exposing the identical roots within a narrow sphere of music — also national deviations, and answer the question: "What is Hungarian, French, Slavic, etc. in music?"

between our Melodies". This chapter, according to the twin-bar system, shows the occurrence of the twin-bars (melodic nuclei) in the songs. The foreign music occurring among the children's tunes (a number of folk songs proper) is also included here, first of all according to the number of lines and to the number of syllables. In case of isometry the final notes of the lines provide the classifying principle. These latter songs will, naturally, be registered in other places too, where they, as folk songs, belong by their line endings (for example, in volumes XV or XXIII). It is owing to the action of the childrens' games that these songs come under the heading of this chapter, where the divergence of folk songs, sung by children, from their original form is also shown.

In Volume II, *Calendar Customs*, the songs are even more bound to occasions than the children's games. It covers eighteen folk customs, nearly as many types of songs, and is a splendid example showing to what an extent different musical materials require their own specific methods of classification.

If a holiday is connected with a single song, the variants and fragments follow the intact, presumably the oldest, form (New Year, St. Blase's and St. Gregory's Day, Easter, Harvest, St. Lucy's Day). The holiday songs built up in twin bars are arranged in a system similar to that of the children's games. At Whitsuntide three songs are sung by children. All three are different in style and absolutely independent of each other, coming from three different regions. Their variants form three different groups. The *"regös"* songs (New Year's songs) form another group containing twin bars and (though having *do* for final note and extending to one hexachord) are almost totally seperated from the children's songs. The group of the *regös* songs is of a higher order in quality, first of all owing to the text which, consequently, involves a more monumental, artistic structure in music. The *"regölés"* (New Year's mascarade) our oldest folk custom dating evidently from pagan times, is in its outward appearance a felicitating visit. Among the good wishes, the lines of love-magic addressed to young couples are the most important ones. A beautiful mythological part of it is the song about the Mythical Stag. All *regös* songs have essentially the same words ; as to their tunes, all must have had the same source. Nowadays we find about a hundred variants separated into five well discernible groups around five melodic nuclei.

The group of the Midsummer Night's songs surpasses in richness and complexity the previous chapters. Every tune sung by the Mid-summer Night's fire must be regarded as a Midsummer Night's song. This is a rather loose definition but involves no difficulties of classification. Tradition acknowledges only some twelve such songs. Each text has, unlike the *regös* songs, a melody of its own. The performance, however, of the Midsummer Night's songs and of the *regös* songs is similar. Five to seven of the ten sections at a *regös* performance are sung in a roughly defined order. The succession of the Midsummer

Night's songs is also defined and varies according to villages. More one of our most beautiful songs belong to this group.

From the musical point of view, the order of performance of the Christmas and Twelfth Night's singing plays is similar to that of the Midsummer Night's songs. The only difference is that the melodies of the former are inserted between the dialogue scenes of the play, and could not be arranged in the musical order. We refer to them in the *Index of strophe types according to the number of syllables*, and later in the Index of cadences. The Christmas songs, collected separately, are naturally published in the musical order (on account of their frequently changing line endings and broken forms, in syllable order); the name-day greetings likewise.

In the next two volumes of songs connected with occasions, the regular Hungarian tune form, *i. e.* the four-line stanza, and the constant number of syllable prevail. From the world of children and adolescents we pass over to the world of adults.

Volume III, the *Wedding*, contains the richest domain of our folkways extending farthest both in time and space. Its music, too, comprises a vast number of elements. A purely musical classification would not have been useful. The songs follow in the order of succession determined by the 27 phases of the traditional wedding, and the book is divided into just so many chapters. The succession of the songs is : *a)* chronological *(Engagement, Asking for the Bride, Greeting the Dishes), b)* governed by the frequency of the phase variants wherein the main type precedes the others *(Filling the Eiderdowns, Farewell of the Bride, Bridal Dance),* and *c)* based on the number of syllables if the songs are heterogenous *(Drinking Songs).* The relationship between the tunes, naturally, precedes all other viewpoints : the variants follow in strict musical order. To facilitate the finding of a tune, we have, considering the many-sided material, included several indexes based on different principles of musical classification (line endings, stanza types, initial words).

In Volume IV, *Match-making Songs*, the texts dominate more than anywhere else. Their explicit task is to connect the names of a girl and a boy with attributes, comparisons, one- or two-sided actions, etc. in as compact a form as possible, in the drollest fashion. This requires not beautifully unfolding melodies, but short, witty ones. The bulk of the volume, the first chapter, consists of such tunes which we regard as *typical*. The second chapter contains *non-typical* match-making songs, the tunes of which are borrowed for the occasion. The line endings and stanza types are classified in an index at the end of the volume.

Volume V, *Dirges*. "The significance of Hungarian dirges lies in their being the sole musical examples of prosaic recitation and the only opportunity for improvization" in our musical folklore, wrote Kodály[21],

[21] *A magyar népzene* (Hungarian Folk Music), Budapest 1952. p. 38.

discoverer and pioneer collector of this genre. He has described the shape of the melody discernible above the freely flowing words and pointed out that even this melody can be considered to consist of lines and final notes allowing to determine strophes, just as in Hungarian folk songs in general. The few tunes in which four lines can be distinguished are followed in the collection by broken variants of three- or mostly two-line tunes.

In Volume VI, *Trades, Occupations, Folkways*, the chief task was to search for the original sources on the basis of tune fragments sung by night watchmen, marketers, beggars, etc., and to group the variants and fragments around the first unbroken forms.

Volume VI is the last to contain songs connected with occasions, whereas Volume VII introduces a series of songs not associated with any particular folk custom. These songs make up the bulk of the collection. Volume VII marks, at the same time, the beginning of purely musical systemization which involves headings like 1 5 2, or 7 5 3♭, etc., undoubtedly less colourful than the titles of the previous volumes. Will such headings imply as much variety and evoke as much interest as, for instance, the Volumes of *Wedding* and *Match-making Songs?* We are convinced that they will, as soon as the reader is acquainted with the contents. Because even an immense quantity of songs coming under the same cadence formula may represent quite a number of melodic groups [of different character. Let us examine a series of tunes in ₜwhich the formula of line endings is, for instance, 7 5 3♭:

No. 1

No. 2

Parlando

Ló-ra, csi-kós, ló - ra,

El-szö - kött   a mé-nes,

Csak e - gye-dül ma-radt

A pány-ván   a nyerges

Vi-gan,vi-gan,víg angyalom,

Víg ó-rá-ban ter-mett ra-jom,

Min-dig i - lyen víg vagyok én,

Víg ó - rá-ban szü-let-tem én.

Collected by L. Lajtha, in 1921, in the village of Vajdácska, county Zemplén.

Collected by Z. Kodály, in 1912, in the village of Deresk, county Gömör.

452

No. 3

Három ic-ce kendermag,

Jaj de büsz-ke le gény vagy!

Mit ér a büsz - ke-sé - ged,

Nem szép a fe - le - sé - ged.

Collected by L. Vikár, in 1954, in the village of Karád, county Somogy.

No. 4

Ederics i ut-cán foly a víz,

Ne menj arra ró-zsám, mer elvisz.

El-vi-szi a cif-ra szűrödet,

Ki-vel be-ta-kar-tál en-ge-met.

Collected by V. Seemayer, in 1932, in the village of Cserespuszta, county Zala.

No. 5

Ki - lyu-kadt a zsé - tá - rom don - gá - ja,

El - ha-gyott a sze - re - tőm bú - já - ba

Ha el - ha-gyott, majd meg-vár, majd meg - vár

A li - ce - i do - bo - gós kő - híd - nál.

Collected by Z. Kodály, in 1913, in the village of Licze, county Gömör.

Hol hál-tál az éj-jel, ci-ne-ge-ma-dár?

Ab-la-ko-don hál-tam, szi-vem asz-szony-kám!

Mér bel-lebb nem jöt-tél, ci-ne-ge-ma-dár?

U-rad-tul nem mer-tem, szi-vem asz-szony-kám!

Collected by A. Péczely, in 1927, in the village of Kiskomárom, county of Zala.

We find different types among the isometric examples, for instance, in the group with line endings 1 5 2, in an eleven-syllable stanza of four lines where we have 54 independent tunes, differing from each other, and most of them having many variants.

These variant groups of a main melody demonstrate the thriving life of the folk song as we have seen in the children's games and wedding customs. What is alive, is changing ; the scholar may, through the countless variants, get an insight into the throbbing life of rich traditions. Several problems may be raised here : did every epoch have its specific manner of varying folk songs? Did the songs vary in a different fashion in Transdanubia and Transylvania? The latter question, — though we may only guess at an answer, — involves another : would it not have been better to arrange the songs according to *certain geographical units?* We cannot dwell upon the definite answer here[22], but those who would like to have, *e. g.*, the songs of county Vas, or those of the Palots, may consult the geographical indexes of the volumes or compare the maps in the chapters.

---

[22] Nowadays, the songs exclusively sung in a given region are less in number than those known all over the country. Not even Transylvania, the richest in "exclusive" songs, is an exception. No generally valid regional limits could be established. We designate the tunes limited to some region (as in *Calendar Customs*, etc.).

"To find any tune easily" — this aim is realized in the *Corpus*, assuming, of course, that one *knows the song* one is looking for and wishes to find the words, place, source, date, and variants. Nevertheless, many people *know* melodic *fragments only* and wish to find the entire tune. Indexes of twin bars can be compiled, as has been done with the children's songs. It would not be possible to prepare such a catalogue for each volume (some thirty of them) of the *Corpus*, for it would mean the publication of the whole musical material once more, broken down to its motifs, and in a different order. However, some *special indexes* may give considerable assistance, e. g. the Index of *B-lines* which in the tunes of the new style (in the structures ABBA, AA⁵BA, etc.) may readily be compared with each other. An index of this kind is, first of all, Béla Bartók's last work in Hungary completed before his emigration, an index of rhythmical formulae based on, and referring to, the entire domain of Hungarian folk music (for part of his manuscript see facsimile on pp. 456—457).

This systemizing by the rhythm covers all the fields of Hungarian vocal folk music. It must be remembered that Hungarian folk music is divided, in respect of rhythm, into two main groups, *parlando-rubato* and *tempo giusto*. The second group again falls in two parts: tunes in *invariable* and those in *variable tempo giusto rhythm*. In the latter the formula ♩♩ can be changed in any part of the melody to ♪♩. or ♩.♪, according to the length of the syllables of the text.

Bartók divides Class A (old style) in his new system as follows: *I. Invariable tempo giusto rhythm.* The four lines of the stanza contain identical numbers of syllables (5 to 14). The metrical form of the lines is manifold. The group of 6, for instance, yields 14 formulae:

1. ♩ ♩│♩♩│♩♩│
2. ♪♩│♪♩│♪♩│
3. ♫♫│♩♩│
4. ♫♩♩│♩♩│
5. ♫♩│♫♩│
6. ♫♩│♩♫│
7. ♫♩│♪♩♪│
8. ♪♩♪│♫♩│
9. ♩♩│♫♩│
10. ♩♩♩│♩♩♩·│
11. ♫♩│♩♩│♩│
12. ♩♫│♩♩│♩│
13. ♩♩│♫♫│
14. ♩♩│♫♩│♩│

Consequently they are not only isometric but also isorhythmic *(aaaa)*. Besides them there are stanzas which are frequently made livelier by lines of different patterns. The formulae of these are: *aaba, abab, abbb, aabb, aaab, abba, aabc, abac, abcb, abcc*. All of them have several forms, on the whole 62 formulae of six syllables. *II. Variable tempo giusto rhythm.* The formulae are roughly identical with those of the first group, but the time is predominantly 4/4 instead of 2/4. The rhythmical patterns ♪♩. and ♩.♪ are characteristic. "One may assert with every chance of certainty that the adjustable *tempo giusto* rhythm constitutes a

Details from Bartók's last scientific work in his country: the register of rhythmic formulae in Hungarian folk songs.

mode of performance born in Hungary and manifestly Hungarian"
says Bartók.[23]

In the group of the new style (class B) the number of syllables
amounts to as much as twenty-five. A rhythmical formula of such a
line is, for instance

The third lines are predominantly different from the others, shorter or
longer.

Class C contains heterometric stanzas occurring in songs that do
not belong to class B. There are a few new formulae (the longer lines
marked Z, the shorter ones z):

1. z z Z z   6. z Z z Z   11. Z Z Z + Z Z
2. Z Z z Z   7. Z z z z   12. z z Z + Z z
3. Z Z z z   8. z Z Z Z   13. Z Z z + z Z
4. z z Z Z   9. z z z Z   14. Z + Z z Z + Z z
5. Z z Z z   10. Z Z Z z

An example for the last formula:

No. 7

Collected by B. Bartók, in 1907, in the village of Felsőireg, county Tolna.

In the index volume devoted to Bartók's system every rhythmical
formula will be referred to by the corresponding number of the songs
to be found in the different volumes.

[23] *Hungarian Folk Music*, p. 30.

From among the other systems applied in the *Corpus* we mention three prominent ones: 1. the system of games connected with children's songs[24]; 2. the system of match-making motifs derived from the text; 3. the system of games attached to match-making songs in Volume IV now in print.

BIBLIOGRAPHY

The most significant publication since the appearance of this study is *The Problem of the Lexicographical Indexing of Folk Tunes*, Adam Rieger, Wroclaw 1957. (Reprint, *Lud.* vol. xlii, with an ample bibliography of the dictionary-like ordering of melodies; in Polish with an English summary). In this we can find further data such as:

G. O. Arlt, *Lexicographical Indexing of Folk Melodies*, in *Modern Philology*, vol. xxvii, 1929, no. 1, pp. 147—154.

G. Brandsch, *Noch ein Vorschlag zur lexicalischen Anordnung von Volksmelodien*, in *Zeitschrift des Vereins für Volkskunde* vol. xxiv, 1914, no. 1. pp. 196—199.

W. Haas, *Systematische Ordnung Beethovenscher Melodien*, in *"Veröffentlichungen des Beethovenhauses in Bonn"*, vols. vii—viii, Leipzig 1932.

W. Heinitz, *Eine lexikalische Ordnung für die vergleichende Betrachtung von Melodien*, in *Archiv für Musikwissenschaft*, vol. iii, 1921, pp. 247—254.

S. B. Hustvedt, *A Melodic Index of Child's Ballad Tunes*, in *Publications of the University of California at Los Angeles in Languages and Literatures*, vol. i, 1936, no. 2, pp. 51—78.

L. R. Lewis, *The Possibilities of Thematic Indexing*, in *Papers and Proceedings of the Music Teachers' National Association, Studies in Musical Education, History, and Aesthetics*, vol. vii, 1913, pp. 180—188.

S. Poladian, *Methods of Indexing Melodies*; manuscript 1937. in *Library of the University of California at Berkeley*, further: *Journal of International Folk Music Council*, vol. iii, 1951, p. 34.

D. F. Scheurleer, *Welche ist die beste Methode, um Volks- und volkmässige Lieder nach ihrer melodischen (nicht textlichen) Beschaffenheit lexikalisch zu ordnen*, in *Zeitschrift der Internationalen Musikgesellschaft*, vol. i, p. 219.

[24] *Corpus* etc., vol. i, pp. 703—789.

JÁNOS JAGAMAS

ON DIALECT PROBLEMS OF
HUNGARIAN FOLK MUSIC IN RUMANIA

Béla Bartók was the first to deal with dialectal differences in Hungarian and Rumanian folk music ; he made the following statement regarding the dialects of Rumanian folk music in the districts of Maramureş, Bihor, Hunedoara, Banat, Mezőség and Satu-Mare (the Rumanian folk music of other regions was, at that time, not yet known to him) : "The Rumanian folk music of different regions has often a different, if not contradictory, character"[1]. Unlike these essential regional differences appearing in Rumanian folk music, he found that ". . .in Hungarian speech-areas we find more or less the same material everywhere, and the old pentatonic melodies alone display some insignificant dialectal differences according to regions"[2].

Bartók divided the territory inhabited by Hungarians into four dialectal regions : I. Transdanubia ; II. Upper Hungary, north of the rivers Danube and Tisza ; III. Region of the river Tisza, *i. e.* the Great Hungarian Plain ; IV. Transylvania, including Bucovina. This division became known through the publication of his work *Hungarian Folk Music*[3]. The features underlying Bartók's division were such regional characteristics of the pentatonic melodies like principal cadences, rhythmic final formulae, rhythmic structure, higher intonation of certain notes, and the occurrence of melismata. Table no. 2 in his work quoted above[4] shows clearly that his statements concerning dialect IV are based mainly on folk songs collected in the counties Ciuc, Odorhei, Mureş-Turda, in the regions of Bucovina inhabited by "Szeklers"[5], a few folk songs from Kalotaszeg (County Cluj) and a small number of folk songs from the counties Salaj, Trei scaune,

[1] Bartók Béla, *Népzenénk és a szomszéd népek zenéje* (Our Folk Music and the Music of Neighbouring Peoples), Budapest 1934, p. 22.
[2] Bartók, *op. cit.* pp. 21—22.
[3] Bartók, *A magyar népdal*, Budapest 1924. — English edition : *Hungarian Folk Music*, London 1931.
[4] Bartók, *op. cit.* p. 134.
[5] A group of Hungarian natives in Rumania.

Aranyos, etc. The statistical table includes but two melodies from Mezőség and none from other territories.

Relying on collections started among the Changos of Moldavia in the thirties (P. Domokos-Pál and S. Veress), P. Domokos-Pál was the first to declare and emphasize[6] that his collection " . . . adds a fifth to the existing four musico-dialectal regions inhabited by Hungarians, one that extends from the East Carpathians to the village of Gaiceana-Unguri in Tecuci county". In the Notes of his work he lays particular stress on the fact that he consciously and consistently insists on the existence of dialect V. On the strength of field work performed in the thirties in Moldavia, Veress made a similar statement in connection with the folk songs of the Changos in that territory. Although he does not openly declare in his report *Collection of Folk Music among the Changos of Moldavia*[7] that he, too, regards Moldavia as the fifth dialectal region, this becomes evident from his repeated references to dialectal differences between this and the other regions.

The exploration of Hungarian folk music in the area of Mezőség dates from 1940, when L. Lajtha's collection from Sic (Szék) was published, adding new — partly unknown — material to already existing collections.

The establishment in 1949 at Cluj of a separate department of the Folklore Institute of Bucharest meant the revival — on a large scale — of folk music collection both in Transylvania and in Moldavia. The material accumulated during the last 6 years[8] furnishes fresh data for the solution of the dialectological problems regarding Hungarian folk music in Rumania. The data in question refer (with the exception of Bucovina) to the fourth dialectal region of Bartók and the fifth of P. Domokos-Pál.

The present article is an attempt at elucidating the peculiarities of the music of the Hungarian people living in the Rumanian People's Republic, especially as regards regional differences or conformities in style, and dialectal deviations. In order to prevent any misunderstanding we want to emphasize that our material is still insufficient to allow of definite conclusions, so that all we want to do, at this juncture, is to contribute some data to the elucidation of the question concerning dialects of the Hungarian folk music in Rumania.

The significant part of our collection comes from Moldavia, Kalotaszeg, Mezőség, and certain parts of the area inhabited by Szeklers. Even in these regions there is still scope for further researches. Some areas are very poorly represented, e. g. Giurgeul, Ciuc, Ghimes, Odorhei, Bihor, Salaj, and the greater part of the region around Baia Mare,

---

[6] *A moldvai magyarság* (The Hungarians of Moldavia), Cluj 1931.
[7] Published in the review *Ethnographie-Népélet*, vol. iv, 1931.
[8] Until 1955 *(Editor's note)*.

the regions of Aiud, and Ludoşul de Mureş; we possess no songs from Tarnava, Trei scaune, Hunedoara, Arad and Timiş.

It should be noted that researches into our instrumental folk music are less advanced than those concerning vocal folk music, since the overwhelming majority of the instrumental material have not yet been taken down from magnetophone records; thus we have to abstain, for the time being, from making far-reaching conclusions or ascertaining dialectal differences in this respect.

The material we are concerned with is in the collection of the Folklore Institute : some 3700 Transylvanian and Moldavian variants of melodies (530 variant groups for the time being) of non-architectonic structure with Hungarian text (corresponding to the material of the old and miscellaneous class in Bartók's system), further 132 Moldavian variants of the new style, thus a total of 3832 melodies. With the exception of occasional references, it is not proposed to deal with the material of older folk music editions, for they show Hungarian folk music as it used to be some decades ago.

Being concerned with the folk music collection of the Folklore Institute we have accordingly grouped the material to be analysed into the following regional categories : Moldavia, Casin, Ciuc, Ghimes, Giurgeul, Odorhei, the neighbourhood of Reghin, that of Aiud and Ludoşul de Mureş, Mezőség, Kalotaszeg, Bihor, and Salaj—Satu-Mare.

*

The greater the number of melodies with variants occurring exclusively within certain regions, the greater will be the difference between the dialects of folk music. This is the problem we propose to tackle first.

1. Basic Melodies (Groups of Variants) Occurring in a Single Region. Moldavia has the highest number of basic melodies which cannot be found anywhere else. So far, 226 out of 337 four-line basic tunes (including a few five-, six-, and seven-line tunes) have been detected that do not seem to occur in any other territory (see Ex. nos. 1, 2, [3], 4, 5, 6, 7). The variants of 67 per cent of the Moldavian four-line melodies (from Rumanian territory) have not been encountered hitherto anywhere outside Moldavia. Within this considerable number we find the Aeolian scale in 75, the pentatonic in 66, the major in 56, the Dorian in 16, the Phrygian in 5, the Mixolydian in 5, and a mixed one in 3 melodies. The most frequent principal cadences are [3♭], [1] and [5], but — with reference to other regions — [4,] [2] and [VII], too, may be regarded as characteristic. The compass of 62 melodies is shorter than an octave, mostly a fifth or a sixth. All metrical patterns, from hexasyllabic lines to those with twelve syllables, are represented (74 per cent isometric, 26 per cent heterometric).

What has been said so far is alone sufficient to show that the melodies in question belong to various types. Some of these types are encountered at some points of Transylvania also, some have but a few occasional Transylvanian counterparts : which are of the same type but belong to a different group of variants. We are not yet in a position to say which of the types appear throughout Moldavia and which in certain places only. Continued research work will surely yield more accurate and reliable results. All we can be sure of at present is that future investigations will bring a modification of the above-said percentage (67%) ; should they bring a reduction, it is highly improbable that the figure will go below 40 to 45 per cent.

The situation is similar in regard to the melodies collected in Mezőség and Bihor. While the percentage of basic melodies unknown in other regions is lower than in Moldavia, still more than 50 per cent of the four- to seven-line basic melodies collected in Mezőség and Bihor are such as have not been traced in other areas. It should be noted that the material collected in the county of Bihor is too negligible (a total of 17 basic melodies) to carry weight.

Of a decided significance are, however, the 248 (four- to seven-line), basic melodies coming from Mezőség. There are 133 among them the variants of which have not yet been encountered anywhere else. Of an especial interest are the structures composed of lines with sixteen syllables. They are isolated phenomena which occur in a few places.[9]

The basic melodies which, so far, have not been encountered outside the area of Mezőség contain preferably the principal cadences [3♭] [5] [1] and [4]. In three basic melodies from two large villages we find the principal cadence [2♭] a phenomenon of utmost rarity in Hungarian folk music. It was discovered in a twelve-syllable structure from Sic, as also in a twelve-syllable and a sixteen-syllable melody of Phrygian character from Suat. The variants were published by L. Lajtha[10] (see Ex. no. 11).

At Rasciuci, [2♭] is found in the variant of a melody sung in various areas with [1] as principal cadence : the former may be regarded as an upward modification of the latter. Apart from our examples from Mezőség, [2♭] appears in a melody from Bihor : it is a close variant — with cadence displacement[11] — of a melody from the county of Békés published by Bartók.[12] Auxiliary cadences on the minor second above the final note occur in exceptional cases as the conclusion of the third

---

[9] The discovery of 16-syllable lines is attributable to L. Lajtha in connection with his collection from Sic (1940). See his *Újra megtalált magyar népdaltípus* (Hungarian Folk Song Type Rediscovered), in *Emlékkönyv Kodály Zoltán 60-ik születésnapjára* (Treatises in Honour of Z. Kodály's 60th Birthday), Budapest 1943.

[10] *Széki gyűjtés* (Collection from Szék), Budapest 1954 nos. 43 and 45, further in notes under no 45c.

[11] See *Ethnographia*, 1947, p. 300.

[12] Bartók, *op. cit.* (in note 3), no. 187.

line. In our collection they figure as conclusions in the third line of two four-line melodies, one from Moldavia and one from Mezőség (village Sic), further as the conclusion of the fifth line in a six-line melody from Alunis. In melody no. 66 of Bartók-Kodály's collection of Transylvanian folk songs[13], too, we encounter [2♭] as an auxiliary cadence. It occurs three times in lament no. 8 of L. Lajtha's collection[14] and figures once more in the same collection as the conclusion of the third line of the funeral song no. 12. [2♭] as principal cadence is unknown in Rumanian folk song collections: it appears in some exceptional cases as the conclusion of the third line[15].

The more detailed analysis and final elucidation of the basic melodies that are encountered exclusively in Mezőség are also tasks which require further investigations.

Half of the old four-line tunes (together with a five-line melody) collected at Magyarlapád (near Aiud), Ozd and Istihaza (in the neighbourhood of Ludoşul de Mureş) are unknown in other areas. We have done field work only in three villages of this region: our harvest resulted in 64 basic melodies, 32 of which appeared to be unknown in other regions. They seem to be worthy of attention because these 32 basic melodies (may be types of melodies), apart from being unknown in other regions, reveal dialectal peculiarities (Ex. no. 16).

The folk music of this region has, so far, been completely unknown. If we want to correlate it with the material of other regions we may say that it shows some affinity with the folk music of Mezőség.

Analysing the material collected in the neighbourhood of Kalotaszeg, at Reghin, Odorhei, Ciuc, Casin and in Salaj—Satu-Mare, we find that about 30 per cent of the melodies are unknown in other regions. Viewed from the standpoint of dialect, the melodies belonging exclusively to any one of these places are of less significance than the material typical of the regions mentioned above.

There is one more, quite unique phenomenon worthy of mention that has hitherto been observed only in three villages in the vicinity of Reghin. Approximately 30 km east or Reghin, along the river Mureş, there are the villages Alunis, Porcesti, and Mureşmort. The so-called "song of the village" in these places is a tune composed of six octosyllabic lines; it is somewhat suggestive of laments as sung at Mezőség. It is traditionally sung alternately by a soloist and by the choir. The first line is sung by the leader of the choir, the second and third by the choir,

[13] *Erdélyi magyarság. Népdalok* (Hungarians of Transylvania. Folk Songs), Budapest 1923.
[14] *Szépkenyerűszentmártoni gyűjtés* (Collection from Szépkenyerűszentmárton), Budapest 1954.
[15] For instance in Bartók's *Volksmusik der Rumänen von Maramureş*, München 1923. no. 110*b*, and as the conclusion of the second line, in no. 127 of *200 cîncete şi doine* (Two Hundred Songs and Doinas), Bucharest 1955, a six-line melody from Banat.

the fourth by the leader, the fifth and sixth again by the choir. A single text line, twice repeated, serves as the first section of the song and another line, likewise twice repeated, constitutes the second section. The older people in the village recall that this manner of performance as well as the melody and this application of the text, was inherited from their parents and grandparents, which proves that this kind of performance was already in use 70 to 80 years ago. There is no restriction as to the words : any old lyrical text composed of octosyllabic verses may accompany the melody. As a matter of fact, it is quite often associated with the text of the recruiting song which begins with the words *Megjött már a parancsolat* (The order has arrived). Besides its six-line form, the melody is sometimes sung in three-line form, with the introductory and concluding verses separately (Ex. no. 17. In an interesting, amplified variant we heard it sung by a woman from Alunis to the text of the *Kontyoló* song — a nuptial song used to celebrate the act when the newly-wed bride exchanges her maiden head-dress for one worn by married women). Future research work might throw light on the question whether this "song of the village" with its numerous texts, its dialogue-like performance by choir-leader and choir, goes back to ancient tradition or has been borrowed from foreign parts (*v.* the *"pripjev"* performance of the South-Slavs).

2. Mode (Scale). Apart from the number of basic melodies belonging exclusively to a definite region, another characteristic of dialectal significance is the extent to which the scales of older tunes reveal regional deviations. We must content ourselves, at this juncture, with analysing this problem from the point of view of the two most significant groups of the old material, *i. e.* the pentatonic and non-pentatonic systems, without going into the details of the modes of non-pentatonic melodies. At best, we may make references to the Phrygian mode, the Phrygian cadence, or the question of the augmented second.

For the analysis of the modes we can — for the time being — rely on a more or less complete collection from three areas.

The division of melodies according to modes is this :

Table I

Mezőség		Moldavia		Kalotaszeg	
old pent. in abt. 109 groups of var. 289 melodies 39%	old non-pent. in abt. 169 groups of var. 275 melodies 61%	old pent. in abt. 105 groups of var. 375 melodies 31%	old non-pent. in abt. 232 groups of var. 562 melodies 69%	old pent. in abt. 64 groups of var. 343 melodies 35%	old non-pent. in abt. 117 groups of var. 386 melodies 65%

466

(The great number of pentatonic variants in the material from Kalotaszeg is due to the fact that the major part of the variants originate from Inucu where, for the purposes of a monograph, an especially exhaustive collection of variants was conducted.

The figures of Table I show that the highest number of pentatonic basic melodies were found in Mezőség and Moldavia. It is at the same time surprising that the extent of old non-pentatonic material is predominant in Moldavia. The pentatonic group of variants derived from Kalotaszeg is substantially smaller.

Phrygian mode or Phrygian cadence, as also augmented second, occur but rarely in Hungarian folk music. The 2^b (mostly before the final note) and the Phrygian mode contained in the melodies amount to 12 per cent in the old Moldavian material, to 8 per cent in that from Mezőség, to 6 per cent in the region of Reghin, to 5 per cent at Odorhei, to 4 per cent in the region of Aiud and Ludoșul de Mureș, and to 3 per cent, each, at Ghimes and Kalotaszeg. Phrygian cadence occurs in 4 cases among the 25 old tunes collected in Bihor, *i. e.* in 16 per cent of the whole material derived from that county. While this number is negligible, we must remember that 2^b forms the principal cadence in two variants. In our collection from Ciuc, Casin, Salaj and Satu-Mare we have not a single melody with Phrygian mode or Phrygian cadence.

The augmented second appears in three forms: $2^b - 3^\sharp$, $3^b - 4^\sharp$ and $6^b - 7^\sharp$. The form $2^b - 3^\sharp$ was found in 9 variants from Moldavia and 7 from Mezőség, and nowhere else. The form $3^b - 4^\sharp$ occurs in 40 variants from Moldavia, 41 from Kalotaszeg (among which there are 27 variants of 3 melodies from Inucu), in 3 from Odorhei, 2 from Ciuc-Casin, 2 from Ghimes, 2 from Salaj. The form $6^b - 7^\sharp$ was found in 2 variants from Mezőség, 2 from Kalotaszeg, and 1 from Moldavia. Thus the augmented second is rather typical of Moldavia and to a lesser extent also of Kalotaszeg and Mezőség. Observations on the spot showed a frequent fluctuation in the intonation of the augmented second: it was usually somewhat narrow. Even if a melody is repeatedly sung by one and the same person, he will sometimes leave out augmented seconds altogether.

Both phenomena (Phrygian cadence and augmented second) are characteristic of the majority of Rumanian folk songs. Though known all over the Hungarian-speaking area, they appear in the Hungarian folk music most frequently in regions where there is a close contact between the two nationalities. Apart from a direct Rumanian influence upon Hungarian folk music one is tempted to think of the still haunting influence of vestigial Turkish traditions.

3. Principal Cadence. Based on the number of pentatonic melodies and arranged according to geographical areas, the following table illustrates the frequency of the various principal cadences. (The bracketed figures indicates the number of principal cadences diminishing from left

30*

to right. The upper figure shows the number of the pentatonic, the lower figure the number of the non-pentatonic basic melodies.)

Moldavia $\quad$ [3♭] $\frac{49}{34}$ [1] $\frac{17}{34}$ [5] $\frac{13}{54}$ [VII] $\frac{13}{7}$ [4] $\frac{10}{24}$ [V] $\frac{1}{3}$ [7] $\frac{1}{1}$ [2] $\frac{1}{30}$ [3] $\frac{-}{20}$ [6] $\frac{-}{2}$ [8] $\frac{-}{2}$

Mezőség $\quad$ [3♭] $\frac{54}{29}$ [5] $\frac{16}{42}$ [1] $\frac{15}{28}$ [4] $\frac{11}{21}$ [VII] $\frac{7}{3}$ [7] $\frac{2}{6}$ [2] $\frac{2}{14}$ [V] $\frac{1}{7}$ [8] $\frac{1}{3}$ [3] $\frac{-}{11}$ [b2] $\frac{-}{4}$ [6] $\frac{-}{1}$

Kalotaszeg $\quad$ [3♭] $\frac{32}{12}$ [5] $\frac{11}{30}$ [1] $\frac{8}{22}$ [VII] $\frac{7}{-}$ [4] $\frac{3}{15}$ [2] $\frac{2}{17}$ [8] $\frac{1}{2}$ [V] $\frac{-}{3}$ [6] $\frac{-}{2}$ [b6] $\frac{-}{1}$

Odorhei $\quad$ [3♭] $\frac{28}{8}$ [5] $\frac{12}{18}$ [1] $\frac{7}{19}$ [4] $\frac{3}{3}$ [7] $\frac{2}{-}$ [3] $\frac{-}{7}$ [2] $\frac{-}{6}$ [6♭] $\frac{-}{6}$ [8] $\frac{-}{1}$ [VII] $\frac{-}{1}$ [V] $\frac{-}{1}$

Casin $\quad$ [3♭] $\frac{25}{4}$ [5] $\frac{10}{14}$ [1] $\frac{5}{15}$ [4] $\frac{4}{6}$ [VII] $\frac{4}{4}$ [8] $\frac{2}{2}$ [2] $\frac{-}{10}$ [7] $\frac{-}{1}$ [6] $\frac{-}{1}$ [V] $\frac{-}{1}$

Ciuc $\quad$ [3♭] $\frac{16}{2}$ [5] $\frac{5}{2}$ [1] $\frac{4}{12}$ [4] $\frac{2}{3}$ [7] $\frac{1}{1}$ [8] $\frac{1}{-}$ [VII] $\frac{1}{-}$ [2] $\frac{-}{5}$ [3] $\frac{-}{4}$ [V] $\frac{-}{1}$

Reghin $\quad$ [3♭] $\frac{11}{7}$ [5] $\frac{3}{17}$ [1] $\frac{2}{14}$ [4] $\frac{1}{5}$ [VII] $\frac{1}{1}$ [2] $\frac{-}{5}$ [3] $\frac{-}{2}$ [6] $\frac{-}{1}$ [8] $\frac{-}{1}$

Ghimes $\quad$ [3♭] $\frac{9}{2}$ [5] $\frac{4}{3}$ [1] $\frac{3}{4}$ [VII] $\frac{2}{-}$ [4] $\frac{-}{1}$ [2] $\frac{-}{1}$ [8] $\frac{-}{1}$

Aiud, Ludoşul $\quad$ [3♭] $\frac{8}{1}$ [VII] $\frac{8}{-}$ [5] $\frac{7}{8}$ [4] $\frac{5}{3}$ [1] $\frac{4}{9}$ [8] $\frac{1}{2}$ [7] $\frac{1}{-}$ [2] $\frac{-}{6}$ [3] $\frac{-}{3}$ [6] $\frac{-}{1}$

Giurgeul $\quad$ [5] $\frac{3}{2}$ [1] $\frac{2}{2}$ [3♭] $\frac{2}{1}$ [6] $\frac{-}{1}$ [8] $\frac{-}{1}$

Bihor $\quad$ [5] $\frac{1}{6}$ [1] $\frac{1}{1}$ [8] $\frac{1}{-}$ [V] $\frac{1}{-}$ [3♭] $\frac{-}{3}$ [7] $\frac{-}{2}$ [6] $\frac{-}{1}$ [4] $\frac{-}{1}$ [3] $\frac{-}{1}$ [2♭] $\frac{-}{1}$

Salaj—Satu-Mare [1] $\frac{9}{12}$ [3♭] $\frac{7}{4}$ [5] $\frac{4}{20}$ [VII] $\frac{3}{-}$ [4] $\frac{2}{12}$ [8] $\frac{1}{1}$ [7] $\frac{1}{-}$ [2] $\frac{-}{7}$ [3] $\frac{-}{3}$ [6] $\frac{-}{1}$

We cannot tell to-day with certainty which of these lines is closest to reality. It seems safe to suppose that further collections will modify these lines, in the first place those based on a small number of tunes. According to the tabulated figures it is still generally true that the old Transylvanian pentatonic material is characterized by the principal cadence [3♭], a phenomenon observed by Bartók some decades ago.

As regards the principal cadence [VII] we think we are at present justified in claiming that — compared to the entire material — it is more frequent in Moldavia, in Mezőség, at Casin, Kalotaszeg and in the area of Aiud and Ludoşul de Mureş than elsewhere. We know from Bartók that [VII] occurs but in the dialectal region IV, and even there only occasionally, as something borrowed from the Rumanians. Recent documents have shown its sporadic appearance in the present territory of Hungary too.

[VII] as principal cadence is quite frequent in Rumanian folk music, and it occurs also in the pentatonic melodies (ending in *so*) of the Cheremisses and the Chuvashes. In Kodály's *Pentatonic Music*[16] 19 out of 70 Chuvash melodies ending in *so* have [VII] as the principal cadence, and it appears in seven of the Cheremiss melodies known to us.

Whether the occurrence of the principal cadence [VII] in Moldavia and Transylvania is to be regarded as the result of Rumanian influence or as oriental inheritance, is a question not yet investigated. The probability of the first theory seems to be favoured by the fact that the principal cadence [VII] is more frequent in areas where lively intercourse exists between the Rumanian and the Hungarian populations. It is, on the other hand, quite possible that part of the melodies with [VII] as principal cadence are not of Rumanian origin but have to be accepted as vestigial phenomena of an oriental tradition which the Hungarian-speaking population — surrounded by Rumanians — may have preserved in certain regions. (Let us refer to the great number of last lines concluding on *so*).

The principal cadence [4] in pentatonic melodies occurs likewise in Moldavia and Mezőség. Regarding [4] we have Bartók's statement that two groups of variants occur in all four dialectal regions, one group occurs only in regions I and III, while four groups occur only in region IV. It follows that [4] plays an important part in Transylvania. Recent collections have enhanced its prominence in Moldavia and certain areas of Transylvania.

Also in regard to [4] we are uncertain as to the possible connection that may exist with the Cheremiss and Chuvash tunes in which the principal cadence falls on the upper fourth from the final note. Such was found to be the case in four Chuvash melodies concluding on *la*, 21 Chuvash ones concluding on *so*, and 12 cheremiss melodies concluding on *so*. This principal cadence in the Cheremiss material is, with but a single exception, always associated with a transposition on the lower fourth. In 12 out of the 21 Chuvash melodies belonging to this category this is more conspicuous. Traces of transpositions on the lower fifth or fourth also in the Hungarian material are sometimes quite sharp, sometimes rather blurred. Ex. no. 8 which, together with its following variant, demonstrates also the change in the character of the final note, belongs to a group of variants fairly widespread in Moldavia. The conclusion on *so* is sufficiently marked in the melody from Frumoasa. (A variant with a similar conclusion occurs also in the collection of Sándor Veress[17].)

The connection between the Hungarian tunes showing [4] as the principal cadence (or, rather, tunes the first part of which concludes on the upper fourth of the final note) and the eastern material is another problem that awaits elucidation.

[16] *Ötfokú zene*, Budapest 1947, vol. iv.
[17] *Op. cit.* (in note 7).

The same as [VII], the principal cadence [4], too, occurs mostly in Transylvania and Moldavia. The fact should not be disregarded that wherever in the course of our field work we encountered [VII] we invariably found also [4]. (Except for three villages where we collected very few melodies and which, therefore, do not count, in this respect).

4. Different Principal Cadences Within the Same Group of Variants. Various principal cadences within one and the same group of variants occur with the greatest frequency in the material from Moldavia, namely in 27 basic melodies. We encounter two kinds of principal cadences in 17, three kinds in 6 and four kinds in 3 basic melodies ; while 8 such cases were found in Mezőség and Kalotaszeg respectively, 5 are known from Casin, and 2 to 3 at the most from other regions. (There are more cases than those enumerated here in which different principal cadences appear within a group of variants, but in these cases the variants, though belonging to the same group, are scattered over different areas.) (See Ex. nos. 5, 6, 7).

5. Final Note. We cannot omit dealing, even if briefly, with the matter of the final note in old pentatonic melodies because a small part of the oldest Hungarian pentatonic tunes ends, apart from the usual *la*, occasionally also on other notes. The majority of our pentatonic examples which do not close on *la* come likewise from Moldavia. *So* is the final note in 6 and *do* in 2 groups of variants. Among the 6 *so*-groups there are 3 in which some variants have *la* as the final note. In Moldavia there is one *do*-group containing also variants ending on *la*. We encountered two *so*-groups in Mezőség and Aiud (each contained also *la*-variants), and a *do*-group at Kalotaszeg. We collected, moreover, two groups of variants in the region of Mezőség and Reghin which contained variants ending in *la* or *do*. One of them is to be found in Kodály's book *Hungarian Folk Music*[18] ; it is a *do*-variant (from Alunis and Caianul Mare) of a psalmodizing melody beginning with the words *"Szivárvány havasán"* (On the snow-capped alps of the rainbow ; Ex. no. 18).

6. Architecture of Melodies. ABCD is the most frequent form everywhere. The frequency or rarity with which structures of a transposition on the lower fifth, repeats of lines, and refrain-structures occur vary from region to region. Of our three largest collections (Kalotaszeg, Mezőség, Moldavia) it is the latter which shows the greatest number of structures with transposition in fifths, amounting to an average of 11,5 per cent (13 per cent of the pentatonic and 10 per cent of the non-pentatonic melodies.) It is, at the same time, among the structures of transposition in fifth and fourth that we encounter the widest range of variations, namely

[18] *Magyar népzene*, Budapest 1952, p. 22.

no less than 15 different types of melodic architecture. AB⁵CB, A⁵B⁵AB, A⁴B⁴AB, A⁵BAB and AB⁴AB are the more frequently occurring forms (referred to variants of melodies). The quintal structure is nearly as varied as in the Cheremiss and the Chuvash material. Only 6 examples of this structure have so far been recorded at Odorhei and Casin, while 7 per cent of the entire material from Mezőség (9 per cent of the pentatonic and 5 per cent of the non-pentatonic variants of melodies) display this structure. It occurs with the least frequency at Kalotaszeg : 2.6 per cent of the whole material.

The A⁵B⁵AB form of the quintal-structure appears with the greatest frequency at Casin : in 23 variants of melodies.

Table II

AABB with repeat of line

	Pentatonic %	Non-pentatonic %	Entire material %
Moldavia	16,53	12,65	14,20
Mezőség	10,04	5,45	7,81
Kalotaszeg	10,49	4,92	7,54

This form appears, though much less frequently, also in the smaller collections. Compared with the form AABB, the forms ABAC, ABAB and ABCB are much rarer throughout the material, and — if they occur — it is mostly in Moldavia. (They are completely missing from the material of certain areas). It should be noted that, side by side with the predominant fifth- and fourth-structure, the said occurs also in Chuvash and — with less frequency — in Cheremiss melodies.[19] The AABB form with repeat of line is, on the other hand, a typical and frequent feature of Rumanian folk music. To what extent Hungarian AABB melodies go back to oriental tradition or whether their existence owes its origin to Rumanian influence is a problem still awaiting elucidation. It is quite possible that there exists a steadily fading oriental tradition gradually replaced by Rumanian influence.

7. Number of Syllables, Isometry, Heterometry. Of the isometric pentatonic melodies those with octosyllabic lines prevail in Moldavia, at Giurgeul, Ciuc, Casin and around Aiud-Ludoșul de Mureș, while eleven syllables are the rule in other areas. The number of eight-syllable

[19] The data regarding the inaccessible Chuvash material have been taken from Parts 3 and 4 of Kodály's *Ötfokú zene* (Pentatonic Music) and from vol. iv of his *Bicinia Hungarica*, Budapest (no year).

and eleven-syllable basic melodies was found equal at Odorhei. The number of octosyllabic melodies exceeds that of the eleven-syllable ones by just one at Casin. Table III offers a good survey of the distribution of the various syllabic arrangements.

Table III

Region	Isometry									Heterometry
	6	7	8	10	11	12	13	14	16	
					%					
Moldavia	24	8,5	46	4	8,5	7	1	1	—	9
Mezőség	9	7	28	6	38	8	1	—	3	15
Kalotaszeg	4	4	30	4	50	6	—	2	—	19
Odorhei	7	7	39	2	39	4	—	—	2	15
Ciuc	27	—	42	—	27	—	—	4	—	13
Casin	11	6	36	6	33	2	—	6	—	20
Ghimes	12	—	41	—	47	—	—	—	—	11
Giurgeul	25	—	75	—	—	—	—	—	—	33
Reghin	14	10	10	—	52	10	—	4	—	16
Aiud—Ludoșul de Mureș	3	7	57	—	33	—	—	—	—	12
Bihor	—	20	—	20	60	—	—	—	—	—
Salaj—Satu Mare	15	5	20	15	40	—	—	5	—	26

This table shows the percentage of the pentatonic groups of variants with any number of syllables within the whole four-line material of an area. It also shows the percentage of the heterometric melodies within the entire pentatonic material.

As regards non-pentatonic isometric melodies, a predominance of the octosyllabic ones is revealed in all regions save Moldavia, where hexasyllabic melodies are most frequent. Their number exceeds that of the octosyllabic melodies in other regions.

A special melodic type is the group of 16-syllable melodies from Mezőség. It occurs within the category of isometric four-line forms in 33 variants (in 17 groups of variants), and in a single five-line melody. Within the group of heterometric "four-liners" this 16-syllable form occurs in 7 variants (6 groups of variants), as also in 5 "five-liners". Four-line melodies: one isometric and one heterometric, each from the region of Odorhei; two heterometric from the region of Reghin; one heterometric from the region of Aiud, and one from Moldavia. The figures seem to prove that melodies with 16-syllable lines have to be regarded as a typical feature of the dialect of Mezőség. Sporadic data make it probable that these 16-syllable melodies may have existed in the past in other regions as well, an assumption substantiated by occasional examples that have survived and are still encountered here and there. We find

472

the 16-syllable forms among the non-pentatonic old melodies in the penultimate group of old dance tunes in L. Vargyas's collection[20]. We have, as an exception, classed three of those contained in our collection with the pentatonic material.

Let us add, as a new datum, that in five isometric 16-syllable groups of variants from Mezőség there appear also variants with other metric arrangements. A 16-syllable group from Rasciuci, with [2] as the principal cadence, contains also 8- and 12-syllable variants; (all variants are from Rasciuci). Another such group contains an 11-syllable isometric variant (likewise from Rasciuci): a third 16-syllable from Rasciuci includes 12- and 11-syllable variants; finally, we know of a 16-syllable group from Mezőség which contains 14- and 11-syllabled variants (Ex. nos. 12, 13). In Mezőség alone there exist three more groups which contain several variants with other than 16-syllable metre. With the exception of Moldavia we have not found a similar phenomenon anywhere else. Variants of a melody that differ from one another in respect of the number of syllables have been found in five additional groups of variants; however, these syllabically different variants originated always from different geographical regions. Our examples offer a convenient material for the study of the relationships between, and the interconnections of, the various syllabic arrangements and should be taken into account when making investigations into the origin of 16-syllable melodies.

The amplification of certain lines in some old 11-syllable melodies is another special feature of Mezőség. Sometimes 2 to 3 lines are lengthened to 15, sometimes even to 19, syllables by repeating parts of the text (Ex. no. 14). This kind of elongation is well known from the new style. In our examples of old 11-syllable melodies it is only the 3rd line that, very rarely, becomes elongated in this manner. The lengthening usually begins with the first line. The richest material of this kind was encountered at Suat.

Bartók adduces examples in which even lines with more than 10 or 11 syllables undergo elongation. Whether the origin of this phenomenon dates from times prior to the birth of the new style or should be regarded as a retroactive effect of the new style upon the old 11-syllable melodies, has yet to be decided by future investigations.

8. Compass. Treating of the ambit of old melodies, Bartók stated that their compass was mostly around an octave. Ranges of fifths, sixths and tenth are comparatively rare. An analysis of the Moldavian material of our collection will reveal the frequency of small compasses: major sixth and still narrower ranges constitute 20 per cent of the pentatonic variants, 24 per cent of the non-pentatonic melodies and 23 per cent of the entire old material (together with variants; Ex. nos. 3, 4, 5).

[20] *Collections of Hungarian Folk Songs* in Kodály, *op. cit.* (in note 18).

The corresponding percentage in Mezőség is about 6 and in other areas still lower.

9. Graces. According to Bartók[21] octosyllabic *parlando-rubato* melodies from the dialectal region IV usually display rich ornamentation. Our present collection — made about 40 to 50 years later — shows a considerably reduced application of melismata in those Transylvanian areas to which Bartók's finding refers, while melodic embellishments are, as a rule, more lavish in the *parlando-rubato* melodies collected by us in Mezőség and Moldavia. Such melodies, whether performed by old or young people, reveal in Moldavia — and to a still greater extent in certain villages of Mezőség — an abundant ornamentation which is well defined even in group-songs. The use of many grace notes is an old custom which we encountered also around Aiud, though not as frequently as, for instance, at and around Suat (Ex. no. 15).

10. The Question of Verses. It is also stated in Bartók's work quoted above that in the majority of the melodies each line of a four-line stanza has a different text, the pattern being a, b, c, d. He calls attention to an old-fashioned arrangement of the verses in dialectal region IV : melodic stanzas still consist of four lines, but contain two verses only : the first is repeated in the second line and the second in the fourth line, the pattern being, a, a, b, b. Our collection reveals such repeats of verses in the material of nearly all regions. It amounts to 45 per cent of the Moldavian variants of melodies, 34 per cent in the region of Aiud and Ludoşul de Mureş, not quite 7 per cent in Mezőség, and to still less elsewhere. This archaic structure is most frequent in Moldavia, where it displays the greatest variability. Quoted in the order of diminishing frequency, the following patterns have been found there : a, a, b, b (152); a, b, a, b (109) ; a, b, c, c (45); a, b, b, c (15); a, a, b, c (13) ; a, b, c, b (11) ; a, a, a, a (1) ; a, b, b, b, (1) ; a, b, a, c (1). Kalotaszeg too, has a multiplicity of types, but the number of melodies there is negligible. The same can be said of the region of Aiud and of Mezőség. It should be noted that the above figures refer mostly to the first stanza of the melody texts. The pattern of the first stanza may recur in the other stanzas or may change in one and the same stanza of a melody if repeatedly sung, even by the same performer. A repeat of verses (lines) alternating with the ABCD-form also occurs sometimes. All this makes it evident that the treatment of the texts is not bound by strict rules.

Refrains play a considerably less significant role. They were found in 61 variants of melodies from Moldavia, in 35 from Mezőség, in 15 from Kalotaszeg and in 8 from Casin. Most of them are non-pentatonic melodies. Their number varies from 1 to 5 in other areas. There were 15 Rumanian refrains in the whole material of refrains encountered in

[21] *Op. cit.* (in note 3).

Moldavia which seemed to have directly been borrowed from Rumanian folk songs. Let us here mention a rare phenomenon which was mostly encountered in Moldavia : the same melody is sometimes sung once with a Hungarian text and once with a Rumanian text, both texts having the same meaning (Ex. no. 9).

11. Two- and Three-Line Melodies. There are, apart from 337 old four-line basic melodies, 147 two-line and 98 three-line groups of variants in our material. These figures do not include those two- and three-liners which must be regarded as distorted melodies of the new style. The occurrence of the said two- and three-liners was found to be most frequent in Moldavia : 87 two-line and 42 three-line basic melodies (with 190 and 104 variants respectively). Their number is much lower in other areas : we know 21 two-line and 23 three-line melodies from Mezőség and still less from other places.

Some of the two-liners have four-line variants ; others have either no such variants or — if they have — these variants have, so far, escaped detection. There are also three-line melodies with four-line variants. Such variants are either borrowed from Rumanian folk songs or else are the products of Rumanian influence (Ex. no. 10).

12. The New Style in Moldavia. From all that has been said above it seems to be evident that it is the Moldavian material that shows the most considerable deviations from the melodies of other areas. If we consider also the melodies that belong to the new style, the discrepancy appears to be still wider. Sándor Veress, one of the earliest collectors in Moldavia, says : "It is obvious that in no region, where the old Hungarian style is still alive and dominates the entire folk music, can the new style strike roots. Accordingly, one seldom finds new-styled songs in such places, and where one or two such songs still appear, they are always associated with a particular person and, therefore, not integral parts of the folk music"[22]. Those few melodies of the new style which are included in his collection were, without exception, sung by male singers who had done military service together with Szekler lads. In evaluating Veress' data we must always remember that his field work was of short duration and covered a comparatively restricted area. Péter Domokos Pál[23], published 10 melodies of the new style from his collections made in 1929 and 1932. They were all melodies sung by young girls or married women. Two of them were recorded at Galbeni, a place where Veress, too, did field work. Domokos' data modify the results of Veress' investigations, though not to a very large extent. Some 20 years later we encountered new-styled melodies in 18 Moldavian villages : their number was 132. (Most of them were from Galbeni where,

---

[22] *Loc. cit.*
[23] *Op. cit.* (in note 6).

for the purposes of a monograph, we made thorough-going investigations. Regarding 22 melodies out of a total of 52 collected at Galbeni it could be established without a doubt that they had been introduced by Hungarian teachers a few years before, after the foundation of Hungarian schools. More detailed data in this respect will be contained in the monograph on folk music at Galbeni, to be published in the near future). The number of such melodies is much higher than any that has ever been published in earlier collections; however, it is still negligible in comparison with the number of new-styled melodies in certain other areas, for instance at Kalotaszeg, where the material includes 1346 variants of the new style.

Documents existing in this respect make it probable that the new style was either unknown or merely sporadically known in Moldavia before World War I (the majority of the melodies traceable nowadays started to penetrate from Transylvania not more than 30 or — at the most — 35 years ago). Future investigations will have to ascertain the extent to which the new style has struck roots in Moldavia. It is certain that it has still not gained ground in quite a number of places. As far as we can judge, the folk songs, as used by the majority of the Hungarian-speaking population east of the Carpathians, represent that dialect of Hungarian folk music which is most different from all others, a dialect in which melodies of the old style are still in full vigour and in great majority as compared with the number of new-styled melodies.

Nearly 16 per cent of the Moldavian new-styled melodies of our collection display a mutilation, or rather distortion, of form. It seems as if we had to do here with the same *"Zersingung"* (deterioration by transmission) of Hungarian melodies as has been observed regarding Hungarian songs taken over by Slovaks and Ruthenians. Writing about the interactions of Slovak and Hungarian folk music, Bartók points out[24] that, in a group of melodies of the new style borrowed by the Slovaks and Ruthenians, "there appear modifications which impress us as structural distortions. Either a line of the melody or a repeat is usually omitted: the typically Hungarian pattern ABBA, for instance, appears as ABA..."[24] Similar distortions found among the Hungarians of Moldavia have presumably also been brought about by a failure to understand the original — one is tempted to say, too modern — form (Ex. nos. 19—24).

*

Documents concerning folk music in the above-treated regions offer the following picture:

The so-called IVth dialect of Hungarian folk music has been proved by recent investigations to consist of several dialects.

Moldavia has to be accepted as having a separate dialect. The maintenance of ancient traditions; the great number of melodies

[24] *Op. cit.* (in note 1).

unknown in other areas; the negligible proportion of melodies of the new style; the strikingly rich ornamentation; the effect of foreign — especially Rumanian — influences which manifested through the borrowing of melodies, texts, Rumanian refrains and certain musical elements — all these phenomena distinguish the Moldavian dialect quite sharply from that of other regions. At this juncture, the question arises as to whether the dialect of Moldavia constitutes a uniform whole or may be further divided into "subdialects".

Statistical data concerning particular musical elements of folk songs in Mezőség reveal much similarity — in some features even a perfect identity — of the respective melodies of Mezőség and Moldavia, but the types of melodies encountered in Mezőség impart to this region a special character of its own. If nothing else, the 16-syllable type of melodies, the elongation of the 11-syllable verses, and the individual grace notes will always distinguish the dialect of Mezőség not only from that of Moldavia but also from the folk song of all other regions of Transylvania. To determine the exact boundaries of this dialect and to ascertain possible deviations within it are tasks to be solved by future investigations.

Even the scanty material collected in the region of Aiud and Ludoşul de Mureş, reveals some striking individual features. The Rumanian influence observed in Mezőség is still more pronounced in this region: it manifests itself both in the form of borrowed melodies and the special character of ancient forms. Moreover, there appears to exist an affinity between some of its songs and the *Jaj-nóta* type of the Mezőség melodies (where the text-lines are completed by repeating the word *jaj* 'oh!').

As regards folk melodies of the Széklers, Bartók's definition of the IVth dialect can still be said to hold good.

Kalotaszeg has given way to the new style to the greatest extent: the old style is being pushed to the background with increasing vigour, a process which involves the decay of musical embellishments. Rumanian influence is the slightest here.

The material derived from Salaj, Satu-Mare, and Bihor is too scanty to admit of drawing definite conclusions: these regions seem to belong rather to the IIIrd dialect.

We want to emphasize that the dialectal differences treated above do in no way impair the uniformity of Hungarian folk music.

Quite a host of questions regarding matters of detail arose in the course of our investigations, and no definite elucidation of the problem of musical dialects among the Hungarian population of Rumania can be expected before each of the said questions will have been solved. It is furthermore necessary that comparisons be made with the results of linguistic investigations, and that also the history of settlements and other historical details be cleared up. A successful solution of the question regarding folk-music dialects may contribute to a better elucidation of the history of nationalities and settlements.

No. 1

Collected by J. Jagamas in Luizi-Călugara, 1950. No. 1920, F 343a.

No. 2

Collected by J. Jagamas in Galbeni, 1953. No. 6707, 6/1

No. 3

478

Hull - ja - tok le - ve - lek, ta - kar - ja - tok in - gĕm, m

Mett az én é - de - sem sír - va ke - res in - gem.

Collected by J. Jagamas in Galbeni, 1950. No. 1762, F 285b.
Variant in Bartók, *Volksmusik der Rumänen von Maramureş*, no. 68.

No. 4

Giusto ♩=92

I - de ki jă csi - hi csi - hi csi - hir - be

♩=96

I - de ki je csi - hi csi - hi csi - hir - be.

Collected by J. Jagamas in Valea Seaca, 1953. No. 8197, M 14/3

No. 5

Parlando ♩=38

a

1.2. A - pám, é - desz - a - pám,   A - pám, é - desz - a - pám.

Parlando

b

1.2.   (ă)

Parlando ♩=cca 144

c

1.2. Hajts el Du - na, hajts el,   Hajts el   Du - na, hajts el,

Collected by J. Jagamas *a)* in Galbeni, 1950. No. 1931, F 348c;

b) in Galbeni, 1953. No. 6624, M 1/2;

c) in Valea Seaca, 1953. No. 8215, M 15/3

No. 6

2. Zab - lak i ba varr va - la, Him - jit varr - ja va - la.

2. Ott es csak úgy ke - rülj, Bú - val (a) meg ne me - rülj.

2. I - lo - nám, I - lo - nám, Lan - gasz sziép I - lo - nám.

Collected by J. Jagamas *a)* in Galbeni, 1953. No. 6695, M 5/12;
b) in Galbeni, 1953. No. 7604;
c) in Cleja, 1950. No. 1751, F 273;
d) in Valea Seaca, 1954. No. 10,712.

No. 7

Giusto ♩=84

a

1.2. M - eg - vi - rág - zott ë di - ó - fa, Meg - vi - rág - zott

Giusto

b

1.2. M - eg - kö - töm az ök - röm szar - vát, (ǎ) Meg - kö - töm az

Giusto ♩ = 138

c

1.2. Huj - zad, huj - zad én ci - gá - nyom, Én es vó - tam

e di - ó - fa,

ök - röm szar - vát,

ki - rály - le - ány,

3.4. Na - gyot haj - latt há - rom á - ga, Na - gyot haj - latt

3.4. Fël - szán - tom e ker - tem alyát, Fël - szán - tom e

3.4. Ki - rály le - ány Ka - ta - li - na Kit meg - öl - tek

há - rom á - go.

ker - tem alyát

má - ná - szó - ba.

Collected by J. Jagamas *a)* in Valea Seaca, 1953. No. 8201, M 14/7 ;
b) in Galbeni, 1953. No. 7910, M 10/8 ;
c) in Vladnic, 1951. No. 2713.

No. 8

Parlando ♩=92

1. Sír az út e - lőt - tem, bán - kó - dik az ös - veny,

Parlando ♩=cca 48

1. Úgy őr - zi, úgy őr - zi szép fe - hér pa - ku - rár

2. Sír az út e - lőt - tem, bán - kó - dik az ös - veny,

2. E - zer bá - rán-ká - ját, néz - te - len sok jo - hát,

482

Collected by J. Jagamas *a*) in Frumoasa, No. 2640, F 432 ;
b) in Galbeni, No. 1767, F 292

No. 9

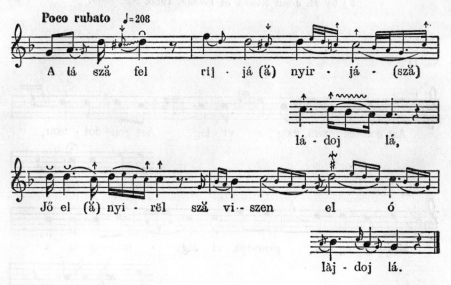

Collected by J. Jagamas in Sabăoani, 1953. No. 8338.

No. 10

Collected a) by P. D. Szabó in Luizi-Călugara, 1950. No. 1615;
b) by R. Joan Nicola in Feleac, 1950. No. 8069.

No. 11

De már lá-tom, ho-gyan e-sik, ha-lá-lo-mat

so-kan le-sik.

A-zért le-sik ha-lá-lo-mat, ve-gyík el a

ga-lam-bo-mat.

Collected by J. Jagamas in Suat, 1951. No. 3145, D 4/b.

No. 12

Poco rubato ♩=cca 104

1. É-des a-nyám sok szép szava, kit fo-gadtam, kit nem soha.

Rubato

1. A-mer-re én já-rok, még a fák is sír-nak,

Poco rubato ♩=cca 84

1. Mikor mentem a fa-lumból ki-fe lé,

485

2. Megfo-gadnám, de már késő, hull a könnyem, mint az e-ső.

2. Gyenge á - ga - ik - ról a le-ve-lek hull - nak.

2. Lányok kisér - nek az ál-lo - más fe - lé.

3. Hull e - lőt- tem, hull a földre, hull a gyászos ke-be-lem-re.

3. Hullja-tok le - ve - lek rejt-se-tek el en - gem,

3. Úgy kísér - nek, mint egy szegény ván - dor lót,

4. Ár-kot mos a két or - cá - mon, mind a zá-por az uc-cá-kon.

4. Mert az én ga - lam - bom sír - va ke-res en - gem.

4. Kinek szi-ve hol-tig gyászba be - bo rult.

Collected by J. Jagamas in Rasciuci, 1950. *a)* No. 1115, F 147a ;
b) 1116, F 147b ;
c) 1117, F 147c.

a 1.Ke-se-re - dik az az a - nya, ki-nek két fi - ja ka-to-na,

b 1.Szegény Barna Pé - ter a lo-vát nyer - ge-li,

c 1.Ös - te-le - dik. sö - té - te-dik.

a 2.Egyik tüzér, másik káplár, pes-ti ka-szár - nyába sétál.

b 2.Ro - mányi két lá - nya jó tá-vo-lán né - zi.

c 2.Az én ró - zsám nem ér ke - zik.

a 3.Pesti ka-szár - nya re-pedj meg, é-des fi -am sza-ba-dulj meg.

b 3.Nézzed lányom, néz - zed fi-uk bosszu - já - ra,

c 3.Nem ér - ke - zik, vagy dó - ga van,

a
4. Sza-ba-dul-nék, de nem le - het, sza-ba-dul-nék de nem le-het.

b
4. Fi-uk bosszu - já-ra, lá-nyok si-ral - má-ra.

c
4. Vagy sze re-tő - je más va-gyan.

Collected *a)* by Z. Kallós in Rasciuci, 1952. No. 3303 ;
        b) by B. Sárosi in Rasciuci, 1951. No. 2280 ;
        c) by J. Jagamas in Rasciuci, 1950. No. 1110, F 145a.

No. 14

Rubato

Sa- jó ku-tyám jaj de ré- gen jaj de ré- gen a-lu-szol,

hej de Nem lát-tad a ró-zsám jön-ni va-la - hol?

hej D'ed-dig ku-vin - tot-tál e-gyet vagy ket-tőt,

Min- dig tud-tam mi-kor jön a sze-re- tőm.

Collected by J. Jagamas in Suat, 1951. No. 3139

No. 15

Rubato

El me - gyek én es-te a-fo - nó - ba

488

Ha-za · jő-vén (ä) szép pi-ros haj-nal - ba L-

-e is fek-szem jól ve - tett á - gyomba.

Collected by J. Jagamas in Ördöngősfüzes 1954. No. 8638, M 35/5.
For a four-line variant see *Moldvai csángó népdalok és népballadák* (Moldavian Csango Folk Songs and Ballads), 1954, p. 211

No. 16

Hej, az óz-di ol-tár e-lőtt Há-romá-gú di-ó-fa nőtt.

Há-rom ágú, hat le-ve-lű, s Az én ba-bám Fe-ri ne-vű.

Collected by J. Jagamas in Ozd, 1954. No. 8751, M 40/18.

No. 17

É- dës a-nyám ró-zsa-fá - jo,

Édës anyám ró-zsa-fá - jo, Édës anyám ró-zsa-fá - jo,

Én vol-tam a lëg-szëbb á - go.

489

"Song of the Village" collected by J. Jagamas in Alunis, 1954. No. 8970 M47a. *Énekkezdő* 'solo', *Mind* 'chorus'.

No. 18

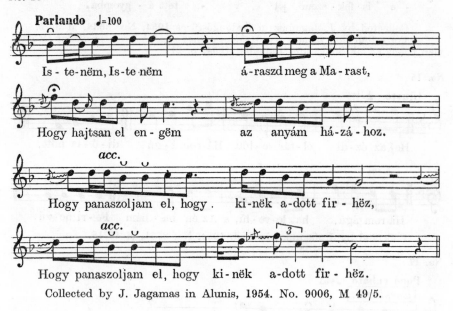

Parlando ♩=100

Is - te -nëm, Is -te ·nëm á -raszd meg a Ma - rast,

Hogy hajtsan el en - gëm az anyám há -zá - hoz.

acc.

Hogy panaszoljam el, hogy . ki -nëk a-dott fir - hëz,

acc.

Hogy panaszoljam el, hogy ki - nëk a-dott fir - hëz.

Collected by J. Jagamas in Alunis, 1954. No. 9006, M 49/5.

No. 19

Giusto

Ki -men - nék a se -lyem-rét - re ka -szál - ni,

Ott a fü - et én nem tut - tam le - vág - ni,

Me nem lát - tam a sok sár - ga **vi - rág** - tól.

Collected by J. Jagamas in Pustiana, 1951. No. 2580.

Bo-roz-dá-ba, bo-roz-dá-ba szépen szól a mo-zi-ka,

Az én ba-bám, az én ba-bám s a le-ve-lit most ír-ja,

S az én ba-bám, s az én ba-bám s a le-ve-lit most ír-ja.

Collected by J. Jagamas in Frumoasa, 1951. No. 2644.

No. 21

Ősz-vel é-rik bu-bám a fe-te-ke sző-lő,

Ne ha-ra-gudj rú-zám, hű-szé-gesz sze-re-tő.

Collected by J. Jagamas in Galbeni, No. 6714, M 6/8.

No. 22

Szól-nak az á-gyuk,(de) ro-pog-nak a kő-fegy-ve-rek,

Majd meg-lát-juk, mit ér meg a kis-gye-rek.

Collected by L. Gurka in Cleja, 1950. No. 2038.

491

No. 23

Ki - csi ma - dár még az é-gen ván-do - rolsz,

Ne lát-tad e ba-bám s a ró-zsámat va-la - hol?

Collected by P. Szabó in Lespezi, 1950. No. 2060.

No. 24

Giusto ♩ = 100

A - lá - fe - lé fa - lu - ba nem me-he - tek,

Mind azt mond - ják, fe - te - ke gyászt vi - se - lek,

Mind azt mondják, fe - te - ke gyászt vi - se - lek.

Collected by I. Szenik in Galbeni, 1953. No. 6467.

LAJOS VARGYAS

INFLUENCE OF THE BAGPIPE ON HUNGARIAN FOLK DANCE MUSIC

Hungarian folk dance music, according to our present knowledge, consists only of folk songs with text ; if there is no musician they sing the songs to the dancing, if there are musicians the songs are played on various instruments and, in the course of time, under the varying effect of the constant instrument playing, they become independent instrumental pieces. But most of them can be shown to have developed from song types. Therefore every instrumental folk tune, either a dance air or other tune, originates, in fact, from a song.

In the following, I shall endeavour to prove that some cases testify to an inverse development : certain songs have originally developed from instrumental music, and certain elements of our instrumental music originate not from songs, but from melodies played on instrument, namely on bagpipe.

Among our folk instruments, the bagpipe alone has its own music. It has been formed by the instrument's peculiarities, and can be performed on the bagpipe only. Every bagpiper knows certain textless figurations, variations of two- to four-bar motives, which are played mostly as a postlude after a folk song or sometimes even separately. This is called *"aprája"*, *"aprózás"* (diminished figurations).

Since these figurations are very simple, and since our bagpipers are without exception peasant or herdsman musicians (never gypsies) handing down their musical material from generation to generation among themselves, we may consider the *aprája* as the most primitive form of our traditional instrumental music.

Here are a few examples of the *aprája* played after songs (nos. 1 and 2).

Example 2 is a well-known minor melody with text. It must be noted that only the most experienced of our bagpipers could play a minor third (as in example 2), because the fundamental scale of the bagpipe is Mixolydian, within the range of an octave, and notes not included in

No. 1

Collected by B. Bartók in Nagymegyer, county Komárom. No. MF.
797a, 798a.

No. 2

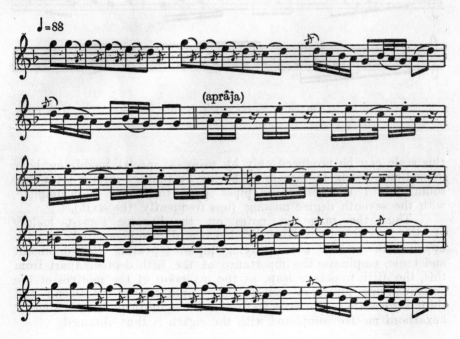

(apråja)

Collected by B. Bartók in Nagymegyer, county Komárom. No. M.F. 796a.

this scale can be produced only by using a special modifying hole.
(Sometimes, owing to inaccurate boring or tuning, certain notes may
sound false.) On certain bagpipes even this scale is incomplete,
with the seventh degree missing (less frequently, the sixth).

Thus the range of notes on the bagpipe consists mainly
of the major pentachord or hexachord, supplemented by the
upper octave. The accompanying pipes, repeating the dominant
and tonic, emphasise the importance of the fifth degree. Apart from
this, the fifth-to-octave leap, as the inversion of the motives of the
accompanying pipes, as well as the periphrasing of the second and
third degrees are conspicuous features in the figurations. In fact, a major
hexachord motive completed with the eighth is thus obtained.

The *apr\u00e1ja* style consisting of repeats and variations of the small motives often influences the performance of the melody, too : the melody is broken up into its elements, it is repeated, varied, sometimes even interwoven with alien motives (see the repeats in no. 2).

Occasionally more developed motives, even periods are formed from the hexachord range of notes.

No. 3

Two bars of unintelligible postlude.

Collected by J. Manga in Doborgaz, county Moson, notation by O. Dincsér. No. M.F. 2822d.

Swineherd's Song

No 4.

Collected by L. Lajtha in Balassagyarmat, county Nógrád. No. M.F. 2434a.

Texts are added sometimes. The bagpiper called no. 3 a "swineherd's song", and no. 4 *Uccu Kanász a Gyepen* (Get On, Swineherd in the Grass). The texts to such tunes are words from the ribald swineherd's song uttered while dancing. Otherwise even the periods do not offer genuine, closed melodies, not even when sung separately. The text mentioned in no. 4 has been recorded at another place too, to a very similar melody.

Swineherd's Song

No. 5

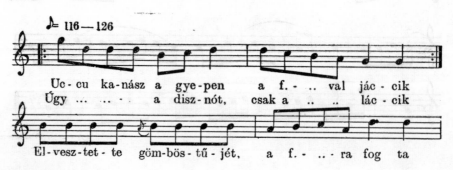

Uc - cu ka - nász a gye - pen   a f. - .. val jác - cik
Úgy ... .   a disz - nót,   csak a .. ..   lác - cik

El - vesz - tet - te göm - bös - tű - jét,   a f. - .. ra fog ta

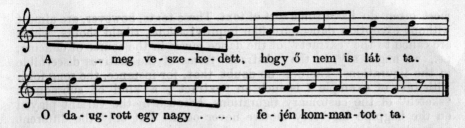

A . .. meg ve - sze - ke - dett, hogy ő nem is lát - ta.

O da - ug - rott egy nagy . ... fe - jén kom - man - tot - ta.

Collected by L. Lajtha in Ipolykelenye, county Hont. No. M.F. 2313c.

But here, too, the repetition of the first motive is the only factor that yields some sort of folk song melody — just as on the bagpipe — while the rest makes it evident that occasional texts are attached to some kind of melodic sketch. These are no definite songs but melodies fashioned more or less in the same way, though the "fashioning" is very free and occasional. Example 6 clearly shows the origin of such melodies. I asked an 84 year old singer what the old bagpipers used to play. "They always piped this":

No. 6

Eggy teli tálló   be - tá - ló - tak (Eggy teli tálló   be - tá - ló - tak.)

Lüttü - lülü - lü   lüttü - lülü - lü   lüttü - lü - lü - lü   lü lü lü lü

Collected by L. Vargyas in Zámoly, county Fejér.

"This was the piper's song, they always played this", he added. Its text is obviously an improvized imitation of sound. Later he dictated additional words: "*Mikor mondtam, még eɟɟyel ho:tak*" (When I asked them, they brought one more). In general the division of the text was not uniform. In example 10 the note of the collector reveals that indeed such "texts" consist of dance words called to some parts of the melody. Kodály also mentions[1] that various dance words are occasionally added to the music. It is obvious, therefore, that examples 3 and 4 are not songs performed on bagpipe, but more settled *aprája* motives which, owing precisely to their more settled form, can bear and

---

[1] *A magyar népzene* (Hungarian Folk Music), Budapest 1952, p. 65. Published in German in 1956: *Die ungarische Volksmusik*, Budapest.

most often do have some sort of text. These texts, however, are almost without exception danceword-like improvisations, ribald shouts, which are called to the "extracts" of the dance music in the course of dancing, *i.e.*, we might say, to the "abstract" forms of the motives discernible in the figurations. There is no doubt that, for instance, the song form with text of example 7 is such an "extract", a kind of subsequent "sketch" of the customary figurations, because in the variant played on the bagpipe this very motive never occurs but only the different succession of the same connections of notes.

Our examples 1 to 6, therefore, represent simple and more developed patterns of *aprája* music.

For dancing our bagpipers, similar to specialists of other instruments, play some sort of familiar dance tune. Such dance tunes are usually attached to the various dances and are thus regarded as their own special melody. But in a few instances they play pure *aprájas* to dancing (nos. 7 to 11), and we even have examples (nos. 7, 10, 11.) showing *aprája* music used as constant accompaniment to particular dances.

Bagpipe Polka

No. 7

Ö-reg-a-nyád i-gen jó, Té-len csi-kó, nyá-ron ló.
Ha fel-ül a tűz-hely-re, On nan mondja,   ne ló ne!

Collected by B. Bartók in Nagymegyer, county Komárom. M.F. 799b, 799a.

attacca:

4 volta

4 volta

6 volta

Collected by Z. Kodály in Lukanénye, county Hont. No. M.F. 1287a.

Bagpipe Dance Tune

No. 9

Poco rubato
♩ = cca 168

Collected by L. Lajtha in Érsekvadkert, county Nógrád. No. M.F. 2744b.

Recruiting Tune for Bagpipe

No. 10

Collected by J. Manga in Naszvad, county Komárom, notation by L. Vargyas. No. M.F. 3309

Collector's note: danced by lads at dance festivities. With hands on hip, they click their heels together to the rhythm of the music, performing intricate steps, lifting their right foot, while singing different texts.

No. 11   **Crossing Dance**

Collected by O. Dincsér in Karancsberény, county Nógrád, notation by L. Vargyas. No. M.F. 3945a.

Such designations as "bagpipe dance tune" (no. 9.) reveal that the tune is not associated with any sort of text, otherwise the informant would have designated it by its initial words. Therefore, this too is *aprája* music without words, which has generally been played to dancing.

Today this kind of dance music is an old-fashioned rarity amidst the well-developed violin pieces or the myriad of folk songs with texts. Long ago, however, it must have been more customary, when the bagpipe had a greater role in the life of the people, in fact, even in the life of the cultured stratum. Kodály[2] quotes Katona Geleji from 1636, according to whom the bagpipe was "the chief music of the Hungarians". It provided the martial music of the hussars until the middle of the 16th century, when it was replaced by the Turkish pipe[3]. It was a permanent instrument in the orchestras of the aristocracy, during the 16th and 17th centuries, even in the courts of the princes of Transylvania.[4] In fact, we even know of its early use in churches at Christmas herdsman Masses.[5] As late as the beginning of the last century the recruiting of soldiers must have taken place generally to the tunes of the bagpipe, like in the recruiting

[2] *Op. cit.* note 139.

[3] Sándor Takáts, *Régi magyarok jókedve* (Merriness in Old-Time Hungary), 2nd ed. Budapest, no year, p. 182.

[4] Bence Szabolcsi, *A 17. sz. magyar főúri zenéje* (The Music of Aristocratic Hungary in the 17th Century), Budapest 1928.

[5] For example, Zrunek's herdsman Masses at Gyöngyös (1767) also indicate the use of the bagpipe. (From the copy of the discoverer, Lajos Pásztor.) See B. Rajeczky: *A gyöngyösi pásztormisék* (The herdsman's Masses at Gyöngyös), in *Zenetudományi Tanulmányok*, vol. iv, Budapest 1955. Kodály also discovered traces of bagpipe music in the musical material of the Szalakusz midnight Mass in Nyitra County. See: *Régi karácsonyi énekek* (Old Christmas Carols), *Ethnographia* 1916, pp. 141—142.

scene shown by Bikessy's contemporary drawing.[6] No wonder that not so long ago in the life of the people the bagpipe was the most important musical instrument, alone providing music at all important festivities. The old descriptions of the herdman's dances of Transdanubia speak constantly of bagpipe music (apart from the long flute); its wide use is corroborated by recent collections also.[7] One or two generations ago this was the situation in the villages even in the region between the Danube and the Tisza Rivers where traditions are discarded earlier than elsewhere. At the beginning of the 20th century the bagpipe reigned supreme in the farmsteads between Szeged and Kiskunhalas: in 1939 there still lived an old bagpiper who had earlier been the sole provider of music at corn-husking parties, wedding feasts, balls, etc. He usually played alone, only rarely joining with a fiddler or a clarinettist to form a duo.[8] Gypsy violinists, and even more so gypsy bands were rarities in quite recent times. It may be said that in certain regions the bagpipe was the "chief music" of the Hungarians almost to our days.

It is no wonder that its characteristic method of playing and its timbre has been imitated. There are phonograph recordings in which gypsy musicians imitate the bagpipe on the violin.

Bagpipe Tune

No. 12

Collected by L. Lajtha in Balassagyarmat, county Nógrád. No. M.F. 2440c

[6] See, for example, Kodály, *op. cit.* (in note 1) Plate IX.
[7] *Somogyi táncok* (Dances from County Somogy) ed. by P. Morvay and E. Pesovár, Budapest 1954, pp. 59—60 and 251—252.
[8] L. Vargyas, *Régi népdalok Kiskunhalasról* (Old Folk Songs from Kiskunhalas), Budapest 1954, p. 11.

509

Collected by J. Manga in Bocsárlapujtő, county Nógrád, notation by L. Vargyas. No. M.F. 3930a.

Collector's note: "I stole the bagpipe", said the leader of the gypsy band *(primás)*. No absolute pitch could be determined. Possible irregular tuning was not marked.

Where the gypsy gradually supplanted the bagpiper there was, for a time, rivalry between them and they must have heard each other rather often. Bagpipe music had to be reproduced on the violin over and over again in order to win the listeners who had been accustomed to the bagpipe. This is evinced by these two imitations and a few bagpipe-like dance tunes, on the violin, which we shall see below (as well as by an imitation of the bagpipe on violin recently recorded on magnetic tape in the Szigetköz region, now in the possession of the Folk Art Institute).

Even more striking is the fact that this popular instrument was imitated even in singing. The following examples are phonographically recorded imitations of the bagpipe from a region where bagpipers could no longer be found at the time of the collection, but where the music of the bagpipe still lived in the memory of the old people.

No. 14

Szi - li jasz-szony ti - kot lo-pott, De ha-mar ki - bi - zo-nyo-dott.

Hjába vitte jiérte az e-ce-tet, A húsából semmit sem e-he-tett.

Döddörödö etc.

Collected by S. Veress in Szany, county Sopron. No. 2829cd.

These imitations reveal the essence of bagpipe music as heard by the performers: the broken-up, varied performance and motives which recall the previously mentioned "extracts". In other words, mostly the *do' so so fa mi fa so* and *so la so do'* type of connections of the hexachord motives. At the same time these features indicate the direction of the subsequent effect of bagpipe music : its descendants may be found both in songs and in instrumental pieces.

In our more incipient songs, said to be "bagpipe tunes", and written down as independent "folk songs", moreover, in major melodies said to be swineherd's songs, we may find much that is closely related to the sung variants of the *aprája* tunes. These, too, are but faintly outlined melodies and can hardly be called closed songs. Also their texts are nothing more than ribald improvizations.

Bagpipe Tune

No. 15

Van itt p.. - .. v.- ... is B...-.. - ... még ma-rad is.

Collected by L. Lajtha in Nemesócsa, county Komárom. No. M.Sz. 1454.

Bagpipe Tune

No. 16

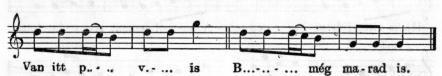

Ö-reg a-nyád ré-gi rin-gyó, ré-gi rin-gyó, ré-gi rin-gyó,

V.- .. - .. ban k., - ... - bim-bó, k.. - .. - bim-bó, k.. - .. -bim-bó.

Collected by L. Lajtha in Nemesócsa, county Komárom. No. M.Sz. 1463.

Bagpipe Tune

No. 17

A - ki du-dás a-kar len-ni, An-nak po-kol - ra kő men-ni.

Ott kő ne-ki meg-ta-nul-ni, (Ej) hogyan köll a du-dát fuj - ni.

Collected by Z. Kodály in Bakonybél, county Veszprém. No. M.Sz. 1689.

Swineherds' Song

Egy ün-göm van, egy ga-tyám, mé-gis sze-gény va-gyok,

Te-li va-gyok te-tü-vel, a-lig ma-rad-ha-tok.

Hü ne! ko-ca ne! Nem a ti há za-tok ez

Collected by L. Lajtha in Szentgál, county Veszprém. No. M.F. 2398b.

I have already discussed elsewhere[9] that instrumental melodies may assume texts subsequently. We know of many dance tunes where the dance-words or some other text follow only a part of the melody, the rest being filled in by syllables like, *tra la la*[10]. In such cases the words have obviously been fitted to a previously existing melody of instrumental origin. This makes it understandable, together with what was said in the foregoing, that certain songs must have crystallized from the *aprája* music, with hexachord motives. Should anyone still believe that we did have songs with *do' so so fa mi fa so* melodies, which were subsequently broken up by the bagpipers into such pieces as shown in examples 3 and 4, then let him take a look at the following *rubato* preludes and postludes where the bagpiper holds only an instrumental try-out, or provides a conclusion to the piece.

No. 19

[9] *Op. cit.* (in note 7) p. 271.
[10] L. Vargyas, *Ugor réteg a magyar népzenében* (Ugric Layer in Hungarian Folk Music), in *Kodály-emlékkönyv, Zenetudományi tanulmányok*, vol., i. Budapest 1953, nos. 43, 48 and 49; or also the melody of the stick dance [of Porcsalma: no. M. F. 2719b.

Collected by L. Lajtha in Érsekvadkert, county Nógrád. No. 2774c.

No. 20

Collected by L. Lajtha in Mezőkövesd, county Borsod. No. M.F. 2383c.

No. 21

Collected by Lajtha in Ipolybalog, County Hont. No. M.F. 2306b.

Collector called no. 19 a "postlude fantasy on bagpipe"; no. 20 is the beginning of a melody and no. 21 a melody-concluding motive.

The outlines of the earlier motives, though without their characteristic rhythm, can be discerned in them. And truly this cannot be said to originate from a song!

Since this wealth of motives originates in the bagpipe's range of notes and technical possibilities, it is immaterial whether it first developed among the Hungarians or, for example, among the Slovaks — as may be assumed on the basis of data presented by Marián Réthei Prikkel.[11] Our neigbours used bagpipes essentially identical with ours, therefore the basis is common. Yet from a few Slovak and Rumanian bagpipe recordings it seems that there is a difference between the very uniform Hungarian *aprája* music and that of our neighbours. These apply the hexachord tonal range with somewhat differing note relations, in different rhythms. According to this the *do so so fa   mi fa so* type of motives would

[11] *A magyarság táncai* (The Dances of the Hungarian People), Budapest 1924, pp. 143—144.

514

appear to be of Hungarian origin. However, the material at our disposal is so scarce that it does not allow a deeper inquiry for the time being.

If now on the basis of our experiences we examine our dance melodies, especially the simpler major-melody types, we can immediately recognise the further development of bagpipe music. The following examples have preserved the memory of bagpipe music not only in the line of their melody but also in their structure: the repetitions of the *aprája* motives live in them, crystallized into a more settled form.

No. 22a

Szél - rül   le - gel - je - tek,   Mert ha fá - nak   ne - ki - men - tek
Fá - nak   ne men - je - tek,   fe - je - te - ket   be - ve - ri - tek

Szi - li kut,   Sza - nyi kut,   Szentand - rá - si   Sob - ri kut.

From Szany, county Sopron.

Weavers' Dance
No. 22b

♩=150

Szé - rül   le - gel - le - tek,   Fá - nak   ne men - je - tek

Mer ha fá - nak   ne - ki men - tek,   Fe - je - te - ket   be - tö - ri - tek

Sa - nyi - kó,   szél - rül le - gel - le - tek

Collected by V. Seemayer[12] in Cserespuszta, county Zala.

[12] Notation by V. Seemayer (nos. 22b, 22c, 24, 25, 26, and 33) are taken from his paper; *Adatok néptáncaink ismeretéhez* (Contributions to our Folk Dances), *Ethnographia* 1935.

Weavers' Dance

No. 22c

Jaj ta-kács o-da vagy, Megy a ta-kács az ut-cá-ba,
Ré-mi-tő csu-da vagy, Lo-tyog a tej a ha-sá-ba,

Jaj ta-kács o-da vagy, Hjá-ba ta-kács az a-pád,
Ré-mi-tő csu-da vagy, Mé-gis ron-gyos a ga-tyád.

Collected by V. Seemayer[13] in Iborfa, county Zala.

Weavers' Cap Dance
(On violin)

No. 22d

Collected by L. Lajtha in Kunszentmiklós, county Pest. No. M.F. 2616a.

Heiducken Dantz
(1592)[14]

No. 22e

---

[13] *Op. cit.*
[14] B. Szabolcsi, *A XVI. század magyar tánczenéje* (Hungarian Dance Music in the 16th Century), in *Népzene és történelem*, Budapest 1954, Ex. 7 (here diminished).

516

No. 23   **Weaver's Dance**

Megy a ta - kács az, uc - cá - ba, Lö - työg a tej   a ha - sá - ba.

Hej   ta kács,   o - da vagy,   Ré   mí - tő   csu - da vagy.

Collected by Z. Kodály in Karád, county Somogy. No. Gr. 31/B/b .

For a variant of no. 23 in a more characteristic, "repeating" instrumental type of form, see *Somogyi táncok*.[15]

No. 24   **Mortar Dance**

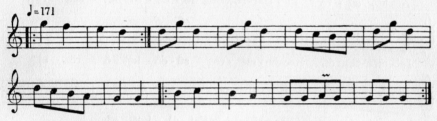

Collected by V. Seemayer[16] in Murakuresztur, county Zala.

No. 25   **Mortar Dance**

Collected by V. Seemayer[17] in Murakuresztur, county Zala.
Collector's note : earlier played by bagpipers, later by gypsy musicians.

[15] *Op. cit.* (in note 7) p. 248, Ex. 50.
[16] See note 12.
[17] See note 12.

No. 26

♩=120

Me- gis-mer-ni a ka-nászt, Me- gis-mer-ni a ka-nászt
É- kës- fé-kës bocsko-rá- rul, É- kës- fé-kës bocsko- rá- rul

é- kës já- rá - sá - rul,
ta-risz-nya-szij - já - rul,

A két ág- ra ki- sod-rott fe- ke- te baj- szá - rul.

Jel- mën-tem én Kecske- mét- re sű- dő- ket ő röz- ni

Lë fa- gyott a sar kam, Fel- ál- lott a .. - ..

É- des-ked-ves ko- mám-asszony, Se- gél- jën kee raj- tam.

Csi - kó sok, gu- lyá- sok. Vagy gyakha- tó kan-dá- szok

3 volta

Cif- ra kö- tőt kan-dász-né-nak Cif- ra kö- tő li- beg-lo- bog
Cif- ra kö- tő li- beg-lo- bog Cif- ra kö- tő li- beg-lo- bog
Kandász ..- ... i - zeg-mo- zog

Hüccs ki disz- nó ja be- rek-ből csak a fü- le lát- szik

518

Kandászbojtár a bo-kor-ba menyecs-ké-vel ját-szik.

El-szö-kött a vén disz-nó ki-lenc ma-la-cá-val

U-tá-na mënt a kan-dász fé-nyes bal-tá-já-val.

Kandász hajt-ja ma-la-cát, Já-ger ...-... a lá-nyát

U-tá-na megy a boj-tár fé-kom te-rin-get-te.

Mér ...-....-.. sze-re-tő-met, eb-ad-ta né-mët-je.

A disz-nó-hús a kan-dá-szé, a disz-nó-hús a kan-dá-szé,

A disz-nó-sz.. a boj-tá-ré, a disz-nó-sz.. a boj-tá-ré

Ap-rót sz.-... a disz-nó, rakd a ta-risz-nyád-ba,

Ha meg-ʊ-nod ma-ga-dat, ra-ko-gasd a szád-ba.

Collected by V. Seemayer[18] in Bajcsa, county Somogy.
Collector's note : It was played on a long flute or a bagpipe and also sung.

[18] See note 12.

They sing a familiar pentatonic swineherd's song to it in a bag-pipe-like, fragmented form, whereas the *aprája* after the song is in major.

Cap Dance from Kunszentmiklós

(On violin)

No 27a.

Collected by L. Lajtha in Kunszentmiklós, cou nty Pest. No. M.F. 2616d

Cap Dance from Kunszentmiklós[19]

No. 27b

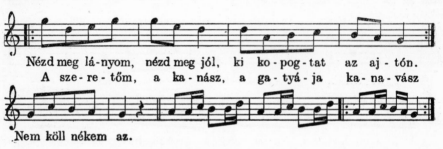

Nézd meg lá-nyom, nézd meg jól, ki ko-pog-tat az aj-tón.
A sze-re-tőm, a ka-nász, a ga-tyá-ja ka-na-vász
Nem köll nékem az.

Magpie Dance from Galgamácsa[20]

No. 27c

Vé-kony vá-szón le-pe-dő, Tar-ka ku-tya ne tü-dő
Ez a tánc, ez a tánc, ez a szar-ka tánc.

[19] For nos. 27b, 27c, and 34 see E. Lugossy & S. Gönyey, *Magyar népi táncok* (Hungarian Folk Dances), Budapest 1947.
[20] See note 19.

Recruiting Dance from Szatmárökörító

No. 28

Fogd meg ci - ca   az   e - ge - ret.   Ha meg - fogtad   meg   e - he   ted.

Hun - cut   a macs - ka,

Sza - ladj ha - mar,   ne   félj tő - le   Ma - ris - ka.

Bear Play

No. 29

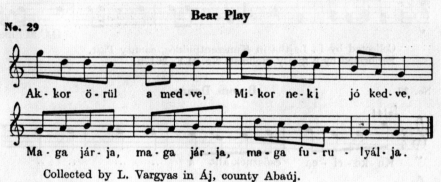

Ak - kor ö - rül   a med - ve,   Mi - kor ne - ki   jó ked - ve,

Ma - ga jár - ja,   ma - ga jár - ja,   ma - ga fu - ru - lyál - ja.

Collected by L. Vargyas in Áj, county Abaúj.

Ungarländischer Tanz

(1689)[21]

No. 30

[21] B. Szabolcsi, *A XVII. század magyar világi dallamai* (Hungarian Secular Melodies of the 17th Century), Budapest, (no year) no, 69.

No. 31   **Sidling Dance**[22]

Fine

No. 32   **Mouse-Catching Dance**

♩=126

Fine

D.C. al Fine

Collected by L. Lajtha in Kunszentmiklós, county Pest.
Performed by a gypsy violinist. No. M.F. 2617b.

No. 33   **Broom Dance**

♩=141

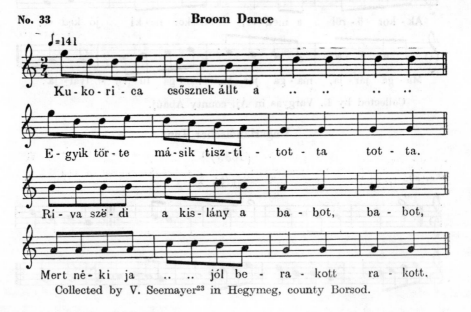

Ku - ko - ri - ca   csösznek állt a   .. ..

E - gyik tör - te   má - sik tisz - tí - tot - ta   tot - ta.

Ri - va szë - di   a kis - lány a   ba - bot,   ba - bot,

Mert né - ki ja   .. ..   jól be - ra - kott   ra - kott.

Collected by V. Seemayer[23] in Hegymeg, county Borsod.

[22] M. Réthei Prikkel, *op. cit.* (in note 11), pp. 202—203.
[23] See note 12.

Wine-Treader Dance

Collected[24] in Váralja, county Tolna.

Nos. 27a, 27 b and 27c have a different rhythm on instrument, a more logical one, than with text. Obviously, the text was added subsequently. In 27b, although the collectors fail to indicate, we have a form which was obviously sung to instrumental playing. There was no text left to the final instrumental figuration.

The last example (no. 34) is reminiscent of certain Nativity-play songs. Some of these are related to the former, and generally to bagpipe music, particularly because the repetitions of small motives in them are more frequent[25]. The use of the bagpipe in church at Yuletide makes this relationship highly probable.

Apart from the previous, typically hexachord melodies, we find more complicated dance pieces, closer to the instrumental type, as the following. (I must note, however, that the Hungarian origin of some of them has not been ascertained.)

[24] See note 19.
[25] See: *Corpus Musicae Popularis Hungaricae*, vol. ii, no. 501, or those on pp. 466—467, or 487—488, and 495, and others like them. Concerning this type see L. Vargyas, *Les mélodies des jeux hongrois de Noël*, in *Folia Ethnographica* 1950, p. 97, and nos. 4a, 4b, 5a, 5b, 6a, 6b, 7, and 8.

Gypsy Dance

Collected by L. Lajtha in Monor, county Pest. M.F. 2769a.

Smooth Swift Dance

No. 36

524

Collected by B. Bartók in Nyárádremete, county Maros-Torda. No. 3702b.

Kercsej

No. 37

Collected by O. Dincsér in Gyimesközéplok, county Csík, notation by L. Vargyas. No. M.F. 4155c.

Korobjászka

No. 38

D.C. dal ⊕ bis

Collected by O. Dincsér in Gyimes, county Csík, notation by L. Vargyas No. M.F. 4154b.

Bagpipe Dance

(On violin)

Fine

D.C. al Fine

Collected by I. Zámbó in Simonfa, county Somogy.[26]
Collector's note : they called it a "bagpipe dance", but executed a brisk
czardas to it.

The violin melody from Simonfa, in a minor key, unmistakably
reveals its origin from the bagpipe, just like its name "bagpipe dance".
Although no. 35 is a tune, as indicated by the meaningless syllables
written under the notes, this performing technique is characteristic of the
gypsies only. They sing the accompanying music of the dance without
words, and with instrumental ornamentations. The others provide an
accompaniment in chorus, by producing puffing noises through their
lips (bilabial rolled sounds) in intricate rhythm. This, therefore, is
essentially an instrumental melody. Most of the elements of this "Gypsy
dance" (no. 35.) are of the Hungarian *verbunkos*-type. Its music is very
heterogenous; many of these pieces are of Hungarian origin. Nos. 37 and
38 are pieces of a Csango fiddler from Gyimes. (The collectors failed to
indicate the tuning of the violin and its original pitch.)

The transfer of bagpipe motives to violin is not without parallel
in the Carpathian Basin. Bartók came across a similar development
in the instrumental dance pieces of Maramuresh.[27]

[26] *Op. cit.* (in note 7), p. 241, no. 41.
[27] B. Bartók, *Die Volksmusik der Rumänen von Maramureş*, München
1923, p. xxi, and nos. 136 — 163 in *"Tanzweisen von freier Form"*.

All this dance material rooted in bagpipe motives comprises a relatively small number of our dance melodies, including but a few important ones. Nevertheless, bagpipe music has a more important effect, both qualitatively and quantitatively. This can be detected in the so-called "figures" of our dance pieces. In quite a number of dance pieces the melody, having a recognizably closed form, is followed by one or more figurations that are in no way reminiscent of melodies with strict forms. These are, practically without exception, major motives, even after minor melodies, sometimes conceived almost entirely in the spirit of the bagpipe's *apája* music; *i.e.*, in a form transferred to the violin as seen in the imitations of the bagpipe. These figurations often appear in a more stylized form, periphrasing the 2nd and 3rd degrees according to the possibilities of the violin, or emphasizing their dominant and tonic character by runs of functional importance. But even in the scale-like runs which swoop to the lower dominant the *apája* type of figurations can be discerned.

The fact that the figuration appears in a major key even after a minor melody is a proof of the thriving memory of the bagpipe's *apája* music. Such figures following a melody occur in large numbers in our dance pieces. Disregarding the special types that are excluded

Recruiting Dance

(On violin)

No· 40

528

Collected by L. Lajtha in Kunszentmiklós, county Pest. No. M.F. 2617a, 2618. The variant of this piece sung with text[28] is presumably a later addition. The clearly instrumental cadences of the sung variant and its unusual form seem to corroborate this assumption. The "melody section" must have originally been sung with text, of the type represented by Pt. no. 363.

No. 41   **Spur Dance**

(On violin)

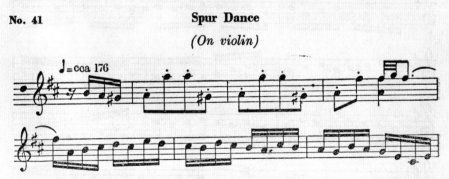

[28] See in S. Gönyey & B. Rajeczky, *111 táncdal* (Hundred-and-Eleven Dance Tunes), Budapest [1949], no. 107.

34

(figura)

Collected by G. Veres in Marosvásárhely, county Maros-Torda, notation
by J. Deutsch. No. M.F. 1160b.

Twirling Dance from Marosszék (On violin)
(On violin)

Collected by A. Molnár in Gyergyóújfalu, county Csík, notation by B'
Bartók. No. M.F. 1528b.

No. 43

Sűrű Tempo

(On violin)

Collected by L. Lajtha in Szék, county Szolnok-Doboka. No. Gr. 83/Bc[29].

from consideration, figures like this were found in 39 of the 292 tunes examined. This corresponds to 13.4 per cent, which means that about every eighth instrumental dance piece is of this type.[30]

This was where the question of the similar phenomenon in the 19th century *verbunkos*[31] music arose. The so-called *"dísze"* (ornamentation) of the *verbunkos* pieces, the interludes with *virtuoso* figures, obviously goes back to this traditional practice. The first masters of the verbunkos style, the great gypsy *primás*, first of all Bihari, evidently played traditional material. Later the *verbunkos* composers, Lavotta, Csermák and Rózsavölgyi, recast, restyled this practice. In these composed pieces, *i.e.*, their *virtuoso* interludes, the modest *"aprózás"* (diminished figurations) of the bagpipers reached its greatest flowering.

ABBREVIATIONS

Gr.   = Grammophone records in the Hungarian Ethnographical Museum
M. F. = Phonographic records in the Hungarian Ethnographical Museum
M. Sz. = Written records in the Hungarian Ethnographical Museum
Pt.   = Collection of Folk Songs (compiled by L. Vargyas) to Kodály's *A magyar népzene* (Hungarian Folk Music), Budapest 1952

Place names are given in the forms as used by the collectors.

[29] Published in L. Lajtha, *Széki gyűjtés* (Collection from the Village of Szék), Budapest 1954, no. 5.
[30] See, for example, L. Lajtha, *Kőrispataki gyűjtés* (Collection from the Village of Kőrispatak), Budapest 1954, no. 5, note 15, nos. 16, 18, and note 18, no. 42 ; *Széki gyűjtés*, no. 14.
[31] A kind of dance music performed by gypsy musicians in the 19th century with rich figurations. Its instrumental musical style was imitated by western composers (Haydn, Mozart, Beethoven, Schubert and others) in works with Hungarian themes.